Barcode in

MW01122449

Lesbian Plays
Coming of Age in Canada

Lesbian Plays
Coming of Age in Canada

Black Friday
Growing Up Suites I and II and *Object/Subject of Desire*
Dykes and Dolls • *Karla and Grif* • *A Fertile Imagination*
Difference of Latitude • *Swollen Tongues* • *Life and A Lover*
Random Acts • *Smudge* • *Privilege*

Selected and Edited by Rosalind Kerr

Playwrights Canada Press
Toronto • Canada

Playwrights Canada Press
The Canadian Drama Publisher
215 Spadina Avenue, Suite 230, Toronto, Ontario CANADA M5T 2C7
416-703-0013   fax 416-408-3402
orders@playwrightscanada.com • www.playwrightscanada.com

Financial support provided by the taxpayers of Canada and Ontario through the Canada
Council for the Arts and the Department of Canadian Heritage through the Book Publishing
Industry Development Programme, and the Ontario Arts Council.

The Canada Council for the Arts
Le Conseil des Arts du Canada

ONTARIO ARTS COUNCIL
CONSEIL DES ARTS DE L'ONTARIO

Cover art by Stephen Fouquet.
Cover design and Production Editor: JLArt

Library and Archives Canada Cataloguing in Publication

Lesbian plays : coming of age in Canada / selected and edited by
Rosalind Kerr.

Contents: Black friday -- Growing up suites I and II and
object/subject of desire -- Dykes and dolls -- Karla and Grif -- Fertile
imagination -- Difference of latitude -- Swollen tongues -- Life and a
lover -- Random acts -- Smudge and privilege
ISBN 0-88754-864-4

1. Lesbianism--Canada--Drama. 2. Lesbians--Canada--Drama. 3. Canadian
drama (English)--20th century. 4. Canadian drama (English)--21st century.
I. Kerr, Rosalind, 1941-

PS8309.L48L48 2006   C812'.54080353   C2006-902615-7

First Edition: May 2006
Printed and bound by Canadian Printco at Scarborough, Canada.

To my girlhood friend Bonnie Prentice and her partner Beth Foster
And to lesbian playwrights everywhere

Table of Contents

Acknowledgements

I would like to acknowledge several people who have contributed to the making of this volume in addition to those playwrights whose plays are included: Kate Weiss, Kelly Thornton, Cynthia Zimmerman, Shelley Scott, Rebecca Burton, Sandy Nicholls, David King, Nairne Holtz for suggestions about playwrights; Renate Pohl for help with transcription and layout; Dawn Tracey, Janine Plummer for research on texts; other members of my graduate class in Queer Canadian Theatres: Judith Anderson, Jeff Gagnon, Tawny Lehan, David Lenard for important discussions; my colleague Piet de Fraeye for helpful advice; Stephen Fouquet for cover art. I would also like to thank the Drama Department of the University of Alberta. Finally, thanks to Angela Rebeiro, the publisher at Playwrights, for helping in so many ways.

Introduction

by Rosalind Kerr

This anthology of plays/performance texts by twelve Canadian artists is the first of its kind and celebrates a new stage in the representation of Lesbian Theatre(s) in Canada. It offers a selection of texts written over the past two or so decades as a sampling of some of the ways in which lesbian or lesbian-positive playwrights have staged their particular visions of lesbian experiences. Increasingly self-conscious in their expressions of diverse lesbian voices and in their choice of their innovative staging techniques, these playwrights have found many ways to make lesbian theatre exciting and provocative. Taken together, the sheer wealth and range of plays serve as a testimonial to the fact that lesbians have indeed arrived as legitimate theatre practitioners. All of these texts have been produced, several of them have won awards, and some of them have already become well-known staples of Canadian lesbian/queer theatre. However, this selection is by no means comprehensive as it offers only a sampling of the many important plays that could have been included. It also suffers from its lack of inclusion of artists writing from diverse race, ethnic, age, ability, education, economic and regional backgrounds. [1] It is hoped that this anthology will stimulate interest in broadening the field of study so that more texts will be published and the contribution that lesbian playwrights have made to Canadian theatre history can be fully documented.

By having a body of plays available to read in relationship to each other, it becomes possible to formulate valuable insights into the ways in which diverse lesbian playwrights have impacted our culture. In trying to find a definition of what being lesbian includes, I have fallen back on Phyllis Lyon and Del Martin's claim that "a lesbian's *primary* erotic, psychological, emotional, and social interest is in members of her own sex." [2] However, I would qualify this definition with Bonnie Zimmerman's observation that "[l]esbian literature, like lesbian culture in general, is particularly flexible on issues of gender and role identification." [3]

Definitions of what lesbian theatre is have also been widely disputed. While British lesbian playwright Nina Rapi proposes that it should ideally refer to "work by out lesbians which foregrounds the lesbian experience," she herself admits that this is not always possible. [4] While most of the play/performance scripts included fit the latter criteria, they do so in varying degrees. To select them, I have been guided by Emily L. Sisley's revised version of a description used to refer to gay theatre with "lesbian" substituted for "gay": "I define [lesbian] theatre as a production that implicitly or explicitly acknowledges that there are [lesbians] on both sides of the footlights." [5] In acknowledging that the plays/performance texts represent lesbian subjects on stage who address themselves to lesbian spectators in the audience, I am proposing that all the texts push at the boundaries of representation and its heterosexualizing norms by making the lesbian subject and the desire that circulates around her the central focus of attention. [6] As Jill Dolan outlines it in *The Feminist Spectator as Critic,* the lesbian subject "denaturalizes dominant codes by signifying an existence that belies the entire structure of heterosexual culture and its representations." [7]

It is precisely the kinds of arguments advanced by feminist performance theorists about the possibilities of challenging the ideologies that obscure the hetero-normativity of most realistic theatre texts that led Robert Wallace to argue for a revisioning of gay theatre in Canada. His important *Producing Marginality* compared the marginal positioning of theatre in Canada with "the marginal positioning of women and gay men inside the dominant culture of patriarchy," and noted that the rise of outstanding new theatrical productions by gay theatre artists from the late '60s owed a great deal to their embracing this marginalization and foregrounding it in their texts. [8] Thus, through their very celebration of their marginality, they were also able to expose the oppressive conditions that had produced it in the first place. While this celebratory claiming of theatrical sites by outstanding gay male playwrights has led to the establishment of a strong gay male Canadian canon, the same cannot be said for lesbian theatre artists. The exciting work of Wallace and others who follow his materialist method of enquiry as they explore the social, economic and political conditions that allow for the development of works by gay artists, and the theatre spaces and audience base to support them may serve as a useful blueprint for mapping the trajectory of lesbian theatre(s) as well.

But even if many intersections with gay/queer theatre production are to be taken for granted, the fact remains that the extreme marginalization of lesbian theatre, accurately reflects the very precarious place that lesbian culture occupies in Canada and everywhere else in the world. In trying to understand this comparative lack of visibility in relation to the cultural representation of male homosexuality it has been helpful to look at theories of the intersections of sexual and national identities in contemporary societies. [9] Nationalism, as Ann McClintock spells it out in *Imperial Leather,* has been "constituted from the very beginning as a gendered discourse and cannot be understood without a theory of gender power." [10] Since nation states have traditionally assigned women to a subordinate childbearing role in an oedipally organized family hierarchy which locates all the power in the hands of male figures, it is no surprise that lesbians are even less likely to register in official culture than their heterosexual female counterparts. Canadian scholar, Patricia Smart, in querying whether or not feminism is compatible with nationalism, points out that "[n]ations have without exception been the creation of fathers, wild spaces tamed and mapped and bordered by them, in order that they may then be passed on to sons … [n]ations … have used women as reproducers and educators and nurturers, all the while excluding them from power and from public space." [11]

Since in this scenario with its idealization of motherhood, the lesbian is considered to pose a national threat because of her unwillingness to subordinate herself to heterosexual marriage, and childbearing, she has tended to be either totally absent, misrecognized, or, possibly, cast as a monstrous outlaw. Although there continue to be many different positions that feminists occupy in relation to the intersections of sexualities and nationalities, the emergence of the representation of a lesbian subject has added a new voice to the discourse of sexual difference. Teresa de Lauretis after describing the relegation of the lesbian to the off-stage space of "socio-sexual (in)difference," posits an *ironic* rewriting by lesbians of the heterosexual contract and the male hierarchy it supports.[12] While the trope of lesbian as monstrous outlaw still casts a shadow over some of the plays included here, they all engage with de Lauretis's project to open up "a conceptual and erotic space" where women could recognize women concurrently "as subjects and as objects of female desire" (155). Revealing their debt to lesbian feminist theories, they show us lesbians in all stages of coming out of the closet in past and present situations, provide a glimpse of the flirtation with the utopic Lesbian Nation movement, and offer reflections of the new kinds of challenges that life in postmodern queer Canadian society presents for the non-conforming "lesbian" subject.[13]

As we move increasing away from any fixed definitions of gendered and sexualized identities towards a queer postmodern Canadian society, it is important to know what part lesbian theatre has played in reflecting these historical developments back to us.[14] The commentary they offer on the ways in which dominant Canadian cultural norms are being shaped, gives valuable insights into ways to resist the coercive and exclusionary power tactics that our national institutions employ in the interests of maintaining the status-quo. The plays that are included here serve the purpose of charting certain historically specific moments that represent a range of lesbian experiences over the past twenty years in various parts of Canada. In many ways they reflect the gradual changes that have brought lesbians into greater prominence within Canada as a result of important legal and social changes.[15] By creating an alternative theatrical contract which requires spectators to acknowledge the importance of same-sex desire between women as they show their characters caught up in social interactions which require painful confrontations, these playwrights have all contributed to the creation of an alternative canon which no longer conforms to the naturalized heterosexual imperative that we take for granted. It is hoped that exposure to these plays can help us to rewrite our national history by opening up the spaces to make room for the experiences of lesbian subjects whose previously denied and erased identities have now entered into representation.

While the plays are very diverse, it is possible to find points of comparison. The first four selections are all concerned with coming-out stories and as such reflect back to us the repression and hostility with which the lesbian presence was regarded. The first play, Alec Butler's pioneering *Black Friday* (1989), is a partially autobiographical coming-out story which involves the return of the protagonist Terry to her birthplace in Sydney, Nova Scotia with her black leather dyke lover in tow. The naturalistic setting and dialogue puts the lesbian relationship right in the face, not only of the family, but the audience as well.

Shawna Dempsey's and Lorri Millan's parodic pieces, *Growing Up Suites Part I* and *II* (1994) provide another look at growing up lesbian in the suburbs of Scarborough in

1968 when there were no available icons or ways to exist in society other than the heteronormative rites of passage that left Shawna, the performer, out in the cold. Her compulsive distortion of the available fetishes forces the audience to examine their own constructed desires. Complementing these pieces is their *Object/Subject of Desire* (1989) which shows us how a lesbian prom queen can thwart the conventional expectations of becoming a perfect love object. Next, Lisa Lowe's solo performance piece, *Dykes and Dolls*, also about growing up in the late '60s, shows her turning her bedroom into a lesbian playground as she rescripts her relationship to Barbie and the other dolls who are supposed to feminize her.

The last and very different coming-out story, Vivienne Laxdal's *Karla and Grif* (1991) tells the heartbreaking story of Karla's rejection by Grif after their intense summer camp experience. Tied in with Karla's conflicted relationship with her hard-drinking working class dad, Danny, this play captures the confused rage that overwhelms Karla when she finds herself cast as the monstrous outsider whose very existence is denied.

Sharply contrasting the tentative and/or heavily ironized coming-out stories of the first four plays is Susan G. Cole's *A Fertile Imagination* (1991) which features the experiences of Rita and Dee, an ideal lesbian couple, as they set out to co-opt the reproductive rights denied to same-sex couples. Loaded with all the markers of lesbian domesticity, this play makes a strong statement about the rights of lesbians to occupy space both on and off stage.

The next three texts all deal with representations of fictionalized historical situations in which the prohibitions against expressions of same-sex desire among women are used to focus attention on liberatory possibilities for the future. Lisa Walter's *Difference of Latitude* (1995) goes back to 1812 to explore how one woman escapes from the stifling restrictions of domestic life by running away to sea. Offsetting the hardships of gender-crossing, Frances's reciprocated love of Rose offers a glimpse of the fantasy of a new world order where lesbians might be able to exist at some future time.

Kathleen Oliver's *Swollen Tongues* (1998), set in Restoration England, uses the dramatic device of rhyming couplets to explore the mistaken identities and trans-gressive circulation of desire that occurs when her lesbian heroine Catherine competes with her brother for the love of the same woman. Making crossdressing a major motif, the play shows the kinds of transformational shifts that can occur when characters are forced to find out what it feels like to play the other gender. The utopic second act where lesbian desire is recognized and fulfilled turns transvestism into a rite of passage for male and female alike.

Finally, Natalie D.Meisner's *Life and A Lover* (1999) recreates the story of the love affair between Virginia Woolf and Vita Sackville-West through the theatrical device of personifying Orlando as their go-between. Having captured the oppressive Edwardian milieu which straitjackets the expression of same-sex love between women, Meisner's treatment of the androgynous Orlando suggests that the artistic imagination can bring about the desired sexual transformation.

The next two plays, Diane Flacks's *Random Acts* (1999) and Alex Bulmer's *Smudge* (2001), bring us back to the present day and offer highly personalized visions of the perils that life in a modern megacity pose to anyone who finds themselves on the margins. Flacks transforms herself back and forth into multiple female personae whose lives intersect with her main character Antonella Bergman, a recently paralyzed self-help guru who finds herself hard put to remain optimistic when dealing with the human misery she encounters. Her attempts to deal with the lovelorn problems of the heartbroken lesbian Lisa brings this alternative life style into prominent focus.

On the other hand, Alex Bulmer's *Smudge* (2001) contrasts the fleeting happiness of the protagonist Freddie with her lover Katherine against the terrifying onset of her blindness. By having a personified Blindness deprive her of the ability to negotiate life in the city, Bulmer leaves us with a poignant sense of the double precariousness of her existence as both lesbian and blind.

Corinna Hodgson's *Privilege* (2004) which closes the anthology revisits the coming-out motif of the first plays but now reformulates the question as to what exactly coming-out has come to mean. In featuring the disturbed adolescent Ginny's resistance to the pathologizing of her sexual relationship with her girlfriend Nat, Hodgson turns the official world of disapproving parents, teachers, lawyers and therapists inside out. The Ginny who reveals the tissues of hypocrisy and lies on which heteronormative values are based is a new breed of "lesbian" subject. Even if the punishment she receives reveals that not much has changed in the society at large, she herself now knows that things could be otherwise.

With each alternative voice that we have heard in this anthology it has been increasingly impossible to deny that lesbians exist. It is hoped that those who read or see these plays performed will recognize that lesbian theatres have come of age in Canada.

Notes

[1] Lynda Hart, "Canonizing Lesbians?" *Modern American Drama: The Female Canon,* ed. June Schlueter (London and Toronto: Associated University Presses, 1990) 285, criticizes the first American Anthology of lesbian plays, Kate McDermott, *Places Please!*, published in 1985, for being "primarily white, middle-class, and realistic." This anthology falls into some of those traps and needs to be complemented by another volume.

[2] Hart, 281, quoting from Del Martin and Phyllis Lyon, *Lesbian/Woman* (New York: Bantam Books, 1972) 1.

[3] Bonnie Zimmerman, "What Has Never Been: an Overview of Lesbian Feminist Criticism," *Making a Difference: Feminist Literary Criticism*, ed. Gayle Greene and Coppélia Kahn (London & NY: Methuen, 1985) 202.

[4] Nina Rapi, "Hide and Seek: the Search for a Lesbian Theatre Aesthetic," *New Theatre Quarterly* 9 (1993): 148, proposes that these are important criteria but not always easy to fulfill.

[5] Emily L. Sisley, "Notes on Lesbian Theatre," *A Sourcebook of Feminist Theatre,* ed. Carol Martin (London & NY: Routledge, 1996) 53.

[6] Kate Davy, "Constructing the Spectator: Reception, Context, and Address in Lesbian Performance," *Performing Arts Journal* 29 .x. 2 (1986): 43-52.

[7] Jill Dolan, *The Feminist Spectator as Critic* (Ann Arbor: U of Michigan P) 116.

[8] Robert Wallace, *Producing Marginality: Theatre and Criticism in Canada* (Saskatoon, Sask.: Fifth House Publishers, 1990) 29-30.

[9] Andrew Parker et al, ed. "Introduction," *Nationalisms and Sexualities* (NY & London: Routledge, 1993) 1-18, raises most of the major issues that scholars have identified.

[10] Ann McClintock, *Imperial Leather: Race, Gender, and Sexuality in the Colonial Contest* (NY & London: Routledge, 1995) 355.

[11] Patricia Smart, "The (in?)compatibility of gender and nation in Canadian and Quebecois feminist writing," *Essays on Canadian Writing* 54 (Winter 1994) 15.

[12] Teresa de Lauretis, "Sexual Indifference and Lesbian Representation," *Theatre Journal* 40.3 (May 1988) 161.

[13] Becki Ross, "A Lesbian Politics of Erotic Decolonization," *Painting the Maple: Essays on Race, Gender and the Construction of Canada*, ed. Veronica Strong-Boag et al. (Vancouver: UBC Press, 1998) 187-214, includes a discussion of the impact of the ideal of a Lesbian Nation on lesbian history in Canada.

[14] Eric Savoy, "You Can't Go Homo Again: Queer Theory and the Foreclosure of Gay Studies," *ESC* 20.2. (1994) 145-46, remarks that the loss of the imperatives of gay studies to bring about real change through "the empowerment of lesbians and gay men by educating them in our cultural heritage and tactics of survival" leaves us with the need to find new strategies to make queer theory accountable as an emancipatory project. This anthology is looking for ways to mediate between lesbian and queer.

[15] L. Pauline Rankin, " Sexualities and National Identities: Re-imagining queer nationalism," *Journal of Canadian Studies* 35.2 (Summer 2000): 176-97. This important article charts the problematized relationship of lesbians within Canada over several decades. While not about theatrical representation, it does make it possible to relate the various plays to the stages of the historical battles that lesbians have waged to promote equal rights.

Black Friday

Alec Butler

Introduction:
Black Friday

The text of Alec Butler's pioneering *Black Friday* included here is substantially that of the 1989 production.[1] A classic coming-out story, it also mirrors the coming out of Toronto as an urban centre with a lesbian subculture. Although Butler had to struggle to get productions mounted, the very fact that his play had two successful runs in Toronto, and travelled to several places around Canada is a measure of its timely appearance and popular appeal. Partially autobiographical, it features the surprise visit of the thirty-something writer Terry, back east to her birthplace, Sydney, Nova Scotia with Spike, her Black biker-dyke lover. Superficially realistic in its portrayal of the family living room in Sydney, the fourth-wall illusionism is constantly interrupted. In the first place, the stage directions tell us that when the characters are not on the set, they sit and watch the action from the church pew located on the upstage wall. (In the revised script, Butler reinforces this sense that the actors when offstage are actively involved in witnessing the onstage events with the audience. This device enhances the constant in-your-face exhibitionism of the lovemaking scenes between the butch-femme duo, just as their larger than life bursting onto the stage in their full leather biker regalia after a mythical bike ride all the way from Toronto.)

While Terry's trip home after a six-year absence also predictably ends with her official coming-out scene with her mother Rita and aunt/grandmother Effie, the clues that they send out are so obvious from the moment of their arrival that even if her family members are in a state of denial, the audience is never in doubt. When Effie, Terry's aunt/grandmother exclaims on first sight, "Youse look like a pair'a Martians!" the joke is actually directed back to the spectators who are positioned to have to identify with Terry as she tries to break into her family's consciousness. So too, Butler by making Spike into an educated, middle-class, totally politically-sexually evolved lesbian has added another iconic reversal to her butch-femme subversion of the perfectly matched heterosexual couple. The failure of Effie and Rita to openly acknowledge that Terry and Spike are lovers allows Butler to keep staging scenes which test the willful prejudice of both the characters and the audience towards not only lesbians but also Blacks. Grandmother Effie's assumption that Spike could only have come from the Pier, the black ghetto in Sydney, becomes a running joke which recalls the actual historical situation that most Blacks were experiencing. Spike's self-consciously "out" portrayal, also radicalizes the position of the still-closeted Terry, making it impossible to the audience to read her apart from her participation in a butch-femme dynamic, which by its very existence, disrupts the pretense that masculine-feminine gendered roles are fixed.[2]

If the play charts the journey that Terry must go on to acquire full agency as a lesbian, it marks her as a questing subject, who operates very differently from the expected passive female position, in her attempt to vindicate her disgraced father and to restore his reputation as a national hero. In this way, she represents the lesbian subject who since she is outside the political categories of "man" and "woman", must forge a new identity in the in-between spaces by pushing at the boundaries of representation.[3] Male-identified in her obsessive pursuit of the father who deserted her, Terry had left home six years earlier to track him down in Toronto where he had retreated to a life as a barroom poet. Terry's quest in returning to Sydney is to find the newspaper clippings which would confirm his heroic stance as a political activist who had served time in Dorchester for the part he played in establishing the union at the steel mill in Sydney. This somewhat chimerical task is only part of her attempt to rewrite the fateful events that followed after the union was formed. This event which went down as one of the darkest days in the history of Cape Breton, the Black Friday for which the play is named, is based on an actual history event which took place on Friday, October 13, 1967, when the union vote was split over whether or not to accept a pay cut.[4] Butler portrays Frank as the man who led the faction who refused to vote for the pay cuts, and hence, as the true champion of the people's rights.

Terry's wish to believe in her father's heroism and her search for the evidence to prove it may ostensibly drive the plot but it also reinforces the more important dramatic motif that all the actions in the play derive from the attempts made by the characters to run from the painful truths of their lives. Offsetting Terry's obsession with her father's greatness is the truth that he is a beaten-down drunk who has filled her with lies about both his betrayal of his fellow-workers and his abandonment of her. As her inquiry forces her to admit that he had never sent her the letter explaining his actions, or made any effort to connect to her, she also arrives at a place of forgiveness and acceptance of his brokenness. Coming to this sort of understanding about her father's place in the larger history of the betrayal of Atlantic Canada, gives Terry a new stature as someone who can now move beyond defining herself only through her father.

Terry's gradual shedding of her illusions about her father is interwoven dramatically with the stripping off of most of the other family secrets that have prevented the characters from fully embracing their lives. Even as Spike and Terry flaunt their lovemaking, Effie and Rita refuse to read the signs as they concentrate on masking the deep love they share in their denied mother-daughter bond. The perverse desire that Teresa de Lauretis uses to describe the reversal of the oedipal prohibition placed on the daughter to renounce her love for the mother's body, is thus played out on several literal and metaphorical levels in *Black Friday*.[5] Reinforcing the symmetry of the women-identified circle that Terry's mother and aunt/grandmother already belong to, is the additional information that the other significant female relative, Sister Teresa, who is now a nun, has a suspicious lesbian past. Kept off stage, and immobilized in hospital, she assumes increasing importance as the family member from whom Effie is estranged, mostly because she tried to get her to reveal to Rita that she is her child.

When *Black Friday* ends, Terry's obsessive identification with her father has been laid to rest and she is able to finally acknowledge the centrality of her mother/ grandmother/aunt's roles in shaping her. It is highly significant that her coming out to them is parallelled with Effie and Rita's coming out to each other as mother and daughter. Thus the shame of having an illegitimate child that is brought to the fore when Effie and Rita admit their real relationship, deeply underscores the shame of being a lesbian that has kept Terry away for the past six years. Butler's choice of adding a question mark to her revised version *Black Friday?* speaks to her wish to leave her spectators with hope that the future will be different. The metatheatricality of the final kiss between Terry and Spike leaves just such a message when audience members are told that it is not for their benefit. As the lights go down, we are left with a sense that their lives are just beginning.

Notes

1 Audrey Butler, *Black Friday,* copyrighted in 1988, first published in *Theatrum* (February/March 1990) S2-S11. The version included here has been updated by the author. However, as her artist's statement explains, she has agreed to include this earlier text with a few modifications, rather than the later *Black Friday?*.

2 Sue-Ellen Case, "Towards a Butch/Femme Aesthetic," *Making a Spectacle: Feminist Essays on Contemporary Womens' Theatre,* ed. Lynda Hart (Ann Arbor: U of Michigan P, 1989) 282-99.

3 Monique Wittig, "One is not Born a Woman," *Feminist Issues* (Winter 1981) 49, argued cogently that by refusing to become/remain heterosexual, lesbians had to be something else, "a not-woman, not-man, a product of society, not a product of nature, for there is no nature in society." Almost forty years later, the society-nature argument is no longer so valid.

4 "Black Friday" refers to October 13, 1967 when Hawker-Siddley, then owner of the Sydney steelworks, announced permanent closure of all steel plants in the city. In answer to fervent community protests, the provincial government stepped in to revive the fledgling industry. Despite increasing reliance on government aid and an industry boom in the 1970s, both the steel and coal industries were eventually deemed unrecoverable. In 2001, the last coal mine and steel mill in Cape Breton closed. Today, the legacy of the steel and coal industries continues to affect Cape Breton. The unemployment and subsequent emigration caused by the closure of the island's two primary industries has left Cape Breton struggling to find an economic alternative. (Note supplied by Dawn Tracey.)

5 Teresa de Lauretis, *Practice of Love: Lesbian Sexuality, Perverse Desire* (Bloomington, Ind.: Indiana UP, 1994) 257-97.

photo by Nicole Kayson

Alec Butler

Bio and Artist's Statement

Alec Butler self-identifies as two-spirit, pagan and a trans man; he is also an award-winning playwright and filmmaker. His plays include *Shakedown, Cradle Pin, Claposis, Black Friday, Black Friday?, Medusa Rising* (nominated for two Dora Awards for theatre in 1996) and more recently a one trans man show called *Ruf Paradise* which he performed at the Rhubarb Festival in Toronto and the Wow Cafe in New York City in 2003. Alec's films include the animated trilogy about growing up "gender variant" and working class in the 1970s called "MisAdventures of Pussy Boy: First Love, Sick & First Period"; and an experimental documentary about transitioning from butch dyke to trans man called "Audrey's Beard". All these films were screened at A Space Art Gallery in his show *Trans Missions: Get your motor runnin'* for the month of November in 2003. Alec's most recent film, "Darla's Goodbye", is another experimental film which samples found footage from the past with a voiceover that is also published as a short story in *Red Light: Superheroes, Saints and Sluts*, an anthology edited by Anna Camilleri.

Alec currently works as the Trans Policy Consultant and Artist-in-residence at the 519 Church Street Community Centre. He lives in downtown Toronto with his animal familiars Daisy the dog and black cat Spike. Alec is working on a touring cabaret show with his new trans community theatre company called TransForm, a short film about his "mixed blood" roots called "Red Medicine: A cutting" and a novel based on his stage show called *Ruf Paradise.*

•

In the seventeen years since I wrote *Black Friday* without the question mark, as I like to call this version of the script (as opposed to *Black Friday?* with said question mark), a lot has changed in my life. Transitioning from female to male at age forty after living as butch dyke for a quarter of a century was not a simple matter of a name change but at the same time it wasn't that complicated either. I had always been called "sir." Not opting for surgery or hormone therapy was against the grain of what gender transitioning meant seven years ago. Some have challenged my self-identification as "trans" because I didn't go that route. I went my own route, as usual.

Looking back it occurs to me that Terry, the working-class dyke in *Black Friday* is Audrey in her "glory days." It's interesting to me, Alec, that back then Audrey chose a gender neutral name, a name that could be either female or male for the character who represented her "voice" way back in 1989.

But this is an anthology of lesbian plays, so I have to think back to what it was like to be a lesbian almost twenty years ago. I always preferred to self-identify as a dyke back then.

The word had an "in your face" quality that had more street cred. I doubt if I would continue to be an activist today if I hadn't identified as a dyke for twenty-five years. This wasn't an easy thing to do in the mid to late eighties when I wrote this first version of a dyke's coming out story, which has parallels with Audrey's coming out story. "The Ellen DeGeneres Show" wasn't even a sparkle in someone's eye when Audrey hosted a series called Late Night Lesbians on stage for three years running that would have given Dave Lettermen a run for his money. These were heady times, the queer revolution was gaining traction and walls were coming down, not just in Berlin, but in the sexual/social/psychic realms as well. But lesbians still had to fight creatively and demand to see positive representations of themselves in the media and in the gay community itself, which had a mostly young white gay male image. The production history of *Black Friday* was part of that struggle. The version published herein was only produced once, any further productions were of the version with the question mark. Re-reading and comparing the two versions, I realize that the version without the question mark is clearer and has a rawness that I find refreshing. I believe that with the handful of lines that I asked to be added from the version with the question mark this version stands as a production-worthy version of the script and melds the intentions of the later version with the earlier.

Production History

Scenes which later became *Black Friday* were read publicly at the Tarragon Theatre in the mid 1980s when Audrey was a member of the Tarragon Theatre's Playwright's Unit.

•

A first draft of the script had a reading at Nightwood Theatre's Groundswell Festival in 1988. The version published in *Theatrum* in 1988 was produced as part of the Foreplay Festival by Buddies in Bad Times Theatre at Actor's Lab, Toronto, in April 1989 with the following company:

EFFIE	Marguerite McNeil
TERRY	Kate Johnston
SPIKE	Marcia Johnson
RITA	Merle Matheson
RODDY	Grant Carmichael

Directed and designed by Bryden MacDonald
Production co-ordinated by Paula Muisal
Stage managed by Veronica Macdonald
Assistant stage managed by Ann Vespry

•

Black Friday? (with the question mark) which was produced by the playwright's own theatre company Tempermental Journey in 1990, and The Great Canadian Theatre Company in Ottawa in 1994, among other productions, was also nominated for the Governor General's Award for Drama in 1991.

Characters

Terry Morrison, a white working class dyke, thirty-one years old, who returns home after a six-year absence. She has been living in Toronto, Ontario, where she has recently met up with her father Frank, who abandoned her and her mother Rita shortly after the events of Black Friday. On Friday, October 13, 1967 the steel plant where Frank worked shut down after a bitter fight to keep it open. The shut-down threw thousands out of work and a community into chaos. Terry was eight years old.

Rita Morrison (nee MacIntyr), Terry's mother, she is also a singer in church choirs and community theatre musicals and makes her living as a music teacher. Rita is a striking woman in her early fifties who has a touch of sadness about her. Rita was left holding the bag when Frank left town after being accused publicly of stealing the union's membership dues.

Aunt Effie MacIntyr, Rita's aunt, who is really her mother and Terry's grandmother. Aunt Effie is the loveable matriarch of what's left of the MacIntyr clan, sister to Sister Theresa, a nun (offstage) in the hospital from falling down after drinking too much communion wine.

Roddy Bishop, a professor at the university, and draft dodger from the States who has lived in his Aunt Shirley Bishop's house next door to the MacIntyr's since 1969. Roddy is also Terry's ex-boyfriend and the first person she came out too. Roddy is still in love with Terry.

Sophie "Spike" Johnson, Terry's lover, a twenty-five-year-old woman of African-Canadian descent. Spike is in love with Terry and has been worried about her since Terry met up with her father Frank.

Setting

Black Friday is set in the spring of 1989 in the MacIntyr family living-room in downtown Sydney, Cape Breton Island, Nova Scotia. Twenty-one and a half years after Black Friday. When the characters are not performing in a scene they sit in a church pew located upstage and watch the action on the set.

When the intro music pumps in after the house lights go down it starts with a throbbing club hit from the late 1980s and morphs into a more down-home fiddle tune by Howie MacDonald. In the black before the stage lights come up the headlight of a motorcycle makes a sweep across the stage. Music fades out to the sound of a motorcycle gearing down to park.

BLACK FRIDAY

A One-Act Play

scene one

EFFIE taking curlers out of her hair. SPIKE and TERRY enter. EFFIE screams.

TERRY Aunt Effie! It's me! Terry! From Toronto.

EFFIE Jesusmaryandjoseph Theresa! Scared me half to death in that outfit! Who's that?

SPIKE Spike.

TERRY My roommate. She drove me up.

EFFIE Youse look like a pair'a Martians!

TERRY Airight if she stays here?

EFFIE Like my new TV? Combination radio. Your Uncle Jerry bought it for me Christmas.

TERRY Bought it. Probably stole it. Spike's stayin' in the attic with me.

EFFIE Oh well, suit yourself. Room's filthy. Can't be bothered to climb all those stairs like I used to—Rita shoulda never let you move up there in the first place. Attics are for ghosts and mad wimmin.

TERRY So where is Ma.

EFFIE I'm not your mother's keeper. Never even breathed a word you were comin'.

TERRY Nobody knows. She doesn't even know.

EFFIE Lose another job didja?

SPIKE laughs.

TERRY No. I quit.

SPIKE They were gonna fire ya anyway.

TERRY Because I told that jerk of a manager off.

EFFIE See, she takes right after her father. Never did a lick of work either—

TERRY He was blacklisted remember. Long before Black Friday.

EFFIE   Just an excuse to run out on you and your mother. There's been plenty Black Fridays since.

TERRY   Ma tell you where she was going?

EFFIE   Mother doesn't tell me anything. Been ages since she put up my hair. Give me a hand will you dear. *(TERRY does.)*

TERRY   You and Ma on the outs again?

EFFIE   Spikey dear, you from the Pier?

TERRY   Effie!

SPIKE   Pier? What pier?

TERRY   Never mind. Spike's from Toronto, Aunt Effie.

EFFIE   Whadda sin—Could you grab that down by your foot there, dear?

TERRY   *Diet Coke?* Since when?

EFFIE   Went off regular for Lent. Don't taste the same anyway. Your mother's been in a terrible state since Christmas—You turnin' down that plane ticket—Ouch!!

TERRY   I told her I had to work—hold still.

EFFIE   Said that the last three Christmases.

TERRY   I couldn't afford it the first time

EFFIE   Good way to treat your mother. And after all she's done for you too.

SPIKE   The fog you guys get in this part of the world. Soon as we hit Nova Scotia, felt like I was ridin' on a cloud. My headlight cutting through it like a knife— When Terry said she wanted to head East I thought she meant Provincetown.

> *Enter RITA.*

RITA   Terry!

TERRY   Ma!

RITA   You didn't lose another job did you?

TERRY   Maaaa. I quit, okay.

RITA   You must be—

TERRY   Sophie.

SPIKE   Spike.

RITA   Spike? You're Terry's—

TERRY   Spike drove me up here.

SPIKE   We live together—

TERRY   We've been on the road all night. Where've you been?

RITA   Visiting Sister Theresa up the hospital—

TERRY   Is she?—

RITA   Took a bad turn last week. Fell down after she had a bit too much communion wine.

> *RITA and TERRY hug.* ·

Sister Theresa asked after you again. Aunt Effie. When you gonna go see her?

That's a sin. Her own sister. Her own flesh and blood. So, why are you here dear? Oh, you found your father. Is that it? I don't wanna have nothin' to do with him. You hear me. Even if he does come back.

TERRY   He's not coming back. All he wants are the columns the *Highland Press* printed in the '50s.

EFFIE   Those f'in Dorchester columns.

TERRY   And a the letter he wrote me after he left. Which nobody even bothered to tell me about.

RITA   What letter?

TERRY   He said he wrote when he got to Toronto.

EFFIE   You sure you're not from the Pier dear?

TERRY   Effie!

SPIKE   Huh?

RITA   No letters came from your father after he left. Might as well've dropped off the face of the earth.

TERRY   Well somebody has it. What about the Dorchester columns? Where are they?

RITA   I gave 'em away.

TERRY   You what? Ma! Those columns started a labour union. You were savin' them for me!

RITA   You said you didn't have any use for them anymore.

TERRY   I never said that.   •

RITA   You never said anything to make me think any different.

> *Pause.*

TERRY   So you gave them away. To who?

RITA   I sure as hell never had any use for them.

TERRY   Ma.

RITA   The Archives. Roddy Bishop arranged it.

TERRY   Oh, Roddy Bishop. When?

RITA   Months ago. Christmas.

TERRY   That's long enough. Get them back.

RITA   Terry! Don't be foolish.

TERRY   Ma. How could you? Roddy's Uncle didn't lift a finger to defend Dad after he left town.

RITA   Cyril Bishop? When your father was first blacklisted and sent to Dorchester Cyril Bishop worked to clear him.

TERRY   Cyril set Dad up. Made it look like he extorted union dues—

RITA   Oh, is that your father's latest story?

TERRY   That letter proves it.

RITA   Cause if it is he's stuck with it—

TERRY   Where is it?

RITA   Terry dear, I do not know what letter you're talkin' about! Roddy's been awful good to me and Effie since you left.

TERRY   I bet.

RITA   He's always askin' after ya. Asked after you the other day.

SPIKE   Who we talkin' about?

RITA   Sorry, dear.

TERRY   Prof I used to TA for.

SPIKE   Oh. Your old boyfriend. The draft dodging Cassanova.

RITA   What's that dear?

TERRY   She's just teasing.

SPIKE   Oh am I now?

TERRY   Don't start—

RITA   Theresa! Go talk to Roddy yourself! Better yet, go see him. He still lives across the way.

EFFIE   *(exiting)* His Aunt Shirley, she's been livin' it up in that new condo for the last coupla years. Oh jezuz, goin' concern that one. He owns that house now. Shirley gave it to him! Still single.

EFFIE exits.

TERRY   I'll go see Roddy in my own time, okay?

RITA   *(sighs)* Suit yourself. Always have. *(to SPIKE)* Welcome to Cape Breton, dear.

Exit RITA.

SPIKE   Terry, what is going on?

TERRY   Look at this place. Graceland North.

SPIKE   Like it. Feels funky.

TERRY   You would. Some of this stuff has been here since my great grandfather, the paranoid patriarch, built it a million years ago. His daughters Effie, her sisters Theresa and Sadie all worshipped the ground he walked on. Scared shitless of him at the same time. Aunt Effie isn't even really my aunt. Did I tell you that already?

SPIKE   So who is she?

TERRY   She's really my grandmother. My mother's mother.

SPIKE   I thought Sadie was your—

TERRY   She's really my aunt. Effie had Rita out of wedlock. Sadie was married—

SPIKE   But she's really your grandmother—

TERRY   Who?

SPIKE   Who are we talking about?

TERRY   Sadie's called my grandmother—

SPIKE   But she's really—

TERRY   My aunt—

SPIKE   So who's Sister Theresa?

TERRY   A nun.

SPIKE   Jesus Christ! But who is she?

TERRY   My aunt. A nun. And my aunt. Her and Aunt Effie ran a hairdressing school downtown. Never married. Two of 'em could've had the pick of the men in this town. Judges, mayors, men who are millionaires now. Theresa turned them all down, became a nun in her forties. Effie ran the school on her own for another twenty years. Jeezus, all these family secrets. Effie'd keel over if she knew that I knew—

SPIKE   Knew what?

TERRY   That she's really my grandmother!

SPIKE   Honey—

TERRY   What?

SPIKE   How do you remember all this?

TERRY   Night before Ma and Frank got married Ma got an anonymous note telling her Effie was her mother. He swears Effie sent it. She never wanted them to get married, Frank wasn't Catholic. Oh, God, thank God my mother rebelled. I was almost Roddy's cousin—

SPIKE   What?

TERRY   If Effie had managed to set my mother up with Mr. Bishop, Roddy's uncle—

SPIKE   Never mind. Forget I even asked—

TERRY   Religion's fucked in the head anyway. Listen to me Sophie, why am I getting myself mixed up in this? Whadda ya think I should do? Sophie. Say something.

SPIKE   *(shaking a snowbubble)* Whadda ya call these things?

TERRY   Snowbubbles. Sophie. What should I do? Huh? I should just stay out of it.

SPIKE   Gimme a break. As if you could. And stop calling me Sophie. I hate that name.

TERRY   I like it, it's cute.

SPIKE   Cute! I musta been nuts to tell you my real name. Never hear the end of it now.

TERRY   You're a real softy Sophie, that's why.

Horseplay.

SPIKE   Am not.

TERRY   Are too.

SPIKE   Am not.

TERRY   Are too.

SPIKE   Am not.

TERRY   Are so. *(Enter EFFIE, she takes her curlers and her Diet Coke. Exit EFFIE.)* Jeezus!! I knew that would happen.

SPIKE   Relax, Terry. We weren't doin' anything wrong.

TERRY   People around here wouldn't see it that way.

SPIKE   What did we say before we left Toronto?

TERRY   You said it, not me.

SPIKE   What did I say?

TERRY   You weren't gonna pretend to be someone you weren't once we got here.

SPIKE   What about you?

TERRY   It's not that simple!

SPIKE   What's the matter? Not femme enough for ya?

Enter EFFIE and RITA.

RITA   Aunt Effie! Don't leave the room while I'm talkin', all I said was: It's about time you stopped all this foolishness. It's been going on for twenty years!

EFFIE   That may be so. But as far as I'm concerned Theresa stopped being my sister twenty years ago—

TERRY   Aunt Effie.

EFFIE   You! You're a good one to talk. Couldn't pick up a telephone. Tell us you were comin'. Coulda took something decent outa the freezer—

TERRY   It's okay, Aunt Effie. Don't go to any trouble.

EFFIE   All I got is last week's chicken stew. Beef's so dear these days. Cut off my right arm before I pay that price, it's scanless.

TERRY   Let's just all go out for Chinese.

EFFIE   You know how much Chinese hates me. Want me up half the night? Oh you're just here to stir up trouble. She takes right after her father that one.

RITA   Effie! You've got no place shootin' your mouth off like that to Terry. The girl hasn't been home 20 minutes!

Enter RODDY.

TERRY   It's okay, Ma.

RITA   It's not—shootin' her mouth off like that in front of... company.

SPIKE   Don't mind me.

EFFIE   Say anything I want in my own home. Papa left this house to me remember.

RITA   Oh, here we go again.

TERRY   Will you two give it a rest! I didn't come 1500 miles to listen to you two fightin' like cats and dogs—

Doorbell.

RITA   I'll get it.

EFFIE   What did you come here for?

> *RITA exits.*

TERRY   Dad's old newspaper columns.

> *RITA and RODDY meet.*

RITA   Well well, speak of the silver-tongued devil.

> *RODDY laughs.*

EFFIE   Those f'in Dorchester columns—

TERRY   And a letter he wrote years ago—

RITA   Have I got a surprise for you—

TERRY   Do you know anything about it?

> *RITA and RODDY enter.*

EFFIE   I don't know where my dentures are half the time. Roddy, darlin'. Talk some sense into this girl! She's goin' on and on about some damn letter—

RITA   Aunt Effie! Let someone else talk for a change.

RODDY   Already talkin' about Frank are ya? Welcome home Ter.

TERRY   Hi Roddy!

RODDY   Saw the big bike out front. Figured it must be Terry.

RITA   Big bike?

RODDY   *(to EFFIE)* How are you today, sexy?

RITA   What bike?

RODDY   Irish Club. Tomorrow. Friday night. How about it?

EFFIE   Ah! Go way with ya—

RODDY   You're not gonna pass up another lip synch contest?

RITA   Terry.

RODDY   I hear they've got three Elvis's lined up.

EFFIE   You big tease!

RITA   Who's bike—

SPIKE   MY BIKE!!

RITA   Don't tell me you two came all the way here on a motorbike—

TERRY   That's right.

RODDY   Well girl, you're lookin' good.

TERRY   Roddy, this is my roommate Spike. Spike, Roddy. Roddy, Spike.

SPIKE   I'm amazed we got here in one piece. Not like those poor fuckers in "Easy Rider".

TERRY   Tea ready yet, Ma?

RITA   Come on, Effie. Let's get that stew in the microwave—

     RITA exits.

EFFIE   Just don't get me goin'. Or I'll stick you in the microwave. Baked a pan of date squares yesterday, Roddy—

RODDY   Wouldn't miss them for the world sweetheart. *(exit EFFIE)* So, this what they're wearing in TO these days?

TERRY   They're bike leathers, Roddy. We didn't come all the way here to make a fashion statement.

RODDY   So, Spike. Where'd you pick up a handle like that?

SPIKE   Bargain Harold's.

RODDY   I like her, Ter. Where'd you find her? Revolutionary Tea Party?

SPIKE   Where'd they find you, sweetheart? Elton John look-a-like contest?

TERRY   Spike. Why don't you go out and get some of our stuff off the bike. Please.

SPIKE   I'll get it later.

TERRY   Now.

SPIKE   Why? Whadda ya need?

TERRY   Please.

     SPIKE exits.

RODDY   Ah, Alone at last.

TERRY   Boy, are you barkin' up the wrong tree.

RODDY   We had quite a thing goin' you and me. We made quite a team.

TERRY   Oh Roddy, I didn't come back to pick up where we left off, okay? I came back for a letter Frank wrote.

RODDY   Oh, one of the Dorchester columns?

TERRY   All of them for a start. Plus a letter he wrote from Toronto. Addressed to me.

RODDY   Was he sober? *(pause)* What does this have to do with me?

TERRY   Have you seen or heard about it?

RODDY   The only letters I know about are the Dorchester Columns. Rita donated them to the Archives.

TERRY   I used to be your TA remember.

RODDY   For one lovely year.

TERRY   Six long years ago. Could get it back for me.

RODDY   Frank put you up to this?

TERRY   He said he wrote home once.

RODDY   Nobody heard from him after he left you know that.

TERRY   He said he wrote.

RODDY   Stories. Rumours. That's all you heard.

TERRY   A letter that proves he didn't extort money from his own union.

RODDY   I don't know what letter you're talking about—

TERRY   You wouldn't admit it if you did. Cause Frank sez this letter proves his innocence. Proves Cyril set him up.

RODDY   My Uncle Cyril tried to save your father's ass—

TERRY   Bullshit!

RODDY   Cyril kept this family out of the poorhouse after Frank left. Just ask Effie.

TERRY   Oh and your wonderful uncle took you in after your parents kicked you out for burning your draft card—I heard it all before—spare me.

RODDY   What's gotten into you?

TERRY   I want my letter!

RODDY   You're like a dog after a bone. *(enter SPIKE)* You're gonna have to learn to live with what Frank did.

TERRY   It better show up soon cause I'm not leavin' this island without it.

RODDY   Looks like you'll be stickin' around for quite a while then.

SPIKE   He givin' you a hard time?

TERRY   He'd like to.

RODDY   Hard time? It's the other way around.

TERRY   I haven't even started yet.

RODDY   Whadda ya gonna do? Sic this one on me?

                Sound of breaking glass offstage.

SPIKE   What the fuck was that?

TERRY Ma!

RITA Effie!

    Blackout.

scene two

The living room. SPIKE staring off. Enter TERRY.

SPIKE Well.

TERRY She's okay. Fainted that's all. They're keepin' her in overnight. They're gonna run some tests tomorrow.

SPIKE What about your mother?

TERRY Took it worse than Aunt Ef. God, those two are a pair, aren't they. One of these days. It's a wonder my mother doesn't spill it out. The whole sordid story. One of these days.

SPIKE Why doesn't she?

TERRY I don't know.

SPIKE What difference would it make?

TERRY Who knows?

SPIKE What about Hot Rod Roddy?

TERRY What about 'im?

SPIKE Nothing.

TERRY That's right. Nothing. Zip. I fucked him to get straight A's.

SPIKE Probably fucked me just to get a ride up here.

TERRY Oh, come on, Spike—Will you stop it. What's got into you?

SPIKE I shoulda stayed home.

TERRY What?

SPIKE Home. Toronto. Where you live now.

TERRY I know where I live.

SPIKE Why am I here? Shock value?

TERRY Spike—

SPIKE Just don't use me—

TERRY   Use you—

SPIKE   To tell your mother—or whoever she is—that you're gay—

TERRY   Don't flatter yourself—

SPIKE   Course I don't even know if you are gay.

TERRY   Oh. Would you like a signed affidavit?

SPIKE   No. *(pause)* Yes.

TERRY   You know what? You have the most talented tongue this side of Montreal—

SPIKE   Bet you say that to all the girls—

> *The girls start making out.*

TERRY   Soph.

SPIKE   What?

TERRY   My mother's bedroom is right at the top of the stairs.

SPIKE   I don't care—

> *Pause.*

TERRY   Soph.

> *SPIKE jumps up.*

SPIKE   This mean—

TERRY   Shhh

SPIKE   This mean we won't have sex the whole time we're here?

TERRY   No, it just means—

SPIKE   What, Terry, what?

RITA   *(offstage)* Terry—

TERRY   Yes, Ma.

RITA   If you girls are hungry…

TERRY   It's okay, Ma, we're just gonna—We'll be up soon.

RITA   Okay, dear. Night.

TERRY   Night, Ma.

RITA   Goodnight… Spike.

SPIKE   Goodnight… *(pause)* What the fuck is Black Friday? An East Coast Holiday?

TERRY   The day somebody spraypainted "commie bastard" all over the front of the house I grew up in.

SPIKE   Why?

TERRY   Because the steelplant shut down.

SPIKE   So.

TERRY   The day before Frank left town.

SPIKE   For Dorchester.

TERRY   No, no. That was before that, Ma was 8 months pregnant—

SPIKE   Why did he leave town?

TERRY   Because of Black Friday—

SPIKE   I still don't get it. What is Black Friday.

TERRY   The day the union bit the dust—

SPIKE   They sent him to Dorchester for that?

TERRY   No, before that, for sedition.

SPIKE   Before what?

TERRY   Before Black Friday. I was nine, almost ten.

SPIKE   So, not before you were born?

TERRY   Yes. No. Yes. What are we talking about?

SPIKE   You tell me!

TERRY   Shhh—Spike. Could we talk about this in the morning?

SPIKE   Jeez, I'm sorry I asked.

TERRY   Spike.

SPIKE   Ummmm.

TERRY   I want you.

SPIKE   What about Hot Rod Roddy?

TERRY   I told you, as soon as I get Frank's letter—

SPIKE   What if Roddy has it—

TERRY   I don't know who has it—

SPIKE   He was hard to make sense of—

TERRY   Who?

SPIKE   Frank. He was pretty pounded that night—

TERRY   Which night?

SPIKE   The night he went on and on about the letter—

TERRY   We'll figure this out in the morning, okay?

SPIKE   If Roddy has it—

TERRY   Yes?

SPIKE   You think he's just gonna hand it over?

TERRY   Not if he finds out. Of course if he has it then he already knows—

SPIKE   Knows what?

TERRY   That there's a letter from Cyril included in it—

SPIKE   Cyril.

TERRY   Roddy's uncle—

SPIKE   So there's two letters.

TERRY   Right. I hope they're still together—

SPIKE   How do you plan on getting it back, that's what I wanna know—

TERRY   I'm not gonna sleep with him, Sophie. You're jealous.

SPIKE   Am not.

TERRY   That's so sweet.

SPIKE   How long we here for?

TERRY   As long as it takes.

SPIKE   Jezuz.

TERRY   Baby.

> *They start making out. Blackout.*

scene three

> *TERRY poring over newspaper clippings. RITA folding laundry.*

RITA   Day before I married Frank I found out who my mother was. People been feeling sorry for me for years. They say I was so much like her when I was younger. Sharp tongued, headstrong. Always wanting my own way. Two peas in a pod.

TERRY   Do you know who sent the anonymous note?

RITA   Cyril Bishop's mother sent it.

TERRY   What?

RITA   She never had much use for me after I threw Cyril over for Frank.

TERRY   Boy, I bet you were a real heartbreaker—

RITA   Theresa! What a way to talk about your mother.

TERRY   Why did you stop singing?

RITA   Because I wasn't good enough.

TERRY   You have a beautiful voice. So when did you audition at Julliard?

RITA   Julliard? Who told you about Julliard? Frank?

TERRY   Aunt Effie. Aunt Effie told me last time I came home for Christmas.

RITA   I don't remember you around much that Christmas—

TERRY   Ma. You know how I feel about this house I don't feel comfortable here. You grew up here not me. I miss the house we lived in with Dad.

> *Beat.*

RITA   I was 17 when I won first prize at the Kiwanis Music Festival. Sister Theresa and Aunt Effie persuaded me to go down to New York City and audition at Julliard. I went and came back the same day with my tail between my legs after squawking my way through the audition. Aunt Effie told you about Julliard?

TERRY   Ma, she was proud of you—

RITA   Two years later Frank and I married. That's what you did back then—

TERRY   But you worked. Damn right you worked. Some of your students are singing professionally now because of you.

RITA   If I'm such a good teacher why am I still folding laundry?

TERRY   What's your favorite memory of Dad?

RITA   Terry—

TERRY   It couldn't all have been bad.

RITA   No, it wasn't all bad.

TERRY   What about the day he came back from Dorchester? You must have been ecstatic.

RITA   Ecstatic. I felt like I'd never been kissed.

TERRY   What?

RITA   I was nervous, dear. It had been a long time. People from all over the island were at the train station that day. You'd think your father was a big war hero coming home. Not a man coming back after six months hard labour at Dorchester.

TERRY   All for writing about starting a new union. Trumped up sedition charge.

RITA   And inciting riot, I know Terry. Nothing ever stopped him from going after what he believed in. Least of all me! He kissed you before he kissed me.

TERRY   Huh? *(RITA touches her belly.)* Why didn't you ever tell me that before?

RITA   Sometimes you forget these things. Sometimes you have to.

TERRY   He started writing poetry at Dorchester too didn't he?

RITA   I suppose.

TERRY   He's writing it again. He didn't for a long time. But he's writing it again. *(pause)* Wanna know how I found him? What he does now? How he looks? Anything? Ma. He still loves you—

RITA   They all say that, dear. Okay okay. What's he do? For money, I mean.

TERRY   He does what he has to. Like me. It's funny, for months I kept seeing his name on posters for poetry readings. But it didn't click until I was dragged along for one myself. There he was: preaching at the Brunswick Hotel. "The light at the end of the tunnel has a stranger's name."

RITA   "Has a stranger's name."

TERRY   Now he wants to write his life story. About the union, the politics. Guess what he's calling it.

RITA   *Black Friday.*

TERRY   He's obsessed with it. I don't blame him. He got a pretty raw deal.

RITA   This whole island got a pretty raw deal if you ask me.

TERRY   He drinks.

RITA   He always did—

TERRY   Ma, he drinks! He looks sad. "In the darkest annals of capitalism few incidents can compare with this example of social irresponsibility. If this represents the way of life for which we so proudly wave the new flag this centennial year then all I can say is God help Canada. It can never save itself."

RITA   Last thing he had published. He recognized you, huh?

TERRY   Well, he thought I was someone who looked like you. We didn't speak to each other. Well, not until we saw each other that third time. He knew who I was by then. Our eyes. I have his eyes don't I? I can't even remember what he said. Or what I said. Whatever it was it was hard to say.

RITA   Didja try "Where you been for twenty years?"

TERRY   Is this the only column you kept?

RITA   Rest went to the Archives, where they belong.

TERRY   Ma. They belong to us! And I have to find that letter. I can't clear Frank's name without it.

RITA   I don't know what letter you mean, dear. Shoulda burned the lot years ago. They called you names in school over what your father did. Just leave it alone!

TERRY   He never stole money from the Union. Cyril Bishop was behind all that. Took advantage of Dad leavin' town. Years later he wrote Dad practically confessing, apologizing. It's in the letter Frank sent me.

RITA   Did your father tell you this!

TERRY   Yes!

RITA   Was he sober?! Your father was no saint either. Not to people around here!

TERRY   To some people around here. Christ! The others had him tarred and feathered! For trying to change things. They were too stupid to know it was change for the better.

RITA   If your father said the world was flat you'd believe him. Yes, your father liked to change things. He could sweep people away with his talk. But if things didn't go the way he wanted he'd ask for trouble. He would make things up that just weren't true! *(pause)* He have a roof over his head?

TERRY   Stayed with us a coupla times. Between benders. He can't remember much because of the booze. When he wrote it, what he said. What happened to it, Ma?

RITA   Terry, I don't believe this letter exits. Will you stop going on about it. On top of everything else—

TERRY   On top of everything else?

RITA   Sister Theresa in the hospital. The goin's on between with Effie. I just can't take it.

TERRY   I don't know how you can stand it Ma. Living all these years in the same house. Pretending she's your aunt.

RITA   I didn't have any choice Terry. And most of all neither did she. We can't imagine what it was like years ago. To have a child out of wedlock. To bring all that up now.

TERRY   I know.

RITA   Sister Theresa tried to get Aunt Effie to acknowledge me 20 years ago, of course that's another thing I'm not supposed to know. Craziness, huh?

TERRY   And that's when it all started between Effie and Sister Theresa?

RITA   More craziness.

TERRY   Do you know who your father is? Ma?

RITA   A sailor off the boats. Of course that's another thing I'm not supposed to know. *(laughter)* Your grandmother was a pretty wild woman in her day. What difference would it make to bring it all up now?

TERRY   You might start getting along better.

RITA   Her and I get along fine!

> *Enter EFFIE.*

EFFIE   Heart in my throat—all the way home. Runnin' the red lights like there was no tomorrow. Taxi drivers!

RITA   What are you doing here?

EFFIE   I live here.

RITA   They finish all those tests this early?

TERRY   Here, let me take your coat.

EFFIE   They're all crazy up there. Not gonna strap any machines on me and poke around. For the love of God—All I did was faint. Watch my hair, dear. Nice girl came in this morning and did it for me.

TERRY   A candystriper?

EFFIE   No, a Newfoundlander.

RITA   I don't want Dr. Wong pitchin' a fit, I'm calling the hospital. Tell them where you are.

> *RITA exits.*

EFFIE   Go ahead! Crazier than Sunday's KOC Flea Market up here. Take 'em months before they notice I'm gone. What's all this?

TERRY   Old newspapers.

EFFIE   Just put them in the kitchen over by the stove dear.

TERRY   They're not for burning. There's stuff in them about Black Friday. I brought them out to show Spike.

EFFIE   Black Friday Black Friday Black Friday. Why you bringin' that all up for? Gettin' people down on their heads. We all nearly lost our homes and our minds over that one. When all those big shots pulled out, didn't know where our next meal was comin' from. And your father, well, Black Friday was a good name for it.

TERRY   Some people felt Black Friday brought this island closer together—

RITA   *(enters)* Dr. Wong's office Monday—and you're going! If I have to drag you there myself kickin' and screamin'. Come on now, have a laydown before your shows starts.

EFFIE   A cuppa tea won't hurt.

RITA   Terry'll bring it up.

EFFIE   Oh dear, I want you to make it.

TERRY   It's okay, Ma. I'll take her upstairs.

EFFIE   I don't need anybody to take me up those stairs, I been climbin' those stairs all my life!

RITA   I have to go visit Sister Theresa at the hospital.

> *TERRY and EFFIE exiting.*

EFFIE   Rush rush RUSH!

TERRY   Come on, Aunt Effie. We're only trying to take care of you.

EFFIE   I want my tea!

TERRY   I'll bring you up a cuppa tea.

EFFIE   Sure, just stick me up the stairs, forget about me.

RITA   I don't wanna hear that kinda talk, you just got outa the hospital.

> *RITA readies to leave. Looks at her sheet music. Sings a bit of the aria from Puccini's "Madame Butterfly." Spike enters.*

SPIKE   Wow! That was beautiful! Good as Leontyne Price.

RITA   Leontyne Price! What foolishness.

SPIKE   I've seen her live three times. That voice! Makes the back of my head tingle. My heart pounds, does somersaults in my chest. Once I coulda swore my womb swelled up to twice its size.

RITA   Oh!

SPIKE   Off to visit Effie.

RITA   Sister Theresa. Effie's upstairs. Up and walked outa the hospital this morning. Can you believe it! More guts than brains. What are you up to?

SPIKE   Changin' the oil on the bike. We really booted it up here. Wanna lift?

RITA   Oh! No no no no no. I'll call a cab.

SPIKE   I'll get the Beast back together before a cab shows.

RITA   Thanks, dear—

SPIKE   No problem.

RITA   What do you do? Up Toronto?

SPIKE   Tend bar. I'm good too. I used to be a mechanic till they found out I was a girl. Wasn't the same after that.

RITA   Where do you work? Same place Terry works? Worked.

SPIKE   Nope. You know what a booze can is?

RITA   A blind pig.

SPIKE   Yeah. Right! Can't call it those names though. The boss gets pissed off.

RITA   Sounds awful.

SPIKE   Naw. It's great! Some real jerks hang out there though.

RITA   Where you work?

SPIKE   Mosta them celebs.

RITA   Celebs?

SPIKE   Celebrities. Lousy tippers. Friends of the boss. If it wasn't for the music. Verdimozartbellini! Puccini! That aria's my favorite.

RITA   Mine too. How did you and Terry meet?

SPIKE   At the blind pig. We heard of each other before though.

RITA   What was Terry doing there?

SPIKE   She came to hear Frank. He reads there sometimes. He's a real character when he's not too pounded. They have performers every Friday. We had a great drag act last week.

RITA   Drag act?

SPIKE   A guy in dress.

RITA   Sounds like a hoot.

SPIKE   One night she asked me out, you know, for coffee. The club doesn't close till six unless the cops close it earlier. One morning I come out to get on my bike to go home, guess whose sittin' on her? Sun was just coming up and it was pissin' rain. She said: "Take me to the ocean" but of course she meant Lake Ontario that time. Then I took her to Fran's for breakfast.

RITA   Another friend of yours?

SPIKE   Nope. S'posed to be a restaurant. Open twenty-four hours. Grilled cheese sandwiches with olives stuck on top with toothpicks. Anyway, we've been friends ever since. Well, hey, let's hit the road!

RITA   Oh no no, I'll call a cab.

SPIKE   I can get you there in two minutes. I won't drive too fast. Grab that helmet.

RITA Well, this will certainly be a first. Tell me something? Is Terry okay?

SPIKE She's got Frank on the brain. I wish he'd never told her about that letter.

RITA I was afraid of that. She's just grabbing at straws. *(exiting)* Do me a favour.

SPIKE Depends.

RITA Don't let on to Aunt Effie where you met Terry.

SPIKE Not much chance of her asking me that. What pier is she always going on about?

RITA Whitney Pier. It's an area of town…

SPIKE Where lots of Blacks live.

> *RITA nods.*

RITA Try not to mind her too much.

SPIKE I like her!

> *Blackout.*

scene four

SPIKE and EFFIE watching TV.

EFFIE Holy-Mother-of-God, that is one smart dog. Only show that's not fulla sex and dope. So where are you coming from, dear?

SPIKE Whitney Pier. I took Rita to the hospital. Went for a drive. Where's Terry?

EFFIE Poor girl's beat. She laid down beside me. Konked right off.

SPIKE What about you, shouldn't you be resting?

EFFIE Fit as a fiddle I am. *(doorbell ring)* Get that for me will you dear. *(enter RODDY)* Roddy! Seen more of you in the last day and a half than I have in the last month.

RODDY Where's Terry?

SPIKE Laying down.

EFFIE Boy she is one popular girl. I'll go put the kettle on.

SPIKE I'll do it.

EFFIE No you won't. You young people stay here and talk. Get yourselves sorted out.

SPIKE You just got out of the hospital. Effie!

EFFIE   *(offstage)* How many lumps do youse want?

SPIKE   None.

RODDY   One. One.

SPIKE   None. None!

RODDY   One.

EFFIE   *(offstage)* Alright! One for one. None for one.

> *Pause.*

RODDY   So. You stickin' 'round here til Terry heads back to Toronto?

SPIKE   Maybe.

RODDY   I was thinking: This can't be a pretty exciting place for a girl like you—

SPIKE   A girl like me?

> *Pause.*

RODDY   Where you from?

SPIKE   Why does everybody around here wanna know where I'm from? I don't get it.

> *Enter EFFIE with a plate.*

EFFIE   Storeboughts! Storeboughts! You girls pigged out on all my homemades.

RODDY   What about those date squares?

EFFIE   Look you little christer, you go visit your Aunt Shirley once in a while. Maybe she'll make you some.

RODDY   I saw her last week. She never bakes.

EFFIE   Never bakes!

RODDY   Now she's busy getting the Winnebago ready to drive off to Florida.

EFFIE   Goin' concern that one. Cyril left her in good shape. More than I can say for the men in this family.

SPIKE   Who?

EFFIE   Shirley Bishop. His aunt. Her and Rita used to step together in school.

SPIKE   Step?

> *EFFIE does a bit of a step dance. She has to stop.*

EFFIE   Oh oh! That's enough for me! *(exits)*

> *Pause.*

SPIKE   What are you up to?

RODDY   Eating a cookie.

SPIKE   Why are you here?

RODDY   To talk to Terry.

SPIKE   Why are you asking me so many questions?

RODDY   "Where you from?" That's how we check people out around here. "So where you been anyway" that's another common one. My favorite is "What's your father's name?"

SPIKE   Well, I been all over, I've been a dude dyke, a Birkenstock dyke, a leather dyke, I'm a virtual dykology, now I'm a bike dyke.

RODDY   Do you have to be so blatant about it?

SPIKE   Why not? Better blatant than latent. Two women may be a turn on for men but for lesbians it's about taking our power into our own hands and coming a lot.

RODDY   It's just the sex? Come on.

SPIKE   Naw, fucking is only part of it, Roddy. The idea of women having sex in a society that hates sex and women, not to mention lesbians, makes it dangerous. For me. For us. I hate the danger but I take it because I love women. That's why I'm a dyke! Does that answer your question?

RODDY   I think that about covers it. What's Terry told you about me?

SPIKE   Everything. She tells me everything.

RODDY   She tell you when she's headin' back yet?

SPIKE   She's going back with me. You have a problem with that?

RODDY   I don't have a problem. Terry's been through these phases before.

SPIKE   I ain't no "phase" she's goin' through, sweetheart.

RODDY   You sound a little worried. I was just wondering whether Terry found what she was looking for. *(enter EFFIE)* Sounds like Frank's been filling her head with stories—

SPIKE   Mind your own fucking business.

EFFIE   I left you two here to sort yourselves out, instead you're cursin each other out like a coupla heathens. Jeezus H Christ! *(exit EFFIE)*

SPIKE & RODDY   Effie!!

SPIKE   We been lovers a good long time. We spent yesterday morning making love on the beach in Igonish just as the sun was coming up. It was great. *(SPIKE exits.)*

RODDY   "It was great."

TERRY enters.

TERRY   Where's Effie?

RODDY   She's in the kitchen.

TERRY   Well Roddy, I just called the hospital. They did a biopsy on Sister Theresa this morning. It doesn't look good. Ma's waiting for the results.

RODDY   I remember waiting for Cyril's biopsy—

TERRY   Cancer from the air in that fucking steel plant.

RODDY   We met two weeks after he died. You helped me deal with that. You were lovely.

TERRY   I was 21 and naive. Do you have something for me?

RODDY   I told you Terry, I don't have that letter. How would I have gotten my hands on it? Look, I used to look up to Frank too, we all did. Everybody loved Frank. The booze did him in.

TERRY   If Frank and Cyril were such good friends why didn't he even stick up for Frank or lift a finger to defend him after they discovered the missing union dues?

RODDY   He was the union's treasurer for Christ's sake! Will you just let go of it! Cyril didn't defend him because Frank was guilty. My uncle took the flak for not pressing any charges. He's lucky he didn't end up in Dorchester.

TERRY   Maybe because he didn't want the truth to come out. Years later he sent Frank a letter confessing! Frank told me!

RODDY   Frank told a lot of people a lot of things—

TERRY   Maybe I should give Cheryl Beck or Diane Sawchuck a call. I wonder what those girls are up to. They were straight-A students too. Like me, right?

RODDY   Yeah, but you were special.

TERRY   If Dean Father Pat ever found out—

RODDY   Terry, this doesn't sound like you at all. Blackmail? You wouldn't.

TERRY   I might.

RODDY   What about the good times? Making love on the beach in Kenington cove. Afternoons in my office. You used to sneak out of this house almost every other night—

TERRY   All I remember is lots of groping and grinding, waiting for someone to knock on the door.

RODDY   What about that birthday party?

TERRY   Yeah, you threw it for me.

RODDY   Invited all your friends.

TERRY   Played guitar.

RODDY   Badly. I've gotten better.

TERRY   Roddy, it was over the night you told me my father was a lush.

RODDY   Let's just put all that behind us—

TERRY   You don't understand. Quit stalling. I want Frank's letter.

RODDY   Terry, this letter might be a fantasy. Did you ever consider that?

TERRY   No! It exists!

RODDY   Then it's somewhere in this house. I don't even have access to the Dorchester columns anymore. To tell you the truth, I don't have any pull out there anymore.

TERRY   Since when?

RODDY   Since cutbacks last fall. Know what they got me teaching out there now? Terrorism. It's about as popular as the PTL Club. Students are terrorists, all five of them.

TERRY   Are you afraid of what you'll find out about Cyril?

RODDY   There's nothing to find out about Cyril. Frank is—maybe Frank made this letter up—but if you think this letter exists, I'll help you find it—okay?

TERRY   Am I way off base?

RODDY   I don't know.

TERRY   When you first walked in yesterday I thought "he hasn't changed a bit" but maybe you have. Thanks.

RODDY   You're still lovely—remember I brought you to New York City? Reading week. You told Effie and Rita you were going with someone else.

TERRY   I wanted to check out the gay bars.

RODDY   I didn't know where any were—

TERRY   I do now.

RODDY   You know, I don't understand what the attraction is. It can't just be the sex. You and I could still be good for each other—

TERRY   Oh Roddy, that's just not gonna happen.

RODDY   Why? I loved you.

TERRY   You loved a different me.

RODDY   You loved me!

TERRY   I did, then. But this is now. I love Spike.

RODDY   Does Rita know?

TERRY   Ma couldn't say "lesbian" if her mouth was full of one.

RODDY   You should tell her.

TERRY   Jezus! Why don't you guys have to tell your mothers you're straight?

RODDY   Want me to tell her?

TERRY   Oh yeah, Roddy, that would go over like a fart in church. I'll tell her soon, okay. *(pause)* You been alone all these years?

RODDY   No. *(pause)* Yes.

TERRY   Oh Jesus! Maybe they don't exist! I don't know! *(RODDY comforts her.)* We can be friends Roddy, that's all. *(They comfort each other.)* Maybe I did tell her, when I was in love with Kathy Gosby in Grade Ten. She said it was just a phase I was goin' through. Like what? I wanted to ask. Life? Since meeting Spike I've come out more and more. She's very brave you know, not a chicken-shit like me. *(SPIKE enters.)* When I finally realized I could talk about what I wanted I just wanted to celebrate. *(RODDY kisses her.)*

SPIKE   Well, well, isn't this a pretty picture.

> *SPIKE exits. TERRY follows.*

TERRY   Jeezus Christ! Spike!

SPIKE   I don't wanna hear it, Terry! I've had it!

TERRY   Thanks a lot, Roddy! *(exiting)* I'm sorry, I didn't mean to do that *(to SPIKE.)* I LOVE YOU!!

EFFIE   *(entering)* Terry! Terry! Roddy dear, you look as white as a ghost. Don't worry, dear.

RODDY   Ah, Effie.

EFFIE   None of this is your fault. That girl takes right after her father. Driftin' from job to job.

RODDY   No, Effie—she's just like you—that's why I love her. *(They hug.)*

EFFIE   Poor Roddy, you know the women in this family never did have much sense, fallin' in love with drifters, and drunkards and dreamers. This family coulda used a man like you, trouble is, you were just too damn normal! Rita never had a decent roof over her head after she married that Frank.

RODDY   Frank was quite a guy.

EFFIE   He could charm the birds right outa the trees alright but he couldn't put food on the table for his family. The minute I laid eyes on him I knew where it was headed.

RODDY   Then why did Rita throw Cyril over?

EFFIE   He was too goddamn normal too!

> *Enter RITA.*

RITA   What in the name of God are those two girls going on about in the backyard?

RODDY   Just a misunderstanding—

EFFIE   Just a misunderstanding—

RITA   All this is Frank's doing. He's got her believing things that just aren't true. That damn letter!

RODDY   Rita, is there a letter?

RITA   No! It's just another one of his pipedreams, the drink talkin'.

RODDY   Effie?

EFFIE   I been takin' in the mail for years, there was never any letters from Frank. Not a cheque. Not so much as a birthday card for his own daughter. Nothin'!

RODDY   How do we convince Terry?

> *All sit. Silence. TERRY and SPIKE enter. Pause.*

EFFIE   I'll get the tea!

RITA   Aunt Effie. Sit. Tea can wait. Terry dear, I know how much you love your father and I don't want to take that away from you but there are a few things you should know. Frank could, would do anything to get what he wanted. He wanted you to believe in him. There is no letter. He was lying.

TERRY   He didn't lie. He needed to believe in that letter. I know that now. Even the night he told me about it I probably had my doubts. But he is my father. I had to try.

RITA   I know, dear.

EFFIE   You're alright then, Terry?

TERRY   Yes… Gramma.

EFFIE   What did you say, dear?

RITA What did you say, Terry?

TERRY Ma, I'd like you to meet your mother.

RITA Theresa!

TERRY Ma, you know she's your mother!

EFFIE His dirty old grandmother told you that!

RITA You mean you knew I knew!

RODDY Everybody knows.

RITA What? That Effie knows I know?

RODDY Yes. No.

RITA Mother! You knew!

EFFIE Of course! Mothers know everything!

RITA You kept it to yourself—

EFFIE I was waiting for you—

RITA All these years—

EFFIE You coulda opened your mouth—

RITA So could've you—

SPIKE Who the fuck cares!!! *(pause)* Hey, Roddy. No hard feelings?

RODDY No.

TERRY *(kisses RODDY)* Thanks.

EFFIE Mother. I been waitin' to hear that a lot of years.

RODDY Well—

RITA Oh, I almost forgot! Sister Theresa.

EFFIE Oh my God! What happened!

RITA She's gonna be fine. The biopsy—

EFFIE Oh, shit! I knew that. Called the hospital myself right after my shows.

RITA You what?

EFFIE I'm not as hard as all that—

RITA Nobody said you were, Mother—

EFFIE After she ran off in the middle of a blue rinse and joined the nuns—

RODDY *(to TERRY and SPIKE)* Here we go again—

TERRY   *(heading RITA and EFFIE off)* Ma, Gramma, Roddy, this is who I spent last Christmas with. We live together, we shop together. We walk down the street holding hands, together. Now I would love to be private but for some of us being private is a luxury we can't afford. We have to be public first. And the day I stop coming out is the day I check out. I kiss in public too! Yes, Ma, I kiss Spike in public. Spike! Kiss me now! In public! *(SPIKE kisses TERRY passionately.)*

EFFIE   Those potatoes have gone to mush by now. I don't know about youse, but I need a drink! Roddy—

RODDY   I'm all yours, sweetheart!

> *EFFIE and RODDY exit.*

RITA   Terry, I knew when you told me you were in love with that Gosby girl in Grade Ten. I didn't understand it at the time and I still don't know if I do, but I want you to be happy.

TERRY   I am.

RITA   As for your father. Don't think badly of him. He needs you. We both do. *(They hug. She speaks to SPIKE.)* Welcome to Cape Breton, dear.

SPIKE   Thanks.

> *RITA exits.*

TERRY   Well, now you know why you're here?

SPIKE   I have a pretty good idea.

TERRY   You're here because I want you here. And don't you forget it.

SPIKE   Not a chance. Could we do that again? This time without an audience?

TERRY   Sure. *(They move in to kiss as the lights go down.)*

> *Blackout.*

> *The end.*

Growing Up Suites, Parts I and II

and

Object/Subject of Desire

Shawna Dempsey and Lorri Millan

Introduction:
Growing Up Suites Part I and II
and
Object/Subject of Desire

Shawna Dempsey's and Lorri Millan's *Growing Up Suite Part I, Part II*, (1994) and *Object/Subject of Desire* (1989) address the experiences that Dempsey and Millan went through growing up in the bleak suburban landscapes of Scarborough and Etobicoke in the 1960s and 1970s. Fictionalized from similar events, the *Growing Up Suites* feature performances by Dempsey in which her body becomes a symbolic map on which the oppressive cultural messages of the time are encoded and exploded. In "Volatile Bodies: Toward a Corporeal Feminism," Elizabeth Grosz notes that "the body is that materiality, almost a medium, on which power operates through which it functions." In the first sequence in *Growing Up Suite, Part I*, Dempsey appears dressed in a full corset with stockings and garters, looking larger than life, as if she had just stepped out of the Eaton's catalogue where her five-old self first glimpsed her picture. Behind her on stage is a large chorus of middle-aged women dressed in conservative suits and hats in 1940s styles whose song swells up worshipfully as if they were embracing their undressed girdled selves in the form of Dempsey's stately icon. Already partially deconstructed by her incongruous buzz-cut, Dempsey's girdled body evokes the kind of slightly kinky erotic attraction that others might also have had to look for in the lingerie section of a catalogue at a time when any kind of sexualized images were regarded as sinful. Speaking retrospectively with occasional reminders that she is only an innocent five-year-old, Dempsey's sumptuous girdled body, speaks of her love for this image of "Winter, page 117" turning herself into both her own object and subject of desire. What she maps for us is this little girl's refusal to give up the female/mother's body as her love object, whom she considers to be "concealing body parts I knew I did not have/Body parts so powerful/They needed hardware to keep them in place." Reclaiming back the phallic female/mother's body from its enlistment in the service of social modesty and restraint, Dempsey claims this image as her own personal lesbian pin-up who carries the promise of future sexual encounters when she comes of age.

In "Collision," the scene that follows, Dempsey continues with her project of mapping out her contradictory entry into girlhood by usurping the more aggressive actions expected of little boys, as she cunningly engineers crashing her trike into the bike of the new little girl who had moved into town. "Birthday Gifts" fast forwards her through her increasing alienation as her adolescent body is subjected to compulsory feminization. Speaking from her eleven-year-old disenchantment with birthday parties that now focus on imprinting her as a girl, she takes us through the succession of gifts she receives every year up to her fifteenth birthday. As she enacts her growing dismay at the "three or four party dresses" and the "tablecloths, bed sheets, and towels" that arrive for her hope chest, she subverts our traditional reaction to these gifts as necessary acquisitions for every young marriageable girl, reconfiguring them as frightening markers of entrapment.

Growing up Suite, Part II, the saga continues through junior high school as Dempsey traces the progression of denial, hatred, and persecution that haunt her teenaged self as she tries on the various insults hurled at her for failing to perform her gender properly. Reflecting the violently homophobic institutional attitudes of Canada in the 70s, where lesbian sexuality was still considered nonexistent by the school authorities. Dempsey's lesbian child now finds herself inscribing the hatred onto her teenaged body, responding to the guy who yells, "Hey lezzie cunt-face, you got a match?" as if such abuse is to be expected. At the dances, she knows not to dance with her girlfriends for fear of being called a loser, but finds herself hesitant to take the lead in asking a boy for fear of being called pushy. Inevitably, Dempsey reveals that all her efforts at being "normal" fail anyway as her masquerade has only convinced others that she is truly a "lesbo bitch."

However, *Growing up Suite, Part II* does not end here because in claiming her name, she has now opened up the possibilities for the non-existent same-sex desire she feels to happen. Sure enough, on a school band trip, the schoolmate she is billeted with, comes through and makes sweet, if secret, love to her through her Holly Hobby nightgown. The prophecy made to the Girdled Women in the Eaton's Catalogue is thus fulfilled and Dempsey has created a performance space for her lesbian adolescent to enter representation.

The private sexual encounter depicted in *Growing up Suite, Part II*, is more than matched by celebratory sex-talk that closes an earlier piece, *Object/Subject of Desire*. Performed by Shawna in a pristine white strapless prom dress which carries the fragility of the crinkly paper it is made out of, this piece takes us through several deconstructions of desire as it parodies the conventional heteronormative to the tentative politically correct lesbian, and ends with the breakout of uncensored explicit expression of joyful lust. Thus Part One begins with Shawna deconstructing the objectified position of the coy debutante by having her speak with a garbled smattering of feminist theory which has revealed that women exist only as the object of men's desire and hence only want to be wanted. Shawna's debutante blows her own cover by admitting that she doesn't really want it to be too demanding on her time, forcing the audience to think about their own formulaic constructions of desire. Part Two continues the parody by describing a similarly rigid but now absurdly unromantic constructed relationship recognizable as that of lesbians recovering from their abusive upbringings. With just as huge a fear of intimacy as the heteronormative debutante, the frightened lesbian coming out of her shell is only able to contemplate expressions of desire that are completely regulated. Part Three echoes Part One in its vicious parody of the middle-class greed driving naturalized coupledom. Dempsey offsets the normalcy here by slowly strangling herself. Finally, in Part Four, the desiring lesbian subject, still dressed in her demure prom dress, is transformed by her lust into speaking/writing all over her own and our lesbian bodies as we receive her lovemaking instructions.

Notes

¹ Elizabeth Grosz, *Volatile Bodies: Toward a Corporeal Feminism* (Bloomington: Indiana UP, 1994) 146.

² Regretfully, I am only working with the written text for the rest of the sequences in the *Growing Up Suites, Parts I and II* and hence cannot reconstruct the performances.

photo by Sheila Spence

Shawna Dempsey and Lorri Millan

Bio and Artist's Statement

We are defined by physical acts with other women: the desires of our bodies label us as homosexual.

"I am what I am." —Gloria Gaynor, pop song

As artists, we are attempting to perform our realities into existence. Just as historically some lesbians have "passed" as men in order to fulfill their dreams/desires, we attempt to "pass" our work into mainstream culture. We seek to interrupt the expected boundaries of cultural forms, such as civic awards (Golden Boy Awards for *Unscrupulous Political Behaviour*, performance, 1993, 1995), music videos (*We're Talking Vulva*, 1990, *What Does A Lesbian Look Like?*, 1994), journalism (A Day in The Life of A Bull-Dyke video, and In The Life artists' book, 1995), tourism (Winnipeg: One Gay City ad campaign, 1997) and even uniformed authority figures (Lesbian National Parks and Services performance, video and publications, 1997-present). By effectively mimicking the packaging of culture, we are able to subvert the familiar with our own feminist, lesbian content.

As for *Growing Up Suites*, we are from Scarborough and Etobicoke (different sides of the same coin). Rough suburbs that were marked by racial unrest and disparity between rich and poor. We were born in 1963 (SD) and 1965 (LM). We each left the suburbs before completing high school—both needed to leave! So the pieces (*Growing Up Suites, I and II*) reflect, say 1968-1979. They are not strictly autobiographical of either one of us, although we feel they embody truths about those times and places.

Production History

Growing Up Suite I: The initial draft was first performed at Le Lion d'Or with Choeur Maha, Montreal, 1994. The first performance of the final text was at The Banff Centre, Alberta, in 1994.

Performed by Shawna Dempsey

•

Growing Up Suite II: First performed at the Neutral Ground Artist Run Centre, Regina, in 1995.

Performed by Shawna Dempsey

•

Object/Subject of Desire: The initial draft was first performed at Om Performance Space with Company of Sirens, Toronto, in 1988. The first performance of the final text was at Red Deer College, Red Deer Alberta, in 1989.

Performed by Shawna Dempsey

Growing Up Suite, Part I

Eaton's Catalogue

In 1968, in Scarborough, it was all I had
In 1968, in Scarborough, I was five
I hadn't heard of erotica or porn
I didn't know those words then
And though I know them now
I really don't know the difference
Between the meaning of the two.
I just know what turns me on:
Girls.

Though what turned me on then
In 1968, in Scarborough
Was the Eaton's catalogue
Ten pages of ladies wearing
Lingerie that resembled architecture
Covered in buckles and zippers and snaps
Industrial strength underwear
Concealing body parts I knew I did not have
Body parts so powerful
They needed hardware to keep them in place.

I didn't know the word lesbian
Lesbianism wasn't very fashionable
In 1968, in Scarborough
Lessie, lesbo was a dirty word
And though my thoughts were dirty
They were not without love
The first love of my life being Winter, page 117.
I didn't know if I wanted to be her
Staring off into middle distance
So beautiful, so blank
Or if I wanted to be her undoing
The one to take the straps down from her shoulders
The row of hooks from their eyes
Teeth of the zipper unfurling.
I just knew that I wanted her, Winter, page 117
In 1968, in Scarborough

My small chubby hands touching the paper
Of the Eaton's catalogue
Knowing how good she'd feel
Not knowing exactly what I would do with her
But assuming she
So calm and so underdressed
Would have an idea or two
And that eventually
In another fifteen years or so
Together, we could figure it out.

Collision

When I bumped my trike against your bike
It was no accident, no mishap.
Sure the sidewalk is narrow, the road forbidden,
And they're hard to steer, three-wheelers.
But I saw you coming a mile away
A half a block at least
And I had time to start up and drag my toes
So we'd meet in front of Hansen's roses.

First impressions are worth a lot.

There was the squeal of two voices
Because I squealed too
Even though I'd planned the collision.
My shin was bleeding,
Unforeseen complication,
But it made my squeals more convincing.

I didn't want you to squeal alone,
Didn't want you to feel lonely.

When the metal stopped crunching
And our voices were still
The silence was awfully silent.
So I jumped right to the point,
I cut quick to the chase
And asked you that hope-filled question.
I'd been a loner in nursery
Kindergarten as well
Never caring who I played with, if anyone.
But when I saw you carry
Your dolls from the moving truck

My stomach felt achey
And I knew that had changed
Because you were so pretty,
You wore red just like me
And could ride a two-wheeler without trainers.

I knew it was time to settle down.

I'd avoided it for the first six years of my life
Never being vulnerable or sharing my secrets
Never needing or wanting
'Till I needed you.

Of course all of this was too hard to explain
As we lay splayed and bruised on the boulevard
So I said it as simply
And as truly as I could
"Will you be my best friend?
Please?"

Birthday Gifts

When I turned eleven, birthdays became difficult
"Happy Birthday" a bitter irony
"The Birthday Girl" what I least wanted to be.
Girls were sissies, girls were stupid
Or maybe not but you'd never know it
From the sissy, stupid presents
That girls get at eleven.

You see, I didn't mind aging.
There was nothing I wanted more
Than the insufferable, awkward years
Between zero and thirty to whip by.
I didn't even mind my body changing
Though it seems unfair there's a mere second lapse
Between when breasts stop growing out and start to fall down.
But at eleven the problem was presents
And though they foreshadowed injustices to come
I couldn't see them as metaphor
But simply as a raw deal, a rip-off, a rip.
When I was eleven, for my birthday,
I began to get clothes.
Not toys
Like every other birthday before that year

Not even something cool like a T-shirt
Not anything fun or special or what I might want
But clothing.
Specific clothing.
Party dresses.
Not just one, but many
Because there's some rule that a group of people
Can't see you in the same party dress
More than once. Ever.
Therefore you need quite a few
And I think they're kinda expensive
So it's real easy for three or four party dresses
To suck up an entire birthday's worth of presents.

Or at least that's what happened when I turned eleven.
And twelve.
And thirteen.
There was a brief respite in my fourteenth year
When I got a digital alarm
With a.m., f.m., and snooze.
But at fifteen,
As if it could get any worse than midi-length pastels,
An even weirder pattern began:
Tablecloths, bed sheets, and towels;
A little something for my hope chest.
Presents not for me, at fifteen,
But for the mythical "us" of years down the road,
Presents I wasn't allowed to use yet
Only look at
And imagine how fun they would be to use:
Tablecloths, bed sheets, and towels.

My friend David Sharp
Got the entire Supertramp library that year.
I got Irish linen dishcloths
In the hope that someday I could use them
To dry a good man's dishes
When nothing was further from my mind.

At fifteen
My hope didn't lay in a chest.
My hope was in me.
Though it was clear that no one else could see me
Or simply refused to see
When it was time to buy me a present.

When it came time to shop they imagined that I was
What they wanted me to be
And their presents made it painfully obvious that I was not.

If I could have chosen
If I could have said
"This is what I want"
And been heard
Then I would have asked for toys again
Lots and lots of them,
Like before I turned eleven.
Because toys were fun,
They were just for me and my pleasure,
Because they had no reason
Filling time with motion and surprises and "what if?".
They were goofy and useless and mine
And had absolutely nothing to do
With preparing me to be a woman.
Because to any eleven-year-old in her right mind
With her eyes open,
With her eyes on presents to come,
Being a woman
Is the last thing that she'd want to be.

Growing Up Suite, Part II

Name Calling

Sexually you are normal.
Which means, really, you are non.
Because you would say NO, loud and clear, if anyone asked,
Not that they do, but you would.
You would say NO to any boy who asked.
Oh, a girl would never suggest to another girl…
A girl would never ask say…
Do you want to… please…
Because it isn't physically possible, girls just don't fit
Right? Together.
They don't tell us about it in health class and they would know
Wouldn't they? If we could… fit?
It must just be a figure of speech, that word, LES.
Like cunt and slut and slave
And all those other things boys call us
Because, as the guidance counsellor says,
It's the only way they know how to express themselves,
To say how much they care.
So if, in the smoking area, a guy says,
"Hey lezzie cunt-face, you got a match?"
It's really your lucky day
And you're looking into the pimpled face of your potential future.

Dances

With the music of "I Will Survive" by Gloria Gaynor (instrumental version).

High school dances provoke dread.
They demand weeks of mental preparation.
Like psyching up before a major sporting event
I run through each potential move in my head:
If he does this, I'll do that,
If he says this, I'll say that.
It is a combination of rigorous strategizing and creative visualization.
Imagining my entrance into the table-less cafeteria
Where, much like in "Saturday Night Fever"
All of those roving disco lights
Will suddenly rest on me,

My white suit reflecting their approval,
My glowing face a cross between the Virgin Mary's
And Olivia Newton John's in "Grease", after she gets sexy.
Except that the white suit of John Travolta would hardly be appropriate for
    a babe.
No, a better choice would be my seams-up-the-front wide-leg jeans,
Wood-soled sandals with ankle straps
And red poly granny blouse that has those strawberries appliquéed on the
    collar.
Cute.
I will be foxy, I will be foxy, I will be foxy!
But wardrobe is not the only concern.
There is the very real dilemma between asking, and waiting to be asked.
Now chances are pretty good that no one will ask me to the dance.
Which is okay, I can still go.
Except, if you go to a dance with somebody, then they have an obligation to
    dance with you at least a few times.
Which is great.
Which means you don't spend the whole night sipping orange pop,
Leaning against the stacked tables.
Which means you don't spend the whole night watching other people's better
    outfits.
Which means you don't spend the whole night dancing with the other girls.
Now that's the kiss of death.
Having a good time dancing with your girlfriends means you won't get asked by
    a boy, ever.
It means you're a loser,
That you're too square to do the proper thing and wait.
For a guy. To ask.
It's just that waiting gets boring.
Waiting takes too long!
And leaning against the stacked tables doesn't really show one to the best
    advantage.
So there is the tricky other option of asking a boy to the dance
Or of asking him to just dance for one number.
I mean, it sounds kinda cool, kinda Peggy Lipton—
Knowing you've got nothing to lose,
Nothing ventured, nothing gained—to say,
(improv) "Do you wanna dance?"
Except, that maybe it means more than just asking.
Maybe it's not so cool for me to ask
Because I'm not cool in the first place.
Maybe it just proves that no one would ever ask me,
Me having to ask them… desperate.
Or worst of all, maybe it means that I'm pushy.

No, it seems like the best course of action is inaction.
To wait, patiently, to be asked.
To wait, patiently, for him.
And while I wait, watch.
And try to memorize the dance steps
As they go hustling by
So I can practice them later, at home, with the mirror.

Name Calling Some More

The problem is that boys don't seem to think of you THAT WAY.
You've never been asked out in your life
And when they say cunt and slut and slave to you
It's with less affection, than to, say,
Robin Diamond who they've nicknamed Party Pack.
No, when they call you lesbo bitch
It's when you fuck up
Because you really don't get it
This business of being a girl.
And they all know it.
They all know that, although, sexually, you're normal
(Because there are no other options)
You wouldn't be a good time
Always saying some opinion
And not playing the game
Because somehow you can't figure out the rules.
And it's kinda scary for the other players
It seems to make them mad
It seems to make them want to say things like lesbo bitch
When not everyone will play along.

Sleeping Together

With the music of "American Pie" by Don McLean.

We're on a band trip.
We're far, far away from home
And we're being billeted with a family who thinks they have a prodigy
An ugly little boy
Who plays "Flight of The Bumble Bee" over and over, faster and faster
Night after night for a week.
Maybe it wears us down.
Maybe it wears us out.
Maybe we are just a little homesick

Or sick in love with those trumpet players who never give us French horn
    playing girls a second thought
But whatever the reason, whatever the cause,
In the middle of the night
On the foamy, in the den, in the suburb of Calgary
You turn to me
And kiss my lips, my cheeks, my neck.
You kiss my eyes and ears and shoulders
Through my Holly Hobby nightgown.
You run your hands down my sides
Down my legs to my hem
Which lifts as easily as a sigh
So you can kiss my never-before-kissed nipples
Your embouchure perfect
As your fingers reach that embarrassing, hairy place
And moved in slow circles
For what seems like forever, but not near long enough
Until I gasp and shake
Without making a sound
Without uttering a peep.
Because your eyes are closed.
Your eyes are shut tight.
I know you are asleep.
You must be.
And I don't want to wake you up
At all.

Object/Subject of Desire

Part One

I want you, to want me. I want you to want me, even though I don't really want you. I don't want you at all, but I want everyone else to. I want everyone else to want you, but I don't want you to want anyone else but me. All I want is your want. I want you to need me, to cry for me, to suffer for me. I want to be your chocolate cake, your hot-water bottle, your savior. As long as it doesn't take too much of my time. As long as I can say, "Thanks, but no thanks." And you'll still love me and want me forever. And I'll be beautiful forever. And I'll live forever in your broken heart. While I remain perfectly intact: wanted.

Part Two

I want to improve my intimacy skills. My therapist says it's about time. So if it's okay with you, I think we should change our pattern of relating. I'll call you, once a week on Tuesday. You'll pick up the message from your machine and will call me back on Wednesday. I'll pick up the message from my machine and will call you back on Thursday, confirming our plans for Saturday. We'll go see a band, a movie, a play: something that doesn't require too much interaction. But then, we will go to a café, drink soothing herbal teas, and exchange stories about childhood trauma and failed relationships. We will become close, but not dependent, and not co-dependent. We will be adult about things. We will split the bill. Now this won't be a relationship, but rather an intimate friendship involving sex where applicable. It'll be good for us. It'll be fun. We won't get hurt. And we will be better people because of it.

Part Three

I want love. I want twoness, and tandem, and we. I want reduced rates for double occupancy. And anniversaries, and valentines. I want to hyphenate our names, buy a puppy, invite you to my parents for supper. We'll get a house. I'll work, you can look after the kids. We'll put in a pool, buy a car, and be normal, because we own things. We will drive off into the rest of our lives, and be happy, and not lonely, and just like everyone else.

Part Four

I want to fuck you. I want to fuck you until you can't cum anymore. I want to run my hands down your sides, squeezing your nipples between my fingers as I bite your neck. My tongue in your ear your mouth, going down, down, your belly, your thighs… I want you. My face parting your lips, biting clit as my finger curls up inside of you, turning, scratching, reaching, then behind you, your legs beneath me, tongue in and out, hands wet under you… I want you. On my face, dripping into my mouth, hair tickling up and down, yes… I want you. On the table, on the chair, on the floor, kneeling beside the bed, I am fucking you with my face, my fists, my hands, my feet, again and again until you can't cum any more. I want you.

Dykes and Dolls

Lisa Lowe

Introduction:
Dykes and Dolls

Lisa Lowe's *Dykes and Dolls*, is another coming-out, coming-of-age solo performance, which complements Dempsey and Millan's *Growing Up Suites*. It differs from them in its lack of a specific location, although Lowe admits that she too was in the bedroom communities of Toronto in the late 1960s and early 1970s. Perhaps it is a measure of the stiflingly intolerant atmosphere of the small town that prompted Lowe to confine the action of the play to the imaginary space of the Girl's bedroom. Reflecting the precarious existence of the child who refuses to perform her gender properly, Lowe's fantastic recuperation of the female-gendered icons and symbols for her own perverse purposes calls attention to the coercive ways in which female children are enculturated to be child-bearers. Full of grotesque exaggerations, *Dykes and Dolls* works theatrically by carrying her distorted reality to increasingly wild extremes which require the audience to rethink their reactions.

From the outset she leads the audience into a kind of hallucinatory space where none of the expected realistic conventions apply. Next, she appears as a Narrator to warn the spectators that she is about to perform the story of "a lesbian, a genetic girl who seeks the love and gender she wants without any reckoning of remorse." In this way she signals to the audience that she is inviting them to look at the stage world through her outlawed lesbian eyes, accepting her terms and reading the signs they see as departing from a heterosexual perspective. When she returns again, this time as a Scientist in a lab coat holding a doll upside down by the ankles, she encourages the audience to follow her even further into the fantasy of the pink nightmare world that the little girl has been forced to inhabit for the first three years of her life. Next, she shifts perspectives again by stripping off her lab coat to reveal "a pink tutu, pink petticoat and a pink undershirt" indicating that her gendering as Girl has successfully taken. Now whatever part of us is still outside the fiction, trying to observe the experiment with scientific objectivity is jolted into a new role as she briefly introduces her Mother into the scene as the person most invested in keeping her daughter feminized.

Just as she had first introduced herself as a doll-like experiment, she is now given her first doll by her Mother as the secret weapon to awaken the motherly instincts she is supposed to have been born with. In the next scene, where Girl slowly destroys the doll by burning off her hair, she also symbolically severs any ties with the disapproving scientists who have continued to watch her as a bad experiment gone awry. In her gesture of holding up the monstrous burning doll with her hair on fire and letting out her monstrous roar as the one-eyed monster, she also indicates that she knows she has performed an act which will put her beyond the reach of the gender police. In naming them and smoking them out from their hiding place behind the one-way mirror, she removes them from the stage and claims the space as her own.

At this juncture, now able to free herself of the tutu and petticoats, she strips down to her underwear and t-shirt, and gets to the serious business of inventing herself within a fantasy world of her own making. Never leaving the bedroom, Girl now forms her own liaisons with the girl-toys she continues to receive. Barbie doll in particular inspires her to take on a butch role in contrast to Barbie's extreme femme. Entering fully into the affluent middle-class way of life that Barbie was supposed to sell to little girls with all her clothing, cars, and household goods, Girl rewrites the hetero-normative inscriptions by bringing Barbie to life and playing out various scenarios where she takes care of Barbie by driving her around and fixing her car or saving her from accidents. Greatly enhanced by having Lowe move in and out of both roles, the burgeoning love affair that takes place between both reminds us of the domestic dream that Barbie sold us while at the same time exposing its limits. Even as her butch lover, Girl finds herself questioning Barbie's extravagant life style, "I didn't really understand what brought us together. I suppose I envied her in some ways, her popular appeal, housing, mobility and her money. Although, where she got it she certainly never said. Not even when I was removing her pants. Which I did on a frequent basis."

Lowe's ultimate ditching of Barbie on the grounds that their relationship was "nothing more than a bad cliché" moves *Dykes and Dolls* into its final fantasy sequence when Girl fashions herself into a swashbuckling pirate and seeks the love of the doll she falls for in a TV commercial. Seeing her own androgyny reflected in this doll whose hair could be transformed from long to short, she finds herself so sexually attracted that she has no choice but to rescue her love from inside the television screen. As the piece ends with a high flown account of their enraptured lovemaking in their oceanic lair, Girl has found the way to make her sexual fantasies come true. Flooding out of the private space of the bedroom setting, *Dykes and Dolls* leaves us with a sense that Girl has found a way to break out of its confines into real representation.

photo by Mary Lou Trinkwon

Lisa Lowe

Bio and Artist's Statement

I am a writer, performance worker and expressive arts therapist living in Vancouver. Currently working with children, I often use play, drama and storytelling as tools for creative expression, self-reflection and understanding. *Dykes and Dolls*, was my first solo performance since my collaborative work with Labrys Rising Dance Academy, a parodic movement based performance troupe, with Mary Lou Trinkwon and Sharon Bayly, from 1991 to 1993. *Dykes and Dolls* was commissioned by the 1994 Women in View Festival's Formations initiative. The Formations initiative invited five emerging writers to write and perform a short 20-minute play about love. *Dykes and Dolls* was the outcome of my exploration on this prescribed theme. Working in a collaborative an improvisational manner with Sharon LeBlanc and Mary Lou Trinkwon, I was able to use a classic feminine signifier and transitional object, the doll, to construct a childhood coming-out story. This story not only explored and validated my own developmental experiences of my emerging sexuality, but also evaluated the social context that attempted to control and re/produce me. References to the emergent self, constructed through powerful fantasies in play, drive the images in this embrace of lesbian identity.

Following *Dykes and Dolls*, *Crowns and Anchors*, a commissioned work by Out West Theatre, for a collection called *Plague of the Gorgeous*, gives voice to a lesbian drug user with AIDS. *Seized Materials*, a performance piece written about censorship for the Little Sister's Defense Fund, where I worked selling poppers and porn after my defection from small-town Ontario to the mythic west coast, was performed alongside Serrano's *Piss Christ* at the Vancouver Art Gallery amid controversy and community anxiety in 1996. In 1997, *Lesbians or Lemmings?* marked a huge departure from the youthful coming out story staged in *Dykes and Dolls*. *Lesbians or Lemmings?* takes aim at the very notion of a cohesive lesbian identity and attempts to deconstruct the lesbian community. Riding rogue waves of anger and cynicism through the context of lesbian identity and community, I address issues of sameness, otherness and belonging. My most recent work, *Mildred A Horn: Sex Hygienist 1942* (2001), with Rosalind Kerr and Mary Polito, returns to issues of social control, the body and technologies of the self through the staging of a 1942 sex hygienist on a public speaking tour advising mothers and daughters on reproductive matters.

Although my work can slip through the cracks in and between categories, being "too theatrical" for performance art and "too performance art" for traditional theatre, I work solidly out of the "solohomo" tradition, role modelled to me by queer writer, performer and friend, David Bateman, in Peterborough, Ontario. Largely self-taught and an independent outsider, all of my work has been written for my own body; that is, for myself to perform in. I have performed every work except, *Crowns and Anchors*, which continues to evade me. In 2004, *Crowns and Anchors* was presented by Act Out Theatre at the National Arts Centre and performed by Janne Cleveland.

Believing strongly in the purposes and persuasions of performance, I have integrated the values of feminist theatre into my practice. I have been fortunate to have worked with many visionary women, who have generously shared the tricks of the trade enabling me to carve out images and moments that attempt to speak to and represent some of our strange and unique complexities.

Production History

Dykes and Dolls was first performed at Women in View Festival, in 1994.

ALL CHARACTERS   Lisa Lowe

Characters

Girl
Narrator
Scientist
Mother
Barbie

Location

Girl's bedroom.

Properties

Bed on wheels, traveller's trunk/treasure chest on wheels, pink electric heater, pink mouse and dolls, dolls, dolls.

Wardrobe

Lab coat, pink tutu, pink petticoats, pink boy's underwear, undershirt, pirate shirt, pants, motorcycle boots.

Dykes and Dolls

> *This one act takes place in GIRL's bedroom. Dolls are strewn about. GIRL plays all the characters and is multi-voiced as she tells her story through fantasy and play. Her story is developmental beginning in infancy and ending in adulthood with dolls acting as transitional objects to her emergent identity.*

> *Horror music plays.*

> *This NARRATOR's warning is given in black with a flashlight to the face.*

NARRATOR   Good Evening. We feel it would be a little unkind to present this performance without a friendly word of warning. We are about to unfold the story of a lesbian, a genetic girl who seeks the love and gender she wants without any reckoning or remorse. It is one of the strangest tales ever told. It deals with two great mysteries of life… dykes and dolls.

We think it will thrill you. It may shock you. It might even horrify you. So if any of you feel that you don't care to subject your nerves to such a strain, now's your chance to ah, ha, ha, ha, *(evil laughter)* well, we warned you.

> *More horror music.*

> *Enter wearing lab coat and holding a doll upside down by the ankles.*

SCIENTIST   It *(gestures toward doll)* was created in an uncontrolled teen sex experiment. Nine months later it was extracted from living flesh. In a well-lit laboratory it was observed that the specimen demonstrated enough characteristics *(genital check)* to distinguish itself as female. It was pronounced Girl. After a modest announcement in the local paper, gender and child went home with the two domestic scientists assigned to it. The specimen was immediately incubated in pink. Pink hats, pink dresses, pink boots, pink fun-fur, pink playthings, pink sheets, pink curtains, pink walls, pink, pink, pink, pink. All gray matters were pink matters. She was clothed in pink petticoats and spoken to in pink tones. On special occasions, particularly during the yuletide, she was fed pink mice. *(removes pink mouse from top lab coat pocket)* Naturally her poo was perfectly pink. And after examination of the solids the two domestic scientists were often heard exclaiming with a delight, uncommon to people of science, that it smelt remarkably like the Rose of Tralee.

Now the key to any scientific theory is controlled repetition. So for three years she lived in this highly controlled environment moving through the maze of pink the way a mouse scurries through a labyrinth sniffing for cheese. The scientists observed her from deep within their lab coats, making silent tick marks with their eyebrows, as they approved and disapproved of her behaviour. From the official records we know that she talked back more than once. That she was stricken with bouts of exaggeration and that she frequently demonstrated resistance over compliance to the domestic scientists' commands. However, when problems of compliance arose the scientific team worked around the clock to correct them. Generally the scientific team was satisfied with all data received and they fully substantiated the claim that when one is flogged in pink, *(slowly begins to disrobe—underneath lab coat, GIRL is dressed in a pink tutu, pink petticoat and a pink undershirt)* they will at the very least appear female. There is no evidence to the contrary.

> *The SCIENTIST has fully disrobed and GIRL stands centre stage in pink.*

One cold dark evening in the dead of winter, after a third party report that Girl had gravitated toward and had made several verbal inquiries as to the use of a long stick with a curved blade, she had found idle at the side of a neighbour's house, the domestic scientist referred to as mother, shamed by her daughter's unconventional interest, panicked and unleashed the most powerful dose of female gender prescription known to humankind. Just before Girl was drifting off to sleep, a time when defenses are known to be down, she tiptoed down the hallway and into Girl's room and presented her with a friend. Someone to play with. She also brought her some ginger ale to help sweeten the delivery.

MOTHER   Ginger ale, your favourite. I have something else for you. Can you guess?

GIRL   Ginger ale, mmm. Yummy bubbles.

MOTHER   *(presents doll proudly)* It's a baby doll.

GIRL   A baby doll?

MOTHER   She comes fully equipped with a bottle and a diaper. She was mine when I was your age and she was my favorite thing to play with and now she's yours. I want you to have her.

GIRL   *(GIRL hesitates, but takes the doll.)* What can she do? Can she pee? Can she poo? What can you do? *(GIRL throws baby doll down in frustration.)* Hey, I know. Do you want to play scientists? Let's pretend you're trapped in a maze and I am a one-eyed monster waiting to capture you and I'm about to... what was that? Did you hear it too? *(GIRL begins to make a low hissing sound.)* Hisssssssss. It's the big snake calling out. It's calling out from its cave. *(GIRL moves to electric heater.)* Snakes like hot places. See the heater's coils they're spiraling into red-hot irons. It's warm in there can you feel it? You want to go closer. Then I do it. I take the baby doll and place her head first against the hot heater coils. The doll's hair singes and sparks, then shoots back like a live ember antenna. Afraid, I stuff the doll's head into my ginger ale. The ginger ale fizzles over with bubbles. I pull her out of the golden liquid and watch it run down my arm. She gots a great big bald spot and is far more appealing to me because of it. I put her head back against the coils. The heat dries the sticky ale and her hair fires again. I dip her back into the bubbles and back to the heater. Into the ale, into the fire, hey, you're not so bad to play with, into the bubbles, into the fire. The room is filling with the smell of burning sugar and spice and everything nice, when suddenly the door of the labyrinth blows open and the scientists are standing there. A hot fiery wind rushes past them ballooning their lab coats and scorching the tips of their ears. By the horrified looks on their faces, it is clear they have been observing through the one-way mirror. I proudly hold up the doll to them. Her hair is on fire, her eyes are sparking white centres and I let out the roar of the one eyed monster. GRRRRRRRRRRRRRRRRRRRR. One of the scientists' points, lets a cry and collapses into the arms of the other as they topple against the charred doorframe.

By the way they were acting you'd have thought they had watched me cook and eat my own child. *(begins to remove tutu and petticoats)* Those of you who are more psychoanalytically inclined may speculate that I was demonstrating some kind of classic complex. But no, my fantasy play was much more powerful than the adult anxieties around me. *(standing in underwear and t-shirt)* The truth is I was merely developing my preference for bald dolls.

My early rearing only served to give me a bad case of pink eye. Despite the atrocities performed on dolls, they were still brought to me. They began piling up and on occasion I would play with them. I even played with Barbie. I might have played with her longer, if she had more interesting tools, *(begins to pulls on pants)* like a rope, knife or axe. But no, the only tool she had was her wardrobe. Barbie had oodles of clothes, which were always wrinkled and/or in a heap. She never folded or hung anything up. Everything was left strewn about or stuffed turkey-style into the closet. It was just too much chaos for me. I just couldn't keep up. The clothes, the pretty hairdos. I liked her car though and she let me drive it too. *(moves bed into place as car)* In fact, she said, she liked it when I did the driving. We spent a lot of our time together going on long drives and then the car would break down and I'd have to fix it.

BARBIE   *(sitting on top of bed primping her hair)* Is it fixed yet?

GIRL   *(flops down on back as if underneath car)* Just a minute. I just have to turn this and turn this and this.

BARBIE   *(continues primping)* I wouldn't have a clue what to do to fix a car.

GIRL   *(turns car on and makes sound of car roar)* It's fixed!

BARBIE   Girl, you're wonderful.

GIRL   Then we'd race down the highway, making our quick getaway from the bad guys and we'd hit a curve *(makes sound of brakes and crash)* and crash and I'd have to save her.

BARBIE   *(uses sheet over head to depict BARBIE's despair)* Oh Girl, help me, help me, please help me.

GIRL   I'll save you, Barbie.

BARBIE   Oh Girl, I don't think I'll make it. Girl, I can't feel my legs. I can't feel my legs.

GIRL   No. You can't. Barbara you must live. Here take this. *(pretends to give medicine from pocket)*

BARBIE   Oh Girl, I feel much better. Look, I can walk again.

GIRL   At the end of our drives, we'd always end up fighting because she wanted to go shopping and buy more clothes, and I wanted to keep driving. Barbie, I'd say, why do you want more clothes when you've got a closet full of ones you never even wear? At first she'd respond "because I want to be beautiful for you" and I could only agree adding that she'd look great in anything. But near the end, after the same conversation for the fiftieth billionth time she began to turn away from me saying I just didn't understand. She was right, I didn't understand.

You know she was the first doll to come with her own condo and she was the first doll I shacked up with. It was a great shag pad and I tried to make it nice, a bed out of a cardboard box, hand-sewn bedding, bottle cap chairs and little side tables with plasticine ashtrays. But nothing was ever good enough for her. She always wanted things new from the store. I didn't really understand what brought us together. I suppose I envied her in some ways, her popular appeal, housing, mobility and her money. Although, where she got it she certainly never said. Not even when I was removing her pants. Which I did on a frequent basis.

These were explosive times that Barbie and I played within. I'd ask, let's turn the condo into a commune?

BARBIE   No I'd rather renovate and turn it into a boutique for other Barbies.

GIRL   Barb, listen. If we could only try to be less exclusive, strip ourselves down to the bare essentials, we might be able to change the disastrous course the world seems to be on right now. I mean aren't you worried about how things are and how they will turn out especially if we keep going in the current direction?

Barbie pushed her hair away from her face and she actually looked thoughtful for a moment before responding.

BARBIE   That's a gross exaggeration, Girl. Did you know that you always exaggerate to make your point and it's getting pretty lame? No, what the world needs are more good designers. Now mix me a martini, prepare my next outfit, we're going out dancing tonight. Wheewe!!

GIRL   Barbie always made that sound before she went out. She was designed for one single event and one single event only. I found myself wishing Barbie could do other things. Like I wished Barbie had been designed to clean up after herself. She was just another classist snob I was supposed to cater to while dreaming to become. Our play was nothing more than a bad cliché. I finally ditched Barbie as she boarded the elevator to her vanity on the fifth floor. I wasn't interested in Barbie's games and I wasn't going to be her lady's maid when I could create more powerful fantasies of my own. Before Barbie even knew she had been abandoned, I had set sail *(moves to bed on casters and turns it into a pirate boat)* cast off my boat and was roaming the seas for treasures. I ran my skull and crossbone flag up the ship's mast. I was alone on the open sea. The wind howled and I bobbed up and down riding the swell… then a big wave sneaked up behind me, it hit me by surprise and washed me overboard. *(GIRL falls off bed and is swimming.)* All around me were giant man-eating sharks, swimming circles and I had to fight to keep off those sharks, using my knife and stabbing them. But their skin was like steel and it almost breaks my knife and I have to stab them in the eyes to blind them. *(GIRL rolls around fighting sharks and stabs several sharks 2 times, once for each eye)*

Play like this transformed me into a pirate of exceptional grace disrupting the conventions of all who looked upon me. Although my pirate play was pure fantasy, my pirate was stowed away at school and family gatherings. If I needed my pirate I only had to squint me scaly pink-eye to call upon my pirate secret powers to plunder expectation and maraud your gaze with pure pirate exhibitionism.

> *GIRL moves toward treasure chest.*

Aye mates. I'd carved me out of boy and girl. Modelling myself after the hermaphroditic shells I found washed ashore. *(opens treasure chest and removes pirate clothes and motorcycle boots)* I weighed what I wanted and took without asking. These were the treasures that I found and I placed them in a sacred chest and buried it on the island of my body. Then I memorized the map to that place remembering my path so I could send others who were cast adrift.

> *Dressed as pirate.*

I was a mid '70s cross-dressing pirate who had sworn off dolls. I was having my own adventures. I was sailing the high gender seas, navigating its currents, finding my own direction.

Then one day, as I was charting a course for a new adventure, I was adjusting my rigging, swinging from rope to rope, when I swung right in front of a television and it happened. A doll turned around in the TV frame and faced me square on. Her hair was down around her shoulders, long thick and gorgeous. Then, in the next frame, it was tucked up, short and perky. The vixen. She too was transformative and that drove me wild. Her magic? At the touch of a button, she could have both long and short hair. Now that's novelty built into a plaything. This was the doll of my dreams. Just looking at her made my body feel like cream on crushed velvet. Her eyes were crystal blue lusciously lashed shores. She was land to my water and I was breaking against her in desire.

It was then that I knew I had to play with her. From then on I always tried to sail on a channel she was on. Sometimes she appeared at lunch hour sandwiched between "Flintstone" reruns and my hungry mouth. I was anchored and sinking in love. Love makes for wild play and wild play was what I was after. It was then that I began to plot a plan. After repeated screenings and close semiotic readings of her television commercial, I began to notice other visual signs besides my literal, clitoral swell. This doll was always at the centre of a smiling bunch of girls. This was encouraging. She even had her own commercial jingle. Unusual, I thought, but strangely enticing.

One night, after deciding on a course of action, I waited for her jingle. I waited through "I Dream of Jeannie", "Bewitched" and "The Flying Nun". I heard her jingle and I grabbed my rope and swung right through the television screen. Landing gracefully in front of her I gallantly introduced myself as her pirate. She said she always wanted to play with a pirate and asked why I hadn't come sooner. I replied, time is no matter, the future is now, so make your hair short and we'll escape and I plucked her from the centre of those smiling girls. But before we could make our swift getaway her dastardly corporate sponsors were fast on our heels… wielding sharp contracts. It was time to take a stand, bridge the imaginary and the real, so I pulled my trusty cutlass from my hip and in one fell swoop… removed their heads. What else can a dyke do but rescue her doll from a life of patriarchal, capitalist greed?

Together we swung back and arrived on deck. We tied the sheet knot and let out the sails. They filled with strong tradewinds and we set our course on a passionate wave. Together we created life, dining on oysters, weaving seaweed and diving for pearls. Charting ourselves by the moon we played our bodies like tides, rising and falling, continuously changing. We sailed outside of fixed boundaries into the uncharted waters of our lust and love, discovering delicate inland passages and weathering dangerous currents. It was not who we were, but what we imagined ourselves to be. To play is the thing. This is the treasure that will cure your bones.

> *Closing music. Classic 40s happy-ending Hollywood sound byte plays while GIRL turns back to audience and, embracing self, with hands on her own back, pretends to neck with her doll.*
>
> *The end.*

Karla and Grif

Vivienne Laxdal

Introduction:
Karla and Grif

Vivienne Laxdal's *Karla and Grif* (1991) shares elements of the coming-out stories of the first three selections but differs in not being partially autobiographical. However, as Laxdal notes, the story does have some basis in fact as referenced by the inclusion of actual locations in and around Ottawa in the 1970s and 80s.[1] Told from Karla's perspective, the play provides another vital portrait of the struggle she faces in trying to makes sense of a world that wants to exclude and punish her. By making us follow Karla's mental processes as she pieces together the high costs of coming to terms with her sexuality, Laxdal throws our naturalized frame of reference out of sync. In so doing she disrupts what Jill Dolan has called the "dynamics of desire" between the performance and its spectators. As Dolan sets it out, "desire is not necessarily a fixed, male-owned commodity, but can be exchanged, with much different meaning, between women. When the locus of desire changes, the demonstration of sex and gender roles also changes."[2]

The present-day action of the play, set in the corridor and interior of Grif's bachelor apartment, concerns Karla's surprise visit there on a night in October, 1991, three years after their fateful sexual encounter on the last night of summer camp. Identified as the stalker, her wait for Grif is punctuated by her reliving of the memories of all the key events in Karla's life which have come to haunt her. Juxtaposed with one another, these scenes which occur in the cabin at summer camp, or in her father Danny's living-room, overlap with each other in increasingly intense ways as Karla's psyche comes closer to putting the pieces of her shattered life together. Thus, even as Karla stands outside Grif's apartment door, her mind is flooded with the simultaneous conflicting memories of the effusively loving greeting that Grif gives her when she arrived at summer camp that final summer, and the gruff apologetic greeting that Danny gives her on her return as he inquires about the broken arm that he gave her before she left.

By the time Grif returns and tries to brush her off, we have been enlisted into supporting Karla's demand to be let into the apartment through the series of flashbacks that have given us insight into her split reality as the disadvantaged poor kid who found her solace by becoming Grif's friend at summer camp. Mingling together a host of memories of their various arrivals and departures from Camp Cedar Rock over the eight turbulent years they shared a cabin, the scenes that Karla recalls quickly admit us in to witness the intense bond that grew up between them. While Grif flaunts her sexual appeal by detailing her increasingly promiscuous encounters with the boys in the neighbouring camp, she binds Karla to her by demanding physical and emotional comfort. At the same time, Karla's rough and tumble knife-wielding ways, and dangerous experimentation with drugs, scarcely mask her worshipful devotion and awe for the socially superior and sexually desirable Grif.

Seeing their burgeoning relationship through Karla's eyes brings the increasing pain she feels in having to deny her "abnormal" desire into sharp focus, especially as it is contrasted by Grif's socially acceptable exploitation of her. Laxdal's inclusion of the "Backwards Strip-Tease" act that Karla and Grif perform on skit night further alerts us to the ritualized same-sex female flirtation that is condoned at girls' summer camps but denied elsewhere. Grif's ruthless flaunting of her bikini-clad body in front of her acknowledged cabin-buddy now disguised as the male "Karlo," foregrounds her need to protect herself from recognizing her sexual feelings.

The careful interweaving of the past and present scenes begins to intensify when Karla is able to gain access to Grif's apartment by winning Grif's sympathy for her news that Danny is dead. As a measure of how interwoven her rejection by Grif is with her rejection by Danny, Danny now begins to appear in Grif's apartment, even peering through Grif's window as Karla tries to wipe it clean. Karla's need to get Grif to admit to what really happened on the last night of camp remains inextricably woven with her need to surmount the ridicule her father exposed her to after Karla confessed to being in love with Grif. As the play builds to the reenactment of that scene, we finally witness the tenderness of their lovemaking followed by Grif's accusations of rape the morning after. In the fictional world of the play, Karla brings the dead Danny into the scene of her anguish as a redemptive figure who first wipes away her tears and then restores the knife she has dropped into her hands. To underline this moment of imagined reconciliation, Danny makes his final exit. Continuing the fantasy, Karla now imagines a scene where she and Grif share an intimate domestic moment in front of a fireplace.

But if Karla is able to put her ghosts momentarily to rest, her tenuous acceptance into Grif's world is quickly denied by the arrival of Grif's long-expected mystery date. When she turns out to be a highly accomplished professional woman, Kathy, we are faced with a whole new reality. Kathy's casual acceptance of Karla's highjacking of her date with Grif forces us to look at everything that has happened in a new light. However, when Kathy leaves them alone, the scene is prepared for Karla to force Grif to come clean with her. Moving from getting a confession from Grif of the pain she had caused her, Karla reverts to threatening her with her knife. The violence that erupts as Karla gets Grif to cut into her palm spirals out of control as Karla then first smears her blood all over the apartment and then onto Grif herself. Naming herself an outcast wolf, she wipes her hand across Grif's breast, crotch and face. These heavily symbolic acts of revenge finally peak and Karla is able to extricate herself and leave the apartment. However, the play offers no easy ending—as her towering rage at having been duped into non-existence cannot be contained.

Tremendously powerful in its portrayal of Karla, Laxdal's inclusion of Kathy as Grif's lesbian lover prevents the play from simply reverting to a reaffirmation of a heteronormative status-quo. But what it does instead is problematize another huge marker of desire—class.

Notes

¹ Vivienne Laxdal, email 03/06/06, explains: a) The Chaud (Chaudière) was a dive bar in Hull—on the Quebec side. Ottawa teens would often go there because the legal drinking age was 18 as opposed to 19, and the bouncers were really slack on ID; b) The Market—Byward Market—Ottawa's historic merchant centre just East of the Parliament Buildings; c) Algonquin College—in Ottawa. Back in the 70s/80s it was thought of more as a vocational school rather than a respectable post-secondary institution; d) Nepean—used to be a suburb of Ottawa (now integrated into City of Ottawa). The mention of this locale, for some reason, got a lot of laughs on opening night of the San Francisco production—don't know why.

² Jill Dolan, "The Dynamics of Desire: Sexuality and Gender in Pornography and Performance" *Theatre Journal* 39. 2 (May), 173.

Vivienne Laxdal

Bio and Artist's Statement

A long-time resident of the famous Black Sheep Inn in Wakefield, Quebec, actor and two-time national award-winning playwright Vivienne Laxdal has had a long association with the Great Canadian Theatre Company and the National Arts Centre. The author of more than a dozen plays including *Goose Spit*, *Personal Convictions*, *Cyber:\womb*, and *National Capitale nationale* (with Jean Marc Dalpé); her works have been produced in theatres across Canada and in the US. Vivienne has also taught dramatic studies at Algonquin College and has mentored first-year playwrights at the National Theatre School. The feature film adaptation of her 1999 play, *These Girls*, opened in major cinemas across Canada in March 2006.

•

It's wild to think that I wrote this play nearly two decades ago. Perhaps because I'm forced to reflect on the reality that my sons are now as old as the play—actually, they are much the same age now as Karla and Grif are in the story—and that just seems, well, pretty "sketch," you know?

I wrote the first act of *K/G* when my son Ryan was a tyke and I was pregnant with my second child (which I was certain would be a girl—after all, I was writing a play about a lesbian triangle!) Act Two of *K/G* was written with baby Will (another boy!) in a backpack to keep him napping while I hunched over the keyboard and Ryan played with his toy cars under my chair. (A note of caution: It is advisable to periodically stretch one's shoulders and neck when writing a play while wearing a backpack containing a small sleeping child, as the pressure applied by the shoulder straps may interfere with the blood flow to one's head and hands.)

Perhaps this is not the creative backdrop one imagines for the author when reading or watching this play about young women behaving badly—but then, few of my "adult" (ha!) plays to date reflect in any way the domestic, country-fied setting of our lives at the time of writing. I can't say how often someone familiar with my work who meets me for the first time has commented with surprise, "You're so normal and nice! I thought you'd be, you know, weird and dark."

If it weren't for the fact that Will eventually grew out of the backpack and most of my plays to follow usually made people suck wind at the social, cultural or theatrical improprieties contained therein, I'd blame it on the restricted blood flow. But since I don't have adequate physiological evidence to that end, I'll just say, that I've always written what I'd want to read, watch, direct or act—even if it isn't acceptable—and probably *exactly* because it's *not* "normal."

When faced with the inevitable question of why I chose to write a play on a lesbian theme, I answer that at the time I was simply following common tutelage to new writers, to "write what you know." A lot of *K/G* is based on who I've known, what I've experienced, and what others have told me—treated with dramatic licence and an applied theatrical form. End of story. Also, in the mid-80s, I had yet to be introduced to the notion of artistic or cultural appropriation and it wasn't until the play had actually won a national award and had been produced in a couple of theatres when the play received some negative coverage from some political gay press when it was revealed I wasn't actually a "functioning" lesbian. (So, did that make me a dysfunctional lesbian, I wondered?) Essentially, they asked how a married mother with children could ever know anything about being a lesbian and what right does she have to write about it? My response: Do all crime writers have to be murderers? Or do they only need to know what it feels like, even momentarily, to want to kill someone? I've known what it feels like to be attracted to another woman or to be attractive to other women. I've known the thrills and chills that are part of any passionate relationship. And, like the young women in *K/G*, I've known what it feels like to be both on the receiving and throwing ends of rejection, abuse and betrayal. Doesn't everyone?

Production History

Karla and Grif was first produced by the National Arts Centre English Theatre as part of the Atelier Workshop Programme, in March 1991, with the following company:

KARLA	Brooke Johnson
GRIF	Cary Lawrence
DANNY	David Fox
KATHY	Sarah Snow

Directed by Barbara Lysnes
Dramaturge: Urjo Kareda
Set/Costumes by James Cameron
Lighting by Gerry Van Hezewyk
Music/Sound by Ian Tamblyn

•

Karla and Grif was subsequently produced by Centaur Theatre Company, Montreal, in February 1992, with the following company:

KARLA	Brooke Johnson
GRIF	Catherine MacKenzie
KATHY	Rebecca Dewey
DANNY	Dean Hawes

Directed by John Palmer
Set/Costumes by James Cameron
Lighting by Don Finlayson
Music/Sound by Ian Tamblyn

•

Further productions:

• Theatre Rhinoceros—directed by Adele Prandini, San Francisco, 1995
• Sea Theatre—directed by Bill Devine, Vancouver 1996

Characters

Karla, early 20s.
Grif, early 20s.
Danny, late 40s.
Kathy, 30 something.

Settings

Apartment Corridor.

Interior of Grif's bachelor apartment on the market: kitchen counter, couch and window necessary.

Interior of a summer residence camp staff cabin for two: bunk beds, wooden spring-hinge door.

Danny's living room: La-Z-Boy chair, side table.

Note: These settings need only be suggested in design. Easy on-stage access is necessary to each setting.

Time

The scenes that originate in Grif's apartment take place in October, 1991.

Summer camp scenes and Danny's living room scenes are scattered throughout the past without particular respect to chronological time.

Production Note

This play is presented from Karla's point of view—or from her mind's eye. Often a scene from her past will intrude upon her present—sometimes bursting on in bits, other times creeping up slowly to result in complete scenes. Occasionally, they occur simultaneously with the present. Karla may be pulled directly into a scene from the past, or it might be played within the setting she is in at the time. For this reason, there is no numbered breakdown of scenes in the text *per se*, as they often mingle—and never is there a need for a complete blackout (except at the end of Act One). Effective lighting design should emphasize where Karla's attention is directed.

The part of the set being used, i.e. The Cabin, or The Apartment, is indicated in the preceding stage direction.

Karla and Grif

ACT ONE

Apartment Corridor.

KARLA stands smoking beside a closed door. She lets the ashes drop to the floor.

SOUND: Wooden spring door slamming.

Cabin.

GRIF   (*offstage*) Karla! Karla!

GRIF appears at camp door and speaks directly to KARLA.

I'm here!

SOUND: Metal door slamming.

Danny's Place.

DANNY is seated in his chair. He speaks directly to KARLA.

DANNY   Hey! Hey! When the hell did you get back?

GRIF   Did you miss me? Did you miss me?

DANNY   Why didn't you call me? I would have come and got you.

GRIF   How are you!? Kiss kiss kiss kiss kiss!

DANNY   Oh, my baby girl. All tanned and beautiful. Let me look at you.

GRIF   Holy Christ! You got a—

DANNY   Hey, uh… how's your—

GRIF   What happened?

DANNY   Stupid accident.

GRIF   You don't want to tell me.

DANNY   It's going to change. I mean it.

GRIF   Twenty questions!

DANNY   Hey, where you going?

GRIF   We are going to have the best summer!

GRIF runs out the door.

DANNY   Don't you want to talk to me? Karla? Eh!?

> ***Corridor.***

> *Upon the sound of someone approaching, KARLA drops her cigarette and extinguishes it with her foot. GRIF hurriedly enters, carrying a bag of groceries, a bag from a lingerie boutique, an umbrella and a briefcase. She doesn't notice KARLA at first as she is fumbling in her briefcase for her keys. Her umbrella drops. She stoops to pick it up.*

KARLA   Hi, Grif.

GRIF   *(shocked motionless)* Karla!

KARLA   Still raining? Here.

> *KARLA takes the umbrella and opens and shuts it quickly to shake off the water.*

GRIF   That's okay, I can—

KARLA   You look good. What did you do to your hair?

GRIF   What? I didn't…. Nothing.

KARLA   It's lighter or something.

GRIF   How long have you been here?

KARLA   I think I liked it the other way better.

GRIF   How did you find my apartment?

KARLA   Dirty blonde. Or sandy brown. Sort of.

GRIF   Did you… you didn't call my grandmother, did you?

 KARLA   I don't know. Maybe I just remember it different.

GRIF   She, she isn't well. She shouldn't have any stress. Her heart—

KARLA   Did you know they put addresses in phone books?

> *Pause.*

GRIF   I didn't think you lived here anymore.

KARLA   Why?

GRIF   I'm in a bit of a rush.

KARLA   I love this city.

GRIF   I have to be somewhere at 7:00.

KARLA   Dinner date?

> *Pause.*

GRIF   Karla, I wasn't expecting…. If I'd known—

KARLA   I wanted to surprise you. Surprise!

GRIF   We could have arranged something. I don't really have time—

KARLA   Just a quick visit. Shoot the shit. Cup of coffee. Here, give me something.

GRIF   You should have phoned.

KARLA   I did. I just kept getting your machine. I can't stand those things. You've been out a lot. Here, let me help you.

> *KARLA reaches out to take something from GRIF. GRIF doesn't move.*

Are we going in, or what?

GRIF   Karla—

KARLA   What's the matter? You hiding something in there? Oh, wait. Is there a man in there? Waiting for you in a muscle shirt and bikini briefs? Trained to kill uninvited guests?

GRIF   No, I…. Why don't you just tell me what you want?

KARLA   To see you. Talk to you. It's been over three years. Three years… and a couple of months, maybe.

GRIF   I just don't think this is—

KARLA   Open the friggin' door!

GRIF   I'm sorry. I'm busy. I'm going out.

KARLA   You don't have to be there 'til seven.

GRIF   I need a shower.

KARLA   That still gives us a few minutes…

GRIF   I have nothing to say to you.

KARLA   Okay, open the door or I'll yell something obscene. In five…

GRIF   What?

KARLA   Four…

GRIF   What, you're not going to yell in here.

KARLA   The old lady across the hall came home ten minutes ago. Three…

GRIF   No Karla, you can't be serious.

KARLA   You're running out of time. Two…

GRIF   Oh, come on!

KARLA   That's the rule. One…

GRIF   Jesus, Karla!

KARLA   *(hollering)* JANET GRIFFITHS HAS RED PUBIC HAIR!

> *GRIF quickly turns and starts to walk away. KARLA grabs her arm.*

Hey. I could have yelled about the time you shaved it all off.

GRIF   What do you want, Karla?

> *Pause.*

KARLA   Danny died.

GRIF   Really?

KARLA   No. I'm lying.

GRIF   I'm sorry.

KARLA   Want to see his obituary? I brought it for you. In case you missed it in the papers.

> *GRIF doesn't take it.*

Actually, it wasn't in the big paper, or anything. I'm not the obituary-writing type. It was in the company newsletter.

GRIF   You could have just told me this first instead of going through all the bullshit.

KARLA   *(mock terror)* You swore!

GRIF   Are you on drugs, Karla?

> *KARLA laughs.*

Are you?

KARLA   Good ol' Janet.

> *Pause.*

No, Grif. I'm straight. I'm clean. I'm dry. I haven't dropped a speck for three years. Now, doesn't that beat all to hell? Unless you count cigarettes and the occasional beer.

> *Pause.*

What, no confetti? No streamers?

GRIF   That's very good.

KARLA   No hugs?

> *Pause.*

So, how about it? Gonna let me in?

>*Pause.*

GRIF *(punctuating)* I have to leave in half an hour.

KARLA That doesn't give us much, does it?

GRIF Half an hour.

KARLA I'll take what I can get.

GRIF A cup of coffee.

>*KARLA offers to take some of the load. GRIF hesitates, then hands her the groceries. She finds her keys in her pocket and opens the door.*

KARLA Ladies first.

>*GRIF goes through the door.*

>**Danny's Place.**

>*DANNY swivels his chair around to face KARLA.*

DANNY I think you ought to wear a dress.

>*KARLA approaches him.*

KARLA When was the last time you saw me wear a dress, Danny?

>*DANNY thinks.*

Right.

DANNY It's just…. It's sort of formal.

KARLA *(guffaws)* Formal.

DANNY Yeah. Formal.

KARLA Schmitke's Tool and Dye Company has a "formal" Christmas party?

DANNY So what's wrong with that, Karla? Eh? What's wrong with people putting on decent clothes once in a while?

>*KARLA smirks.*

What? What?

KARLA Nothing.

DANNY You know, it wouldn't hurt you, Karla. To make yourself more…

KARLA What?

DANNY You could be a real looker, you know. Lots of guys would think you'd be a real catch.

KARLA I'm not a muskie for Chrissake.

DANNY   A little bit of rouge, earrings maybe—

KARLA   I suppose you'd want me to clean under my fucking fingernails, too.

DANNY   Hey, hey!

KARLA   Look, you want me to go with you, I said I'd go. You want a dress, find a date.

DANNY   Aw, c'mon Karla…

KARLA   And anyway, what are you going to wear? You don't even have a jacket.

The Cabin.

GRIF enters with a "majestic" air, capturing KARLA's attention. DANNY continues speaking to KARLA.

GRIF   You should have seen us at the grad, Karla. We were a vision.

DANNY   Well, forget it then.

GRIF   An absolute vision!

DANNY   We won't go.

GRIF   Gram took me to this little German boutique.

DANNY   I'll be sick or something.

GRIF   They made such a fuss. Opalescent satin. Off-the-shoulder puff. Deep V in the back. Floor-length skirt…

DANNY   I just thought it would be fun for us.

GRIF   …Like Cinderella!

DANNY   Do something special.

GRIF   It took me hours to get dressed. It took Al thirty seconds to rip it off. Want to see the picture?

GRIF exits.

DANNY   When was the last time we went out together, eh? Can you even remember? I remember. It was last summer. After you came back from camp. We had steak. I let you have some wine, too. You were underage. To celebrate your bronze cross.

KARLA   *(frustrated)* Bronze medallion, Danny!

She turns away from him.

It was my bronze medallion!

KARLA exits.

DANNY   *(yells after her)* I was real proud of you for that, Karla! Real proud! That camp was a good place for you. I knew that. A place to learn something good. Get out of the city. Get away from those degenerates you called your friends! Healthy air. Clean water. Sun. Exercise…

> **The Cabin.**
>
> *KARLA enters the cabin with her bedroll, backpack and boom box. She has a cast on her forearm.*

…knee socks, running shoes, t-shirts and shorts. And girls! Lots of girls your own age, Karla. It'll be fun! That's what my little girl needs.

> *KARLA dumps her gear. She slaps the bunk mattress. Dust clouds upward. On her hands and knees she checks under the bed. She scans the walls looking for the past year's signatures.*

GRIF   *(off)* KARLA! KARLA! I'M HERE!

> *KARLA quickly assumes a nonchalant position on the bottom bunk, hiding her cast. GRIF enters with a flourish. On her t-shirt is printed: "CAMP CEDAR ROCK—GRIF—SENIOR WATERFRONT" She drops her gear.*

(almost without taking a breath) AAAAAHHH! LOOK AT YOU! Kiss kiss kiss kiss kiss. Did you miss me? DID YOU MISS ME? Congratulate me, you are looking at a survivor of first-year psychology. OH, GOD, I'M SO GLAD TO BE UP HERE! PRE-CAMP PARTY! WOO-HOO! I had to do some sweet-talking to get Boss Lady to let us share a cabin again, you know. I promised her no late night raids in the tuck cupboard. Hey, did you see the new bell on the mess hall? How the hell are we going to steal the gonger when it's on top of the roof? I'll bet you Boss Lady did that. BIIITCH! Oh, man! Look at this place! It's so clean! I wonder if Mr. T's still alive.

> *She bangs on the bottom bunk and peers under it.*

COME ON OUT YOU ROTTEN RODENT! Bet he's got a whole nest of them under here. Little Mr. T's to scare the shit out of us at night. Hey, you little bugger! Better watch it or Big Bad Karla will get you with her knife. *(to KARLA)* You still got the Sabre?

> *KARLA takes her beaten old pocket-knife out of her pocket.*

All right! "Camper Threatening Device." Remember last year, when we were on night duty, we scared the pants off of Cabin Ten. I've never seen a more still bunch of thirteen-year-olds in my life. God that was funny! They're sitting there, having a seance in the middle of the floor and in slams Grif and Karla with the SABRE! You were so funny, Karla… standing there, your knife glistening in the spot of my flashlight, a wild glare in your eyes. God, if Boss

Lady had ever found out about that we would have been fired for sure. HOLY CHRIST! YOU GOT A BROKEN ARM!

KARLA   Swift.

GRIF   AAAAHH! SHE TALKS!

KARLA   When I have a chance.

> *KARLA sticks her knife into the bunk post.*

GRIF   So, how'd you break it?

KARLA   You want the top?

GRIF   Karla, we've been coming to Cedar Rock for eight years. I've always had the top bunk.

KARLA   So, do you want it again?

GRIF   Why? Do you want it?

KARLA   I was being polite.

GRIF   Well, you already got your stuff on the bottom.

KARLA   It's not unpacked.

GRIF   And how would you climb up there with a broken arm?

KARLA   No problem.

GRIF   Piss off. I want the top. Oh, you forgot to pick up your t-shirt at the office.

> *GRIF throws KARLA's staff t-shirt to her. KARLA holds it up against herself. It reads "CAMP CEDAR ROCK—KARLA—KITCHEN."*

Well, put it on!

KARLA   Later.

> *They start to unpack their bedrolls.*

GRIF   So, what fine items are on the menu for our gourmet campers this summer, hm? More chicken-à-la-shit?

KARLA   Tuna casserole with puss sauce.

GRIF   All you can eat Road-Kill Meat!

KARLA   And Grif's personal favourite:

BOTH   Phlegm flambé!

> *They simultaneously pretend to hork and spit.*

KARLA   There it is!

> *GRIF screeches and leaps onto the bunk, frantically checking the floor.*

GRIF   Where!

> *KARLA points to a spot on the wall where they had engraved their names a few years ago.*

KARLA   No, bonehead, "Grif and Karla, 1987".

GRIF   Don't do that!

KARLA   Wimp.

GRIF   We are going to have the best summer.

KARLA   Right on.

GRIF   So, are you going to tell me what happened?

KARLA   My father broke it.

GRIF   Your father.

KARLA   Yup.

GRIF   Your father broke your arm.

KARLA   You got it.

GRIF   Karla!

KARLA   What?

GRIF   You don't just stand there calmly, and tell me your father broke your arm!

KARLA   What do you want me to do? Cry? It doesn't hurt anymore.

GRIF   How did it happen?

KARLA   How's your grandmother?

GRIF   No. Don't change the subject.

KARLA   She still have that Caribbean cook?

GRIF   You don't want to tell me.

KARLA   The one with the "nice" buns?

GRIF   Okay. "20 Questions."

KARLA   Does he still make "Miss Janet" her favourite "sugar sweets"?

GRIF   Was it an accident?

KARLA   And teach you how to "play his drums"?

GRIF   Was it an accident?

KARLA   *(sighs)* No.

GRIF   Were you fighting?

KARLA   Yes.

GRIF   About your mother?

KARLA   No.

GRIF   About your friends?

KARLA   No.

GRIF   About school?

KARLA   Well, in a way…

GRIF   No, no! You can only answer "yes" or "no"!

KARLA   Yes.

GRIF   Yes. Okay. Wait a minute, I lost count. Did I have five or six?

KARLA   Fuck this.

GRIF   Oh. By the way. I'm making a rule for us for this summer.

KARLA   Who died and left you in charge?

GRIF   No swearing allowed.

KARLA   In front of the kids.

GRIF   No. At all.

KARLA   So what are we supposed to say instead of shit, fuck or piss?

GRIF   Hey, hey!

KARLA   Well?

GRIF   Piffle.

KARLA   Piffle?

GRIF   Piffle.

KARLA   Stupidest word I ever heard.

GRIF   That's the rule.

KARLA   And what happens if we break it?

GRIF   You get spanked.

KARLA   What happens if you like spankings?

GRIF   You would. So, tell me about your fight.

KARLA   Well, I got booted from school—

GRIF   Again?

KARLA Took too many classes off.

GRIF Karla.

KARLA I called the vice principal an asshole—

GRIF You did?

KARLA He caught me and Spider sharing a splif under the football stands.

GRIF You're still doing that stuff?

KARLA He said I was to keep my feet off school property until I "straightened" my ways. I said, "You got it, asshole!"

GRIF Cripes!

KARLA So, I went home. And I'd just broke into my Dad's new case of Brador… He's really protective of his Brador…. If it's 50 or Canadian he really doesn't give a shit—

GRIF Hey—

KARLA But touch his Brador and you're up SHIT creek!

GRIF *(warning)* Karla!

KARLA Then, Danny walks in. He's as red as a lobster. The principal called him at work. So, he tells his boss he has a family emergency and he has to get home immediately.

GRIF Oh, man.

KARLA He walks in… and I'm standing there, drinking his precious Brador. He starts yelling that I should buy my own beer. I tell him to take a hike, and I try to finish the beer. Then he grabs my arm, and smashes it on the door frame.

GRIF Oh, shit!

KARLA Ha!

GRIF Piffle! Piffle! I mean piffle!

> KARLA raises her hand, and tries to corner GRIF.

KARLA Bend over!

GRIF No, no!

KARLA Pull your pants down!

GRIF Not with pants down!

KARLA That's what a spanking is.

GRIF My grandmother never spanked me.

KARLA She should have.

GRIF   Come on, Karla. It was a joke.

> *KARLA drops her hand.*

KARLA   Next time, I pull out the wooden spoon. Or, no, the kitchen paddle—the one I use for stirring the oatmeal.

GRIF   Alright, alright!

KARLA   I mean it.

GRIF   Okay! So, he smashed your arm on the door frame?

KARLA   The bottle flies out of my hand and smashes right through the window.

GRIF   Jeepers. And your arm's broken.

KARLA   Thin little bones there, you know. You should have heard it.

GRIF   Gawd!

KARLA   Cast comes off next week.

GRIF   *(sympathetic)* Oh, Karla.

KARLA   *(mimicking)* Oh, Grif.

> *GRIF tries to hug KARLA. KARLA squirms away.*

Stop it.

GRIF   What are you going to do about it?

KARLA   Oh, I'm going to sue him. Or maybe, I'll report him to Children's Aid. Except I'm eighteen now.

GRIF   I'm serious. You should—

KARLA   I should what?

GRIF   He should pay for that.

KARLA   Well, I'm on his medical plan.

GRIF   He can't just go around breaking your arm like that, Karla.

KARLA   I'm the one who fucked up, Grif. And I don't give a shit about your stupid rule at the moment.

GRIF   What about the police?

KARLA   He's my father!

GRIF   He broke your arm!

KARLA   And I drank his beer! And failed another year!

GRIF   Boy, if my father ever…

KARLA Your father's dead, Grif.

GRIF Or my grandmother, then!

> *KARLA smirks.*

This isn't funny! I can't believe he did that to you. Over a stupid beer!

KARLA He didn't mean to break it!

GRIF What exactly did he mean to do, then?

KARLA It doesn't matter!

GRIF He shouldn't be…

KARLA Let's just drop it, okay?

> *KARLA abruptly turns and leaves the cabin.*

GRIF Karla!

> *SOUND: House door slamming.*

> **Danny's Place.**

> *DANNY is watching late-night television. On the side table beside his chair, there is a half-eaten, store-bought freezer cake, an empty pack of cigarettes, and a bottle of Brador.*

DANNY That you, Karla?

> *KARLA enters.*

KARLA No. It's Freddy Krueger.

> *KARLA stands behind DANNY watching the television. She picks up the bottle and takes a swig. DANNY takes the beer from her without looking away from the TV.*

DANNY There's Canadian in the basement.

KARLA Want a cigarette?

DANNY Eh?

KARLA Your pack's empty. Here.

> *She hands him a cigarette. He accepts.*

DANNY There's Brador in the fridge.

> *KARLA picks up the cake box.*

KARLA What the hell are you buying this shit for, Danny?

DANNY Watch your language.

KARLA   Look at this crap. You look at what's in here? Listen. Sodium aluminum silicate. Triethyl citrate. Propylene mono fatty acid esters. Sorbitan mono stearate—

DANNY   Shut the fuck up, I can't hear the television.

KARLA   You don't have to eat this garbage. You want a cake, ask me. I'll make you a cake.

DANNY   She'll make me a cake.

KARLA   I would.

DANNY   Where you been?

KARLA   What's it matter?

DANNY   It matters 'cause I wanna know.

KARLA   You wanna know when I shit and piss too?

DANNY   She gets defensive on me because I ask her where she's been!

KARLA   At the Chaud (*pronounced "shawd"*), okay?

DANNY   With who?

KARLA   Same people I always go with.

DANNY   You gotta stop hanging around those goofs, Karla.

KARLA   Don't tell me what to do.

DANNY   They're no good, Karla.

KARLA   Goodnight.

> *KARLA moves to exit.*

DANNY   You know who made good cakes? Joyce made good cakes. Big chocolate ones.

KARLA   I remember.

DANNY   She remembers. Tell me how the hell you remember when you were only three years old for Chrissake!

KARLA   I remember! Big two-layer jobs. And she decorated them with goddamn gumdrops!

DANNY   Gummy bears, Karla. Gummy bears. She put gummy bears on them because I liked the contrast. Sweet and sour. She remembers. Hey! You know why you remember? I know why. You don't remember anything. You've seen the pictures.

KARLA   No, I remember getting a cake like that on my birthday.

DANNY   Jesus! It wasn't your birthday, Karla! It was mine! The one you're remembering was my cake!

KARLA   She probably made it more than once, Dan.

DANNY   Look. I'll show you the cake you're "remembering" Karla.

DANNY reaches for a worn photo album from the side table.

KARLA   Forget it.

DANNY   I ought to know what cake Joyce made for me on my birthday. It's right in here.

KARLA   Okay. Alright. You're right. Don't get out the stupid photo album.

DANNY   Don't tell me what to do, Karla. Where the hell's that picture?

KARLA   I'm going to bed.

DANNY   Just get back here, Missy. Here! Look! Here it is! The chocolate cake with the gummy bears. And it's sitting right in front of me.

KARLA   Look at it close, Dad.

DANNY   What?

KARLA   There's three candles on it.

DANNY   So what? Maybe I turned thirty-three and she just shortened it.

KARLA   And I'm sitting there, Danny, with my cheeks all puffed up, like I'm going to blow out the candles!

DANNY   You were always butting in. It was MY cake, and you were trying to blow out MY candles.

KARLA   I don't believe you! It's my birthday cake, on my third birthday. And I remember it without the fucking picture.

DANNY   Shut up, Karla.

KARLA   Look! Look! The next picture. What is it, Dan? It's me. Me opening a present. A present on MY third birthday!

DANNY   You couldn't keep your mitts off anything. Everything was "mine, mine, mine." It's my birthday present you're opening.

KARLA   The wrapping's got pictures of teddy bears on it!

DANNY   Joyce was cheap. She saved wrapping paper.

KARLA   And balloons on the wall!

DANNY   Can it!

KARLA   She put balloons on the wall when you turned thirty-three? Eh, Danny? EH!?

DANNY   YOU GONNA SHUT YOUR YAP?!

> *DANNY violently grabs KARLA's arm and breaks it. KARLA yells in pain.*

Oh, Jesus. Oh, what did I do?

KARLA   It was MY birthday, you BASTARD!

> *KARLA exits holding her arm.*

DANNY   Oh, Jesus. Oh, Karla…

> *DANNY holds himself and rocks in his chair.*

> *KARLA returns to the cabin. She and GRIF are silent for a moment.*

The Cabin.

GRIF   Hey, you know what I heard? Half the camper population this session is on Social Aid.

Hey, wanna lay bets on the number of runaways? Or no… let's do suicide attempts. Yeah. Five bucks on… seventeen boffed suicide attempts from the social aid population.

Remember that fat girl last summer? Drank two bottles of rubbing alcohol? And that other one? From cabin seven? The one with only one pair of shorts? Tried to slit her wrists with a butter knife?

Only on social assistance.

> *Pause.*

(ashamed) Oh, Karla. I'm sorry…

KARLA   No. You're just rich.

GRIF   I'm not rich.

KARLA   A house on Embassy Row isn't exactly middle-class, Grif.

GRIF   It's very old money, Karla.

KARLA   Is it too old to spend?

GRIF   Look, I lived in a split-level in Nepean until I was three years old.

KARLA   Life's rough.

GRIF   My parents had to work, you know. They both had jobs. They weren't just handed the family money. That trip they were taking was the first vacation they'd had in four years.

KARLA   I know.

GRIF   My grandmother has been very good to me. I love her. But, I'd rather have my mother and father, you know?

KARLA   Okay!

GRIF   Oh, my God!

KARLA   What?

GRIF   We were fighting.

KARLA   We weren't fighting.

GRIF   Yes, we were!

KARLA   No we weren't!

GRIF   Yes we were!

KARLA   That was not a fight.

GRIF   Yes it was. And now it's time to kiss and make up. Come on. Give me a little kissy!

KARLA   Forget it!

GRIF   Kissy kissy kissy!

KARLA   Get lost!

GRIF   Pweese… a witto kissy for Gwiffy!

KARLA   Cut it out!

> SOUND: *The mess hall bell rings.*

GRIF   Piffle! Staff meeting.

KARLA   She's bell-happy already.

GRIF   Let's go.

KARLA   Wait, wait!

GRIF   What?

> *KARLA removes her leather bracelet and presents GRIF with it.*

KARLA   You wear it.

GRIF   *(reads)* It says "Let's get high."

KARLA   It has great sentimental value. I traded for it at the Ex. With Lenny the Leatherman.

GRIF   That's nice.

KARLA Put it on.

> *GRIF, embarrassed, puts it on.*

Now, give me your ring.

GRIF Are you crazy? You can't have this ring!

KARLA Why not?

GRIF Because my Grandmother gave it to me when I was ten! My mother used to wear it. It's a family heirloom!

KARLA Just for the summer.

GRIF You'll lose it!

KARLA I will not! It will be my most treasured item.

GRIF But, Karla…

KARLA Give me the ring, or I'll switch cabins with Charmagne. She farts all the time in her sleep.

GRIF You would not.

KARLA The ring or I'm gone!

> *Pause.*

GRIF With Charmagne?

> *KARLA verbally makes a flatulent noise.*

Okay! Alright! For the summer. Then I want it back. You promise?

KARLA Yeah, yeah.

GRIF If my grandmother ever finds out I let someone else wear this ring…

> *GRIF gives KARLA her ring. The mess hall bell rings again.*

That's for us. We're going to get shit already. Whoops…. Piffle!

KARLA *(raising her hand)* Your rule!

> *GRIF runs out, shrieking playfully. KARLA stops to pull her knife out of the bunk.*
>
> *DANNY turns in his chair, and speaks to KARLA as if she were a child.*

DANNY What have you got in your hand, Karla?

> *KARLA puts her hands behind her back and responds as a young girl.*

KARLA Nothing.

DANNY Don't you lie to your father. Show me what you have in your hand.

KARLA It's just a knife.

DANNY A knife! Let me see it. Now. Or you're going to your room.

KARLA Can I bring it with me?

DANNY Don't be a smartass with me, young lady. Show me the knife.

> *KARLA quickly shows him, then hides it behind her again.*

Where d'you get that?

KARLA I found it.

DANNY You playing in my chest again in the basement? Huh? Give it to me.

KARLA No, Daddy. I want it! Please?

DANNY Karla, what is a nine-year-old girl going to do with a knife?

KARLA Keep it in my pocket.

DANNY Why?

KARLA Because I like it! I like the way the blade comes out like this. See, look. It's all sharp and shiny. I polished it up with a face cloth. And then it goes back inside. Like it's hiding.

DANNY Karla...

KARLA I promise I'll be careful. I'll take good care of it. I won't do anything wrong. I just want to keep it in my pocket. Okay?

> *KARLA runs out. DANNY shakes his head, smiling.*
>
> *A telephone rings. GRIF's message is heard on the answering machine: "Hi. You've reached 236-3048. I'm not in right now, but if you leave your name and number..."*

Grif's Apartment.

> *GRIF enters the apartment followed by KARLA. GRIF hurriedly dumps her bags at the entrance and answers the phone, turning off the machine.*

GRIF Don't hang up I'm here!... Oh, hi swee—

> *GRIF looks over at KARLA, then continues.*

How was your day...? I'm fine...

> *While GRIF talks, KARLA hangs up her jacket, then brings the bags to the counter. She opens the lingerie bag and holds up and examines a sexy, feminine brassiere.*

...Oh. Darn. Well, can you still make it for seven? I can wait for you. I'll order at seven-thirty. No, it's okay. See you. Bye. Yeah... *(self consciously)* Love you back.

GRIF hangs up and turns to KARLA.

KARLA *(about brassiere)* This is very nice, Grif.

GRIF Yes.

> *Annoyed, GRIF takes the brassiere from KARLA and brings it to the bathroom. KARLA begins unpacking the groceries. There is a bowl on the counter with a few old vegetables sticking out of it.*

KARLA *(calling)* You want the tomatoes in this bowl here, or in the fridge?

GRIF I'll do that!

KARLA You should keep them in the fridge. Fresh produce spoils fast.

GRIF *(returning)* I like them in the bowl.

KARLA Nutritional loss.

GRIF Would you let me do this?

> *KARLA watches GRIF put away the rest of the groceries—a few vegetables, some fruit.*

KARLA You on a diet? You don't need to lose weight. Where you going to lose it from?

> *GRIF is bent over.*

Your butt? There's nothing wrong with your butt. It's a perfectly acceptable butt. You still swim a lot, right?

GRIF Yes.

KARLA Hey, you know what I'm going to do? I'm going to make you the best Greek salad you've ever had. You got any feta?

GRIF No, you're not.

KARLA It's low-fat.

GRIF I hope you don't mind reheated coffee.

> *GRIF turns on the coffee machine. There is some old coffee in the carafe.*

KARLA You got an ashtray?

> *GRIF hands her one.*

GRIF Would you open the window, please?

> *KARLA opens the window and looks down.*

KARLA You like living on the market?

GRIF It's convenient.

KARLA   You can watch all the hookers from here.

GRIF   I could.

> *KARLA leans out the window.*

KARLA   How's business today, ladies!

GRIF   Please... Karla.

KARLA   Hey, you got any vinegar? Do a great job on this.

GRIF   Pardon?

KARLA   Vinegar. It's the best stuff for cleaning windows. All this crud from the traffic.

> *KARLA searches in the cupboards.*

Where's your vinegar?

GRIF   Karla. Don't clean my windows.

KARLA   No, no really. Watch this, you'll be amazed. It'll only take a second. Where's your paper towels?

GRIF   I ran out.

KARLA   A tea towel will do.

> *KARLA takes one from the counter.*

GRIF   Why do you want to wash my windows?

> *KARLA begins to wipe. DANNY appears on the other side of the window. KARLA stares out at him.*

DANNY   I notice these things, Karla. About you. Things, that I can't figure. Your clothes: Torn. Ripped. Worn. You wear the same, damn, black t-shirt every day... but you wash it every night. Your running shoes: Broken laces. Tied in knots. Holes wearing through the bottom... always placed perfectly, neatly on the boot tray by the door. You never throw away a plastic container. They're all organized by size in the cupboard. You change the aluminum things under the stove burners every week. But, what gets me Karla... is the windows. You're always washing the bloody windows. Why are you always washing the windows?

> *DANNY stays watching her.*

KARLA   Because they're dirty.

> *KARLA continues washing.*

I had a janitorial job at the Met Life building for a while. That's where I learned about vinegar. This old lady? She'd been a janitor for thirty-seven years. Can you believe it? She was great. Told the dirtiest jokes. Cleanest old lady I ever met. She could clean anything. There.

GRIF   Where are you working now?

KARLA   The Delta. Salads and desserts.

GRIF   Do you like it?

KARLA   Oh, yes. It's my calling. How's psychology?

GRIF   I'm an elementary school counsellor.

KARLA   Do you like it?

GRIF   Well, it's sort of… it's fine.

KARLA   Just fine.

GRIF   You don't get to see the happy ones.

KARLA   *(finished)* There.

GRIF   Thanks.

DANNY   You missed a spot.

> *DANNY exits.*

KARLA   Don't mention it.

> *Pause.*

Got anything to drink?

GRIF   The coffee's almost hot. You wanted to talk about your father.

KARLA   Yeah. You got anything to drink?

GRIF   You said you were straight.

KARLA   I'm in mourning. I'm entitled to the odd depressant.

GRIF   Do you feel you need a drink to talk about your father?

KARLA   Yes, Dr. Grif, I do feel that way.

GRIF   And why do you think that is?

KARLA   Sets the mood, I guess.

GRIF   What mood does it set?

KARLA   Fuck the shrink shit, Grif. I wanted to talk to you. Like we used to. I don't want all this "how does it make you feel?" crap.

> *Pause.*

GRIF   I have some wine.

KARLA That'll do.

>   *GRIF pours her a glass.*

Aren't you going to have some?

GRIF No.

KARLA Come on. It'll loosen you up.

>   *KARLA pours GRIF a glass.*

GRIF I don't like to drink before dinner.

KARLA Here you go. Cheers.

>   *KARLA offers to clink glasses with GRIF. GRIF turns away.*

GRIF Please, have a seat, Karla.

>   *They move to the couch. KARLA sits casually on the arm.*

KARLA Where's your bedroom?

GRIF The couch folds out.

KARLA You got a good job. Why are you living in a bachelor?

GRIF I'm saving.

KARLA For what? A house?

GRIF Yes. *(beat)* You find that amusing?

KARLA I always figured some guy with a BMW would provide the house.

>   *Pause.*

GRIF Your father. How did he die?

KARLA Heart attack. What else? Smoked like a chimney. Drank like a fish. He'd put lard on his toast if there wasn't any butter.

GRIF Were you with him when he had his attack?

KARLA Yeah. We were… arguing.

GRIF What about?

KARLA Something about the dragon.

GRIF He was still…?

KARLA Here we were, been without her for 20 years. Whenever he got pissed all he'd do is talk about her. How pretty she was, what a good cook she was, what a slut she was…. And then he'd get out the wedding pictures. Can you believe he kept the friggin' things? And then he'd dribble and cry all over them. It pissed me off. What a waste, you know? All that time. So stupid!

DANNY enters the scene, brandishing a wet facecloth. He is stumbling drunk.

DANNY   I want to know, Karla! I want to know what the hell happened to your nose! Eh? Why is it bleeding!

KARLA   Leave me alone, Danny!

DANNY   How many times I tell you not to hang out at the Chaud?

*KARLA rises and crosses to **Danny's Place**, trying to get away from him. DANNY stumbles after her.*

KARLA   I wasn't at the Chaud!

DANNY   It's no place for a girl, Karla.

KARLA   I haven't been there for over a year!

DANNY   Everyone's looking to scrap there! You scrapping with someone?

KARLA   No!

DANNY   Girls shouldn't scrap!

KARLA   I wasn't scrapping! I wasn't at the Chaud!

DANNY   Now look at you! Scrapping at the Chaud. Y'into some "gang" kind-o-shit, maybe? That's just what I need, thank you very much, my daughter in one of those street scrapping gangs!

KARLA   There's no gang, Danny! I told you already I slipped on some ice. I bashed into the outside railing, okay! Right here! Outside! The stair railing! Scout's honour!

DANNY reaches for her with the facecloth.

DANNY   Here...

KARLA tries to take it from him, but he is insistent on wiping her nose himself.

KARLA   Would you just give it to me?

DANNY   Let me do it.

KARLA   No!

DANNY   Here, look at me!

KARLA   NO!

DANNY   For Christ sake, girl. When are you going to grow up? I'm going to clean your nose, whether you like it or not. Stay STILL!

KARLA   Danny, just FUCK OFF!

KARLA punches him hard in the chest. DANNY recoils, gulping and gasping, feigning a heart attack.

DANNY   Karla...

KARLA   Get lost, Danny.

DANNY   You hit me, Karla.

KARLA   I told you to leave me alone!

DANNY   Pain, Karla... my heart... call the hospital.

KARLA   Aw, come on.

DANNY   Call them.

KARLA   Call them yourself.

KARLA gets him the phone.

Here. Well, go ahead, Danny. Dial! Dial the phone, asshole!

DANNY keeps gasping, his eyes fixed on her. KARLA begins to doubt.

Daddy? Daddy! Oh, God...

KARLA moves to him. He looks away from her.

Oh God, I'm sorry! Daddy...

DANNY turns back to KARLA looking horrified.

DANNY   Boo!

He laughs hysterically.

KARLA   *(enraged)* You son of a bitch! Don't you ever...!

KARLA violently shoves him.

DANNY feigns a second attack. This time, KARLA stands back from him. He staggers to the phone and attempts to dial. He gives up, beseeching with animal-like noises. Again, KARLA doubts.

Oh, Jesus... Jesus, Daddy... don't...

KARLA grabs the phone, fumbling with the number. DANNY stands and laughs again.

You asshole!

*DANNY's laughter suddenly stops. His face becomes grotesquely contorted, he holds his left shoulder and falls back into his chair. KARLA moves away from him, back towards **Grif's Apartment**.*

(moving away from him) You're a lunatic. You hear me, Danny? You're a fucking asshole, lunatic, BASTARD!

DANNY struggles to form his words.

DANNY   ...Balloons on the wall...

KARLA   *(quietly)* ...what...?

DANNY   Balloons... on the wall...

*DANNY dies. KARLA moves back to **Grif's Apartment**.*

KARLA   He'd get so twisted. His heart all in knots.

GRIF   So, an argument about your mother brought on the attack.

KARLA   Yup.

GRIF   And what did you do? When you realized what was happening?

Pause.

KARLA   Remember that CPR course we took? I was positive it was a heart attack.

GRIF   So, you performed CPR.

Pause.

Karla?

KARLA   Probably wouldn't have saved him anyway. His gig was up. He was a mess.

GRIF   It's not unusual to feel responsible for the death of a loved one.

KARLA   *(smirks)* "A loved one."

GRIF   Particularly if your relationship was... unstable. Afterwards, we want to have them back, to solve all the problems. To say the things we perhaps never said... or do the things we never did. And if you were there, seeing it all... well, it's a true shock. You were in shock, Karla.

Sometimes when we're presented with an emergency situation, even one we've been trained for, like the CPR, our senses just don't work. Don't blame yourself. Your father's death is not your fault.

KARLA pours herself another glass of wine.

KARLA   Remember that CPR course? What a grind. All the practice we did on each other. You were so mad at the final test, when I scored higher than you.

GRIF   I wasn't mad.

KARLA   Yes, you were.

GRIF   Why would I get mad about that?

KARLA   You never liked anyone doing better than you.

GRIF   That's ridiculous.

KARLA   No it's not.

GRIF   I just like to do my best.

KARLA   You did your best. Just my best was better.

GRIF   I was disappointed in myself.

KARLA   You were really pissed off.

GRIF   Karla, I know of a very good support group. Or if you would prefer a private counsellor—

KARLA   *(laughs)* Right!

GRIF   Sitting here for a couple of minutes isn't going to help you cope with your grief.

KARLA   You always had such low self esteem.

GRIF   No, I didn't!

> *KARLA smiles to herself.*

You know why you're doing this?

KARLA   What am I doing?

GRIF   You feel angry and guilty.

KARLA   Maybe.

GRIF   You want a fight.

KARLA   No I don't.

GRIF   You want someone to hurt you.

KARLA   I want a friend.

GRIF   You want a friend to hurt you. Subconsciously, it would alleviate your guilt.

KARLA   Is this what they taught you?

GRIF   Yes.

KARLA   You should ask for your money back.

GRIF   I am not going to fight with you, Karla.

KARLA   Fuck, man. I don't want to fight!

GRIF   You barge into my house…

KARLA   I didn't barge.

GRIF   Go through my groceries…

KARLA   I was helping.

GRIF   Clean my windows…

KARLA   They were dirty!

GRIF   Against my will…

> *KARLA freezes and softly emphasizes and directs her words straight to GRIF.*

KARLA   I would never do anything against your will.

> *Pause.*

Would I?

> *Pause.*

GRIF   I'm not the right person to help you.

> *GRIF stands.*

I have to get ready to go.

> *GRIF takes a small swig of her wine and dumps the rest in the sink.*

KARLA   So, who is he? Another one of your big men? Hey, you still feel the same about little dinks? What did you used to call them? "Little minnows." That was it. You used to say little men's bodies made your skin crawl. You still feel that way? About dinks?

> *DANNY suddenly rises.*

DANNY   I think it's time we had a little talk.

GRIF   We're adults now, Karla.

> *DANNY crosses to GRIF's couch and leans against the back of it. He is uncomfortable with what he has to say.*

DANNY   This sort of thing isn't easy to talk about. But, you see, you're uh… well… getting older, and… you know what I'm trying to say…?

> *KARLA ignores him and continues talking to GRIF.*

KARLA   You always had big guys. Jocks. Weightlifters. They all had big bones didn't they? Except that one. What was he? That student. Yeah. He studied something that he didn't need a big dink for—

DANNY   But most important, Karla…

KARLA   But, he didn't last long anyway, did he?

DANNY   Are you paying attention? This is important.

GRIF   I have to get changed.

KARLA   He just couldn't fill you up.

DANNY   Just…. Well, just make sure you don't love the guy. Especially the first time.

KARLA   But then, you remember what everyone said about the size of your…

DANNY   'Cause then you're just setting yourself up to get hurt.

KARLA   …"Peter Heater."

> *DANNY turns directly to her.*

DANNY   And I wouldn't want to see you get hurt by some useless scum.

> *DANNY exits.*

KARLA   Remember the night we sat up making up names for it? Peter heater. Love bush. Clam clamp.

I'll never forget how proud you were when you informed all of us in Cabin Eight that you had been poked for the first time at boy's camp day. And we were all of what? Twelve, thirteen years old?

GRIF   I have to get ready to go, now.

KARLA   Okay. Go ahead.

GRIF   I need to have a shower.

KARLA   Fine.

GRIF   I said half an hour.

KARLA   According to my watch I still have six minutes. And the coffee should be ready.

> *KARLA goes to get the cup of coffee.*

Go have your shower. I can answer the phone if it rings.

GRIF   No, that's okay.

> *GRIF turns the answering machine on.*

The machine's on.

KARLA   I could take a message.

GRIF   No, thank you.

KARLA   But what if it's an emergency? Like, your grandmother having a stroke.

GRIF   My grandmother is not going to have a stroke.

KARLA   Who are you, God? You just said she wasn't well. What kind of a grand-daughter are you? Who doesn't want to know if their grandmother's had a stroke or not?

GRIF   I'm going to take my shower.

KARLA   Okay. I'll let myself out when I'm finished my coffee.

GRIF   I would prefer that you leave now.

KARLA   I promise I won't steal anything. I'll leave you my address and phone number in case anything is missing when you come out. Oh, and thanks a lot. You were a big help. I won't feel guilty any more.

GRIF   You should think about seeing someone.

KARLA   So, I'll see you around. I'll call next time.

GRIF   I'm pretty busy these days.

KARLA   Yeah.

GRIF   Goodbye, Karla.

> *KARLA smiles brightly and waves her off. GRIF goes into the bathroom. When KARLA hears the shower go on, she goes to the phone and unplugs it. Then, she takes GRIF's keys out of her raincoat, takes her own jacket and exits.*

> **The Cabin.**

> *GRIF bursts into the cabin wearing a bathrobe. Out of the pocket she takes a cassette tape which she pops into the boom box. She takes off the robe. She wears a very tiny bikini bathing suit and practices a few dance steps. KARLA enters the cabin with an old tuxedo jacket over her arm, holding a ratty top hat and a long stick to use as a dance cane.*

KARLA   TA-DAAAA!

> *She places the hat on her head with a flourish.*

GRIF   Oh, that's so great! I thought for sure the costume cupboard would be empty by now.

KARLA   I had to fight for them.

GRIF   Oh, "Karlo," you're my hero!

KARLA   And you my little bubble-head, are… uh… almost naked.

> *GRIF is fiddling with the straps of the bikini top.*

GRIF   Can you tighten this up for me?

KARLA   Here.

> *GRIF is swivelling her hips in a "bump and grind" fashion.*

Hold still, you silly bitch!

GRIF   I'm just warming up.

KARLA   I can't believe we're doing this. Minnie and Frankie did this same act for Staff Show three years ago.

GRIF   And? It was a smash hit. Everyone loves revivals! Anyway, this is KARLO AND GRIF, not Minnie and Frankie. Besides, I've got better goods than Minnie did, right, Karlo?

> *GRIF bumps KARLA with her hip.*

Or are you a breast man?

> *GRIF slides her finger suggestively inside her bikini top. Embarrassed, KARLA turns away.*

Oh, I think you are.

KARLA   I think you need more stuffing.

> *GRIF whacks KARLA.*

GRIF   Hey!

> *KARLA hits "play" on the boom box. It plays Chris De Burgh's "Patricia The Stripper."*
>
> *Using the song, they rehearse their ridiculous "Karlo and Grif" act— The Backwards Strip-Tease. KARLA plays the part of the narrator—and sings the first part of the song to the audience, indicating to GRIF as "Patricia"—who poses and "vogues" coyly to the side.*
>
> *With the chorus "...and with a swing of her hips..." GRIF begins to dress over her bikini in oversized rain pants, coat, gumboots and sou'wester. KARLA hands her the clothes and helps her with the boots. It should be playfully choreographed fun.*
>
> *When GRIF finishes dressing with some sort of flourish to indicate the end of the act, KARLA drops the "Karlo" persona and attempts to turn the music off. GRIF, instead, continues to dance in a sexually overt fashion and rubs herself against KARLA, taking off KARLA's hat and coat, giggling, cavorting, etc., making KARLA terribly embarrassed and uncomfortable.*

KARLA   Grif. What are you.... Come on. Stop it!

> *She becomes angry and forcefully pushes GRIF away.*

Cut it out!

GRIF   What?

> *KARLA exits.*

Karla! I'm just... I'm just...!

SOUND: Slamming house door.

Danny's Place.

DANNY is looking at the photo album. KARLA enters with her gear as if she has just returned from camp.

DANNY *(surprised)* Hey! Hey! When the hell did you get back?

KARLA Just now.

DANNY I didn't know when to expect you. How'd you get here?

KARLA I took the bus.

DANNY With all your stuff? Why didn't you call me? I would have come and got you.

Pause.

Well, come here and hug your old man. Come here, come here, I'm not going to bite you.

KARLA allows herself to be hugged.

Oh, my baby girl! Look at you! All tanned and beautiful! You look so… healthy! How was your summer, eh? Hey, uh…. How's your arm? Hm? All right?

KARLA Yeah, fine.

DANNY Stupid accident. I had a hell of a summer thinking about you, Karla. But you know what? It's going to change. I'm going to change. All this fighting between you and me. That's it. It's through. No more. I can't stand it when you're not here for so long. No more arguments, no more accidents. Okay?

KARLA I'm moving out, Dad.

DANNY Come on. Don't start that.

KARLA I'm going to start looking for a place tomorrow.

DANNY Come on, Karla. You just got in.

KARLA I thought you'd want to know.

DANNY Hey. You moving in with a guy? What guy is this?

KARLA I should get a place closer to Algonquin maybe.

DANNY What for?

KARLA It takes forty-five minutes to get there by bus, that's what for.

DANNY What? What? You're going to college? What the hell is this? A miracle?

KARLA I worked it out over the summer. I'm going to take Hotel Management.

DANNY   Hey! That's great! Hotel Management, eh? You know, Joyce used to work the night desk at—

KARLA   Dad.

DANNY   Yeah. Well. That's good, Karla. I'm proud of you, Baby. But why move out? I could help you with a down payment for a car if that's the problem.

KARLA   No, no. Thanks, Dad.

DANNY   So who's this guy you're moving in with? You meet him over the summer?

KARLA   Nobody! I didn't say that—you did!

DANNY   Well, let's not talk about this now, okay?

> *Pause.*

Hey, how about we go out for dinner? Eh? Would you like that? We'll get dressed. I could wear that jacket you got me last Christmas. Never seen me in that jacket. Looks real nice. Yeah. *(sniffs)* You'd better have a shower first. *(laughs)*

Where would you like to go? Huh? The Keg? Eh? Grab a steak? I bet you haven't been eating too much steak this summer, eh? What do you say? Salad bar. Litre of red. You and me. Okay, Karla? Let's go.

KARLA   Danny, I… I'm really tired.

DANNY   You still mad at me, Karla? Is that it? I told you already. I'm really sorry. It's going to stop. I'm slowing down on the drinking. It's true. Come here. Let me hold you.

> *DANNY holds her and rocks her tenderly. KARLA holds back tears.*

You're my baby. You always will be. I want you with me, sweetie. We need each other, you know? I love you, honey.

Let me buy you a car.

KARLA   Dad, no. That's not it.

DANNY   Well, what then? What is it? Hey, are you crying? Why are you crying like this?

KARLA   I'm not crying. I'm going to bed.

> *KARLA exits.*

DANNY   But you haven't eaten yet! What's your problem?

The Cabin.

> *GRIF enters the dark cabin, dishevelled and tired.*

GRIF   I'm back…

DANNY   Eh, Karla?

GRIF   Karla?

DANNY   You not hungry?

GRIF   I can't see!

DANNY   Don't you want to talk to me?

GRIF   Turn on your light!

DANNY   Eh?

> *GRIF is feeling the bottom bunk for KARLA.*

GRIF   Karla? Hey. Where are you when I need you? Where's my welcome? Where's my backrub?

> *KARLA enters, shining her flashlight in GRIF's eyes.*

KARLA   You made it.

GRIF   *(whining)* Yeah. Where were you?

KARLA   Putting out a grease fire. I'm a hero.

GRIF   Bull.

KARLA   Staff lounge.

GRIF   Why?

KARLA   What do you mean?

GRIF   I wanted you here.

KARLA   So, I'm here.

GRIF   Were you rubbing someone else's back?

KARLA   You want one?

GRIF   Were you?

KARLA   Would it matter if I was?

GRIF   Maybe.

KARLA   I was teaching Fran how to roll Drum tobacco in strawberry rolling papers. You know, you can chew those papers if you get really bored.

GRIF   Gross.

KARLA   Roll over. So how was it?

> *GRIF moans.*

Great thunderstorm, eh?

GRIF Spectacular.

KARLA How were the lakes?

GRIF Enormous.

KARLA One little overnight should be a cinch for "senior waterfront."

GRIF Rub, please.

> *KARLA straddles GRIF's back and digs in. GRIF makes loud, sexual-sounding moans of pleasure as KARLA rubs.*

KARLA So, what's the scoop? How did it go? Any jumpers?

GRIF No Kamikaze canoers.

KARLA Tribal wars?

GRIF No fights.

KARLA Leaking tents?

GRIF Uh-uh.

KARLA Well, why are you so beat, then?

GRIF You don't want to know.

KARLA Yes, I do.

GRIF No, you don't.

KARLA *(digging hard)* Yes… I… do!

GRIF Ow! Ow! Okay, okay!

Wigapee Boy's Camp was doing their overnight on the other side of the island.

KARLA So, why couldn't you find another island?

GRIF Are you crazy? We've been up here for seven weeks, Karla. All girls, remember? Besides, we were there first. And you should have seen their trip leader.

KARLA Uh huh.

GRIF Adonis in person.

KARLA Really.

GRIF Six foot one, pure blond. He was ripped! Six-pack, biceps…

KARLA You saw all this in the rain?

GRIF We went for a swim.

KARLA   A swim?

GRIF   A dip.

KARLA   In a thunderstorm?

GRIF   OW! OW! Jesus!

KARLA   What?

GRIF   That really hurt.

> *KARLA lifts up GRIF's shirt and shines the flashlight on her back.*

KARLA   Holy shit! What happened?

GRIF   What?

KARLA   You should see this!

GRIF   I can't! Tell me!

KARLA   Shit. Your back is a mess.

GRIF   What, Karla, would you tell me what it is?

KARLA   It's all scratched and there's a big bruise right here…

GRIF   Ow!

KARLA   What happened?

> *GRIF giggles.*

What?

GRIF   I'll bet his knees are like raw meat.

> *Pause.*

KARLA   You are such a slut!

GRIF   Under a blue spruce.

KARLA   You sure it wasn't a balsam?

GRIF   It was amazing, Karla. I have never done it outside in a thunderstorm, before.

KARLA   Yes, it is amazing that you'd never done it outside in a thunderstorm, before. Couldn't you just carve your initials in a tree for a change?

GRIF   If you're not going to rub, you can get off my back.

> *KARLA resumes rubbing.*

Just watch that bruise. Oh, Karla. It was so perfect. When the thunder rolled I could scream my heart out. God, did I scream.

KARLA   That's nice.

GRIF   I am so sore.

KARLA   I really feel for you.

GRIF   I am so tired.

KARLA   Go to sleep and shut up.

GRIF   Okay.

> *KARLA keeps rubbing as GRIF falls asleep. She gently strokes GRIF's hair and longingly, preciously holds a lock of it. She then rises and tiptoes out of the cabin. As she gets to the door, DANNY calls out. She turns to face him, but he is calling to KARLA down the hallway.*

Danny's Place.

DANNY   So, Karla! About this guy. What is he? A lifeguard? Or… a canoeing instructor? Don't tell me…. You were sneaking out at night and meeting up with the lads from the boys' camp, weren't ya? *(chuckles)* Weren't ya? I wasn't born yesterday you know.

So, when do I get to meet him? Eh? When do I get to do the "heavy father stuff"? Ha ha. Scare the shit out of him. Come on, Karla. Bring him home. I promise I won't bite.

> *KARLA exits the cabin, shaking her head.*

Aw, come on!

Grif's Apartment.

> *GRIF, with a towel wrapped around her hair, pokes her head out of the bathroom, checking to see that KARLA is gone. She goes to the door to ensure it is locked. As she turns to go back to the bathroom, she hears keys fumbling clumsily in the door. A moment of recognition. She smiles.*

GRIF   *(cheerily)* Hey, Darlin'! What are you doing here? I thought we were going to meet at the DeLuxe? *(beat)* You're going to snap the key if you keep forcing it like that! You turn the key to the left, the knob to the right and you push it in before you pull it out!

> *The door is successfully unlocked.*

See?

> *She realizes she is wearing only her lingerie.*

Oh, wait a second! I don't want you to see my surprise yet!

> *She runs back into the bathroom.*

Okay!

> *KARLA steps in the door with a small bag and a bottle of wine. She hangs up her jacket and brings the items to the counter.*

GRIF   *(loudly)* I'm just going to finish drying my hair...

> *A blow-dryer is heard.*

I'm glad, you're here. I'd rather eat in tonight, anyway, wouldn't you? I had a weird day. Hey, I could make us a salad. Greek. Would you like that? Except I don't have any feta. But, I could pop down to Kardish's and get some. And we could just watch television or something. I sure could use one of your rubs. Oh, yeah.

> *The blow-dryer stops.*

And then I'll rub yours...

> *GRIF pokes her head out of the bathroom. KARLA smiles and holds up the bag.*

KARLA   I already got the feta.

> *GRIF is shocked.*

I checked. You were out. Here's your keys. I'll just leave them here.

> *KARLA starts getting the things out to make a salad.*

So, what's the surprise?

GRIF   What do you think you're doing?

KARLA   Oh, and I bought some more wine. You want a glass while you're waiting?

GRIF   No! Look. You can't... Karla, you.... Okay. You obviously have.... You have a problem. I recognize that. But, this is not.... This is no way... okay... alright.... Look...

KARLA   Just say what you mean, Grif.

GRIF   Let's you and me make a real appointment, and we'll work this out in a mature fashion.

KARLA   An appointment?

> *KARLA looks in the fridge.*

GRIF   Okay, Karla. You want an apology? Is that it?

KARLA   I did see a lemon in here, didn't I?

GRIF   Alright. Karla, I'm sorry. I acted immaturely. And irresponsibly.

> *KARLA finds a lemon.*

KARLA   Aha! You squeeze it on the romaine.

GRIF   It was unfair. I'll admit it. Unfair. But, I was confused. Confused and immature. It should never have happened.

KARLA   Keeps it crisp and gives it a nice kick.

GRIF   Did you hear me?

KARLA   You really are tense.

GRIF   It was over three years ago!

KARLA   Have a seat. I'll do your neck.

GRIF   I have to go in five minutes. And would you stop tearing my lettuce?

KARLA   Where's your colander?

> *GRIF goes to the kitchen and starts putting things away.*

GRIF   I don't want you to make me a salad.

KARLA   Don't worry. I'm a professional.

GRIF   You are not making me a salad!

KARLA   You just said you wanted a salad!

GRIF   I am meeting someone for dinner! I will order a salad at the restaurant!

KARLA   So, this "someone" has keys to your apartment? Must be a pretty important someone. Damn, do you have black olives?

GRIF   This is unbelievable.

KARLA   Tell me, do you often just sit at home and watch TV? That's quite a switch from the old party-girl, isn't it? Party, party, party. Guys, guys, guys. You always had to be the centre. The more guys dripping off you the better. No conscience at all for all those weasels who fell for every sway of your ass, every jiggle of your tits. You'd wear your skimpiest bikini to Boy's Camp Day. Christ, even the eight-year-old boys were wagging their tails after you.

So, what happened to you, anyway? What's happened to change you into a "homebody". Someone who's happy with just one person. Watching TV. Eating salad. You are happy, aren't you? You sure sounded happy when I walked in.

That is so weird. I never expected it, boy.

Ah! Good taste in olive oil.

GRIF   Get out of my house.

> *KARLA pulls out her pocket knife and holds it above her head.*

KARLA   The Sabre! *(diabolically)* Ha ha ha ha ha!

> *KARLA viciously slices a tomato with it.*

Take that! And that!

GRIF   Stop it!

KARLA   *(stops)* Oh. Do you prefer it in wedges?

GRIF   You have to leave. I'M GOING OUT!

KARLA   Oh. Right. Your date called. He got held up. Won't be able to make it after all.

> *GRIF looks at KARLA carefully.*

While you were in the shower? The phone rang. I couldn't help myself.

> *She slaps her own hand.*

Bad, Karla, bad.

> *Pause.*

So. Looks like you're free for dinner. But uh, you might want to put on something a little more... comfortable?

> *End of Act One.*

ACT TWO

The Apartment.

KARLA is alone in the kitchen, assembling the salad. DANNY leans over the counter.

DANNY   What are you doing, Karla?

KARLA   Making a salad.

DANNY   No, no. What are you doing, Karla?

KARLA does not look at him.

KARLA   Making... a... salad.

DANNY   What are you doing to yourself, Karla?

KARLA turns to look at him.

The Cabin.

GRIF exuberantly enters the cabin with a handful of letters.

GRIF   Mailman!

KARLA and DANNY remain locked in eye contact.

DANNY   I miss ya, honey.

GRIF   I said, the mail came!

KARLA crosses into the cabin.

KARLA   Anything for me?

GRIF   Oh, now, let's see. Janet Griffiths. Miss Janet Griffiths. Ms. Jan Griffiths. Oh, wait a minute.... Something illegible written by a "Victor Staletti? Stiletto?... I can't...

KARLA   STILT!

GRIF   Victor Stillecki?

KARLA   Just Vic Stilt.

GRIF   And no return address. What's he in, Grade Two?

KARLA   Give me the letter.

GRIF   Truth or Dare.... Who's Vic Stilt?

KARLA   A buddy.

GRIF   Just a buddy?

KARLA   Yeah, just a buddy.

GRIF   Give me the scoop, or it gets the torch.

KARLA   Just give it to me!

>   *GRIF hands her the letter.*

GRIF   Woo. He must be some important buddy, this "Stilt" person. What is he, tall or something?

>   *KARLA lifts the letter up to the light and examines it. Then she carefully pulls the stamp off the letter.*

Have you become a philatelist, Karla? I find this quite remarkable. I mean who would have ever thought…

>   *KARLA looks closely at the underside of the stamp.*

KARLA   YES! Way to go, Victor! My ticket to dream land!

>   *KARLA drops the envelope. GRIF picks it up and opens it. It is empty.*

GRIF   Didn't he learn that the letter goes *in* the envelope?

KARLA   This is a gift of love. No words are necessary.

GRIF   What is it?

>   *KARLA is delicately removing the acid from the back of the stamp.*

KARLA   It's a hit of Window pane.

GRIF   What?

KARLA   Lysergic Acid Diethylemide.

GRIF   No. No way. You're not going to take acid up here.

KARLA   Tomorrow's my day off, remember?

GRIF   You were going off that stuff. You promised. Last year. No more acid.

KARLA   And you promised no more one-nighters. You broke it first. Ha ha!

GRIF   Give it to me.

KARLA   Yeah, right.

GRIF   Come on, Karla.

KARLA   Hey… you want half? Come on, do half with me.

GRIF   No way.

KARLA   A quarter. I'll give you a quarter. Just a weenie trip. It'd be fun!

GRIF   Forget it!

>   *GRIF pushes KARLA's hand away.*

KARLA   Hey! Oh, shit! I dropped it!

> *KARLA frantically searches for the hit on her hands and knees. While KARLA searches, GRIF sees it and manages to pick it up and hide it.*

If I lose it, I'll kill you. Two months. Two months, Grif, I haven't had a hit!

GRIF   Look at you.

KARLA   Get down and help me find it!

GRIF   You're pathetic.

KARLA   This is my night out! It doesn't come and pick me up in a BMW! It comes on a little rectangular tab. And I want it. NOW! So, help me find it!

> *DANNY approaches KARLA. She ignores him, directing her comments to GRIF.*

DANNY   What are you doing to yourself, Karla?

GRIF   Are you addicted, Karla? I could help you if you're addicted.

DANNY   Look me in the eyes.

KARLA   No, I'm not addicted. You are so goddamned ignorant!

GRIF   I'm not ignorant.

DANNY   What do you think, I'm stupid?!

KARLA   You're stupid! You don't know anything about it.

DANNY   You want to ruin your life on this shit!

KARLA   Shit! I'm never going to find it in these cracks. I'm going to kill you!

GRIF   You swore.

DANNY   I won't have it in my house!

KARLA   I don't give a flying fuck about your shitty rules.

GRIF   Karla, don't you enjoy my company?

KARLA   Not at the moment.

DANNY   Drinking I can understand. But this—

GRIF   We could do something else for your night off.

KARLA   I don't want to play cocksucking Scrabble!

GRIF   I can't believe you're acting like this.

DANNY   You need some help or something?

KARLA   LIKE WHAT!

GRIF   Like that. I was only trying to help you.

DANNY   I can't stand seeing you like this, Karla.

KARLA   Get down on your knees and look, then.

> *GRIF kneels down beside KARLA.*

GRIF   Karla, I really care about you, you know. As strange a person as you are, I worry about your well-being.

DANNY   I'm your father. I worry.

KARLA   Shut up and look.

GRIF   Remember last summer when I thought I was pregnant, and you snuck into town to buy a pregnancy test for me?

KARLA   No.

GRIF   Yes, you do. Remember, when Boss Lady took that group for the day trip, and you stole her keys, and drove the van into town—

KARLA   Are you looking?

GRIF   I owed you. I lost that hit, because I care about you.

DANNY   Look, I know I don't always show it too well.

KARLA   You care about me.

GRIF   You're a good person, Karla.

DANNY   You're still my little girl in there.

KARLA   Fuck off.

GRIF   This stuff takes that away.

KARLA   *(despairing)* Oh, God, it must have slipped through the boards.

GRIF   Are you crying, Karla?

DANNY   What's the matter?

KARLA   No, I'm not crying.

DANNY   Why are you looking at me like that?

GRIF   Yes you are.

KARLA   I'm not!

DANNY   Stop it Karla. It's just me.

GRIF   Don't be mad.

DANNY   Hey! Look! This is ME!

KARLA   You've ruined my night off!

GRIF   No, no! We'll have fun. We could have a pow wow on the beach.

DANNY   It's the drugs, Karla! Just the drugs making you think that!

KARLA   Fuck that! I want to get fried!

DANNY   I wouldn't hurt you!

GRIF   You don't like me.

DANNY   Listen to me! You straighten out! Now!

KARLA   SHUT UP!

>   *DANNY retreats. Pause.*

GRIF   Want me to rub your back?

KARLA   No.

GRIF   Brush your hair?

KARLA   No.

GRIF   We could pierce our ears.

KARLA   I'm going to pierce your tit if you don't leave me alone.

GRIF   All right, fine. You're hopeless. *(beat)* I know where it is.

KARLA   What? Where!

GRIF   Say you're sorry.

KARLA   Eat shit. Where is it!

GRIF   Hot and cold.

KARLA   Just tell me you stupid bitch.

GRIF   You're cold, very cold.

KARLA   Come on!

GRIF   Still cold.

>   *KARLA begins moving slowly around the room.*

KARLA   I'll get you for this.

GRIF   Warm. Cold. Warmer. Warmer. Cold. Freezing. Hot… HOT… BOILING!

>   *KARLA finds the hit of acid wherever GRIF has hidden it.*

KARLA   Oh, God!

>   *She places the hit under her tongue.*

GRIF   You're doing it now?

KARLA   There's no time like the present.

GRIF   How can somebody who's not addicted be so desperate for a stupid hit of door pane?

>   *KARLA bursts out laughing.*

What are you laughing at?

KARLA   *(hysterically)* "Door pane!"

GRIF   Well, excuse me.

KARLA   "Door pane!"

GRIF   I'm going to staff lounge.

KARLA   I'm going, too.

GRIF   Not on acid, you're not.

KARLA   You can't leave me here.

GRIF   Why not?

KARLA   Because.

GRIF   Because why?

KARLA   Because I always do it with someone.

GRIF   Too bad. You should have thought about that before you took it.

>   *GRIF turns to leave. KARLA grabs her arm.*

Ow!

KARLA   Please stay.

GRIF   Would you let go of my arm?

KARLA   Stay with me.

GRIF   You want a babysitter, Karla? You afraid of a bad trip? Like last year, when you were sure your father was in the closet?

KARLA   That was an accident.

GRIF   You wanna do that stuff, you do it without me.

KARLA   Come on, Grif. I've covered your ass every time you trip over to the boys camp. One night. That's all.

GRIF   It's not my day off tomorrow. I'm not staying up all night.

KARLA   If you're here…. Just be here. I won't bug you. I promise. Please?

Pause.

GRIF   Why do I always get sucked in?

KARLA   Because you're a nice person.

KARLA smiles at her.

GRIF   Wanna play a game?

KARLA   Sure.

GRIF   I spy with my little eye, something that is red.

Danny's Place.

DANNY brings a suit bag to his chair. A large red Christmas bow on the bag catches KARLA's eye. She stands still, watching DANNY, talking to GRIF.

(*waiting*) Karla?

KARLA takes a deep, satisfied breath and addresses GRIF.

KARLA   There is nothing like the feeling of the impending wave.

GRIF   What?

KARLA   Oh, shit. I didn't eat. I should eat something. There's leftover chicken in the breezeway fridge.

GRIF   You want me to get it, right?

KARLA   Be quick.

GRIF   You owe me.

GRIF exits.

KARLA watches DANNY as he unzips the bag and pulls out the casual jacket KARLA has given to him for Christmas.

He puts it on. He is very proud and a little embarrassed as he displays it to her. KARLA is very happy. DANNY then pours two glasses of wine, and holds one out to KARLA, who crosses to take it. They clink glasses. DANNY gives her a small kiss, then settles into his chair and turns on the television.

The Apartment.

GRIF is seated on the couch, picking at the salad that KARLA has made. KARLA stands behind GRIF, sipping her wine and watching her.

KARLA   You know what this reminds me of? Monk's dinner. Remember Monk's dinner at camp? The night no talking was allowed at the table? And the table that lasted the longest was given double Rice Krispy Squares for night snack?

Except you're the only monk.

More wine?

GRIF   No.

KARLA   Oh, well. More for me. So. How was the salad?

GRIF   Good.

KARLA   That was better than good, Grif. That was excellent.

> *GRIF rises to take her dishes to the counter.*

No, no. Sit down. Sit down. Tonight, I am at your service. *(a little threateningly)* SIT!

> *GRIF sits. KARLA takes the dishes to the counter, then comes back and stands behind GRIF and puts her hands on GRIF's shoulders.*

You still seem pretty tense. I think you should let me rub your neck. Then I'll do the dishes. Then I'll go.

GRIF   No.

KARLA   "No" to rub your neck? Or "No" to do the dishes.

GRIF   Why don't you go home?

KARLA   Because I'm lonely at home. No Mamma, no Poppa. Hey, I know. You wanted to watch TV. What do you like? Eh?

> *KARLA takes the remote and turns on the television, surfing channels.*

GRIF   I don't really…

KARLA   You said you were just going to stay in. You like this? I do. We'll just watch the pictures. So we can talk.

> *KARLA begins to massage GRIF's shoulders.*

GRIF   Karla, my neck is fine, really.

KARLA   *(squeezing)* You call this fine? You call this…

GRIF   Ow!

KARLA   See? Don't fight it, Grif. Don't fight it. When you've got a sore spot, you gotta take care of it. Smooth it out. Work it over. Until the pain is gone. Right?

> *Pause.*

You know, you were important to me, Grif. I thought I was important to you. Part of your show. "Grif's Wacky Sidekick." I made you more interesting. You wanted it that way. You needed it. I was happy to be it. Really happy, Grif. Really, really happy.

Pause.

So. I was thinking maybe we could just pick it up. Like before. I mean, I don't exactly remember what happened, do you?

GRIF   My life is really full right now, Karla.

KARLA   I'm not asking you to marry me, Grif. I just want to be friends again.

GRIF   *(carefully)* I feel we've moved in different directions.

KARLA   We were always different, Grif. That's what you liked! So, forgive and forget?

GRIF   I don't want to continue this! I don't appreciate the way you've manipulated this situation, and I feel it would be best for you to go now.

KARLA   Oh, come on now, Grif! Don't get all tense here, or we'll have to start all over. Just be quiet. Don't say anything.

Danny's Place.

From his chair, DANNY clears his throat and directs his remote control to GRIF's television, turning it off. KARLA reacts to him from her position in the apartment.

Hey, I was watching that!

DANNY   It's a re-run.

KARLA   Well, what else is on?

DANNY   Karla, I want to talk to you for a minute.

KARLA   What.

DANNY   It's Friday night.

KARLA   So?

DANNY   So, why aren't you out? With your friends? At the Chaud?

KARLA   You don't like my friends.

DANNY   That never stopped you before.

KARLA   I don't feel like it.

DANNY   Why not?

KARLA   I just don't. Would you turn the TV back on?

DANNY   Look, Karla, I know we sometimes don't talk too good to each other, but you gotta let me in here. You haven't gone out for weeks. Now, why is that?

KARLA crosses to Danny's Place.

KARLA   Look, Danny… you were right. Okay? I'm sick of those people. I'm sick of the Chaud. I go to school all week. I'm tired.

DANNY   Well, what about this "Grif" person?

     Pause.

KARLA   What about her?

DANNY   Why don't you go out with her somewhere?

KARLA   She's at University. She's busy.

DANNY   You try to get in touch with her?

KARLA   Once or twice.

     Pause.

DANNY   Why are you lying to me, Karla?

KARLA   What? I'm not—

DANNY   Don't bullshit me. What's going on?

KARLA   What's going on where?

DANNY   With this Grif person?

KARLA   Nothing.

DANNY   You're lying to me.

KARLA   About what?

DANNY   You haven't called her once or twice. You been calling her every day. For weeks. Sometimes two or three times!

KARLA   Who told you this?

DANNY   I got a call today. From an old lady. A Mrs. Griffiths. Said you'd been harassing her granddaughter. Saying some ugly things about her. Is this true? You harassing her?

KARLA   It's none of your business.

DANNY   It sure as hell is my business. When I get called from someone's Grandmother, it's my business. Why are you harassing her?

KARLA   I just want to talk to her.

DANNY   Two or three times a day?

KARLA   She won't come to the phone.

DANNY   Why not?

KARLA   I guess she doesn't want to talk to me.

DANNY   Why not?

KARLA   Just drop it, Danny. Okay?

DANNY   No. You tell me. You tell me why she doesn't want to talk to you.

KARLA   Because she doesn't like me, I guess!

DANNY   Why not?

KARLA   We had a fight at camp!

DANNY   So, why don't you drop it, then! Someone doesn't like you, then fuck 'em! You can't have the whole world, Karla!

KARLA   I'm not asking for the whole world!

DANNY   So, what's so special about this Grif person! That you should be harassing her grandmother! Eh? Karla! Talk to me!

KARLA   No.

DANNY   You can tell me. I'm your father for God's sake. I'm sick of seeing you sitting here every Friday night. What's your problem? Boys?

KARLA   There's no fucking problem. Just keep your stupid face out of it, okay, Dan!

DANNY   Don't you use that tone of voice with me.

KARLA   You don't like my tone of voice, I'll just leave, okay?

> *KARLA moves to exit. DANNY grabs her arm.*

DANNY   Don't you walk out on me here, Karla.

KARLA   *(menacing)* Let go of my fucking arm!

DANNY   What is it about this Grif person!

> *KARLA pushes him.*

KARLA   Grif! GRIF! It's her name! She's a girl! Not a "Grif person," you stupid ass!

DANNY   Why you doing this, Karla? Eh? ANSWER ME! WHY!

KARLA   Because I love her!

> *Pause.*

DANNY   Pardon me?

KARLA   Listen real carefully here, Danny. 'Cause I'm not telling you again. I love Grif.

DANNY   Like a friend.

KARLA   Like a lover.

Pause.

DANNY   You're in love with a girl, Karla? You're a goddamned lesbian? A DYKE? Explain this to me Karla! How the hell does my daughter end up being a queer? Do they even call girls "queers"?

KARLA   IT'S NOT LIKE THAT! It's not girls. It's HER!

DANNY   Her! HER! Well SHE'S A GIRL. And you're a girl. So that makes you a lesbian, right?

KARLA   You just can't shut up and leave me alone, can you, Danny? You can never keep out of it. So now you know. I love her. And she doesn't love me. Is that so hard to understand? You should know about this, Danny!

DANNY   So, this is what goes on in those girls camps, eh? I sent you all those summers to an all-girls camp thinking I was protecting you from being jumped by little boys!

KARLA   It's got nothing to do with the camp, Dan.

DANNY   I should have got married again. That's what you needed wasn't it?

KARLA   No!

DANNY   A woman in the house. A goddamned mother, instead of me!

KARLA   NO!

DANNY   And now, you're turning to this Grif bitch.

KARLA   JUST GRIF!

DANNY   *(crying)* Oh, Jesus. Oh, JESUS!

KARLA   Don't cry, Danny. Please. I can't stand it when you do that!

DANNY   You're gonna end up just like your mother.

Pause.

KARLA   Don't you ever, ever say that again.

DANNY   Hanging around bars. Picking up strange men. Oh, God... strange WOMEN!

KARLA   For Christ sake, Danny!

DANNY   And then one day... poof! Gone!

KARLA   I'm not going to leave you like that.

DANNY   She'd slime in after she'd been out all night.

KARLA   I'm not like her!

DANNY With anyone. Anyone but me. And I'd make her a goddamned cup of coffee. You believe that, Karla?

> **The Apartment.**
>
> *Dim lighting. KARLA stays in Danny's Place.*
>
> *GRIF is curled up with a pillow on the apartment couch, as if she were on the bottom bunk, speaking up to KARLA.*

GRIF Karla? Karla are you awake?

DANNY She'd be out prancing around with some other man all night, and I'd make her coffee.

GRIF I had a bad dream.

DANNY One morning, she comes in. Gets a suitcase, says she's leaving.

GRIF About the airplane.

DANNY That was it.

GRIF My mother. On the airplane. She was looking down at me. And her teeth were falling out…

DANNY She just left.

GRIF I saw her teeth, Karla. Falling from the sky.

DANNY But, did I leave you, Karla?

GRIF Can I sleep with you?

DANNY Eh?

GRIF Please?

DANNY Did I leave you?

KARLA No.

GRIF I'm scared.

> *Lights out on GRIF.*

DANNY You were five years old. I fought off the goddamn Children's Aid. They wanted you in a foster home. They said it would be easier for me to let someone else look after you.

> *DANNY grabs KARLA by the shoulders.*

But, did I let them take you away? Did I let them!

KARLA NO!

> *DANNY holds KARLA painfully close.*

DANNY You're goddamn right I didn't let them take you. I can do it!, I said. I can look after my own daughter! Let me look after her! I have a job! I have a brain! Leave us alone! Get out of my house!

KARLA Danny... please.

DANNY I was the one, Karla. I was the one who raised you. Me. No one else. I braided your hair. I washed your face. I gave you your medicine. I went to the parent-teacher meetings. I took you shopping for clothes. Didn't I?

I made sure you had enough. You had what you needed. Didn't you? You got what you wanted. Didn't you? Did you eat? Did you have Christmas presents? Did you have birthday cake?

DID YOU HAVE FUCKING SUMMER CAMP!

KARLA YES!

DANNY AND FOR WHAT? FOR WHAT?

KARLA tries to hug DANNY.

KARLA ...Daddy...

DANNY shakes her off.

DANNY What are we doing here, Karla. What are we doing here?

The Cabin.

It is the last night of camp.

GRIF takes the bottle of wine from the apartment, and staggers into the cabin, singing into the bottle as a microphone. She is really drunk.

GRIF "And nowwwww, the end is neeeaaarrr, and so I face the final cuuurrtainnn...

KARLA regards GRIF, somewhat amused.

La laaaa, la la la laaaa, la la la laaa...

KARLA crosses to her and tries to take the bottle.

KARLA Give me that.

GRIF holds the bottle above her head.

GRIF Fuck you, Babboo!

KARLA Come on, we gotta sign the boards. You won't feel like doing it tomorrow.

KARLA climbs up the bunk with a big magic marker. GRIF stands, wobbling, looking around the cabin.

GRIF Tomorrow.

Tomorrow, we leave.

We're out of here.

Not a trace. Not a speck.

Except for our names.

Names painted on the walls. Names without faces.

In years to come, people will come in here and read our names.

> *She collapses on the bottom bunk.*

What the hell does it all mean, eh, Karla? I mean, who's gonna give a shit ten years from now who "Karla and Grif" were. EH? I mean…

> *She reads a signature on the wall.*

…who the fuck is "Charlotte and Binny?"

KARLA   You're breaking the swearing rule.

GRIF   Tonight, we're allowed to break the rules.

KARLA   Are you going to sign?

GRIF   I bet these walls have seen a lot of things. A lot of secrets. Secret walls.

KARLA   You want me to do it?

GRIF   Shhhh! Walls with secrets.

KARLA   Fine, I'll do it. You never could hold your liquor.

GRIF   Oh, yeah? Oh, yeah. My liquor.

> *GRIF takes another swig from her bottle. KARLA comes back down.*

KARLA   There. "Karla and Grif. 1988." Look.

> *GRIF hollers, drunkenly.*

GRIF   WooooOOOOOO! WooooOOOOOOO!

KARLA   Hey, give me that. I don't want to clean up your puke again this year.

> *KARLA takes the bottle.*

GRIF   Like last year.

KARLA   I never figured out how it got on the ceiling.

> *They laugh.*

Give me your foot.

> *KARLA takes GRIF's shoes off.*

GRIF   Oh, Karla. You take such good care of me.

KARLA   Yes I do.

GRIF   You care about me, don't you?

KARLA   Yes, I do.

GRIF   You're my best friend, aren't you? Are you my best friend?

KARLA   I'm your best friend.

GRIF   *(whining)* I hate the end of camp. Now I have to go back to school. Waaaa!

KARLA   And you'll do great, as always.

GRIF   And you're going to college.

KARLA   Yeah, yeah.

GRIF   You promise now?

KARLA   I promise.

GRIF   No screwing up.

KARLA   I'll be a picture of scholarity.

GRIF   And we're coming back again next year, right, Karla?

KARLA   Sure.

GRIF   You promise.

KARLA   Scout's honour.

GRIF   Hey, I know…

> *GRIF pulls her sleeping bag down to the floor.*

… let's have a sleepover!

KARLA   What about Mr. T.?

GRIF   Fuck Mr. T.

> *GRIF grabs her hairbrush.*

I'm armed!

> *GRIF pats the floor beside her.*

Come on!

> *KARLA carefully pulls her bag down beside GRIF's.*

Brush my hair?

KARLA   What for?

GRIF   Because it feels good. And I won't have you to do it for me for a whole year.

KARLA   Nine and a half months.

GRIF   Pleeease?

> *KARLA kneels behind GRIF, brushing her hair.*

Mmmm. I love that.

> *Pause.*

Have you ever wondered why we don't see each other between summers?

> *Pause.*

KARLA   No.

GRIF   I'll tell you why. Because you're my secret.

KARLA   Right.

GRIF   Am I your secret?

KARLA   You bet.

GRIF   No, really. Have you ever told anyone about me?

KARLA   I don't know.

GRIF   Come on!

KARLA   I don't remember!

GRIF   Nobody outside of camp knows about you. They wouldn't get it. My Grandmother would freak.

KARLA   Why?

GRIF   Because! You're odd.

KARLA   Gee, thanks.

> *Pause.*

GRIF   Will you still love me again next year, Karla?

KARLA   Sure.

> *GRIF reaches back and holds on to KARLA's hand.*

GRIF   I love you, Karla.

KARLA   I love you too, Grif.

GRIF   I love you like a friend, you know?

KARLA   Me too. Like a friend.

GRIF   You love me more than that, don't you?

> *GRIF turns to KARLA.*

Don't you? Don't you love me more than that?

KARLA   What do you mean?

GRIF   Yes you do. Tell me. How do you love me?

KARLA   *(melodramatic)* Let me count the ways!

GRIF   *(laughs)* You're so funny. I love you because you're funny.

> *Pause.*

Why do you love me?

KARLA   I don't know. I just… love you, that's all.

> *GRIF gently strokes KARLA's leg.*

GRIF   Karla?

KARLA   What?

GRIF   You want to be my girlfriend?

KARLA   …what…?

> *GRIF caresses KARLA's face.*

GRIF   You want to be my lover?

> *KARLA moves away from her.*

KARLA   Stop it, Grif.

GRIF   Come on. It's our last night.

> *KARLA rises.*

KARLA   Go to sleep.

GRIF   I don't want to go to sleep. I wanna… you know.

KARLA   Grif. You're doing this because there's no guys around.

GRIF   I'm doing it because I want to. With you. What do you want to do?

KARLA   This is me, Grif. Karla? A girl?

GRIF   I know…

> *GRIF gently kisses KARLA. Pause.*

KARLA   Grif. I love you. I really do love you.

GRIF   I love you too, Karla.

> *They kiss again. GRIF leads KARLA down and pulls the sleeping bags over them.*

Danny's Place.

DANNY stands wearing a clown nose and holding a bunch of balloons.

DANNY   Hey, Karla! Why are lesbian's houses so strong? Because they use tongue-in-groove construction! Ha ha ha ha ha ha!

Did you hear the one about the Dutch lesbian? She put her finger in the dyke! Ho ho ho ho ho!

Hey! Why don't lesbians become alcoholics? Because they know how to hold their "licker". Ha ha ha ha Ho ho ho ho He he he he!

His manic laughter turns to painful crying.

The Cabin.

It is morning.

KARLA is lying beside GRIF, watching her sleep. The mess-hall bell sounds. KARLA takes a lock of GRIF's hair as before.

KARLA   Grif.

GRIF moans.

The bell.

GRIF   Huh?

KARLA   Grif.

GRIF slowly wakes and tries to sit up.

Good morning.

GRIF moans and holds her head. KARLA reaches out to stroke her head.

Poor Grif…

GRIF   Don't.

KARLA   Why?

GRIF   Just don't.

They begin to dress in awkward silence. GRIF pulls her things on using the sleeping bag to cover herself. GRIF takes off the wrist band and holds it out to KARLA.

Here.

KARLA   It's okay.

GRIF   Take it.

KARLA   Keep it.

GRIF   I can't wear it at home.

> *KARLA takes it and puts it in GRIF's bag.*

KARLA   Then hide it somewhere.

> *Pause.*

GRIF   Can I have my ring?

> *Pause.*

KARLA   Grif…

GRIF   What?

> *Pause.*

I need my ring back. My grandmother would be really upset.

KARLA   Tell her it fell off when you were swimming.

GRIF   I don't lie to my grandmother.

KARLA   You mean you tell her everything?

GRIF   I mean I don't say things that aren't true.

> *Pause.*

I want my ring.

> *KARLA slips the ring off her finger and holds it in her hand. She stares at it.*

KARLA   Can we see each other? Meet at a mall or something?

GRIF   I don't know.

KARLA   I really want to see you back home. It's different now. I can't wait until next summer.

GRIF   Give me my ring.

KARLA   So that's it? We sleep together and then we don't see each other again?

GRIF   I didn't say that.

KARLA   You wanted to, remember.

GRIF   Look, it's no big deal, okay?

KARLA   We said we loved each other!

GRIF   Jesus, Karla, I was drunk.

KARLA   Wait… you wanted to. You said you wanted to.

GRIF   You knew I was drunk.

KARLA   You knew what you were doing! You said!

GRIF   I was wasted, okay? It doesn't matter!

KARLA   It matters to me Grif! IT MATTERS!

GRIF   Keep your voice down, Karla.

KARLA   Why should I! What difference does it make! You don't care what you do to people! What you do to me!

GRIF   I do so! I just don't want to make a scene about it, okay?

KARLA   Maybe I should tell your Grandmother! Maybe she should know!

GRIF   Just give me my ring, dyke.

>   *This stuns KARLA.*

KARLA   What?

GRIF   Well, look at yourself! The way you dress. The way you act so tough. Drink beer. Do drugs. A father who breaks your arm. Hang out with people called "Stiff"!

KARLA   Stilt!

GRIF   Face it, Karlo, you're a dyke!

KARLA   And you're a SLUT!

>   *GRIF slaps KARLA. KARLA slaps her back. GRIF tries to hit KARLA again, but KARLA restrains her.*

Admit it. Admit it! You wanted me!

GRIF   Let go!

KARLA   We made love!

GRIF   I mean it, Karla!

KARLA   Loud and clear so the whole camp can hear! KARLA AND GRIF ARE LOVERS!

GRIF   LET GO!

>   *KARLA releases GRIF.*

You ever do that again, Karla…

KARLA   And what?

GRIF   I'll say you raped me.

KARLA   *(smirks)* Come on…

GRIF   I got really drunk playing caps with Karla.

She started pushing me around. She pulled off my pyjamas, and pinned me down on the floor. Then she held her knife to me, and wouldn't let me go. She made me lie still on the cabin floor while she…

KARLA   Grif…

GRIF   *Without* my consent.

KARLA   No…

GRIF   Against my will!

KARLA   I didn't…

GRIF   Rape, Karla.

KARLA   Grif, you can't—

GRIF   RAPE!

KARLA   You came on to ME! YOU started it!

GRIF   FUCK OFF!

KARLA   And you liked it! You said it was better than any of those guys you lay every weekend!

GRIF   BULL SHIT!

KARLA   It was the best! It was wonderful!

GRIF   NO!

> *GRIF angrily kicks the pile of sleeping bags. KARLA grabs her jack knife from its sticking place on the bunk post and holds it menacingly at GRIF, blocking her exit. Her hand shakes.*

What are you doing?

KARLA   I love you. Ever since we were ten years old in Cabin Eight, I've loved you. From the first time you chose me for your swimming buddy, and we had to hold hands in the water and yell: "BUDDIES!" You were my friend. MINE!

Don't do this. Don't walk out like this. It's okay, you know? We don't have to do it again. We don't have to DO anything. But don't… please… don't go.

GRIF   Let me out!

KARLA   Mother may I.

GRIF   Get lost, Karla.

KARLA   Say you love me.

GRIF   Let me out.

KARLA   Say it!

GRIF   I hate your guts.

KARLA   No you don't, Grif...

GRIF   You hear me, Karla? You make me sick! I HATE YOU!

> *GRIF kicks KARLA in the stomach. KARLA buckles over and drops the knife. GRIF runs out the door.*

KARLA   GRIF! Grif...

> *KARLA holds herself, crying. DANNY rushes over to KARLA as if she were a little girl. He holds her face up and wipes away her tears as he sings "You Are My Sunshine" (Davis/Mitchell) comforting her.*
>
> *DANNY picks up her knife, puts the blade in and hands it back to her.*
>
> *He helps her up and wipes the dirt from her knees.*
>
> *He gives her a final hug before leaving the stage.*

The Apartment.

> *GRIF is sitting on the apartment couch as from previous apartment scene, but the light from the TV is as firelight.*
>
> *She gently sings the last-night-of-camp song—"I Wanna Linger" (Murphy/Marshall). KARLA moves with the same emotion from DANNY's song to GRIF's song. She sits behind GRIF on the back of the couch holding GRIF closely, who is relaxed and leaning back against her, gazing into the fire.*
>
> *LIGHTS snap immediately to present, as keys are heard fumbling in the door.*
>
> *GRIF stands, arranging herself.*

How quaint! I finally get to meet the man with the key.

GRIF   Karla...

KARLA   And the million dollar answer to the question.... How really big is he?

> *Enter KATHY, with briefcase. A smartly dressed, very attractive, professional, confident woman. KARLA remains sitting on the back of the couch.*

KATHY   Jan?

GRIF   Hi.

KATHY   Hi. You're home.

> *KATHY kisses GRIF.*

GRIF   Yeah... I... uh.... This is Karla.

KATHY offers to shake hands.

KATHY   Karla.

GRIF   Kathy Westbury.

KARLA   Kathy.

KATHY   *(to GRIF)* I waited for an hour…

GRIF   Oh… I'm… uh… Karla just dropped in.

KATHY   Oh…

GRIF   We… went to camp together.

KATHY   Oh, yes. *(beat)* I called…

GRIF   You did?

KATHY   There was no answer.

GRIF   It didn't ring…

KATHY   That's strange.

KATHY checks the phone.

It's unplugged.

GRIF   Oh…

KATHY   Is everything alright?

GRIF   Yes, fine.

KATHY notices the plates.

KATHY   Oh. You ate?

GRIF   Um. Yes. Karla made a salad.

KARLA   Greek.

KATHY   Well. Oh.

KARLA   Would you like a glass of wine?

Pause.

KATHY   Yes. Please. I can't stay long, though. I have some preparing to do.

KARLA pours the wine. GRIF tries to speak in confidence to KATHY.

GRIF   Kathy, I'm sorry. It got… confusing.

KATHY   You could have called the restaurant.

KARLA   What for?

KATHY Pardon me?

KARLA What are you preparing for?

KATHY Oh. A case for Children's Aid.

KARLA Oh, yeah.

> *KATHY hands her the wine.*

KATHY Thank you.

KARLA Welcome.

KATHY Do you live in town, Karla?

KARLA Yup. Always have. Actually, I just inherited my father's house. In Overbrook.

KATHY Oh. I'm sorry.

KARLA Hey, no. It's an okay house. Better than paying rent.

> *GRIF laughs nervously.*

KATHY Uh huh…. So, what do you do, Karla?

KARLA I'm a sous chef. At the Delta.

KATHY Really? Well. We'll have to have you prepare us a meal sometime.

GRIF Karla was on kitchen staff at camp.

KATHY Oh… right! I remember now. Are you the girl with the knife?

KARLA Probably.

KATHY Jan has some funny stories.

KARLA What stories?

KATHY Didn't you put a bunch of dead flies in the camp director's soup, or something?

KARLA Moths.

KATHY And spread Handi Wrap across the toilet bowls?

KARLA No, that was Grif.

GRIF No, that was you.

KARLA No. You did the Handi Wrap. I did the Vaseline on the seats. *(beat)* She always did get confused with the details.

KATHY What did you call her?

KARLA Pardon?

GRIF   Oh, "Grif."

KATHY   "Grif."

GRIF   It was a…. It was my/nickname

KARLA   *(at the same time)* /It's what I called her.

KATHY   Oh. It's catchy. I like it. "Grif." So you haven't seen each other for a while, then?

GRIF   No, we kind of lost touch.

KARLA   Kinda.

KATHY   It's a shame when that happens, isn't it? I used to go on student exchanges. You know, live with a family in another country for a month or two? It's like you become sisters. So close. And you swear you'll be best friends forever. And write every month. And visit when you're adults.

>   *KATHY tenderly removes a strand of hair from GRIF's face.*

And then, of course you never do.

KARLA   No.

KATHY   *(to KARLA)* So, you just surprised Jan? Grif? Dropping in unannounced?

KARLA   Yes.

GRIF   She looked up my address in the phone book.

KATHY   *(chuckles)* Oh, that's great.

GRIF   Mmm hmm.

KATHY   Oh, Jan… *(to KARLA)* Excuse me. *(to GRIF)* I brought the listing I mentioned.

GRIF   Oh, good.

KATHY   Pamela says that if we want to make an offer, we have to move quickly. They just turned one down for 92,7. She thinks they'll take 93,5. It's going to go. We can see it tomorrow.

GRIF   After work?

KATHY   I can make an appointment for four.

GRIF   Okay.

>   *Pause.*

KATHY   You sure?

GRIF   Absolutely.

KATHY   Great. Okay. Well. I guess you have a lot of catching up to do.

KARLA   Yup.

KATHY   I should go then.

GRIF   I'll call you in the morning.

KATHY   Okay. Well. It's good to meet you, Karla.

KARLA   Bye, now.

KATHY   Okay. Well. Goodnight.

> *KATHY kisses GRIF.*

GRIF   Goodnight.

> *KATHY exits. Pause.*

KARLA   So…. Crazy Eights? Scrabble? *(beat)* Spin the Bottle?

GRIF   Karla, listen—

KARLA   Hey, I know! How about a rousing game of Truth or Dare?

GRIF   No, Karla.

KARLA   Oh, come on, Grif. It was your favourite. Truth. Dare. Double Dare. Challenge or repeat?

GRIF   Stop it.

KARLA   Didn't you hear the bitch? We've got a lot of catching up to do. I dare you to tell me the truth.

GRIF   Not like this.

KARLA   TRUTH!

GRIF   What do you want to know?

KARLA   Kathy!

GRIF   She's my friend.

KARLA   She was your date!

GRIF   She's a good friend.

KARLA   She has a key to your door!

GRIF   She's a very good friend.

> *KARLA picks up the listing.*

KARLA   And what's this? A co-operative investment?

GRIF   Yes.

KARLA   You're moving in together!

GRIF   Yes. We are.

> *Pause.*

KARLA   Repeat.

GRIF   You don't need to do this.

KARLA   Repeat!

GRIF   Get the hell out of my house! NOW!

> *KARLA grabs her knife off of the counter and holds it threateningly at GRIF.*

KARLA   REPEAT AFTER ME!

GRIF   Karla, think about what you're doing.

KARLA   Shut up! Repeat! "Kathy is my lover."

GRIF   Put the knife down, Karla!

KARLA   KATHY IS MY LOVER!

> *Pause.*

GRIF   Yes.

KARLA   SAY IT!

GRIF   Kathy is my lover.

KARLA   Very good. Now. "Karla did not rape me."

GRIF   Let's… just talk. We can talk—

> *KARLA grabs GRIF's top and pulls her close.*

KARLA   Karla did not rape me!

GRIF   Karla did not—

KARLA   Look at me!

GRIF   Karla did not rape me.

KARLA   We loved each other.

GRIF   We loved each other.

KARLA   I hurt Karla's feelings very much.

GRIF   I hurt Karla's feelings very much.

KARLA   I am very sorry.

GRIF   I am VERY…!

> *KARLA presses the knife to GRIF's throat.*

KARLA Don't… yell.

GRIF I am very sorry.

> *KARLA releases GRIF and straightens her top.*

KARLA There now. Don't you feel better? Now that the truth is out?

> *Pause.*

Well. What do we do now?

GRIF You leave.

KARLA Kiss and make up?

> *GRIF picks up the telephone. KARLA cuts the cord with her knife.*

Oops.

> *GRIF goes for the door. KARLA is faster. She holds the knife out at GRIF.*

It's time to kiss and make up.

> *KARLA moves close to GRIF and strokes her face.*

You are so beautiful.

> *GRIF recoils from KARLA's touch.*

I don't want to hurt you, Grif. I didn't come to hurt you. I only wanted to see you. To ask you.

Three years, I've been wondering, Grif. If I got it wrong. If it was me who started it. If it was the truth. Or if it was the dare.

What was it, Grif?

> *Pause.*

GRIF It was both.

KARLA You used me! Used me for the attraction. Like a tattoo. And then you just peeled me off, and I shrivelled away.

Why'd you do that? Why did you leave me?

GRIF I was afraid!

KARLA Of me?

GRIF I didn't want you to need me.

> *Pause.*

KARLA Well, I don't need you, Grif. I just want you. I want you back.

GRIF No.

KARLA   I was here first!

GRIF   I'm happy with her!

KARLA   You mean you're loyal? You have an ongoing relationship? You've slept with her more than once? How long, Grif? How long have you been happy? How long?

GRIF   Eight months.

KARLA   Eight months. Eight months. EXTRA! EXTRA! "Grif Remains a One-Woman Girl For More Than A Week!" This is big news.

GRIF   It's called commitment!

> *KARLA smirks.*

KARLA   So, when did you make the big switch? Eh? After me? Or, maybe you lied. Maybe even before me.

GRIF   No. After.

KARLA   You could have called. You could have told me. "I'm out of the closet." Or maybe you're not. Are you?

GRIF   It depends.

KARLA   On what?

GRIF   On where we are.

KARLA   Does your Grandmother know?

GRIF   Not yet. Soon.

> *Pause.*

KARLA   So, what's she like?

GRIF   What does it matter?

KARLA   'Cause I wanna know why she gets you and I don't.

GRIF   It's different. She's more... she's... we're...

> *KARLA, in angry exasperation suddenly kicks a vase, lamp, chair or similar object.*

KARLA   WHAT!?

> *Pause.*

GRIF   Gentle.

> *KARLA is on the verge of tears.*

KARLA   Gentle? I can be gentle.

GRIF   It's more than that. We respect each other. I admire her. She's talented and successful. We fit!

KARLA   I can't get rid of you. Of remembering you. I remember what if felt like to be around you. To be with you. And that night. What it felt like to be touched by you. Your smell. Your skin. Warm. So… soft. Melting.

Take me back. Please, take me back.

GRIF   No, Karla.

KARLA   You can break up with Kathy. You want a house? I have a house. We could have fun. Endless fun, Grif. We know how to have fun!

GRIF   I love Kathy.

> *Pause.*

I love her.

KARLA   Well.

She doesn't love you. She told me. She said to tell you it was over. Get lost. Fuck off. You're ugly.

GRIF   Come on, Karla.

KARLA   You're fat. Fat and ugly.

GRIF   Stop it.

KARLA   Fat and ugly and gay. A fat, ugly, gay slut! But, I still love you anyway.

> *KARLA touches GRIF sexually.*

Now what are we going to do? Hm?

> *GRIF looks directly at KARLA, allowing KARLA to continue caressing her.*

What do you want?

GRIF   I want my ring back.

KARLA   No.

GRIF   My ring, Karla. Now.

KARLA   Finders keepers.

GRIF   You promised to give it back at the end of the summer.

KARLA   Where's my wrist band?

GRIF   I threw it out.

KARLA   Then fuck you!

GRIF   I want my ring.

KARLA   It's stuck.

GRIF   It was my mother's!

KARLA   You try.

> *GRIF tries. She can't remove it.*

GRIF   Take it off!

KARLA   You'll have to cut it off. Here.

> *KARLA offers GRIF the knife.*

Come on. Cut me.

> *GRIF looks at the knife. KARLA holds out her hand, palm side up.*

Cut me!

> *GRIF begins to slowly cut across KARLA's palm.*

Deeper!

> *KARLA takes GRIF's hand and forcibly pushes down harder on the knife.*
>
> *As she cuts, GRIF begins to shake violently, making a strange guttural noise. KARLA inhales sharply, staring all the time into GRIF's face.*
>
> *After the knife is drawn all the way across the palm, GRIF drops the knife. KARLA begins to bleed.*
>
> *Pause.*

GRIF   *(weakly)* I'm sorry.

KARLA   Pardon me?

GRIF   You're bleeding.

KARLA   So?

GRIF   Well, stop it! Put some pressure on it!

KARLA   No.

GRIF   Clench your fist!

KARLA   No.

GRIF   Jesus Christ!

> *GRIF grabs the tea towel from the kitchen and hands it to KARLA.*

Here, wrap it!

> *KARLA drops it on the floor.*

KARLA   That one's dirty.

> *GRIF runs into the bathroom. KARLA walks slowly around the couch dripping her blood purposely on the floor and over the couch; her hand in a claw-like position.*

> *GRIF emerges with a handful of first-aid supplies. She stops and stares at what KARLA is doing.*

GRIF   ...Karla...?

> *Holding her hand in the air, KARLA speaks with climactic intensity.*

KARLA   I... AM... A... WOLF! THIS is MY territory!

> *KARLA wipes her hand across GRIF's breast. GRIF doesn't move.*

Mine!

> *KARLA presses her hand to GRIF's crotch.*

Mine!

> *KARLA wipes her hand across GRIF's face.*

Mine!

> *GRIF collapses, crying. KARLA takes off the ring and places it back on GRIF's finger. KARLA picks up her knife. GRIF sees this and tries to get up to run. KARLA is quicker and puts her hand on GRIF's back. GRIF freezes.*

I'm not going to hurt you.

> *KARLA grabs a large swatch of GRIF's hair and holds the knife to it. She begins to shake. Her aggressive hold of the hair turns into one of admiration, longing and sorrow. She throws the knife aside. She gently puts GRIF's hair back down. She stands.*

I love you.

> *KARLA moves to the door and puts on her jacket. She stands in the doorway. The last line indicates her pain and vulnerability. She is trying for bravado, but it fails.*

But, I liked you better... as a dirty blonde.

> *KARLA walks out leaving the door open. Lights fade on GRIF.*

> *The end.*

A Fertile Imagination

Susan G. Cole

Introduction:
A Fertile Imagination

Susan G. Cole's *A Fertile Imagination* (1991) tells the story of a lesbian couple's quest for recognition of their rights to live as equal, if separate, members of society. In keeping with its aim of carving out a lesbian space, the play capitalizes on the seductive powers of stage naturalism to legitimize the existence of an idealized lesbian couple seeking to have a child. Set in the late '80s in the apartment of Rita and Del, the play contains main topical references to well-known Toronto landmarks. Thus, reading against Cole's disclaimer that the set is not intended to be naturalistic, I would argue that it is precisely because it draws attention to verifiable off stage referents that it is able to problematize the naturalized heterosexual conventions that rule both on and off stage. Admitting its debt to actual events that had happened to the characters, it documents a groundbreaking period in lesbian history when lesbians actively demanded a counter space. [1]

In focusing its attention on the struggles of Rita and Del to have a baby at a time when lesbian unions had no status and lesbians no access to fertility clinics, the play follows them through all the stages of their determined battle to conceive, carry and deliver a child without the benefit of the institutions available to their heterosexual counterparts. By representing all the difficulties that arise when lesbians try to participate in the most sacrosanct of heterosexual rituals, Cole forces us to look closely at the kinds of exclusionary rules that reward traditional family structures. The highly articulate debate that is carried on by the characters about lesbian issues is justified theatrically by portraying Del as a radical feminist journalist whose inflammatory daily columns have become part of their daily conversation. Rita and Del's constant speculations about their situation are also complemented by the expertise that Zee, their hip young Black midwife, contributes to the mix. Having the Black actor who plays Zee take all the other female roles also reminds us that the play is operating on more than just a naturalistic level. While her Blackness marks her as "other," her appearance as the liberal feminist lawyer, Ms. Martel, the baby dyke separatist Marge, and the straight married mother-to-be Erica, keeps us conscious of the place that Rita and Del occupy in the lesbian continuum.

Its frequent referencing of the world outside the play requires constant interaction from spectators who are confronted with the larger-than-life stage presence of lesbian members from their community—whom they may resemble, identify with, or despise as unwelcome usurpers of heterosexual prerogatives. If lesbian space had been confined to an unseen private sphere before this time, *A Fertile Imagination* takes up the challenge of inviting the spectator in to it and, by so doing, making it public. Right from the top of Act One, it is clear that all the traditional taboos around talking about sex and reproduction are being overthrown as Del's opening speech warns us that she is out looking for semen. Graphically describing all the failings of the available candidates, Del and Rita demystify the ejaculation process and talk about their plan to try "alternative fertilization." Del's new empowering politically correct explanation that "it's not artificial and it's not just about semen" is undercut by the phone conversation that Rita is having with her skeptical mother at the same time. Each scene continues in this way by playing up the stereotype and then confronting the ignorance that produced it in the first place. Del herself as the Jewish intellectual is often the butt of the joke as her prejudices against hiring a midwife spiral from fear of her being a granola dyke to worry about her being too sexually attractive. The bisexual Zee plays along with her by holding up a turkey baster to debunk the myth that it is the instrument of choice.

As Del continues to play straight-man through all the next stages of getting a legal agreement where the father signs off his rights, to debating with Rita about whether they should "mess with nature" in order to have a girl, spectators find themselves drawn into having to think about their own positions on all the serious issues that arise when reproductive rights are thrown into question. On the level of the dramatic fiction, we see them making love and bickering away about what having a child will do to their relationship. While these scenes may strike us as typical domestic fare, they also force us to recognize that Del and Rita are behaving very much like their heterosexual counterparts whose rocky love lives provide the plots for the ever popular situation comedies that dominate the entertainment media. Thus, we are forced to question why it is so shocking to see lesbians take up this space.

The next intrusion after Zee's up close and intimate physical examination of Rita's body, is the arrival of the sperm courier, Marge, recognizable as a zealous new convert by her up-to-the-minute baby dyke clothing. A believer in the need for the creation of a "lesbian nation," She justifies working as a sperm courier by offering her wildly exaggerated vision of the utopia to come:

> Oh this is the way of the lesbian future. Revolutionary reproduction.
> Pretty soon there'll be enough dykes with tykes to fill a co-op. Then
> a city block. Then a whole city. There'll be no more violence against
> women. We'll have control over our lives, the streets, the schools.
> Amazon history will be mandatory. The local video stores will carry five
> copies of "Desert Hearts," a reel containing every single lesbian moment
> on "LA Law" as well as the complete television catalogue of "Laverne and
> Shirley"… (Act One, Scene Five)

Cole uses Marge's extreme position to alert the spectators to this little lesson in lesbian history, including Marge's ignorance of Martina Navratilova's iconic importance to the older Del and Rita. While this scene definitely speaks primarily to the lesbian community, it also opens up the discourse to everyone else. Rita's disclaimer, "She actually thinks we're creating a lesbian nation. I'd settle for one child," puts the politics in perspective and refocuses our attention on the individual experience of Rita and Del.

In the following scenes in Act One, we are shown a blow by blow account of the trials of Rita's insemination with all the hits and misses involved in getting fertilization to take place. For the many lesbian couples who underwent this process, finding their gruelling experiences represented on stage allows them to enter into the discourse of alternative fertilization. Act One takes the harrowing ups and downs further by recreating the heartbreaking circumstances of Rita's miscarriage from the moment when she discovers the baby is dead to her bloody home delivery. Leaving the spectator nowhere to hide, these scenes force us to acknowledge that this situation is also tragic for couples who have traditionally been regarded as unsympathetic to childbearing. Rita's lament that they are being punished for trying to make a baby with a plastic syringe may confront the prejudices of many spectators, just as Del's response will also force us to rethink our positions: "And what's natural? A cock? How many women really choose that? I'll take a syringe over rape any day" (Act One, Scene Thirteen). Having the act end with the sounds of the voices of their lesbian friends leaving comforting messages on the answering machine reminds us that their experience has not gone completely unnoticed and unmourned. In whatever modest way, lesbian motherhood has entered into representation.

Act Two reflects this new state as Rita and Del return with renewed confidence to try again. The scenes in Act Two which mark the stages of Rita's pregnancy are punctuated with reminders that lesbian pregnancy is still outside the popular imagination. Thus we follow them through scenes where they have to discover their own ideas about same-sex parenting in a world largely dominated by heterosexual conventions. Paralleling the changes in Rita's swelling body are the now competing discourses about what kind of family Rita and Del will now enter. With Marge now urging them to join the "dykes with tykes brunch" group, and Erica from prenatal class asking what will happen if the baby is a boy, they find themselves facing the fact that they will be very much on their own in a community of three. As Rita prepares to go to the hospital, Del writes the final problematizing words to her column as she announces: a brave new world of lesbian coupledom:

> Our baby doesn't have a father, or even a father substitute. I'm not Daddy Del. I'm a woman and that's how I want it. I'm a woman who loves a woman and we're going to have a baby. I'm going to be a mother. (Act Two, Scene Two)

Note

[1] Becki Ross, "A Lesbian Politics of Erotic Decolonization," *Painting the Maple: Essays on Race, Gender, and the Construction of Canada,* ed. Veronica Strong-Boag et al. (Vancouver: UBC Press, 1998) 199-202, traces various stages of lesbian activism.

photo by David Hawe

Susan Cole

Bio and Artist's Statement

Susan G. Cole is a political and cultural activist, author and editor. She has written two books on violence against women, *Pornography and the Sex Crisis* and *Power Surge* (both published by Second Story) and continues to lecture on the subject. She was instrumental in organizing Nightwood Theatre's 5-Minute Feminist Cabaret in its early years and appeared as both performer and host.

She has a regular column in the Canadian magazine *Herizons* and is currently the Senior Entertainment and Books Editor at *NOW* Magazine in Toronto. Though many have asked for a sequel, *A Fertile Imagination* is her only play. She lives with the inspirations for the play—her partner Lesley Chudnovsky and her daughter Molly Chudnovsky who, unbelievably, is now 18—in Toronto.

•

When I wrote *A Fertile Imagination* in 1989—just after our daughter was born—Ellen Degeneres was buried in her closet, there was no same-sex marriage debate and there certainly were not over 20,000 families in North America led by lesbian mothers. While it's true small-town lesbians still have a hard time being themselves, the play— especially when the characters feel so alone with their motherhood project—is now almost a period piece. I updated all the pop cultural references so as to make the play current whenever it was produced but now I don't think I would bother. Let *A Fertile Imagination* stand as a statement on what preoccupied lesbians in the late 80s— lesbian invisibility in pop culture and the challenge of being a lesbian mother in a homophobic society, within a queer community that is not exactly child-positive.

On another subject, I always insisted and still do that one Black actor play all the roles other than Del and Rita (which does not preclude a woman of colour taking either of those roles, though the total absence of race-related dialogue between them would make the relationship seem a little false). There were two intentions for this strategy: one was to promote Nightwood's diversity agenda, artificially inflating the presence of Black performers in a cash-strapped medium and the other was to give a Black actor the opportunity to display her virtuosity. Not surprisingly Patricia Idlette was Dora-nominated (as was Robin Craig) for playing the multiple roles.

Production Information

A Fertile Imagination was originally produced by Nightwood Theatre and performed at the Poor Alex, Toronto, in February 1991, with the following company:

DEL	Kate Lynch
RITA	Robin Craig
ZEE and OTHERS	Patricia Idlette

Directed and dramaturged by Kate Lushington
Sets and costumes by Christine Plunkett
Lighting by Lesley Wilkinson

Characters

Del

Rita

Zee/Ms. Martel/Marge/Erica

Casting note: All roles other than Del and Rita are to be played by one Black woman

Setting

The play takes place in Del and Rita's apartment during the late 1980s. The set is not intended to be naturalistic although certain set pieces are essential.

Act Two takes place five months after the end of Act One.

Author's Note

Although the story is based on autobiographical incidents, the characters are not related to any person living or dead. The politically fantastic elements include, for example, the fact that radical feminist Del writes a regular column for a daily newspaper; in earlier versions of the play, Zee was appointed head of a provincial task force on midwifery.

The author has the option to update topical references, in particular references to *People* magazine and/or various tennis and pop personalities.

The Morgentaler clinic is Toronto's free-standing abortion facility. The Honey Dew is a now-defunct midtown Toronto coffee shop. The Life section of the *Toronto Star* is what used to be the Women's section. Roots, No No No, are designer labels for children's clothes. Names can change to suit production locations.

Del's readings are near direct quotes from *Pregnancy and Childbirth*, by Tracy Hotchner (Avon). Although it's not necessary to see this, no other author's name should be visible.

A FERTILE IMAGINATION

ACT ONE

scene one

The kitchen. DEL and RITA come through the front door filled with purpose. They sit at the kitchen table. DEL leafs through a recipe box.

DEL   Can you believe this? For the past ten years I've done everything I can to avoid semen, and now I can't wait to my hands on it. I'm actually sitting here wishing that I knew more men. Uh Uh. Don't mess with my system. That one is for fertility clinics. This one is for donors.

RITA   Your system? It's my body.

DEL   Right, it's a challenge. How to conceive a baby as far away from the penis as possible.

RITA   Did you talk to Max?

DEL   He wants to co-parent. I told him tough luck.

RITA   It's not a totally ridiculous idea.

DEL   For someone else. Greg?

RITA   He doesn't want to take the AIDS test.

DEL   Allan?

RITA   He said he'd have trouble keeping his distance because he'd feel too responsible.

DEL   Responsible, my ass. For what? I feel responsible means I want control. We should feel lucky that he warned us away.

RITA   Why is this so hard?

DEL   Yeah, since when did sperm get so precious? I feel so out of it. I'm trying to remember… men. Maybe you can help me.

RITA   Don't give me that more lesbian-than-thou-for-longer business. You weren't the first woman in my life.

DEL   Cast your mind back. Now, I was on the pill. Weren't you?

RITA   Yeah, or something, or guys wouldn't come inside.

DEL   Okay. So did they worry about what happened after they came, I mean to the semen they lost?

RITA   No, as long as they lost it.

DEL   Really. When you think of all the jacking off they do. But we want to get hold of one tiny tadpole, and these guys get hysterical. There must be ten zillion sperm in this naked city and we want just one of them.

RITA   Can you imagine how I feel walking by the Morgentaler clinic every day on my way to work?

DEL   What about what's his name... your ex...

RITA   Paul.

DEL   You know, the one you were with before...

RITA   ...before you swept me away?

DEL   Before you jumped me.

RITA   I asked him. He said of course. He didn't want to co-parent or anything and I thought the hunt was over. The he started acting as if it was decided. I'd never seen him so... determined. It must be the gene thing. He started talking about names. And when I realized that he expected to be at the birth...

DEL   Come on.

RITA   That made me nauseous. Maybe we should consider an anonymous donor.

DEL   Gee. I dunno. What about Errol?

RITA   The spirit is willing. His wife isn't. This is what it would be like if we didn't know.

DEL   It's too important a variable to leave unknown. I want to know who's hanging around waiting to pounce after you deliver and I want a legal agreement signed. I want to keep an eye on the guy I don't want to see.

RITA   Maybe we should be worrying about genes.

DEL   If half this baby's genes are yours, it will be gifted. Anyway, who has this anonymous sperm? Fertility clinics charge something crazy like a thousand bucks a pop. And even if we were millionaires no clinic in this province will do business with lesbians.

Fade to blue.

scene two

DEL   Check out this story on Kristy McNichol, you know, the one who used to be on Family? She's a lesbian.

RITA   According to *People* magazine?

DEL *People*'s always been an excellent source of information. You just have to know how to read it. There's no mention of any love interests. They talk about her workout pal. Liberace's niece no less. There's a clue.

RITA Now I see it's gay by association. You'll claim anyone for your list. All they need is short hair.

DEL And big watches. And they don't have to have short hair. Look at Lily. Maybe I should go the distance in my next column and bring all the entertainers I know out of the closet.

RITA You don't know. You think any woman that you think is attractive is a lesbian. And you get so upset when you're wrong. Remember when Whoopi Goldberg got married?

DEL She just joins the ranks of ex-lesbians, or, what do they call them? Hasbians. Women who were but couldn't take the pressure.

RITA I can't recall the last time I read the words "I am a lesbian" in your column.

DEL I don't use the first person and I don't intend to.

RITA I noticed. Your last column was pretty abstract.

DEL I was writing about reproductive technology. Of course it got technical.

RITA I said technical, not abstract.

> *The phone rings. RITA answers.*

Mom…. Yeah, I got the tickets. Eighth row.

DEL I got the tickets.

RITA No, we haven't changed our minds…. Oh, no, we're using artificial insemination.

DEL It's alternative fertilization.

RITA *(to DEL)* what difference does it make?

DEL It's not artificial, and it's not just about semen.

RITA *(to the phone)* What? Listen I can't talk now, we're expecting a visit from our midwife…. Of course I'm seeing a doctor…. She…. She's affiliated with a hospital…. Mother, she's aware of our situation…. Uhuh…. Mmhmm…. I love you too…. Bye. *(hangs up)* She's disappointed that I'm not going to sleep with the donor.

DEL She hates me.

RITA Don't be silly. She's crazy about you.

DEL I'm the predator that turned you into a pervert.

RITA   At least you're a Jewish predator, and so smart. She gets a real charge out of reading your byline every week. Face it, she thinks you're fascinating. I'm the underachieving slug who works in daycare.

DEL   I take it she didn't love the midwife idea.

RITA   Not in the least.

DEL   Finally, we agree on something.

RITA   Look, the midwives have a line on sperm.

DEL   I don't want an earth mother in Birkenstocks, wafting patchouli oil through the house.

RITA   "As the medical establishment seizes control of the birthing process, the only truly effective advocates for women are midwives."

DEL   I don't like it when you quote me to me.

RITA   You know we can't do this alone.

DEL   But a fourth party? It's bad enough we have to go sperm-hunting a third.

RITA   Del, we've been through this before. Why are you making it so complicated?

DEL   Midwives don't have to help other couples get pregnant.

RITA   Since when do you care what other couples do?

DEL   Well, the whole thing makes me feel… unnatural. I hate that feeling. I hate feeling marginalized.

RITA   So, we could use the support. Now, I talked to the woman on the phone. Her name is Zee.

DEL   Zee.

RITA   She was very open.

DEL   Zee. Get ready for Ms. Nice, radiating Nurturence, looking like she's never had a haircut in her life. She'll eat tofu burgers. Tofu… burgers. The great contradiction in terms. Like carrot… cake.

RITA   You think a cheese danish is a hit of protein.

DEL   She'll want herbal tea and pull all the sugar off the shelves. Those aren't the crystals they're into.

> *Doorbell.*

Tell her I don't do circles.

> *RITA opens the door. Framed in the doorway is ZEE dressed in
> a beautiful combination of urban funk and African colour. She is very
> much in her body.*

RITA   Hi. You must be Zee. I'm Rita.

RITA & ZEE   We talked on the phone.

RITA   Come on in.

ZEE   You must be Del. I'm Zee.

DEL   I'm Del. Would you like to sit down? Can we get you something?

ZEE   Coffee, please.

DEL   Coffee. How do you like it?

ZEE   Hot, strong and black. *(DEL goes to get it.)* I've seen you somewhere. Your picture, in the *Star*. I have, haven't I?

RITA   Yeah. She writes that feminist column. Sort of a Ms. Manners for the militant set.

ZEE   Oh, I love your stuff. I thought your column on the Winter Olympics was a riot. What was it? "The Winter Olympics—the luxury playground of white male privilege."

RITA   She watched every second of it on TV.

DEL   Rita tells me you have a sperm connection.

ZEE   Yes we do. We have some contacts. In fact, there's a donor in the picture. He's ready to roll.

DEL   Who is this guy?

RITA   Where's he from? Oh I can feel my estrogen levels rising.

ZEE   He wants to remain anonymous.

DEL   I have a problem with the sperm from another planet concept.

RITA   But Del, we've been having such a hard time. Do we really have that much choice at this point?

DEL   I feel like I want to know something about this guy.

RITA   Tell us one thing, just one thing…

ZEE   Well, he's…

RITA   Don't tell us what he does or what he looks like.

ZEE   Actually, he's…

DEL   Just something that will make us feel good about him.

ZEE   He wants to do something for life. His friends are dying of AIDS. He's all tested and everything. *(silence)* How about this? We'll do the practice run now. That way you'll be ready.

DEL   Practice run? *(to RITA)* You didn't say anything about…

ZEE   Yeah, I show you how so you can do it yourself. I'll do the internal now if you want.

RITA   Sure.

ZEE   Where would you be most comfortable?

RITA   In the bedroom, I guess.

ZEE   I'll need to wash up.

RITA   Over there. *(ZEE exits to the bathroom.)*

DEL   See what I mean. First we need help getting pregnant and then some woman I don't even know is going to put her hands…

RITA   She's a professional, Del.

DEL   She's a gorgeous professional.

RITA   Come on. Can't you feel it? We're getting so close. *(She exits to the bedroom.)*

> *ZEE enters and begins pulling plastic wrapping off a syringe.*

DEL   What's that for?

ZEE   It's a syringe to inject the sperm.

DEL   What about a turkey baster?

ZEE   You have one?

DEL   Yeah. Here.

ZEE   *(holding the baster to the side of DEL's body, as if she were measuring the vaginal canal)* Does that look like fun to you?

DEL   Uh uh.

ZEE   *(She removes paraphernalia out of her bag, rubber gloves, etc.)* We need a bottle. This one will do.

DEL   That one's not sterile.

ZEE   People fuck in pretty squalid conditions.

DEL   She said fuck. Midwives don't say fuck.

ZEE   White hippies didn't invent midwifery, you know.

DEL   I know. *(ZEE puts on rubber gloves.)* So when you do this work you find out a lot about people, their intimate secrets and things.

ZEE   Sometimes.

DEL   So what do we ever find out about you?

ZEE   Whatever.

DEL   I'll pick any random thing. Are you a lesbian?

ZEE   I've slept with women. Who hasn't? But I live with a guy.

DEL   Ah yes, pre-lesbian.

> *Fade to blue.*
>
> *Transition.*
>
> *The answering machine is playing.*

—Hi gals, this is Audra. I'm getting on with the legal paperwork. Your guy's lawyer wants to come Tuesday at 5:30 p.m. Make sure you're home.

—Del, it's your editor. I have question about your sexual harassment piece. You say that a male professor's comment on a female student's clothing might constitute harassment. Don't you think it should read that it could constitute sexual harassment?

—Rita, dear. It's Mum. I wish you wouldn't put on that machine. I'm taping the "Donahue" show for you. He's interviewing some women who are, you know, in your situation.

—Hey Del. Dykes on "Donahue". Turn it on.

scene three

> *DEL is pacing the apartment. RITA's in the bedroom.*

DEL   So, I want to make sure that we agree on this. We want to make it clear to this lawyer person that we don't want this guy anywhere near us or our baby. If he tries anything, to contact us, or the baby, even for a peek or a pang of paternal bonding, we'll get a court injunction to get him out of this family's face. I don't know how you put that in legal terms...

RITA   You don't have to worry about that now. We just have to wait to find out what he wants. I just hope he has good mobility.

DEL   Do we care about his career potential?

RITA   I mean his sperm. It better have swift movement.

DEL   Oh, motility.

> *Doorbell.*

I don't like lawyers.

RITA   Try not to be too defensive.

DEL   I am charm itself. (*She opens the door. MS. MARTEL is framed, her presentation, impeccable.*) A woman. Terrific. Did this guy think a lady lawyer would put us off guard?

RITA   Del!

MS. MARTEL   I'm Ms. Martel. You're just what I expected. I read your column.

DEL   Well, I'm glad you're ready, because I intend to be a stereotype of myself if that's what's necessary. No amount of manipulative verbal maneuvering coming out of your dog-trained mouth can move us from our position. Your client has only one thing that interests us. We do not care about his biological needs, his wrenching desire to see his offspring or to know his offspring. We don't care if this baby winds up being the last blood tie in his life. There will not be a single area of this child's future over which he will have control. Over which he will have impact or input.

MS. MARTEL   Agreed.

DEL   And if anything happens to Rita, this baby goes into my care. I don't want to hear from Mr. Right sweeping in and becoming father of the year. If anything happens to both of us, your client does not budge. We will have made all the necessary arrangements. We don't need Mr. Hero. We need the sperm, okay?

MS. MARTEL   Agreed.

DEL   You say so now. But what if he changes his mind? What if he gets hostile? Look at those guys who try to stop their ex-girlfriends from having abortion. They're so pathetic. Just because some blood rushes into that sacred muscle of theirs and an opaque liquid comes out, they call themselves fathers. They're inseminators, period.

RITA   Maybe we can give our guy a break and call him a donor.

MS. MARTEL   My client has only one condition.

DEL   Hah! A hitch. There's never any free lunch.

MS. MARTEL   Don't ever ask him for money.

RITA   What?

MS. MARTEL   No paternity suit.

DEL   He thinks we'd come to him for money?

MS. MARTEL   I have been sent by my client to ensure that under no circumstances will either of you see application from the court to extract funds from him for any purpose—educational, medical, or anything else. He wants to be left alone as much as you want to be left alone.

RITA   Ha ha.

MS. MARTEL   Here. I've drawn up papers. Have your lawyer contact me. I should tell you if your own lawyer hasn't, and especially since at least one of you has worked up a considerable amount of passion over the matter, that these agreements don't carry much legal weight. If my client should decide he wanted to claim any rights, he could still do so, and a court could support his claim.

DEL   What the hell are you talking about?

MS. MARTEL   I'm talking truth.

RITA   But if we sign and he signs…

MS. MARTEL   If my client did decide to take such action, however, I would not represent him.

DEL   Well, you're a credit to your gender.

RITA   She means thank you.

> *MS. MARTEL leaves.*

DEL   *(calling after her)* Tell your client to start exercising. We want him in shape so he can produce a splendid specimen. And no recreational drugs, especially marijuana. It lowers the sperm count. And no sex for three days before the donation, either. It says so in all the books. He's got to conserve his energy.

RITA   She's not going to tell him anything except that you're crazy. Do you want this to happen or not?

DEL   Why do you feel you have to ask me that?

RITA   You are a train.

DEL   What?

RITA   The Del Express, clanging down the track…

DEL   Ah, make me the heavy for a change. No wonder people assume you're the sensitive one in this household. You leave me with all the unpleasantness of implementing your ideas.

RITA   You acted as if I wasn't in the room.

DEL   You know I hate lawyers, they're all sharks.

RITA   But she wasn't one.

DEL   Why, because she's a woman? Law school nukes women.

RITA   You put our arrangements in jeopardy.

DEL   If Ms. Martel is as terrific as you think she is, she'll understand.

RITA   What the hell's going on? You've said clearly that you wanted this.

DEL   Now that that's established there are a few more wrinkles aren't there? Apparently our legal rights are in question…

RITA   So you blow through Ms. Martel as if she were air? And Zee tells me it took you thirty seconds to find out who she sleeps with.

DEL   I didn't find out who, just the gender.

RITA   Just after making that lunatic comment about how she looks? Turning my midwife into a sex object. It's unbelievable.

DEL   Oh, and you've never made a comment on how somebody looks. Give me a break. Nobody checks out body types the way you do. You have a woman's bra size down after three seconds.

RITA   Oh stop. You're not talking to me. You're just running at the mouth. Are you threatened by this or what?

DEL   Of course, I'm threatened.

RITA   By everyone who walks in the room?

DEL   By this person we're creating, Rita. It's hard for me to imagine.

RITA   You've said that about other things. When we met you were Ms. Bachelorette and you weren't going to go steady with anyone. Then you went out with me.

DEL   That's right, but…

RITA   But you said you'd keep going out with others.

DEL   I did.

RITA   For a week. And what was it then? Oh yes, you would never live with anybody because you could never give up your cheap Queen Street apartment. And then we moved here.

DEL   But this is different.

RITA   Why?

DEL   You needed me to do all those things. We went out—together. We chose to give up other lovers—together. We live—together. None of those things could happen without me. But you and baby. It is different. You told me once that, of course you'd rather that we did it together but that even if we didn't, you'd have a baby on your own. I've never forgotten that. It makes me feel… peripheral.

RITA   It won't be that way. We'll be together, the three of us.

DEL   I just want it to be clear. I'm doing this as part of loving you. Got it?

RITA   Got it. *(They get close.)* Don't you sort of wish we could have a girl?

DEL   What?

RITA   Is it so terrible to care either way?

DEL   I thought a baby was enough.

RITA   But there's a way to try for a girl, isn't there?

DEL   This is too much. Aren't you the fighter for boys' rights? You almost ruined our only trip to the women's music festival. We drove for eight hours to get there and you wouldn't go in.

RITA   Well, that's because they were putting boys in a separate play area. The first thing they said to us when we got there was "any dogs or boy children?"

DEL   And now you don't want a son?

RITA   I want a daughter.

DEL   This is almost too weird. It's not because you think you can empathize better with girls, is it?

RITA   I'm a little more comfortable with girl culture than boy culture. I was crazy about my Barbie.

DEL   You're planning to buy our daughter a Barbie doll?

RITA   No, but dolls for sure. They're good for the imagination. For boys too. But wouldn't it be fun to have a daughter. There's a way to try for a girl, isn't there?

DEL   Really, Rita, honey, there are so many people screwing around with genetic balance. I have this feeling, don't laugh, a sense that they're messing with nature.

RITA   Hah, look who's going fundamentalist on me. Don't people usually go for boys?

DEL   You bet. Did you know that they were working on selecting out for boy babies a full ten years before they even started to think about selecting for girls?

RITA   Wow. We could balance it out.

DEL   Rita, that's not how statistics work.

RITA   Maybe you're just a liberal.

DEL   Don't ever call me that.

RITA   You've gone all mushy on this one. Come on. You've read up on this, Ms. Research.

DEL   Maybe. Okay, okay. To select for boys, they spin the sperm so that the heavier ones with the Y chromosome end up at the bottom. Then they inseminate the sperm.

RITA   And for girls.

DEL   They fill you up with a dreadful, cancer-causing drug called chlomid that…

RITA No drugs.

DEL No kidding. But there is another option, my clean machine. Timing. If you inseminate right at the time of ovulation, you increase the chances of getting pregnant.

RITA Sounds like my kind of strategy.

DEL But you also give the male sperm more of a chance if you do it then.

RITA Why?

DEL They swim faster. They get to the egg first.

RITA So that must be why most lesbians have boys.

DEL Right, because they inseminate on the day of ovulation and get male children. But, if you inseminate a few days before ovulation, then you increase the chance of the female sperm hitting the egg.

RITA They're slow?

DEL Think of it this way. You have a twenty-six day cycle. You ovulate on day thirteen. We inseminate on the eleventh day. The boy sperm begin tearing to the finish line. There they go, aiming for the target, slashing their way through the canal, winning the race, for after all winning is everything. But no, not in the birth sweepstakes. The Y sperm hit the site of the egg and guess what? The egg isn't there yet. Now the Y sperm have speed yes, but they have no stamina. They die. Cruising down the canal behind them are the X sperm doing the breaststroke. Gliding along, they seem surprisingly calm. But underneath that serenity is a determination unmatched in all of biological life. For when they arrive at the site of the egg, the egg indeed is right there. Ping. Done.

> *Fade.*

scene four

> *RITA and DEL are in the bedroom after making love.*

DEL I wonder if they ever hear us next door.

RITA You know I thought we did it then. It felt... momentous.

DEL Is that what you were thinking?

RITA Sometimes I feel like I could get pregnant.

DEL You can. The sperm will be here tomorrow.

RITA I don't want the fucking sperm. I want to do it ourselves.

DEL Well, we can't.

RITA   Why not? It's so unfair. They just have to stick it in and bingo.

DEL   Jesus Rita, listen to yourself. Why can't we be like normal lesbians. They go to work. They come home. They have a nice drink. They have brunch on the weekends. They make love to make love.

RITA   I know, it'll be different won't it.

DEL   No kidding. We won't have sex for years.

RITA   More of your research?

DEL   Does anyone with kids say different?

RITA   You won't attack the sperm courier will you?

DEL   I'll behave. *(fade)* Rita, stop it. Rita, go to sleep.

>   *Black.*

scene five

>   *DEL is with ZEE outside the bathroom. RITA is in the bathroom.*

DEL   I was against all this from the start. Organic sponges. It's this obsession with having a girl. Rita and her hippie manuals. She read somewhere that if you douse a menstrual sponge with vinegar and insert it...

ZEE   ...it creates an inhospitable environment for male sperm.

DEL   But it turns out that the vaginal canal, one of her most fabulous feature, is very hospitable to the sponge.

RITA   I can't get at it.

>   *ZEE waves a set of latex gloves and exits to help RITA. DEL leans in as ZEE and RITA try to solve the problem. ZEE emerges from the bathroom.*

DEL   Tampax may have been lax on toxic shock, but you have to hand it to them for the string idea.

ZEE   The miracle of latex gloves. Did you try to get it out?

DEL   Yes. I could just feel that sponge on the ends of my fingertips, but I couldn't get a grip. If only I didn't bite my nails. Thanks for coming over, Zee. Rita thinks you and every other professional consulted on this pregnancy wouldn't want to set foot in here again.

ZEE   I wonder why.

DEL   Oh, I don't know. She thinks I have an attitude problem. I told her you were one of my favourite bisexuals.

ZEE   Come on, Del. Bisexuality is open-minded.

DEL   Bisexuality is half-hearted. *(enter RITA)* This woman can't make up her mind.

RITA   Thank you, Zee.

ZEE   No problem. I brought you a diaphragm. This size should fit you. Put it in after you inseminate. It will keep the sperm close to the cervix.

DEL   That oughta keep them guessing. How did you get pregnant?

RITA   I used a diaphragm. *(ZEE's beeper goes off.)*

ZEE   Can I use your phone?

RITA   It's over there. *(ZEE dials.)*

DEL   Now what did she do that I didn't do?

RITA   She went in like a midwife. You have a lover's touch. I love your hands.

ZEE   I gotta go catch a baby. Now remember, when you're getting the specimen into the syringe, make sure to avoid bubbles. Air in the pipes is bad news. Go good. *(exit)*

>   DEL and RITA go into the bedroom.

DEL   Okay, let's get set. Where are the purple candles I bought.

RITA   I put them in the top drawer.

DEL   God, what a mess.

RITA   Well, it's small. Your papers are all over the living room. I have to have somewhere to spread.

DEL   Well, I wish your socks wouldn't spread into the underwear drawer. It drives me nuts.

RITA   Why? Socks are underwear. *(Hands DEL a sweatshirt.)*

DEL   Why are you giving it to me? You wore it.

RITA   It's yours.

DEL   How would I recognize it? Listen, if you're going to wear my clothes, don't give them back inside out.

RITA   Is this how you plan to create the mood?

DEL   Let's see. Music. How about "My Way". Or, "You're Having My Baby", or…

RITA   Forget the music.

DEL   Okay, pillows, candles.

>   Doorbell.

RITA   This is it.

They open the door to reveal MARGE. She is dressed in up-to-the-minute baby dyke style. Butch would be the operative term. She is young with that recently converted edge.

MARGE You guys picked a real winner.

RITA It's empty.

MARGE He missed the bottle.

DEL What?

MARGE *(to DEL)* Hey, I heard you speak at International Women's Day last year. Not bad.

RITA Now what do we do?

DEL *(looking at the bottle)* No wonder he missed. Didn't anyone tell him to practice?

MARGE Personally, I have nothing to do with gomers…

RITA Gomers?

MARGE Yeah, you know, gomers. Burgers. Men.

DEL Oh.

MARGE *(displaying a short squat bottle)* But I gave him one of these for next time. I think you should give him a couple of hours. *(exit)*

Fade out. Fade in.

DEL and RITA are waiting again. The doorbell rings. MARGE enters with a mutilated plastic bottle.

Your guy is amazing. I was five minutes late and he panicked. He thought the speciperson—I would never say specimen—would get too cold. So he went into his car and tried to keep it warm.

RITA His car?

MARGE So I guess he couldn't resist. You know how guys are with their toys. They think they know everything. He tried attaching it to the adapter on his car lighter. He fried the sperm. This guy has a severe case of testosterone poisoning.

DEL If you can't stand men, whatever possessed you to become a sperm courier.

MARGE Oh this is the wave of the lesbian future. Revolutionary reproduction. Pretty soon there'll be enough dykes with tykes to fill a co-op. Then a city block. Then a whole city. there'll be no more violence against women. We'll have control over our lives, the streets, the schools. Amazon history will be mandatory. The local video stores will carry five copies of "Desert Hearts", a reel containing every single lesbian moment on "LA Law" as well as the complete television catalogue of "Laverne and Shirley"...

RITA   "Kate and Allie"...

MARGE   And "Cagney and Lacey". The way I see it, it shouldn't take more than ten years.

DEL   Excuse me, I thought you gave him that glass bottle.

MARGE   He said he'd figured out a foolproof technique for hitting the target. I didn't ask. If you want my advice, I wouldn't ask him to try again 'til tomorrow. A third shot just won't have any pop.

DEL   Tomorrow? I can't.

RITA   You can't?

DEL   I've got tickets to see Martina play an exhibition tomorrow.

RITA   Don't you think this is a little more important?

DEL   But Martina. She may not have many years left.

MARGE   Martina who?

DEL   What do you mean Martina who? She is one of the only professional athletes alive who is totally recognizable by her first name.

RITA   It's starting. I can see it starting. You're going to have to learn to make compromises for your own child.

MARGE   Isn't she the one who hassled Magic Johnson when he tested positive...

DEL   She didn't hassle him...

MARGE   What do you mean she didn't' hassle him? She was out of control.

DEL   I thought you didn't know who she was?

MARGE   Martina? She's old news.

DEL   Pardon me if that teenaged brat Monica Seles does not move me. Who are you? What's your name?

MARGE   Marge.

DEL   I tell you, separatism ain't what it was. You used to only have to hate men. Marge hates all men and Martina.

RITA   Tomorrow will be fine. We'll call and confirm a time. *(MARGE exits.)* She actually thinks we're creating a lesbian nation. I'd settle for one child. *(pause)* Who's she playing, Gabriella Sabatini?

DEL   Now what difference, oh pure one, would that make?

RITA   Well, I may be pure, but I'm not blind.

   Fade.

scene six

   Doorbell rings. RITA opens it, snatches bottle. DEL slams door before MARGE can say a word.

RITA   Well there's something in there this time.

DEL   Not much though.

RITA   Gee I don't know.

DEL   Well, don't be hard on yourself. I'm sure that even a heterosexual wouldn't know how much of this there should be.

RITA   So far just to get this much. It's changing.

DEL   It's supposed to. When it becomes clear, then it's time to insert.

   DEL begins to flex her thumb.

RITA   What are you doing?

DEL   Calisthenics. Getting ready for the big moment. After this, my role in the creation process goes sort of downhill. Okay, go light the candles.

   Into the bedroom. Preparations.

   It has a slight odour, you know.

RITA   Del, now's not the time to get queasy.

DEL   Well, you always had more tolerance for this kind of thing. *(hums "I'm Forever Blowing Bubbles" by Kenbrovin/Kellette)* My hand is feeling fertile. Come on! Up high on the pillow so I can get a good view. *(RITA spreads her legs.)* God, you're gorgeous.

RITA   Zee said aim to the right. My cervix is a little wonky.

DEL   I remember everything. *(inserts and throws away the syringe)*

RITA   Should I be thinking fertility? I wonder…

DEL   Don't think. *(pause)*

RITA   Zee didn't do that…

DEL   Is that so?

RITA   Or that.

DEL   I hope not.

RITA   Huh. And certainly not that.

DEL   Did you know that if you have an orgasm you help the semen along.

RITA   Part of your research I suppose.

DEL   The best part.

RITA   Come here.

DEL   Uh uh, don't move. And certainly not sideways.

RITA   I want to touch you.

DEL   You have to stay where you are so the sperm flows to desired destination.

RITA   I can't not move.

DEL   You'll find a way.

RITA   I guess I will.

>   *Fade.*

scene seven

>   *RITA in the bathroom, DEL working at her laptop.*

RITA   Shit *(RITA enters.)*

DEL   Rita, Rita, what's wrong?

RITA   Blood!

DEL   Where?

RITA   Out of my body.

DEL   Oh shit.

RITA   Oh, shit and we don't even have any Tampax.

DEL   I have some in a plastic bag…

RITA   No, you don't. I threw them out…

DEL   At $8.95 a box?

RITA   Plus tax. If men menstruated there wouldn't be a tax on Tampax. If men menstruated they'd deliver Tampax, every month, on schedule.

DEL   Why?

RITA   For their own damn convenience. What's wrong with you?

DEL   Why did you throw out the…

RITA   Because I thought they were bad luck.

DEL   But there are two of us here.

RITA   Right.

DEL   Rita, you can't do this to yourself every month.

RITA   What do you mean every month?

DEL   The average couple takes three cycles to get pregnant…

RITA   Do you see anything average going on around here? I can't believe you can just pass us off as a statistic. My body doesn't feel like a statistic. You don't have the same investment. *(goes into the bathroom)*

DEL   It's that sex selection, I'm telling you. Mess with nature and she'll keep you waiting. I told you if you inseminate early in the cycle to get a girl, you also reduce the chances of getting together with that old ovum.

RITA   *(comes out of the bathroom)* I want a baby more than a girl.

DEL   Well you say that now.

RITA   Next time, we'll inseminate early and then we'll inseminate right on the dot of ovulation. If it takes the first time, great. Otherwise, it'll work the second time. We'll go both ways.

DEL   I don't go both ways.

Snap to light for insemination sequence.

scene eight

Insemination sequence.

Music plays over an increasingly mechanized process.

RITA and DEL to door. It's MARGE with sperm. She gives it to DEL, and exits. DEL fills syringe, inserts. RITA goes to the bathroom.

Music stops.

RITA   *(re-entering)* Shit!

Music resumes. To door. Arm in. Receives. Inserts. RITA to bathroom. Music stops.

(re-entering.) SHIT!

Music resumes. To door. Arm in. Receives. Inserts. RITA re-enters. Music stops. Silence.

Ping! Done!

Fade to blue.

scene nine

DEL is cooking. RITA's reading a baby name book.

DEL   Rita, do they still have those one-piece things, with the little feet and the snaps.

RITA   Sleepers?

DEL   Yeah. Are we gonna have those?

RITA   Sure, all you want.

DEL   Here you are. Protein, carbohydrates, roughage, vitamins and minerals. *(RITA looks at the food, nauseous. DEL dives in.)* How old does a kid have to be before read them "The Lion, The Witch, and the Wardrobe"? *(by C.S. Lewis)*

> *RITA pushes the plate away. DEL goes for the crackers and throws one on the table.*

Why do I bother?

RITA   Del, you have to stop counting on things always turning out. You have to be… in the moment.

DEL   I don't cook in the moment. This took me 2 hours.

RITA   *(back to the book)* Why don't we call the baby Sidney if it's a girl. It has such elegance.

DEL   Just what our daughter'll need—more gender ambiguity.

RITA   How about Laetitia. Just kidding.

DEL   No names ending in A for girls. Too femmy.

RITA   My name is Rita.

DEL   You're not responsible for that.

RITA   I tried Sally Claire on my mother and she said it sounded like a dessert.

DEL   She's right. Let's find one name that works both ways. I mean really works. Sidney isn't exactly great for a boy.

RITA   Sascha. it has a ring.

DEL   Kelly.

RITA   It's too… white.

DEL   It's Irish. It breathes dissent.

RITA   Sascha swashbuckles.

DEL   I like Kelly. Kelly will teach me skateboard.

RITA   Sascha will have passion.

DEL   He'll need it.

RITA   Yes, she will.

> *Fade to transition.*

scene ten

> *DEL goes to the bedroom and pull out a box. She opens it to produce a sleeper which she walks onto a pillow. She pulls the book* Pregnancy and Childbirth *by Tracy Hotchner, out of the bag and begins flipping the pages, reading the titles aloud.*

DEL   *Pregnancy and Childbirth.* Deciding to have children. Getting pregnant. Pregnancy and Body Image. *(She flips to the chapter, skims than alights.)* "The strangeness of your new body shape may make it hard for you to accept this new image of yourself." They're talking to the pregnant woman, of course. The average on of these manuals doesn't say much to her lesbian lover.

"You may lose confidence in your ability to attract your mate." What planet is this person on? Don't you know what happens to a woman's breasts when she's pregnant?... They grow enormous, more than enormous, ginormous—quickly. And the belly gets hard and ivory smooth.

"You have to be willing to discuss the fact that your mate may be turned off to your changing body shape." Turned off? And they call me anti-male. I don't get it. I thought guys were crazy about breasts. *(The front door opens. RITA enters.)* Rita! *(RITA doesn't respond. DEL goes to her.)*

RITA   There's no heartbeat.

DEL   There's no...

RITA   Heartbeat.

DEL   So, we've never heard one before...

RITA   We're supposed to now.

DEL   But not necessarily.

> *RITA shakes her head.*

Wait a second. No heartbeat can mean any number of things. You don't always hear the heartbeat at 16 weeks. The baby could be turned around so that the heartbeat is faint. Besides you're in the fourth month. If anything goes wrong, it's usually during the first trimester.

RITA   You researched miscarriage?

DEL   Only a few paragraphs...

RITA   How could you? Just thinking about it can…. They've scheduled an ultrasound for this afternoon.

DEL   I'll go with you. It's going to be alright. It's the middle of the fourth month. We should be free and clear.

RITA   Zee says don't worry. But that's sort of her job.

DEL   No, she's right.

RITA   Didn't you mention this morning that you thought I wasn't growing so much?

DEL   It was just…

RITA   Del, I don't feel pregnant anymore.

Fade to blue.

scene eleven

The same day. DEL furiously cleaning out a cupboard, RITA's still.

DEL   Rita, we don't know for sure. We haven't got any information. We should be at the doctor's office right now.

RITA   Whatever the results, I want to hear it from Zee. Anyway, I don't need to see a doctor. I know what's happening. The technician doing the ultrasound gave it away. She couldn't look me in the eye—

DEL   Don't be so certain.

RITA   It's physically, here, so obvious. I'm not waiting to find out. I'm waiting for… something… I don't know what I'm waiting for.

Door knock. RITA opens it. Enter ZEE.

ZEE   I'm sorry.

DEL   If the baby's dead why doesn't it come out. I thought when you miscarry, you bleed and then the baby comes out. Why doesn't the baby come out?

ZEE   It's not ready. Some wait. Your body's not ready to let it go. I know you went through a lot to get this far.

DEL   But Rita's past the first trimester. And she's never missed a period in her life. She has a great body. Her body wouldn't do this.

ZEE   From what we could see, it looks like the baby's been dead for two weeks now.

RITA   My baby was dead and I didn't even know it? Inside my own body, dead?

ZEE   Rita, it's not uncommon…

RITA   For two weeks.

ZEE   …for the body to take this long. Your doctor will schedule you a D and C with a gynecologist.

RITA   You know how I feel about hospitals.

ZEE   I do know, but if the fetus stays inside too long you risk infection. The appointment is in two weeks.

DEL   And not in ten minutes? I can't believe it. A surgeon who can wait to go in. He's one of a kind.

ZEE   She.

DEL   Surgeons have no gender.

ZEE   We'd have to wait a week or two anyway, until your uterus has shrunk enough to make the procedure safe. If your baby comes out before that and there's no complication, you won't need to go to the hospital.

DEL   A dead baby racing the clock.

RITA   So what am I waiting for?

ZEE   Cramps, contractions, actually.

RITA   Like in birth?

ZEE   Yes. But you'll only dilate half as much. *(RITA turns away.)*

        Fade to blue.

scene twelve

One week later. DEL on the couch, watching baseball. RITA sits down beside her.

RITA   Who's winning?

DEL   They are.

RITA   Well, it's not over 'til the end, or whatever Yogi Bear said.

DEL   It's not over 'til it's over. It was Yogi Berra not Yogi Bear.

RITA   I know. It was a joke. *(pause)* We'll try again.

DEL   How can you even think about it while we're waiting like this?

RITA   I can't think about anything else. I want it. You know how I get when I want something.

DEL   But nothing is working.

RITA   Let's keep going.

DEL   I don't feel ready for any of this.

RITA   We'll be ready.

DEL   Because you want us to be ready?

RITA   That'll help.

DEL   This is making it worse. You shouldn't be taking care of me right now.

RITA   Why, I don't feel physically sick. It's still our baby inside of me and I'm taking care of it. Del, you're slipping away from me.

DEL   I'm not slipping away. But this… project may be too hard.

Fade to blue.

scene thirteen

One week later. RITA's in the bedroom, DEL's on the couch working on her laptop. A late-night talk show plays throughout the scene.

RITA   This must be it. It's here. Del.

DEL   Huh?

RITA   Del, it's here.

DEL   Are you sure?

RITA   It's cramps now not twinges. Call Zee. *(DEL dials.)*

DEL   Page Zee. It's Del and Rita. Thank you.

RITA has a contraction. DEL returns.

RITA   Of course, it's close to midnight. Perfect timing.

RITA has another contraction. The phone rings. DEL picks it up.

DEL   Hello. Yes. Okay. I'll leave the door unlocked. *(hangs up)* She says we'll need towels. What do you need?

RITA   Don't ask me what I need. I don't know what I need. Offer me something. I have to go to the bathroom. *(DEL goes to help her.)* I can't be with anyone. *(goes in, shuts door, passes fetus)* There. So red. I need more towels. *(DEL goes to get towels.)* So much fucking blood. *(She comes out. DEL hands her a towel.)* Where the fuck is Zee?

Fade to blue.

RITA in the bedroom. DEL in the kitchen. ZEE comes out of the bathroom with the fetus wrapped inside a towel.

DEL   What should we do with it?

ZEE   You could look.

DEL   It's a boy.

ZEE   It usually is with a miscarriage.

DEL   Fragile creatures. One leg.

ZEE   There must have been more than that that wasn't quite right.

DEL   We'll bury him. But it's not our house and what about after we leave. Rita? We should bury him, right? *(RITA does not reply.)* Later.

>   *Exit ZEE.*

RITA   We got what we deserved. Messing with nature.

DEL   You don't think what we do is natural.

RITA   We made a baby with a plastic syringe.

DEL   We made a baby with love.

RITA   We're being punished.

DEL   Rita!

RITA   To have a baby like this, out, open, on purpose.

DEL   And what's natural? A cock? How many women really choose that? I'll take a syringe over rape any day.

RITA   We had a son, didn't we?

DEL   Yes.

RITA   Why were we trying?

>   *Slow fade.*

>   *The answering machine is playing.*

—Hi. It's Bev. Carmen told me what happened. We're thinking about you.

—Hi, It's Oona. Rita. Take as much time as you want. The kids miss you but I can hold the fort. We're thinking about you.

—Hi. It's Ada. I'll be over with dinner.

—Hi, Eleanor I just heard. We're thinking about you.

>   *Black.*

>   *End of Act One.*

ACT TWO

scene one

DEL and RITA can be seen dancing to a k.d. lang tune. They come roaring through the front door and fix themselves a drink.

DEL Whoa, I love that woman.

RITA But that bar.

DEL Don't those C and W guys get it yet?

RITA One of them put the moves on Bev.

DEL They just don't seem to grasp the social dynamics.

RITA They must have figured it out eventually. Korinne and Ada were practically doing it on the speaker.

DEL *(sarcastic)* Don't you love going into straight bars with new lovers?

RITA They were a little out of control. Do you miss that beginning buzz?

DEL It's for beginners.

RITA What a charge, taking over the room that way. I could see the beer ad of the future. *(in Labatt's mode)* I was over at La Bar. Catching La Country, when while maneuvering past Les Gomers, I spotted.... La Lesbian. I should have tried that tonight. Rochelle would have hit the roof.

DEL She caught you talking bodies, eh? I heard that.

RITA I only said k.d. should get back to dresses so we could see her legs.

DEL You didn't. You wondered what's under her jodhpurs.

RITA I'd like to help her off with her cowboy boots.

DEL Recreating male behaviours. How dare you survey women in that heartless, objectifying way. Fuck it! You look great.

RITA I know. I can get into my favourite pants again.

DEL Will I be seeing more of you?

RITA Perhaps.

DEL I hope so. You are a very good time.

RITA I know. *(They get ready for bed under the following dialogue. It is easy and domestic, RITA brushing her hair, DEL brushing her teeth.)* I haven't been much fun have I?

DEL Compared to whom?

RITA Compared to me. My body's never failed me before.

DEL It never failed me either.

RITA After the miscarriage, everything shut down. I wasn't hungry. I had no intense sensations. The juice was gone. Now my body's opened up. And I want to try again. I miss being pregnant, but I keep seeing that deep red water and I don't know if it was fluke or if there's a flaw in me.

DEL It was not a flaw in you, Rita. It was nature taking care of business.

RITA But if I don't try, I'll never know. I couldn't bear that. I work with other people's kids every day. I want a child of my own. And look at all those cards and notes we got.

DEL I didn't know we'd told so many people.

RITA You did. Ms. Communications.

DEL No, you had that glow. It told everybody within ten feet of you.

RITA This baby meant a lot to people. It makes me feel that we're part of something. They think I can do it. I have to try. I got my period today. That makes three.

DEL It's been calm here.

RITA Yes. But it's as if we've gone somewhere, a new house or something, and forgot to take something with us. Zee says the donor's willing.

DEL I guess we should find out what Marge has been up to. And the lesbian nation.

Fade to blue.

scene two

RITA's reading People *magazine. Enter DEL from outside with a carton of milk.*

DEL Ho, ho, holier-than-thou. *(displays* People*)* What's the scoop?

RITA Princess Caroline's tragedies.

DEL Anything on her sister?

RITA How did you know?

DEL Let's hear it.

RITA "Princess Stephanie has fed a tabloid frenzy by breaking off her engagement and last month vamping on the beach in an erotic embrace with a girlfriend."

DEL Yes! You never believe me.

Doorbell.

I'm nervous. Even more than I was that first time.

RITA   I know what you mean.

DEL   I keep making every detail significant.

RITA   Like everything's an omen.

> *They open the door. Enter MARGE with bottle. She has a sweatband on her head and on both arms.*

MARGE   I am converted. Tennis.

DEL   You're kidding.

MARGE   Martina.

RITA   Seriously?

MARGE   I was out of the room and someone had it on. Two different voices grunting. Huh. Huh. I was mesmerized. I got some videos now. Did you see her win Wimbledon in 1990?

DEL   Yes, I wrote a long column on it actually.

MARGE   She threw her hands up in the air and her racket away, and then leaped over the first row of spectators. Heads turned to follow her movements. Climbing, climbing. With every step she came closer to that moment when she would be making history.

DEL   She already made history by winning it.

MARGE   To that moment when she would be face to face with her girlfriend. You were watching it.

RITA   Oh, Del made sure of that.

MARGE   And then, the embrace. Better than the hotel room scene in "Desert Hearts". Better than CJ and her latest. Better even than "Silkwood", when Cher put Meryl Streep's bathrobe belt in her mouth. Better not keep that wad waiting. I know you've been having a hard time but... I'm glad I could tell you that you were on the money as far as Martina is concerned.

> *Exit.*

RITA   Very low-key you were over that tiny victory.

DEL   Well, I don't like to gloat.

RITA   Very cool. Especially since you practically brought the house down with every step Martina took into the stands. Yes! Yes! Rita! She's going to do it. Yes!

DEL   And the clinch. It was something. You just don't get that kind of drama every day.

RITA   But honey, she and Judy broke up last year and now they're fighting over money.

DEL   Details.

RITA   Breaking up is not a detail.

DEL   It doesn't take away from that left arm of Martina's.

RITA   Right now I want to know about your thumb.

DEL   My thumb is poised.

> *Fade to black.*

scene three

> *A maternity store changing cubicle. RITA holds a dress up against herself.*

RITA   Oh would you look at this. Who designs these things? They lay the frills on your shoulders or around your neck, anything to draw attention away from your belly. I look like the baby.

SALES CLERK   *(offstage)* What colours does your husband like?

RITA   I don't have a husband.

SALES CLERK   I'm so sorry.

RITA   It's alright, really. I prefer it that way.

SALES CLERK   You're brave to try to do it by yourself.

RITA   I'm not a single mother.

SALES CLERK   Oh. Did you try the other one on?

RITA   Never mind.

> *Fade to black.*
>
> *Transition.*
>
> *The answering machine is playing.*

—Hi, Del, it's Carol from the university student council. We're getting set for your lecture on the changing family. REAL women will be there in full force and there'll be media for days. If you have any questions call me at 595-1411.

—Hell Rita, it's Mum. Oh, I hate these machines. I was over at the children's store and I saw something really wonderful. You will let your baby wear pink won't you? I mean if it's a girl.

scene four

DEL is in the bedroom skimming chapter headings in Pregnancy in Childbirth, *reading aloud to herself.*

DEL   Becoming A Father. Preparing For Twins. Pregnancy and Sexuality. *(flips to a chapter, skimming, and alights)* Increased sexual desire. "Many women feel less sexually inhibited during pregnancy because they don't have to worry about birth control." Many men have trouble during sex because they are afraid the baby will bite their penis. Late Second Trimester. *(reading)* "A major reason why pregnant women feel an increased desire for sex is because a pregnant woman's body state is the same as the state of sexual arousal." Excellent. "You will be surprised, somewhat embarrassed by the intensity of your response.

Knock at the door.

RITA   Will you open the door, my hands are full.

DEL   Will I? *(DEL opens the door.)* Welcome to heart of the second trimester.

Enter RITA, obviously pregnant with her arms full of groceries.

RITA   Dykes don't smile at me anymore. *(She goes to the kitchen to unpack.)*

DEL   What?

RITA   On the street. You know you see a nice, lesbian-looking woman, and you smile at her…

DEL   What?

RITA   And you get a little smile back. It used to work. I'd grin a little and get one back, you know just that flicker of recognition. But now—nothing. The only ones who smile at me are the lunatics picketing Morgentaler's clinic. You warned me.

DEL   I did?

RITA   You didn't want to get pregnant because you didn't want anyone to suspect even for a second that you were heterosexual.

DEL   It'll only be for a few months.

RITA   Del, then we'll have the baby. Do you think that's gonna make us look like butch of the year? Besides, when you're with the baby, they're gonna think you're straight too.

DEL   We'll be together with the baby. Confusing everybody. This is subversive work. Have you read this? You are in the heart of the second trimester. "The second trimester is the time when most women feel increased eroticism."

RITA   And can you tell me please who designs pregnancy clothes? I was everywhere, from the Ritz to the pits and there is nothing to wear.

DEL "You may feel overwhelmed and perhaps frightened by your new sexual appetites."

RITA Kitsinger says the pushing stage in labour is orgasmic.

DEL I'm not going to wait until then. Listen to this. "The first orgasm may go on longer than you've experienced before or, you may have an additional orgasm on the heels of the first one or, you may still feel aroused after the first orgasm and want to continue energetic lovemaking." Can you wait?

RITA I don't know.

DEL It sounds to me like something worth pursuing.

RITA Zee says it's time for us to check into pre-natal classes.

DEL I'll go out of my mind. Half a dozen tumescent women in an advanced state of eroticism.

RITA And their male partners.

DEL What?

RITA There aren't enough pregnant lesbians for a whole class.

DEL Well then we can't go.

RITA We can't just not go. Zee is our midwife.

DEL You know how I feel about group gropes.

RITA You won't have to touch anyone but me.

DEL Exactly, you and I will be touching. And we have to breathe, don't we? In front of people we don't know?

RITA Del, we don't want to be invisible.

DEL You new lesbians. You want to flaunt everything.

RITA Didn't you just say we would be confusing everybody? Subversive work?

DEL But this is… intimate.

RITA No, it's basic. A baby, a child, is going to be in this house. With us. If we don't like being lesbians together…

DEL I do. That's what I'm trying to tell you.

RITA Umm. Better cookies. Melt in the mouth. Know why?

DEL Why?

RITA Butter melts at body temperature. And body temperature's high in pregnancy. *(moves to kiss DEL)*

DEL   You have crumbs in your mouth.

　　　　Fade to black.

scene five

　　　　A pre-natal class.

ZEE   Early labour can last up to 24 hours. A lot of women like a nice warm bath during these early stages. Take it slow. You don't have to take a bath, just consider it a good relaxing option. Ernie?

DEL   Listen to him. Never trust a guy in a peach sweatshirt.

RITA   He's still pressuring Erica into having a home birth.

DEL   He just called me Daddy Del.

RITA   I heard him.

ZEE   Yes, a partner could try that, but women in labour aren't usually interested in food. What, James?

DEL   There's two of them. Feminist men. Next thing you know they'll call themselves lesbians because they sleep with women.

ZEE   Just before you start to push, you'll go through the stage called transition. The contractions will be getting heavy by now. They'll take over. Your body will know what to do. Let the sounds drop down and through. Remember—an open mouth is an open vagina. *(She demonstrates the sounds of labouring.)* Huhh. Huhh. Huhh. Huhh.

RITA   Oh wow. I hope I'll feel relaxed enough to do that.

DEL   I think you will. You can get pretty relaxed.

ZEE   Huhh Huhh… Erica, make whatever noises you want. You'll find your own voice. Don't make any if you don't feel like it. Huhh. Huhh.

RITA   Why aren't they teaching us to breathe?

DEL   Don't they hypnotize you or something, to get you to focus.

ZEE   Transition is the time when birthing mothers can get really anxious and begin to lose faith in their own abilities. They can get pretty bitchy. Women have been known to say some wild things, so partners, be prepared.

DEL   I can't wait to hear what you'll come up with.

RITA   Just don't tell me any jokes.

ZEE   I was at one wonderful birth when the woman in labour started crawling on her hands and knees bellowing through the contraction, "Adoption… is…

the… best… option." And after the contraction she said, "You know people say giving birth is a psycho-sexual experience. Makes you wonder what kind of sex they're having." Partners, I have a little exercise for you to ease some of the tension.

DEL   Here we go.

ZEE   Think about how to touch your partner in a way that you think is supportive, but not intrusive.

DEL   We have to touch each other.

RITA   Come on, try it.

DEL   We'll practice at home.

RITA   Where would you touch me?

DEL   *(hand on RITA's head)* Here I think.

RITA   Gently, now.

ZEE   Good. Take you time. Yes, Ernie. Nipple stimulation can help contractions along, but it's not usually needed in transition. Okay, our time is almost up. Next week we'll work on pushing and breastfeeding.

DEL   Oh boy.

ZEE   I'm staying around for a few minutes if you have any questions.

RITA   There. That's good. 'Night, James *(DEL's hands fly away from RITA's head.)*

ZEE   How're you doing?

DEL   He called me Daddy Del.

ZEE   I think he was just trying to be friendly. At least none of the men came on to you.

DEL   You sure do a realistic impression of labour.

ZEE   Intense, eh?

RITA   It seems so overwhelming. I thought you were supposed to focus.

ZEE   You'll focus alright. Your body will see to that. But it's hard to imagine. To trust your own body is a big thing to ask of people. That's why we show 'em.

ZEE   Goodnight, Erica.

RITA   Goodnight, Ernie.

DEL   *(out the door)* Yo, Ernie. Congratulations on making home birth the new macho terrain.

Fade to black.

scene six

DEL has a laptop on the kitchen table, papers and paraphernalia spread all over the couch. She's reading her words, public speaking style.

DEL   "The language of birthing procedures imbues the medical practitioner, usually male, with powers he in fact can never have. Doctors do not deliver babies. Women birth them. Indeed, physiologically speaking, most men would cave in if they experienced the intensity of a single menstrual cramp." God, I'm good. Just another 500 brilliant bytes, and I'll come in under the wire.

RITA enters and goes to the fridge for ice cream.

DEL   Aren't you going to work?

RITA   No. Zee's coming.

DEL   Oh shit.

RITA   We'll go into our room.

DEL   Can't she come another time?

RITA   No. *(She begins clearing the couch.)*

DEL   What are you doing?

RITA   I'm clearing the mess so that I can sit on our couch.

DEL   But it's all organized. I can't have things moved around when I'm on deadline. *(DEL goes back to work. RITA picks up another of the clippings.)* Put it down.

RITA   *(RITA takes her time finding something to eat, rummaging, banging cupboards, etc., all distracting to DEL. She pulls out some ice cream, and takes her time eating it. She sits on the floor and does some kegels.)* Do you think you'll ever write about miscarriage?

DEL   No.

RITA   Not right this moment. But we've been through it.

DEL   I don't want to go through it again.

RITA   Nobody talks about it much. It wasn't until it happened to me that other women told me it happened to them. You don't have to use the first person or anything radical like that.

DEL   You don't even write. How is it you get to tell me what to put on paper.

RITA   Because I read.

RITA heads for the bathroom.

The phone rings.

DEL   Rita, will you…

RITA   Del, will you get that? *(She exits to the bathroom.)*

DEL   I guess. *(picks up the phone)* Hello. Yes, operator. This is Dolores. Mother… fine…. Yes, I'm fine…. Work's fine…. No, I can't do the lecture tour this year…. Because Rita's…. That's nice for Dad…. Look, he thinks I'm still fifteen and that Rita and I do our homework together…. It's not a lifestyle, it's our life…. You always tell me what Dad thinks. What do you think?… Hello…. Mother, are you there?… Look, I'm writing to deadline. Can I call you back? Great. Sure. Bye. *(She hangs up and goes back to the laptop. The doorbell rings.)* Rita, Zee's here.

   RITA opens the door.

RITA   Marge!

MARGE   I've gotten into journalism. Sperm carrying is not really a full-time thing.

RITA   That's too bad.

MARGE   I want to show you something. I wrote this article on the dykes with tykes brunch.

DEL   Don't you have a phone?

MARGE   It's for a newsletter I'm launching.

DEL   I haven't time for this.

MARGE   I was counting on your opinion. You're sort of a role model for me.

DEL   I'll give you five minutes. *(She exits to the bedroom with the article.)*

MARGE   You'll come to the dykes with tykes brunch won't you?

RITA   How many women go?

MARGE   More every day. And after my article it'll be standing room only. *(She clears the papers from the couch and makes herself comfortable.)* Getting ready for the B-day eh? I have a friend who has a great birthing stool. It's from Holland.

RITA   Thanks, but I'm going to the hospital.

MARGE   How can you go into the medical military after all this?

RITA   Unfortunately, my doctor can't attend a home birth.

MARGE   What do you need the doctor for?

RITA   Excuse me. *(She leaves. DEL returns to the sight of a cleared couch.)*

DEL   Not bad. Too personal. I've marked the grammatical errors. *(goes back to the laptop and continues working)*

MARGE   Grammatical errors? Grammar is a patriarchal straitjacket. We have to shatter the literary chains that have muzzled women for so long. This is a revolutionary new form.

DEL   The confessional's been around since The Inquisition.

MARGE   That's when they burned women, isn't it?

DEL   Not for splitting infinitives.

MARGE   Then show me how it's done. Give us your story for the newsletter. Sperm search, pregnancy, everything. All grammatically perfect.

DEL   I don't do human interest.

MARGE   Why not? The personal is political, haven't you heard? "I feel" are the bravest words ever to hit the page. You can't make change unless you lay yourself on the line. But you wouldn't know that. You're too out of touch. *(DEL finally looks up.)* You're living a revolution and you're not gonna tell anybody. *(exit)*

> *RITA returns and settles down.*

RITA   Just think, when the baby's born, I'll be home for six whole months.

> *Fade to blue.*

> *Transition.*

Del, come here. *(places DEL's hand on her belly)* She was moving around like crazy just a second ago. Honest. *(DEL moves her hand.)* Oh, you missed it.

DEL   Give me a break.

> *Fade to blue.*

scene seven

> *DEL is struggling with one of those seats that slips on to the table. She's trying to pull it off while she's on the phone.*

DEL   You'll never believe it. It took me 45 minutes to put this contraption together and now I can't get the damn thing off. I should have agreed to buy a new one. Then I'd have instruction... Bev, you're kidding. When can I see it? Oh, here comes Rita. Talk to you later. Rita!

> *Enter RITA and another hugely pregnant woman through the front door. they are laden with shopping bags.*

RITA   Put them near the couch.

DEL   And...

ERICA   Erica, from the pre-natal class.

DEL   Erica.

RITA   I was over at Erica's picking up some clothes.

DEL   With some results I see.

ERICA   I have three sisters. They've been handing down to me for years.

RITA   Then we went out on the town.

DEL   Shopping doesn't qualify as nesting, you know.

RITA   This stuff isn't new.

ERICA   We hit every second hand store in the city. What a great place. Mind if I look around?

RITA   Sure. It's small, so it gets messy.

DEL   She's looking at our bedroom.

RITA   Ssh.

DEL   Listen, Bev called.

ERICA   Great colour on the walls. That the kind of colour I'd paint the baby's room but Ernie wouldn't go for it. Where are you going to put the baby?

DEL   We'll keep it with us for a while.

ERICA   *(pausing at the Georgia O'Keefe)* What a gorgeous picture. It looks like…. It's a great colour.

RITA   Let me show you these. I took the labels off and sewed on stars.

ERICA   Took the labels off? They'll lose their resale value.

RITA   Oh, I'd never sell them. I'll pass them on to friends.

ERICA   Aren't these Roots things darling?

RITA   With the polka dots. Fantastic.

ERICA   These No No No shirts are great too. I have to pee. You know how it is. Every half hour my back teeth are swimming.

RITA   Don't I know it. Over there.

We need some ice cream.

ERICA   Yes, we do.

       Exit ERICA.

DEL   Bev called. She says Madonna deep kisses a woman in her new video. Do you think she might be…

RITA   I think she likes the attention. Last time she was fucking Jesus for Pepsi.

DEL   And is she not Catholic to the core!? Add it up. She and that gal pal comic get close on David Letterman.

RITA   They were just trying to fake him out.

DEL   And there they were again in "Truth or Dare". You know where she found that guy for the "Papa Don't Preach" video? On the set of "Desert Hearts". And what was she doing on the set of "Desert Hearts"?

RITA   Picking up the only guy there.

DEL   Bev saw the video last night and says Madonna look like she's into it. Bev, genius, has it on tape. She freeze-framed it and got a full view of her tongue.

RITA   Really? *(ERICA comes back down.)*

ERICA   Oh, I love those old-fashioned tubs. I want one. Big enough for two, I bet.

RITA   Three, actually.

ERICA   I haven't fit into our tub in months.

RITA   Have you seen Madonna's new movie? Del thinks she is a lesbian.

ERICA   Well, I don't like to label.

RITA   We don't want her anyway.

DEL   I do.

RITA   Ice cream?

ERICA   Yes, please.

RITA   These padders are great.

DEL   Our baby already has more shoes than I do.

RITA   That is not true.

DEL   Count them. The sandals, the red runners, the white runners, the high tops, the slip-ons, the slip-ons with the stars. Whereas all I have is black, the brown…

RITA   The loafers.

DEL   They were given to me. I didn't buy them.

RITA   Well, our baby didn't buy any of these.

ERICA   Are you hoping it's a girl?

DEL   No.

RITA   Yes.

ERICA   Ever thought about what's going to happen if it's a boy?

DEL   Never.

RITA   You don't need men at home to know who you are.

ERICA   No shit. We were raised at home by my aunt and my mother.

RITA   Two women. Hey, that's neat.

ERICA   Can I ask you a question? What if she's a girl? Do you hope she'll end up gay?

DEL   My parents were straight and look at me.

RITA   We hope she finds someone to love.

ERICA   But what if she asks about her father?

DEL   We'll tell her the truth. She doesn't have one.

ERICA   Oh, but she'll be curious.

DEL   About what? I don't get all this biological roots stuff.

ERICA   Yeah, but you're in an unusual situation. Are you giving your child an even break?

DEL   Who gives their kid an even break. How's Ernie?

ERICA   It took me ten years to find a straight guy my age who wants to have a family. Do you know how hard that is? I don't think things can change unless men get involved…

DEL   We'll manage without.

ERICA   I don't mean here.

RITA   I know what you mean. We make sure half the workers in the daycare are men.

DEL   Many of them are gay.

ERICA   Really!

DEL   Why, you wouldn't trust your kid with a gay man?

ERICA   It's not that. I just never imagine gay men interested in kids…. It's different for gay women.

DEL   Lesbians.

ERICA   Lesbians. (*pause*)

RITA   Have you been doing those kegel exercises?

ERICA   I don't know why the books say you can do them anywhere. I was doing them in the car and almost had an accident.

RITA   Strengthening the pelvic floor. It takes concentration. Ever tried kegels while you're peeing? They say that's the best way to get precision control.

ERICA   I tried them during sex. Ernie really liked it. You know men.... You know my ligaments down here feel so weird.

> *DEL tries to get the seat off the table.*

RITA   They're loosening.

ERICA   Making way for the miracle creature. I feel like I'm completely insulated. Wrapped up.

RITA   Like in a cocoon.

DEL   Does anybody know how to get this damn thing off the table?

ERICA   Lift it.

> *DEL does and it eases right off.*
>
> *Fade to black.*

scene eight

> *The living room is covered with gift wrap and shower gifts. RITA is at the front door, wearing a cap of bows and ribbon waving goodbye. DEL is cleaning up.*

RITA   'Night Eleanor. Thanks Rochelle. Have a good time at the cabin, you guys. Wish we could go. See you at the birth, Audra, ha, ha. *(comes back in)* What a fabulous day. I had a great time. Thanks, Del.

DEL   You're welcome.

RITA   Now here's an item. *(picks up the breast pump)* Pump, pump, pump the volume. GENTLE EXPRESSIONS. Battery Operated Breast Pump and Feeding System. Personal Comfort Control Valve. Intermittent suction release for rhythmic suction, unique training cup. Soft tease adapter! One Hand Operation!? *(turns it on)* And it vibrates.

DEL   Go nuts, Rita. *(RITA takes the hat and puts it on her own head.)* Ow.

RITA   This is where recycling began. What a haul. What a party.

DEL   It's a party wherever you take your clothes off.

RITA   It was Ada who snapped the button off my shirt.

DEL   And it was pure joy watching the community line up to get their hands on your belly.

RITA   I love that.

DEL   I noticed.

RITA   Oh that's just the physical part.

DEL   As in—I had an affair but it was just physical.

RITA   As in it feels good to be pregnant and confident. Don't you thing I deserve that?

DEL   Absolutely.

RITA   I feel like this baby's in here for keeps now. I've stopped worrying all the time about bleeding.

DEL   I'm aware that it's been hard for you.

RITA   So I want to enjoy my body, now. I'm pregnant.

DEL   No shit.

RITA   What's the matter, media star? Not getting enough attention?

DEL   Hey, I get lots of attention. I go to the hospital with you, and they ask, "Are you the sister?" "No, I'm her partner." "So you're the labour coach." "No, I'm her partner." I go to get the infant car seat and they say, "Isn't it a little early to be looking for a car seat?" and I say, "I'm going to be a mother in about a month." But who am I kidding? It's your body. You have the investment. You have the biological bond.

RITA   My situation isn't exactly mainstream.

DEL   Maybe. But at least you'll be a mother. Like five billion others. There are thousands of manuals telling you how to be pregnant. They chart every hormonal level, you blood temperature, how much to eat and when, how to breastfeed, how to care for your nurturing body. There's no manual for me. What am I supposed to feel? I can't even see myself in the picture.

RITA   Well, you better try. It'll be your baby too.

DEL   Oh yeah. Audra seemed the think it was hers. Or Rochelle's. Or Ada's. "Our baby, Our baby" they kept saying. "I can't wait for our baby to be born."

RITA   Why didn't you say something instead of stewing like this?

DEL   And spoil the solidarity of your shower. What could I say?

RITA   Hard up for words? That's a riot coming from you.

DEL   There aren't any words. You can walk into a dyke bar or a meeting or anywhere and your body makes a statement. I don't have any way to make a statement.

RITA   Write about it.

DEL   I'm sorry but I don't think this problem can be solved on the front page of the Life section. Besides, after the baby's born I'll probably never write again. My life will be taken over by a baby I'll never see because it's being passed around the greater women's collective. And what will it call me, Daddy Del?

RITA   Wait 'till I hear "my mother the dyke." How do you think that'll make me feel.

DEL   But you chose this. It was your idea. *(pause)*

RITA   Do you want this baby? *(silence)* Del?

DEL   Well, we don't have a helluva a lot of choice now, do we?

RITA   Is that your answer?

DEL   We don't, do we?

RITA   Del, I can't do this alone. I thought once I could but I can't say that anymore.

DEL   Well you don't have to do it alone. You are a community treasure.

RITA   This isn't a fucking community baby. It's ours. We created it. We'll be living with it. Not Eleanor, or Audra, or Ada. It's just us. Listen to me. I spent the day with people I'm close to, women I love, but they haven't a clue. My straight friends had theirs fifteen years ago. Erica doesn't like to label, and our dyke friends had their kids before they came out and think we're out of our minds.

DEL   They're probably right. But you're a pioneer.

RITA   I don't want to be a pioneer. I wanted to have a baby and now I am. I wish I had friends who were going through this too. My mother used to go to the Honey Dew coffee shop with her girlfriends and jiggle the strollers. I'm not going to have that. We'll be going over to Eleanor and Audra's and our kid will say, "Are there going to be any kids there?" What are we going to say? What are we going to do?

DEL   Socialize with Ernie and Erica.

RITA   See what I mean? We're going to be on our own, the three of us.

DEL   Yes.

RITA   No chance to change our minds now.

DEL   No chance.

   Fade to blue.

scene nine

RITA is sitting in the bedroom, hands on her belly. Enter DEL.

DEL   You're slipping into that fecund void.

RITA   I like it there.

DEL   I miss you.

RITA   Ever wish it was you?

DEL   I don't want to be pregnant. I want to be close to this kid, though. He'll be crazy about you. You don't have to worry about that. The body bond.

RITA   It'll only be for about a year.

DEL   I think you always feel that way about your mother.

RITA   You'll be the mother.

DEL   Maybe we just never forget that first year. He'll love you for that unconditional embrace.

RITA   She'll love you for being there.

DEL   He'll love you because you can think up a game for everything.

RITA   She'll love you because you can explain things simply.

DEL   He'll hate us both because we're lesbians.

RITA   No, no she won't. That too simple. She'll hate us for some reason we can't even dream of.

> *DEL's hand is on RITA's belly. She feels movement.*
>
> *Fade to blue.*

scene ten

DEL is writing a speech, trying it out loud as before. While she's doing this, RITA is getting labour sensations. Their positions on stage, like their line at the end of the scene, should mirror their positions at the beginning of ACT ONE scene thirteen, just before the miscarriage.

DEL   Most people are shunted into the family by social conditioning that begins at day one, creating a situation in which prospective parents do not think very much, if at all, about why they marry and why they have children. They must do it. This is very dangerous. *(tries again)*

Because women get pressured into the family, they often stay in living situations that aren't safe for them. *(tries again)*

Feminists think the family is really vital, but which family? Not the one defined by frustration and violence and control. We're working on something quite different. I feel passionately about this. *(crumples the paper)*

RITA   *(to herself)* This must be it. *(She moves to the doorway. She can hear DEL.)*

DEL   My lover and I are going to have a baby. She's pregnant. *(goes to laptop and types)* Some of you may find this hard to imagine. It takes a lot for a random person to admit they're looking at a lesbian. A pregnant lesbian stretches things—especially my t-shirts.

Rita and I think that our kid'll want to know how she was created. We'll tell her where she came from. She—or he—will also know why—which, when you think about it, is probably more than a lot of kids can say.

Our baby doesn't have a father, or even a father substitute. I'm not Daddy Del. I'm a woman and that's how I want it. I'm a woman who loves a woman and we're going to have a baby. I'm going to be a mother.

RITA   Del.

DEL   Yeah.

RITA   It's here.

DEL   Are you sure?

RITA   Yeah. It's cramps now not twinges. Call Zee.

Contraction. They lean into it together.

Fade to finis.

Difference of Latitude

Lisa Walter

Introduction:
Difference of Latitude

The sixth play, Toronto-based writer, Lisa Walter's *Difference of Latitude* (1994), turns to the past to look for new ways to bring hidden lesbian experience into representation. As unnamable, Walter's lesbian protagonists can appear only as "hallucinations within the Symbolic," but, as such, can, nonetheless, serve the valuable purpose of exposing the Symbolic as a "male imaginary" that paradoxically only tolerates a lesbian presence if she remains unrealized. [1] Walter wrote *Difference of Latitude* after being inspired by the real-life accounts of nineteenth-century women who had carried on successful careers as military men over extended periods of time. Finding her models in the true accounts in *Seafaring Women* and *Amazons and Military Maids,* she creates a composite character, Frances, who arranges to be pressed into service and sent off to serve in the War of 1812 as a mizzen-man on His Majesty's frigate *Courageous.* Starting out with a series of scenes in which Frances plans her escape from the suffocating boredom of the gentlewoman's drawing-room existence she is condemned to, the setting then shifts to the sharply contrasting rough life of the sailor at sea. Written for a cast of two with the character Frances transforming into the toughened sailor "Nobbie," and the other main character, the very feminine Rose, taking all the other roles of the seasoned sailor Slinger and the cabin boy Daisy, the play's economic doubling of parts has the effect of heightening the theatrical impact in several ways. In undercutting any sustained realism, it strengthens Walter's dominant motif that gender is performative. Since the two roles are written for female performers, their ability to transform themselves into the various male roles either by transitioning, in the case of Frances, or transvesting, in the case of Rose, keeps the spectators alert to the possibilities and potential dangers involved in practicing gender deception.

Walter sets up Frances's transition to Nobbie slowly and deliberately in the first six scenes by showing her various states of rebellion and her gradual winning over of the more conventional Rose as an ally. Rose also gets lessons in performing gender roles when she finds that putting Frances in the role of Beatrice to her Benedict in their amateur theatrical fails to elicit a ladylike performance from Frances. When Rose asks, "Who's the instructor, you or I?," Frances's response, "It depends on the subject" suggests the kind of give and take that Walter is setting up to problematize fixed gender roles. The passionate kiss that Frances gives to Rose when they reverse the roles goes further in drawing attention to the power of theatrical institutions to shape or break with expected responses. The culminating point of these early scenes arrives when Frances tries on her male disguise and stands in the dark to see if Rose will be able to see through it. At this moment, she also invites the audience to make the same judgment call as to whether she can pass. It is telling that it is Rose who signals that she understands that Frances's successful transition to male will depend on "his" acquiring all the important markers of masculinity. Her surprise offer of a stolen pair of trousers to complete "his" outfit, and her willingness to accompany "him" into town dressed as "his" female companion help to put "his" plan to disappear into a new identity into effect.

The setting now switches abruptly to the deck of the *Courageous* where a series of scenes will initiate "Nobbie" into the harsh realities of naval life. Just as the earlier scenes trace the progressive withdrawal of Frances from the social inscription of a leisured upper-class woman, these scenes enact his rebirth as common sailor whose existence depends on his ability to perform hard labour. The delicate submissive gestures that Frances fails to exhibit with Rose are now shown to be dangerously irrelevant in a new system of power relations. Represented as courageous to the point of being foolhardy, Frances's attempt to untie the top masts in a heavy storm marks her successful passage into her new male identity. In reversing her failure to pass as a gentlewoman, "Nobbie's" survival as a male brings into focus Walter's problem- atizing of the rigid rules governing the division of labour along gendered lines. She now complicates the discourse by showing how doubly difficult it is for "Nobbie" to outperform her male counterparts and conceal the evidence that she has a female body. "Nobbie's" successful subterfuge is also challenged by the introduction of another androgynous seafarer, the Captain's "girl", Daisy. When Daisy recognizes that she is female, "Nobbie" finds herself having to face her counter-image in the cross- dressed boy. When Daisy appeals to him to provide the Captain with her "real" female sexual services, Nobbie can only threaten to kill Daisy if she gives her impersonation away. However, this threat of exposure highlights the precariousness of his position as someone whose male privilege could be stripped away simply by having her clothing removed.

To mark "Nobbie's" increasing awareness that he is still trapped within gendered boundaries, Walter now switches the setting back to England. By juxtaposing scenes in which "Nobbie" flashes back to her rejection of Rose's love for her, she forces us to think about the ways in which we are also constrained in our expressions of sexual desire. When the Rose-Frances plot resumes with the lovemaking scene which follows their exhilarating trip to town, it is Rose who initiates it. Caught up in the rush of power that she feels in the company of the male Frances, Rose is overcome with sexual desire. Although Frances makes love to her, she finds it impossible to acknowledge that she and Rose could be partners given that they are both women: "You're confusing me with the clothing. You think that if I'm in men's clothes I must want what a man does" (251).

Rose's practical counsel "To stay exactly as you are... as long as you can join in the masquerade from time to time" (244) echoes in Frances's ears in the only solo scene when "Nobbie" faces the terrifying aloneness which her gender explorations have brought her to. Her attempts to find her "difference of latitude" all come down to recognizing that she cannot escape from the vulnerability which having a female body reduces her to. Sent to the Captain because "she knows her letters," she is forced to defend herself with a marlinspike to stop his sexual assault. Saved from prosecution because, as "Nobbie" she is allowed to protect herself, her need to stop his hands in time is made even more urgent by the fact that if he finds out that she is female, she will have no rights at all.

This critical event, followed up by her discovery that Daisy has been murdered and thrown overboard by the homophobic crew, break down her bravado, and eventually force her to reveal her biological sex. Beaten by Slinger, raped by the Captain and imprisoned in the hold to await execution, Frances now comes to terms with her self-identification and owns her lesbian desire for Rose. The love letter that she dictates to Slinger is spoken aloud to him as the ship is broken up by a storm. Walter's sensationalized portrayal of the tortured end that the lesbian outlaw could expect to face is balanced by a coda in which Rose and Frances are reunited as lovers. By closing with the same lines with which it opened, the play reminds us of the need to rewrite the future in order to bring about change.

Note

[1] Peggy Phelan, Reciting the Citation of Others: or, A Second Introduction," *Acting Out: Feminist Performances,* ed. Lynda Hart and Peggy Phelan (Ann Arbor: U of Michigan P, 1993) 116.

photo by Lucy Snider

Lisa Walter

Bio and Artist's Statement

"What kind of artist are you, anyway?"
—A bewildered friend.

Lisa Walter is female, 37 years of age, and has a prominent scar on her chin. Aliases include: "Lisa Walters" and "*&#?!@." She was last seen in Dominica working for the Ontario Public Service Employees Union/NUPGE on a popular education pilot project entitled *HIV/AIDS and the World of Work*. She is also believed to be responsible for the illustrations in Bread Not Circuses' *Stop Playing Games With Toronto: The People's Anti-Olympic Bid Book*, and banners opposing the rollback of employment standards for Ontario's minimum-wage workers. In an affidavit, an eyewitness claims Ms. Walter attempted to ward off tear gas at the FTAA protests in Quebec City with a balsamic vinegar-soaked bandanna. Theatrical priors include writing *Sold Out* for Tarragon Theatre's Spring Arts Fair, performing in *Oedipus* for Die in Debt and Nightwood Theatre, and stage managing *Summerfolk* for Equity Showcase Theatre. She is often accompanied by a smooth Collie and should be approached with caution.

•

September, 2005.

I had only been *out* for a few years when I sat down in 1994 to write my first play. In Toronto, the community of other-than-heterosexual peoples was bursting with energy: new therapies were providing the first gleam of hope in the fight against AIDS, Pride Day was exploding, and drag kings were a new counterpoint to drag queens. They, accompanied by a resurgence of *butch* fashion, were reheating debates about women who wear manly clothes.

In this fruitful milieu, I was impatient to hear these questions and issues reflected—if only in a brief flicker—in the world around me. I was also intrigued by how war has so often had the effect of creating chasms that women who are intrepid enough can leap into. And though *looking mannish* and *sexual orientation* are very distinct concepts, combining the two gave me the right vehicle for this story of self-invention.

Production Information

Difference of Latitude was first workshopped and presented as a staged reading at Nightwood Theatre's 93/94 Groundswell Festival with the following company:

Ann-Marie MacDonald
Maggie Huculak
Stefanie Samuels

Directed by Alisa Palmer
Dramaturgy by Brian Quirt

·

Difference of Latitude received a workshop production at Buddies in Bad Times Theatre's 4-Play Festival. Toronto, in 1994, with the following company:

FRANCES	Soo Garay
ROSE/SLINGER/DAISY	Julie Stewart

Directed by Sarah Stanley
Set & Costume Design by Dany Lyne
Dramaturged by Brian Quirt
Music by Jamie Stanley

·

A public reading of the final draft was held at the Tarragon Theatre May 1, 1995, with Stephanie Morgenstern as Frances and Diane Flacks as Rose/Slinger/Daisy.

Acknowledgements

Kind thanks to Diane Roberts, Alisa Palmer, Ann-Marie MacDonald, and Rosalind Kerr; thanks also to Sandra Saddy and the Huronia Historical Parks Resource Centre, and the staff at the Marine Museum of Upper Canada and at the Military & Naval Establishment at Penetanguishene.

To Brian Quirt, I must express my debt of gratitude for his unwavering support, gentle questions, and breadth of vision: thank you.

The playwright gratefully acknowledges the support of the Ontario Arts Council.

Characters

Frances

Rose/Slinger/Daisy

Playwright's Note

Although there are four characters in this play, it's written to be performed by two female actors; one taking the role of Frances, and the other playing Rose, Slinger, and Daisy.

Difference of Latitude

England, 1811. A heath in the countryside.

FRANCES   Rose.

ROSE   Frances. You're back.

FRANCES   Yes.

ROSE   Your journey was pleasant?

FRANCES   Tedious.

ROSE   But we're so delighted to have you! We've got a number of lovely soirées and parties planned.

FRANCES   Soirées?

ROSE   In your honour. You'll be radiant, all the young men for miles around will be lining up to meet you. But enough of that—you're weary. Dinner's at eight and we must get you settled in and looking civilized.

FRANCES   You're too kind.

ROSE   Yes, I am.

FRANCES   It's been some time.

ROSE   You must have been fifteen…?

FRANCES   And you would have been fourteen.

ROSE   I've always gone south to visit you since.

FRANCES   You visited the city, not me.

ROSE   The city was more welcoming than you.

FRANCES   I suppose our interests parted as we grew older.

ROSE   Or did one of us simply not grow?

FRANCES   Into a simpering ingénue? Thank God.

ROSE   Your mother was right. She warned me you were willfully immature.

FRANCES   Careful, Rose. Using too many polysyllabic words might damage your intellect.

ROSE   You look so pastoral when you bluster, Frances. It must be that ruddy, working-class glow on your cheeks.

FRANCES   I wouldn't mind a nap before we eat.

ROSE   I'm not surprised, after such a long voyage. I would have shown you your room when you arrived, if you hadn't disappeared from the carriage like that. What a funny thing you are!

FRANCES   I wanted to stretch my legs.

ROSE   Aren't they long enough already?

> *They leave.*

•

> *ROSE's garden. Enter FRANCES running, with a pair of heavy boots wrapped in a shawl. She tears off her shoes and stockings, and hurls them away. She considers trying the boots on, but instead places them near the bench. ROSE enters, unnoticed by FRANCES.*

FRANCES   Freed from bondage, he treads noiselessly along, through forest paths and sweeping meadows. Not the clever fox nor the keen bloodhound hears his approach. Miles of countryside unwind beneath his feet. Sometimes he runs... sometimes he creepeth apace... as swift and as slow as time itself. Suddenly he stands at the foot of the ocean, and waves of possibility lap at his toes... Rose!

ROSE   I'm sorry—

FRANCES   Stop laughing.

ROSE   I know, it's not nice to laugh at people when they're engaged in strange barefoot rituals—are you finished your little game?

FRANCES   It's not a game.

ROSE   Is this what you do at home, take off your shoes and stockings and run around in the garden?

FRANCES   No. It's none of your concern, anyhow.

ROSE   But how can I reform you if I don't root out all your little habits? I must know my subject thoroughly before I can begin to effect a change.

FRANCES   But I've already begun to learn from your example. For instance, I've seen how you couch contempt in a veneer of politeness, and how everyone mistakes that for cleverness.

ROSE   Whereas you mistake childishness for integrity.

FRANCES   At least I make an attempt to have some integrity; your only concern is yourself.

ROSE   It wasn't for myself that I agreed to be your nursemaid for the entire summer.

FRANCES   But you needed something to amuse yourself, didn't you? Someone to sharpen your wit on, to feel superior to?

ROSE   You think I'm selfish, when your foolishness is costing your entire family its reputation?

FRANCES   I'm only responsible for my reputation, not my family's.

ROSE   Well, that's it then.

FRANCES   What is?

ROSE   I can't possibly smooth over your rough spots if your brain is a crater.

FRANCES   If you weren't a girl, I'd slap you right across the face.

ROSE   Go ahead. I'd rather see you shipped to the convent now than have to endure you for the rest of the season.

FRANCES   Thank you, Rose, for a dose of insight. Now I know how I must conduct myself.

ROSE   How?

FRANCES   Badly enough to make your life a misery, but well enough that I'm allowed to remain the entire season in your sweet company.

ROSE   Bah! Who were you pretending to be, anyhow?

FRANCES   What do you mean?

ROSE   When I found you you were referring to yourself as "he."

FRANCES   I wasn't pretending anything, I was reciting. Something. From a novella. I don't suppose you read them. They're far too shocking for the well-bred.

ROSE   Of course I do; I didn't always have you around to illustrate my superiority.

FRANCES   You haven't read this one.

ROSE   Summarize it for me.

FRANCES   Why should I?

ROSE   So I can be certain it's a convent and not a madhouse we should send you to come autumn.

FRANCES   In this story, a person—

ROSE   A man.

FRANCES   Yes, a man; they're not extinct, you know! In this story a man... who was a slave, escapes from his evil captors... and makes his way to the foot of the sea, where he contemplates what it's like to be free.

ROSE   Why did you take your shoes off?

FRANCES It's a symbol, a symbol of freedom.

ROSE He's free of his footwear?

FRANCES In part; he's free of everything, including the nasty ugly pinching shoes his evil mother—masters made him wear.

ROSE You're making this up. It's nonsense.

FRANCES It isn't.

ROSE Free from his shoes? A person can't even walk out of doors without shoes.

FRANCES Of course they can; not only can it be done, it actually feels better.

ROSE Walking without shoes?

FRANCES Yes.

ROSE Prove it.

FRANCES Prove it yourself.

> *ROSE sits; FRANCES removes ROSE's shoes and stockings. ROSE walks about.*

ROSE Do you do this often?

FRANCES I never did until today.

ROSE Ow—I can see why!

> *She sits and pulls on her shoes and stockings.*

It's time for tea. Don't keep us waiting.

> *She leaves. FRANCES waits until she's gone, then crosses to the boots. She makes sure they're well hidden, then exits.*

•

> *ROSE, wearing a men's shirt over her dress, as Benedick from* Much Ado About Nothing. *FRANCES, as Beatrice, with a fan.*

ROSE "Soft and fair, friar. Which is Beatrice?"

FRANCES "I answer to that name. What is your will?"

ROSE Not like that; gracefully, like this.

I'm sure the convent wouldn't be so bad, once you were used to it…

FRANCES Like this? I'm not leaving, Rose. You've sealed your doom.

ROSE We'll see. "Do not you love me?"

FRANCES "Why no; no more than reason."

ROSE   Don't put your hands on your hips. You look like a fishwife. You could turn away coquettishly, *comme ça*. Good Lord.

FRANCES   I don't do this on a regular basis the way you do.

ROSE   No, you slap people instead.

FRANCES   He was rude. If I'd turned coquettishly away, he would have thought I was just teasing.

ROSE   Never you mind what he thinks; he's a baronet.

FRANCES   If a blacksmith asked you if your breasts were real, would you turn coquettishly away?

ROSE   Sssshhh! That's different.

FRANCES   Why?

ROSE   Because I'd never marry a blacksmith!

FRANCES   I'm not going to marry anybody, so I'd just as soon slap a baronet as a blacksmith.

ROSE   Here we go again.

FRANCES   I'm not going to get married and I'm not going to become a nun.

ROSE   Then would you mind telling me exactly what you are going to do?

FRANCES   Something else.

ROSE   Such as?

FRANCES   Go on the stage, perhaps. Wouldn't you all be mortified. I might do it simply to see the looks on your faces.

ROSE   "Why, then your uncle, and the Prince, and Claudio
Have been deceived—they swore you did."

FRANCES   I've lost my place.
    "Do not you love me?"

ROSE   "Troth, no; no more than reason."

FRANCES   "Why, then my cousin, Margaret, and Ursula
Are much deceived; for they did swear you did."

ROSE   "They swore that you were almost sick for me."

FRANCES   "They swore that you were well-nigh dead for me."

ROSE   You can't step up to me like that. Ladies don't do that.

FRANCES   She's different.

ROSE   She's still a lady, though; and ladies don't push gentlemen.

FRANCES   I didn't push you. I simply stepped towards you.

ROSE   As if you were going to push me.

FRANCES   If I'd wanted to push you I would have.

ROSE   "'Tis no such matter! Then you do not love me?"

FRANCES   "No, truly, but in friendly recompense."

ROSE   This is where they give us each other's letters.

FRANCES   Conniving devils.

ROSE   "A miracle! Here's our own hands against our hearts. Come, I will have thee; but, by this light, I take thee for pity."

FRANCES   "I would not deny you; but, by this good day, I yield upon great persuasion, and partly to save your life, for I was told you were in a consumption."

ROSE   "Peace! I will stop your mouth." Then Pedro comes in—

FRANCES   You missed a part.

ROSE   What?

> *FRANCES points in her book. They resume their positions and ROSE kisses FRANCES's hand.*

ROSE   So Pedro—

FRANCES   You can't do it like that.

ROSE   What do you mean?

FRANCES   He says, "I will stop your mouth," and then the stage direction says "Kisses her," so I don't think he kisses her hand.

ROSE   I hardly think it matters.

FRANCES   It does matter. It's the climactic moment of the play—after all their bickering they're finally getting married. He's not going to shake her hand and walk away.

ROSE   Who's the instructor, you or I?

FRANCES   It depends on the subject.

> *ROSE kisses FRANCES.*

A man wouldn't do it like that.

ROSE   That isn't the point of this exercise.

FRANCES   You've been telling me how to act like a lady for the last five acts. I think I should at least get to tell you how to act like a man from time to time, if you're going to presume to play one.

ROSE   You play the man, then.

FRANCES   I thought you'd never ask.

> *ROSE removes the shirt and gives it to FRANCES in exchange for the fan.*

"A miracle! Here's our own hands against our hearts. Come, I will have thee; but, by this light, I take thee for pity."

ROSE   "I would not deny you; but, by this good day, I yield upon great persuasion, and partly to save your life, for I was told you were in a consumption."

FRANCES   "Peace! I will stop your mouth."

> *FRANCES kisses her.*

Then Pedro comes in and he says—

ROSE   And then it's the end of the play.

FRANCES   But there's still—

ROSE   It doesn't matter. I want my things back.

> *FRANCES gives her the book.*

And the shirt.

> *FRANCES removes the shirt and gives it to ROSE.*

We have to go in now. Too much exposure to the sun will coarsen our skin.

FRANCES   Rose—!

ROSE   Now.

> *They go.*

•

> *Night. FRANCES enters with the shirt from the previous scene, a cap, and a lantern. She takes the boots out from their hiding place and changes into the new clothes.*

FRANCES   *(sings)* I had a dream the other night
Lowlands, lowlands away, my chum
I had a dream the other night
Lowlands away.

ROSE   *(off)* Hallo?

> *FRANCES collects her clothing and hides, forgetting the lantern. ROSE enters. She pauses and looks around, and at length sees the lantern.*

Odd.

> *She takes the lantern and leaves.*

FRANCES   She looked right at me, but it was as if I was invisible. I'm untouchable! It won't take much more. When all is complete, then we'll see…. What, I don't know, but we'll see it. Me.

> *She changes back to her regular clothes, bundles her costume, and hides it with the boots before leaving.*

> •

> *Rain. ROSE and FRANCES, sitting indoors with books.*

ROSE   Stop humming. It's driving me to distraction.

What have you done?

FRANCES   What do you mean?

ROSE   I mean what have you done to yourself?

FRANCES   Nothing, I don't know what you're talking about.

ROSE   There's something different about you. You look suspiciously… radiant lying there.

FRANCES   I'm happy.

ROSE   Impossible.

FRANCES   Why?

ROSE   You're always sulking. I've never once seen you look even remotely happy.

FRANCES   Oh.

ROSE   You see? You won't even argue with me anymore.

FRANCES   Oh. Hm.

ROSE   Stop it! It's not polite to be happy when others aren't.

FRANCES   Why aren't you?

ROSE   It's raining, for one thing.

FRANCES   Too much exposure to the sun will coarsen your skin.

ROSE   How amusing.

I shouldn't even be here. I should be in Bath, with all the other young ladies of fashion.

FRANCES   Go, then.

ROSE I can't. I've got guests. Guests upon whom I have to perform a miracle, and transform from scullery maids to ladies-in-waiting.

FRANCES What are they waiting for?

ROSE Ooooh, I'd like to throw my book at you!

FRANCES Do it, if it makes you happy.

ROSE One doesn't throw books at one's guests.

FRANCES You once told me that the definition of good manners is behaving in a way that makes those around you feel comfortable. Is that true?

ROSE I suppose.

FRANCES So if I throw my book at you, it will be good manners for you to throw yours back at me, won't it?

ROSE Don't be ridiculous.

> *FRANCES throws her book. ROSE throws hers back.*

FRANCES Do you feel better now?

ROSE No. Well, a little perhaps.

FRANCES You know where the library is.

ROSE Don't tempt me.

FRANCES Are there many targets?

ROSE Are there books in the library?

FRANCES I thought so.

ROSE You did not.

FRANCES Certainly I did. You're too polite to be sincere.

ROSE People say a lot of silly things without noticing, or at least without seeming to.

FRANCES Why don't you tell them, "That's rubbish!"?

ROSE And wind up in your position? No thank you.

FRANCES I don't think it's any worse than yours. At least I'm not consumed with rage.

ROSE I'm not consumed with rage! It's not a nice day, it's raining, that's all there is to it.

FRANCES Fine.

ROSE Fine.

You're humming again.

FRANCES   Oh, am I?

ROSE   Yes, you are. Stop.

I said stop.

Why do you collect boy's clothing?

You were in the garden the night. I heard a noise and went to investigate, weren't you?

FRANCES   I often go for walks in the evening.

ROSE   Leaving your lantern behind?

FRANCES   That would be silly.

ROSE   Not if you were hiding. If I stumbled upon you and you were wearing boys' clothes, wouldn't you hide?

FRANCES   If I were, perhaps I might. But why would I be?

ROSE   That is what I'm trying to discern. You won't tell me?

FRANCES   I don't know what you're talking about.

ROSE   I'm sorry. I suppose then that you won't want these.

> ROSE *extracts a pair of trousers from under the cushion of her chair.*

FRANCES   Where did you get them?

ROSE   We have a trunk where we keep castaways for our games of charades. That's where the shirt came from as well. Mamma is packing it all up to donate to the church. I daresay someone will want these since you don't.

FRANCES   Wait.

I think I could find a use for them. They look new; there's no sense throwing away a perfectly decent pair of trousers, is there?

ROSE   But what would you do with them?

FRANCES   I'm sure I'll think of something.

ROSE   Confess and they're yours.

Oh well then.

FRANCES   It's a plan.

My plan.

ROSE   I'm listening.

FRANCES   When I have everything together I'm going to go to town one evening dressed like a boy.

ROSE   Why?

FRANCES   I'll only do it once, I promise, if you give me the chance.

ROSE   But everyone will know you're not a boy.

FRANCES   No, they won't.

ROSE   How can you be so certain?

One thing.

FRANCES   Yes?

ROSE   Take me with you.

FRANCES   What?

ROSE   I mean it. You'll look less suspicious with a girl.

FRANCES   Are you joking?

ROSE   No, not at all.

FRANCES   If we're caught—

ROSE   You said you wouldn't be.

FRANCES   But if we were, it would be very serious. Have you ever thought of becoming a nun?

ROSE   Do you want them or don't you?

FRANCES   Very well, then, you can come. But only—and I'm making this absolutely clear—only if you obey me to the letter.

ROSE   Agreed. When do we go?

FRANCES   Some cloudy night, when the world is shrouded in darkness.

ROSE   Tomorrow?

FRANCES   Agreed.

> *ROSE gives her the trousers.*

•

> *FRANCES sleeps.*

ROSE   *(sings)* I had a dream the other night
Lowlands, lowlands away, my chum
I had a dream the other night
Lowlands away.

I dreamt my love came standing by
Lowlands, lowlands away, my chum
Came standing close to my bedside
Lowlands away.

She's sailing o'er the lowland sea
Lowlands, lowlands away, my chum
And will she e'er come home to me?
Lowlands away.

> *She is gone. The gun deck of His Majesty' frigate* Courageous, *38 guns.
> A bosun's call sounds, awakening FRANCES in her hammock. SLINGER
> enters, sees FRANCES and crosses to her.*

SLINGER Outa that.

FRANCES I beg your—

SLINGER That's Sharkey's place. Who are ye?

FRANCES My name's Francis, I'm new.

SLINGER Oh aye? Wher wer ye afore this?

FRANCES In Liverpool; I was—

SLINGER Ay mean what ship?

FRANCES This is my first ship. And I hope it won't be my last. And you are…?

SLINGER So yer not onlie a pup, yer green to boot. What ar wi supposed to do wit ye?

FRANCES The press sergeant seemed desperate for sailors.

SLINGER Saylors, aye, but yer a scrawny green pup of a landsman. An ye come here an sleep in a donkey's breakfast what don't belong te ye?

FRANCES Do you mean the hammock?

SLINGER Ay mean Sharkey's hammock!

FRANCES Ah yes, well you see the gentleman who sold me my… "hard-weather gear" also sold me this hammock. Perhaps your friend exchanged it for a better one…?

SLINGER Do ye know 'penaltie layed out fer hammock-thieves in 'Articles a War?

FRANCES I didn't—

SLINGER "Any man who shall commit 'detestable sin a thieverie of a hammock, shall be sewn into 'said hammock an cast te sea… God love 'im."

FRANCES But I—

SLINGER   Ye didn't wayst anie tyme afore ye commenced yer thievin, did ye? Speak up!

FRANCES   Please, sir, I didn't steal this hammock! I bought it from the purser with the bounty money they gave me for volunteering!

SLINGER   Bountie? Andrew Miller ferbad bountie monie last year!

FRANCES   They offered it to me!

SLINGER   Yer skinked, mate. A confessed hammock-thief an bribe-accepter? Ye'll bi flogged, shot, drawn, quartered, n sunk in yer own thieved beddin when wi reach Cadiz.

FRANCES   Please, sir, I didn't know! The press-sergeant said they needed sailors and they would give eight pounds to any man that would join! Then when I came aboard the mate said I had to buy my gear from the purser and he sold me this hammock! How could I know it still belonged to someone?

SLINGER   Well... ye may bi a bit of a grass-combin' bugger, but ye'v got an honest look te ye... ay might put in a gud werd fer ye wit Captin if...

FRANCES   If what?

SLINGER   If ye give up 'bountie te show ye didn't mean te break 'Naval Code.

FRANCES   But I already spent it.

SLINGER   Well then.

FRANCES   No wait, I can take it out of my savings...

Who are you anyway?

SLINGER   Slinger. Captin a 'fo'c'sle.

FRANCES   With all due respect... are you having me on?

SLINGER   Havin ye—ye piss-eyed, snatch-eatin little fart! Havin ye on? Here am ay, riskin mi bleedin neck fer yer green arse, an ye think aym screwin ye?

He pulls out his marlinspike.

On 'deck, ye bloodie ingrate!

Listen te mi carefullie now. It don't matter none if a mate bi takin ye fer a ride in 'jollie-boat or no; a stiff-bent sayl as yerself is better off playin along. If ye don't, ye might find yerself at 'short end of a long rope.

An don't call mi "sir"!

He leaves her.

The Courageous *gun deck. A storm can be heard battering the ship.*
SLINGER enters, supporting FRANCES, who coughs and gasps.
SLINGER helps her into her hammock.

SLINGER   Easy, boy, yer safe now. Ye stupid bugger.

FRANCES   Thanks.

SLINGER   Yer not bloodie welcome.

He crosses to his hammock and rifles through his belongings. He finds
a dry shirt and changes into it.

Yer damned luckie ye didn't land in 'drink.

FRANCES   Did they get the mast down?

SLINGER   Yeh, they got it down. What in hell wer ye doin on 'foretop anieways?
Yer a mizzen-man.

FRANCES   The mate had his cane out, he was whipping all hands up to take down
that part of the mast...

SLINGER   Topmast. Gale woulda pulled it down otherwise.

FRANCES   I was helping some fellows undo those rope things attached to the
top—

SLINGER   'Shrouds.

FRANCES   —then suddenly there was a crash and everyone vanished, but the
shrouds were still attached. I didn't think they could take the mast down if it
was still fastened at the top, so I kept working at it.

SLINGER   How'd ye get it?

FRANCES   I used my teeth.

SLINGER   Stupid git. Yer gonna lose em all te scurvie anieway, y'in some kinda
hurrie?

FRANCES   I thought they had to be undone.

SLINGER   They did.
Ye'd better get outa them wet rags.

FRANCES   You know, I don't think I have a change of clothes.

SLINGER   What, some hooker run off wit em?

Well, ye can't stay dressed like that.

He starts rifling through his things again.

FRANCES   Oh, no, I mean, I don't have a change of clothes here. They're in my
chest, back there.

> *She coughs violently.*

SLINGER Jesus Murphy.

> *He goes. FRANCES makes sure he's out of sight, then quickly pulls a change of clothes out from her bedding and gets into them. SLINGER arrives back with a steaming wooden pot.*

Ay could't find—

FRANCES Never mind, they were here all along.

What's that?

SLINGER Supper. They was just dishin out.

> *He goes to a table and pulls down some plates and spoons from a shelf above.*

FRANCES I'm starving! Stuck up there, I thought I'd never see another meal.

SLINGER An here y'ar. Calls fer a gilravage.

FRANCES What's that in English?

SLINGER Bein a two-bit hero fer a day dont mean ay aynt gonna knock ye down if ye make smart-ass quips.

A celebration.

> *He serves out two portions of oatmeal.*

FRANCES What is that?

SLINGER Burgoo.

FRANCES Oh my God!

SLINGER Eat, boy. And doñt pick them bugs out, theyr gud fer ye.

FRANCES I would have fallen if you hadn't helped me down. Thanks.

SLINGER Nah.

Ye wer 'sole fella te stick it out up ther, least ay could do was fetch ye down. Mind, ye freeze up like that again aynt no one, nor me included, 's'gonna risk theyr neck fer ye. Must a lost mi bloodie head, goin up fer ye.

FRANCES Thanks.

SLINGER Shut up.

Next tyme ye be worryin a knot, use this stead a yer teeth.

> *He detaches his marlinspike from a thong from his belt and hands it to her.*

FRANCES What is it?

SLINGER   Marlinspike. Keep it on yer belt, then its always ther when ye need it.

FRANCES   You're giving it to me?

SLINGER   Ye ken borrow it till ye get one of yer own.

FRANCES   What will you use?

SLINGER   I ken make another.

FRANCES   Thanks… I'm very grateful.

SLINGER   Yer bloodie nobbie is what.

FRANCES   Slinger… what happened today, it makes me think… if something does happen to me, could I ask you to write to someone for me, to let her know…?

SLINGER   Ay dont know mi letters.

FRANCES   …oh.

SLINGER   Like sum.

But if ye give me 'paper I can try te get it te her.

FRANCES   Could you? I'd be—

If you'd like, I could teach you to write.

SLINGER   Whats a dog want wi letters?

FRANCES   I just thought—as a thank-you—

SLINGER   Ay dont want yer thanks.

FRANCES   Fine.

A bell sounds, eight double-rings.

SLINGER   Tyme fer a doss. It'll be our watch again soon.

FRANCES   I've never been so tired in my life.

They turn into their hammocks.

We're not going to sink in this storm, are we?

SLINGER   This bit of a blow? Nah. Tis naught but a splash next te 'fuilteach—ha! Come Februarie, then wi'll bi swimmin!

•

The bosun's call sounds. SLINGER and FRANCES shake out a sail.

All hands! All hands, out or down, all hands! Livelie there, boys, thers a fair breeze an two leagues from Cadiz! Show a leg ther, out or down! Man 'holiestone!

FRANCES   Flemish sheets!

SLINGER   Hammocks up!

FRANCES   Stomp 'n' go!

SLINGER   *(sings)* When I was a little boy, so mi father told mi—

BOTH   Way haul away, we'll haul away, Joe!

SLINGER   That if ay didn't kiss the girls me lips would turn all moldie—

BOTH   Way haul away, we'll haul away, Joe!

> *A double-ring of a bell. They set to work mending the sail. FRANCES inhales sharply.*

SLINGER   Prick yerself?

FRANCES   No, it's mi hands, look. Mi skin is crackin an every time I bend mi fingers the scabs break open.

SLINGER   That's gud.

FRANCES   Good?

> *Offstage, the sound of a dog, whining and growling.*

SLINGER   Aye. By 'tyme wi bi breakin ice off 'canvas yer fists'll bi gud n tuff. See they get soked in 'brine, keep em from gettin all pussee.

FRANCES   What's wrong wi the dog?

SLINGER   Bin takin wit fits.

FRANCES   How come?

SLINGER   Dont like 'food—how in 'hell shuld ay know?

FRANCES   Can they make im better?

SLINGER   Theyr givin im 'deep-sea cure.

FRANCES   What's that?

> *There is a sudden howl, a pause, a splash. The sound of thrashing water rises then fades. The bosun's call sounds.*

All hands to make sail!

SLINGER   Up 'ratlins ye louse-eaten lard-asses! Up! Up!

FRANCES   Ready ho!

SLINGER   Put helm down!

FRANCES   Helm's a-lee!

SLINGER   Off tacks and sheets!

FRANCES Mains'l haul!

SLINGER Let go and haul!

FRANCES Haul!

SLINGER Haul, boys!

FRANCES Haul!

Three double-rings of the bell. They pull out flasks, which they drink from.

SLINGER Sun's over 'fore-yard.

BOTH Aaah.

FRANCES Do you have a girl?

SLINGER Yeh. Ruth. Shi's mi long-haired chum. Aym a bundle-man.

FRANCES A what?

SLINGER Bundle-man, aym married.

FRANCES Oh, for how long?

SLINGER 'Bout ten years.

FRANCES Don't she miss you?

SLINGER Ay s'pose shi do, but monie's monie, even in 'Navie. Ye hav a wee girl? Ah, one a them. Shi didn't like ye leavin.

FRANCES No.

SLINGER Shi'll bi likin it less when ye gets back.

FRANCES Why's that?

SLINGER Caus ye'll look like dog-meat, like mi. Ladies like theyr men yung n soft like ye, but ye'll bi neither by 'tyme wi make 'Grand Banks an back—if wi get back.

FRANCES Have you bin to America before?

SLINGER Oh aye, manie tymes, afore ay was pressed inte 'service—though ne'er by way a Cadiz afore. Huh. 'Merchantmen always found ways te get around 'embargo—it's never stopped anie trade as far as ay can see. But te Haliefax ay onlie bin once, fer a load a timber. Onlie thing that place seems te bi gud fer; that, an cod.

FRANCES Hope wi're not long there.

SLINGER It may bi ar station, but wi'll mostlie bi cruisin, as far as ay can see. That's what frigates does best, an *Courageous* is as tight as a whore's arse.

FRANCES   Will we make it down to the West Indies?

SLINGER   A foul place! Manie a ship ther's lost er whole crew te 'yellow sickness. Wi go ther ye'll never see yer girl again, certain sure. Nort Alantic may bi cold but at least it brings down a fever.

FRANCES   Hurrah.

SLINGER   Yer too yung te know what's gud fer ye. Yer in a snug little ship, far away from Mediterrenean wher all them big battles ar. No convoys, no blockades, jus cruisin 'devil's own sea lookin fer a fight—us an them, an may best man win. An if wi win, wi'll bi linin ar purses wi gold.

FRANCES   An if wi don't?

Four double-rings of the bell.

SLINGER   'Larboard watch is up, God bless 'em. Ye comin? Spud's promised us a hornpipe.

FRANCES   In a spell. Gotta see about some new rags.

SLINGER   Right then.

They leave, in opposite directions.

·

Down in the cable-room of the Courageous. *It is pitch black. FRANCES enters from a hatch, above, with a lantern. She descends the ladder and crosses to a clothesline strung with rags, from which she chooses a dry one. She undoes her trousers, pulls them down, and removes a bloody rag from between her legs. She replaces it with the clean rag and drops the bloody one into a bucket of water nearby.*

FRANCES   Who's there?

Show yourself!

DAISY   It's only me.

FRANCES   Who are you?

DAISY   Name's Daisy, if you please.

FRANCES   There aren't supposed to be any girls on this ship.

DAISY   I know.

FRANCES   Are you a stowaway?

DAISY   I'm the captain's girl.

FRANCES   His daughter?

DAISY   His girl. You're a girl, too. A real girl.

FRANCES   You musn't tell anyone, understand? If the captain finds out, he'll hang me from the yard-arm.

DAISY   No, he wouldn't. He likes girls. He tells me that all the time.

FRANCES   Not when they're supposed to be sailors.

DAISY   He'd like that especially, I think.

FRANCES   I don't care, promise me you'll never tell anyone.

DAISY   All right.

FRANCES   Swear!

DAISY   I swear!

FRANCES   Someday when you're older you'll understand.

DAISY   Don't leave!

FRANCES   They'll be piping us to supper soon.

DAISY   No, please. It's so lonely, I'm not allowed to speak to anyone. They even took my dog away.

FRANCES   Your dog?… It was sick.

DAISY   He poisoned her.

FRANCES   The captain?

DAISY   He's trying to make me crazy.

FRANCES   You're—

DAISY   You look like a ghost. You look just like a ghost I saw once. I looked into a pond and saw a ghost standing beside me. She looked just like you.

FRANCES   There's no such thing as ghosts.

DAISY   There is too. The seabirds that fly out to ships are the ghosts of dead sailors. Do you think that when I die I'll become a bird?

FRANCES   You're too young to be thinking of that. Go on up now, and just forget about all this.

DAISY   You could save me. You could distract him from me, make him forget all about me.

FRANCES   You need some fresh air to clear your mind.

DAISY   Can't you even try? Please?

FRANCES   Try what? What are you talking about?

DAISY   If he knew that you were a girl—a real girl—

FRANCES If you even think of telling him—

You're a boy! What are you doing in a dress? Who are you?

DAISY I told you. I'm the captain's girl.

FRANCES Oh my God.

DAISY But he doesn't want me anymore, he's trying to make me disappear. If you pleased him, he might forget about me and leave me alone.

FRANCES If I ever see you again, or if you ever breathe a word a this to anyone, I'll slice you open from arsehole to breakfast. Get out of here, now!

Damn.

Damn!

> ROSE's garden at night. FRANCES and ROSE enter, FRANCES dressed in the clothes she's collected, and ROSE with a shawl and bonnet.

You were splendid!

ROSE You were magnificent!

FRANCES You were tremendous!

ROSE You were astonishing!

FRANCES We dazzled!

ROSE We shone!

FRANCES We confounded!

ROSE We conquered!

FRANCES We did it!

ROSE You were right: no one even suspected.

FRANCES That sailor certainly didn't; we must have spoken for a quarter-hour or more.

ROSE More, I should say. One would think you'd been to sea yourself, the way you carried on. Where did you learn about the King's shilling, or the state of His Majesty's victualling yards?

FRANCES I live in a port town. All men talk about is Impressment and the latest corruption in the Naval outfitters. He never would have been so frank had he been talking to a woman; but I deceived him completely!

ROSE I doubt I'd have recognized you myself, if I didn't know any better. Strangely enough, these clothes flatter you.

FRANCES As do you.

242 • *Lesbian Plays: Coming of Age in Canada*

ROSE   Don't let it swell your head. It's fortunate for you I was by to help you out.

FRANCES   If you're referring to that boor, I could have managed him—he was only full of drink and hot air.

ROSE   He was four times your size, regardless what he was full of.

FRANCES   I couldn't let him speak to you like that; no man would tolerate such behaviour toward his mistress.

ROSE   It's a good thing for both of us, then, that my wit saved your dignity and our secret before you met him on the field of honour.

Do you fancy we make a good couple?

FRANCES   We're attentive, protective even, of one another.

ROSE   People would think we're doting.

FRANCES   We intercede on each other's behalf, gently correcting any little lapses in memory.

ROSE   We're a team, in the best sense of the word.

FRANCES   Isn't it curious how people might assume from these simple things that we're lovers, even though realistically speaking we might just as well be cousins?

ROSE   Ah, but mere cousins wouldn't do this—!

> *She leaps at FRANCES and smacks her on the lips. They stare at each other.*

Forgive me.

> *She strokes FRANCES's face.*

FRANCES   What are you doing?

ROSE   Should I stop?

FRANCES   Yes—

> *She kisses ROSE, then breaks away.*

ROSE   What is it?

FRANCES   This isn't right; you're not kissing me—you're thinking of me as a boy—

> *ROSE caresses FRANCES's breasts.*

ROSE   They feel just like mine. Like mine do but different.

> *She places FRANCES's hands on her breasts; FRANCES touches them gently.*

What are we going to do?

FRANCES I don't know.

They kiss again, fall in the leaves, and make love.

•

The garden is transformed by the buzz of voices, the tinkle of fine china, and strains of harpsichord music. FRANCES sits on a bench in a quiet corner, watching the goings-on. ROSE enters.

ROSE I've found you at last—so this is where you've been hiding.

FRANCES I'm not feeling well. I think I've got 'flu.

ROSE Oh?

You don't feel warm. Have you got an upset stomach?

FRANCES A little. My head is pounding.

ROSE When did all this start?

FRANCES About an hour ago.

ROSE Just when the party began, what a coincidence. Come. The best cure for garden-party influenza is to eat, mingle, and try to forget that you're not enjoying yourself.

FRANCES No, let's stay for a moment.

ROSE A moment, then, but no more.

FRANCES Look at Mrs. Tibs. Why doesn't someone tell her that her hair looks ridiculous? No one has the nerve, not even her own daughter.

ROSE It reminds me of when you discover upon retiring that you've had a glob of dessert on your chin all night, and everyone was too polite to mention it.

FRANCES Have you ever seen such an ungainly threesome as the misses Garthsnaid?

ROSE Oh no. The elder is going to take a turn at the harpsichord.

FRANCES I despise this fashion of flirting over the keyboard despite one's inability to play the thing.

ROSE And see? There's Lady Savanwie and Mrs. Hoant gossiping with each other—and about you, I should think.

FRANCES What? Where?

ROSE There.

FRANCES What makes you think they're talking about me?

ROSE By the fact that they're looking at everyone but you.

FRANCES   Let them look, or talk, if there's nothing else in their shallow, inconsequential lives to keep them amused.

ROSE   We'd better rejoin the party now.

FRANCES   I'll withdraw.

ROSE   Don't you dare.

FRANCES   There's no point in staying. I think it would suit everyone, myself included, if I left.

ROSE   Dear Frances, social maneuvering is truly quite beyond you, isn't it? As long as you present a facade of respectability, their whisperings remain just that: whispers. But by leaving, you remove any opposition to the gossip and suddenly the whispers solidify into what is considered common knowledge, whether they have any bearing on the truth or not.

FRANCES   I should just be myself and shock them all to high heaven. I'd give them something to talk about.

ROSE   That wouldn't be very imaginative of you.

FRANCES   I don't care, Rose!

ROSE   Keep your voice down for heaven's sakes.

FRANCES   Should I be afraid someone might hear me? God forbid!

ROSE   Yes, you should be, quite frankly. May I remind you that your visit here this summer is more than a mere lark in the country, at least insofar as your parents are concerned?

FRANCES   Ha!

ROSE   I'm not asking you to change; in fact I want you to stay exactly as you are. And you can, as long as you join in the masquerade from time to time. Ultimately, that's not such a big price, is it?

Well, is it?

FRANCES   I suppose not.

ROSE   And it's infinitely preferable to losing the protection of your family and spending the rest of your life in a cell, isn't it?

FRANCES   Yes.

ROSE   Then keeping that in mind, is there anybody here that you'd like to pay a courtesy visit to?

FRANCES   Lady Savanwie and Mrs. Hoant, I expect.

ROSE   You're a quick learner when you put your mind to it. Give me your arm. Smile!

•

The gun deck of the Courageous. *FRANCES sits by herself.*

FRANCES Dear Rose,

Fear and longing seems to be all there is on this warship. I am punishing myself, but why, really? I don't know, but I see the meat on my bones becoming smoked and seasoned in this cruel place. The feeling part of me is hardening into the spiritual equivalent of salt-beef, a rawhide caricature of myself. I tried to escape to a place where I could not succumb to my body's yearning for you, and I succeeded beyond my wildest dreams.

Rose?

SLINGER enters.

SLINGER Rose? Is that er name?

FRANCES No.

SLINGER Don't fret, Nobbie, wi all misses ar women.

FRANCES Shi's nought!

SLINGER Fine, hav it yer way.

FRANCES What's wit ye? A cat it looks like ye've got in yer clothes.

SLINGER Ayv got news.

FRANCES What kind a news?

SLINGER Gud news.

FRANCES What might that bi? All the burgoo turned into chickens?

SLINGER That'd bi even better, but this is still gud: if all goes well, ye might get a higher ratin'.

FRANCES A promotion? Why me?

SLINGER Captin wer lookin fer a mate fer is clerk—a boy te go over log-book. Ay piped up an said ay knew just feller—you.

FRANCES Ye didn't.

SLINGER Bi dammed if ay didn't. Think a where it could place ye cum a few years. A warrant officer ye'd bi, along wit rest of 'idlers—no more night watches, no more takin in canvas when shi's over on er beam-ends, an no more burgoo, or not so much, at least.

FRANCES What makes ye think a good clerk I'd be? It's sumthin I've never done.

SLINGER   Didn't stop ye becomin a saylor. Yer just a mate, fer now—Mr. Hume will show ye 'ropes. An after all, ye'v got yer letters, ye said ye did. Ye said ye culd teach mi.

FRANCES   I'm not so sure now.

SLINGER   Ye'd better bi, acause ay told 'captain ye were crack on.

FRANCES   It takes practice, like knottin an splicin.

SLINGER   Knottin' an splicin? Is that all?

Try this then. It's from mi Ruth.

FRANCES   Looks like ye washed it stead a yer hammock.

SLINGER   Ayv had it a while, ye culd say. Whats shi say?

FRANCES   I'm not sure I can make it out…

—oh.

SLINGER   What?

FRANCES   "Dear Jimmie. I hav to get this to you quick cos Im afeard Im no much longer for this worald mi luv. I had a miscarruj I didnt even know I was with child. The smallest funniest thing it were too. Midwif says the womb become septic leeches werent no good neither. Im restin now but verie tired wishin you was here. Mrs Bonnie bin takin care May so dont you worrie nun cuz it wont do no good aniehow. Maybie the Captin can put in a gud werd for you at the Pay Office so I can draw more than your half-pay. I hate to but I cant bi takin in laundrie now an the docter's powders is so dammed costlie. I miss you an luv you. Ruth."

It's dated three months since.

I'm sorrie, Slinger.

SLINGER   It's nought.

FRANCES   Ye know, practisin mi hand would do mi no harm, if it's a letter ye want te send her.

SLINGER   Ay aready troubled ye enuff.

FRANCES   No trouble. I have to bi readie for the captain.

SLINGER   What to say?

FRANCES   Think a her sittin here stead a me.

SLINGER   Mi dear Ruth.

Ay got mi a feller knows his letters… so ay thot ayd better see how yer doin. Ay wer distressed te hear ye'd bin teken sick. It's better ay pray this letter find ye, an sef from Harm's way…. Seven quid is all ye ken draw a mi pay at anie tyme but Grenich Hospittle mite fetch ye sumthin. If ye ken get ther.

Wi'll hav lotsa monie when aym back acause wi're bound te square off wit Yankee Doodle anie day now an when wi do ar pockets'l bi jinglin wi prize monie. Gud ol wifie, ay'll bi home later in 'year if things stay as gud…. Fight it best ye ken, mi luv. Tell May her dad's got her a special treat on a account a her bein sech a gud giral. Ay…. Yer own. James.

What's 'date?

FRANCES   February Fifth, Eighteen Hunnerd an Twelve.

Make yer mark here.

SLINGER   Yer giral must bi missin you. Shi wer a fool to let ye go te sea.

FRANCES   More the fool I fer goin.

SLINGER   Won't bi long afore wi're homeward bound.

FRANCES   Is that true?

SLINGER   It cant hurt te think so.

Ye'd better trim yer sheets. Captin wants ye next watch.

•

The cable-room of the Courageous. *The wind whips through the rigging.*

FRANCES   Day of the Week. Day of the Month. Course…. Speaking is not like finding your place on a map. There is no way to know where you are, no columns, no instruments, the stars are gone. Where I am there are no words for things. Only questions. What am I? This flesh here, this scrawny, cold, weak body, why do I care about it? It betrayed me, and so did those words in the log, the ones that promised me—Distance. Difference of Longitude. Longitude by Account…

"Keep reading. You read very well." Those were his words. I had none when I felt his finger running down my back—Latitude by Account. Latitude by Chronometer. Difference of Latitude…. My waist, my bum, my thigh…. Don't stop," he said, his body behind mine, his breath, clothes grating in my ear—Departure. Remarks on Board…. "Keep it on your belt," Slinger says, "then it's always there when you need it." Not on my belt now, in my hand, into the captain's hand as it tries to undo my trousers, the point driving into the red space between the bones. I want to scratch words into his skin I am not yours you will not press me in your book of empty promises I will go where you cannot steal me—a noise: the log-book crashing to the floor, his yell, my heart tearing through the cabin door

ME

ME ME ME ME

the only word left that's mine

I'm here, I'm here, somebody please help somebody help me please, oh

•

ROSE and FRANCES, each with a book.

ROSE   Stuff.

Have you ever heard of someone being described as "hyacinthian?"

FRANCES   Mm-mmm.

ROSE   As in the flower. Drivel.

Why is this man such a popular author? This is one of the worst novels I've ever read.

FRANCES   Don't read it then.

ROSE   Too late, I'm finished.

How is your book?

FRANCES   Fascinating.

ROSE   What are you reading? It looks technical.

FRANCES   It is.

ROSE   What is it?

Oh my lord, Frances, have you lost your senses? There must be a thousand volumes in our collection and you choose this!

FRANCES   It's interesting.

ROSE   Really? Why?

FRANCES   I'm not going to bother explaining it to you.

ROSE   But I want to know why you're so engrossed.

FRANCES   Will you make a sincere effort to appreciate it?

ROSE   Yes, certainly. I love it when you look so stern.

FRANCES   You're messing my papers!

ROSE   Oh my. I'm listening.

FRANCES   This book explains three principle methods of marine navigation. The most common is known as dead reckoning.

ROSE   It must have been what Lord Nelson reckoned with.

FRANCES   Are you going to listen?

ROSE   Sorry—do go on.

FRANCES   The basic principle is simple. You determine your position on a chart by calculating how far you've travelled along the Parallel of Latitude and Meridian of Longitude each day. The amount in nautical miles you've travelled from North to South is called the Difference of Latitude, and from East to West is the Difference of Longitude. Clear?

ROSE   As a foghorn. Is this the part I'm to appreciate?

FRANCES   When you cross-reference the Differences of Latitude and Longitude, they pinpoint your position on the sea. From there you can plot a course to anywhere; to Russia, if you want, or Indo-China, or the Spice Islands.

ROSE   But why would you want to go to any of those places? Wouldn't they be awfully warm?

FRANCES   That's beside the point; what matters is that once you know where you are, you can go anywhere.

ROSE   An attractive idea indeed—

FRANCES   You see?

ROSE   —if you know how to get wherever it is you choose to go.

FRANCES   You have to know where you're going before you can decide how to get there.

ROSE   And you? Do you have a destination?

FRANCES   Away.

ROSE   Can you be more specific?

FRANCES   Far away.

ROSE   I see. It shouldn't be hard to find, at any rate. Wait—there's a ballad in this, I'm certain of it. One moment—

—yes. Here it is; an "Ode to a Grecian Beauty", in the Byronic Mode, by Rose Langley, entitled:

"Miss Frances's Pilgrimage."

"Up high, upon yon silver dusted cloud,
Or snared, despaired, 'tween sun and moon and stars,
Her path pursues her, weary but yet proud,
Her quarry almost 'tained, yet ever far.
Avoiding gilded hearts along the way
She seeks a star to guide her wand'ring bark,
A silver voice to complement her lay."

"At last those weary eyes may rest their gaze,
For which the restless ages have rolled by.
She laughs—you'd think it is a horse which neighs—
For she has what she's come for, namely: I.
Our families may smile in condescension:
Two girls, arm in arm, happy as can be.
The truth would choke them with apprehension
But little do they think we lovers be."

FRANCES   Sublime—

ROSE   Thank you.

FRANCES   —and utterly ridiculous.

ROSE   Yes, but what about the romantic part, "she has what she's come for, namely I"? It could be true; I could go with you and we could live far away together.

FRANCES   But you don't really want to leave home.

ROSE   I never used to, until I fell in love with you. What a queer look you've got on your face!

FRANCES   What are you talking about?

ROSE   Just imagine: a newlywed couple arrives in a village with a small amount of capital, not much, just enough to rent a cottage and establish themselves. But soon they have a garden with a fine crop coming in; she teaches at a nearby school, he works in town. They live a simple, happy life, growing old together year after year. Why would anyone guess they were both women; who would ever imagine such a thing? We would succeed because of our audacity.

FRANCES   You couldn't make do without your servants, let alone work for a living.

ROSE   We could make it a dream come true, if we wanted to. Think for a moment. What's to stop us?

FRANCES   We would be living a deception; our lives would be lies.

ROSE   To outsiders, yes, but not to us. Between you and I there would be only love and the bare truth.

FRANCES   I think you are labouring under some sort of misapprehension.

ROSE   What do you mean?

FRANCES   I mean… what makes you think I want to go away with you?

ROSE   Isn't that what all lovers want?

FRANCES   But we're not lovers.

ROSE   We're not? What are we then?

FRANCES   I'm not certain…. Special friends.

ROSE   Isn't that the same thing?

FRANCES   No, it's not the same at all!

ROSE   Why not?

FRANCES   It's obvious, Rose—we're both women; we cannot be lovers.

ROSE   No—we're not supposed to be lovers, nor are we supposed to dress in men's clothes and traipse around the countryside. But we've done both those things, so it's a little late to say we cannot.

FRANCES   You're confusing me with the clothing. You think that if I'm in men's clothes I must want what a man does.

ROSE   But it's precisely because you are a woman that I love you.

Oh. Is that it? Oh dear.

FRANCES   If it were possible for me to love you, I would. But how can I love another woman?

ROSE   I don't believe it.

FRANCES   Please try to understand. You are very special to me.

ROSE   A "special friend."

FRANCES   Yes.

Say something.

ROSE   Such as?

FRANCES   What are you thinking?

ROSE   I cannot think.

FRANCES   What are you feeling, then?

ROSE   I want to die. No, I want you to die. I want to kill you. How can you be doing this? You're wrong. You do love me. You do, I've seen it! I've seen it in your eyes when you've listened to me talking, or when we've had to behave ourselves around others. I've felt it in your hands when you've stroked my hair. You can lie to yourself if you wish to, but your body has told me the truth.

FRANCES   That's not the truth, it's just what you want to believe. I don't blame you; our friendship has become tangled up like a ball of wool in a way that never should have happened.

ROSE   And when has the word "never" been a part of your vocabulary?

FRANCES   Look at us from the outside: here we are, me pretending to be a man, doing things to you only men are supposed to do; not me, not another woman.

ROSE   But do you like touching me?

FRANCES   Rose—

ROSE   I want to know. Do you?

FRANCES   No—

ROSE   Are my lips and cheeks soft on your skin, does that please you?

FRANCES   No—

ROSE   And when you explore the warm secret world inside my belly do your fingers like it there? Does that make you feel good?

FRANCES   How could it? Your touch was like a whiplash, it made me sick!

Scream, why don't you; cry, hit me, kick me! What am I but a freak, how could it matter? I don't love you, Rose; I couldn't if I wanted to. Can't you see?

ROSE   Yes. I see a coward.

FRANCES leaves.

•

In the gun-room of the Courageous. *FRANCES and SLINGER listen to the sound of the ship being wracked by a storm.*

SLINGER   Now bi tyme if ye want to write yer giral a letter. Mightn't get another chance.

Aym jus makin funnie, ye know that. Nah, wi're snug aright.

Ye never sayled in 'fuilteach afore, eh?

Everie Februarie it seems worse. But wi've ne'er a worrie so long as wind's at ar back. It's them cross-waves what spell trubble.

Ye ne'er said how it went on wit Captain.

FRANCES   He didn't like mi hand.

SLINGER   Oh. Ay spose it don't hav it's sea-legs yet. Ye'll do better next tyme.

Spirits live in water, ay think. Not that aym filled wit fancies like sum, but when it comes on to blow hard like this, ay think a mi mates what hav drowned. Must bi gilravagin down ther, stirrin things up.

FRANCES   Ay was out takin a walk one day. The sun was shinin bright. I was strollin by the bay; the air was calm an the water was shinie as glass. Then suddenlie I felt like I weren't alone aniemore. I turned around—there were nobodie there, but I still had that strange feeling... an then I don't know why, but I looked into the water, an in the reflection I saw a yung woman standin biside me.

SLINGER Who wer it?

FRANCES I don't know.

SLINGER Did shi speke?

FRANCES Not a word.

SLINGER Keeper a 'deep dont giv er secrets away. Aye, an ay fancie onlie shi knows secret a that boy wi lost.

FRANCES What boy?

SLINGER That's just it. Nobodie knows wher he come from—he musta been stowed away all this tyme—God knows how.

FRANCES What did he look like?

SLINGER Wi thot im a girl till wi got im on 'deck: he wer wearin a frock! No dowt he wer leavin his people, what done cast im out. Sea-bed's 'onlie fit place fer im—ay'd a thrown im over miself if ayd found im.

Eh? Jesus, Nobbie, it wer just some bleedin faggot, not one of ar mates.

FRANCES He was my mate.

SLINGER That's what ay'm sayin': he weren't.

FRANCES Get away from me! Faggot!

SLINGER Yer daft!

FRANCES You wanted to touch me.

SLINGER We're raggies, ye nit! Whats got inte yer head, weevils?

FRANCES Would you touch a woman that way unless you wanted her?

SLINGER Yer not a fuckin woman!

FRANCES Yes, I fuckin am!

SLINGER Aym fetchin surgeon. Yev cracked yer nut.

FRANCES I am not a boy.

SLINGER Outa mi way!

FRANCES Cocksucker.

> *He hits her. She removes her shirt.*

Give this to the dead boy. I'm the one that should have died wearing a dress.

> *SLINGER throws a blanket over her and beats her.*

SLINGER I should fuckin kill you, I should fuckin kill you you fuckin whore lyin bitch! Bring im back!

FRANCES   It's me

SLINGER   Bring im back!

FRANCES   me

SLINGER   Nobbi!

•

The cable-room of the Courageous. FRANCES sits in darkness. The storm battering the ship is at its height; from below, the sound of the groaning hull is even louder. The hatch is unlocked; SLINGER enters with a lantern.

SLINGER   Speak up. Ay got things te do.

FRANCES   A paper.

SLINGER   What?

FRANCES   A piece of paper. And a pen, please.

SLINGER   Ye brings me down here so ay can do yer fetchin? Christ.

He turns to leave.

FRANCES   Please, Slinger, you must.

SLINGER   Must?

FRANCES   No I'm sorry I didn't mean… they won't give me anything to write on. You know where I keep my pen and paper. You could bring them to me. Please.

SLINGER   Ay don't want nothin te do wit ye. Got that? Don't send fer mi again, fellers is aready lookin funnie at mi.

FRANCES   Who is?

SLINGER   Spud, fer one, that cross-eyed, Dutch-built ol lard-ass.

FRANCES   He'd look sideways at his own shadow.

SLINGER   Yeh—Ay cant get yer papers.

FRANCES   Why?

SLINGER   Ay aynt gonna bi seen runnin an fetchin fer ye! Get someone else te do it.

FRANCES   No one will help me.

SLINGER   Can't blame 'em.

FRANCES   They're going to hang me. The captain raped me and next he's going to hang me. When the storm is over.

Do you care?

SLINGER   Who ar ye that ay culd care? Ay bin livin on this ship wi ye fer four months an ay dont even know yer name.

FRANCES   Yes, you do. My name is Frances. Nobbie.

SLINGER   Nobbie was a boy. Ay can't even tell now—aym hopin wi muster naked next tyme so's wi can see who's a boy an who aynt.

FRANCES   She has to know. If I'm going to die she has to know.

SLINGER   Maybe shi don't want te know. Maybe shi's better off not knowin.

FRANCES   She has to know that I love her.

SLINGER   Yer mum? Yer sister? Who then?

FRANCES   My long-haired chum.

SLINGER   Jesus.

FRANCES   Please get my paper.

SLINGER   It ayn't right, don't ye get it? Ay shuldn't even bi standin here listenin te ye. 'Lads all say yer a silkie, or a mermaid.

FRANCES   Why did you come then?

SLINGER   Te get outa 'weather.

> *Yells and shouts from above, the sound of ropes and timber under terrible strain.*

Ay gotta go.

FRANCES   My paper.

SLINGER   Ther's no tyme.

FRANCES   What if I were Ruth.

SLINGER   Ruth?

FRANCES   What if I were Ruth lying abed and slowly dying, and I asked someone to write to you for me and they said no?

SLINGER   Yer daft.

FRANCES   What would you say to that person to convince them?

SLINGER   It ayn't 'same thing.

FRANCES   Why isn't it?

SLINGER   Bicause shi's mi wife, aym a man, shi's a woman, shi's mother a mi girl!

FRANCES   But that's not it, that's not what really matters.

SLINGER   A course it is!

FRANCES   No! What matters is that you love her. Nothing else would mean anything if you didn't love her. Which you do, don't you?

SLINGER   Yes.

FRANCES   And I love Rose; we love each other as much as you and Ruth do. What would you have done if you'd returned to England a year from now to find Ruth dead, what would you have said or done to the neighbour who refused to help her?

SLINGER   Ayd bi pretty mad.

FRANCES   So think of me in Ruth's place, think of Rose as a boy if it helps, just help me write to her, please.

SLINGER   Ay don't see how a woman can love another woman.

FRANCES   It doesn't matter how, it just is.

SLINGER   Aright then. Ay will.

With a roar, the ship's planking is broached by sea—the water rushes in.

FRANCES   Slinger!

SLINGER   Shi's goin down!

He picks FRANCES up and folds her over his shoulder, carrying her out. Darkness and thunder as the ship sinks.

•

FRANCES   Dear Rose.

ROSE   Day of the Week. Day of the Month.

FRANCES   "I love you" is what we long most to hear, and are most afraid of saying. I never intended to love you.

ROSE   Course. Distance.

FRANCES   Without love I am a skinless dolphin, skimming my way through life.

ROSE   Difference of Longitude. Longitude by Account.

FRANCES   Love catches me at the heels, weighs down my trunk, causes me to linger too long at my own reflection.

ROSE   Latitude by Account. Latitude by Chronometer.

FRANCES   This thing, love, has insinuated itself inside me while I was looking the other way.

ROSE   Difference of Latitude. Departure.

FRANCES   What I long most to hear I am most afraid of saying.

ROSE   Remarks on Board.

FRANCES   I live in the hope that if I see you again, my voice will have the courage to speak from my heart.

> *A heath in the English countryside.*

Rose.

ROSE   Frances. You're back.

FRANCES   Yes.

> *Blackout.*
>
> *The end.*

Swollen Tongues

Kathleen Oliver

Introduction:
Swollen Tongues

Kathleen Oliver's *Swollen Tongues* (1998), a conscious parody of a Restoration comedy of manners, draws attention to its sustained use of rhyming couplets to underline its *tour de force* manipulation of restoration staging conventions. Thus spectators are never allowed to forget that they are participating in a creative process in which the characters are required to come up with the next rhyming line, as well as participate in several poetry competitions. This playful improvised effect is reinforced in every other aspect of the play since all of the characters will at some time or other find themselves improvising not only verse but also a gender role that goes with it. In its endless proliferation of transvestite disguises, Oliver keeps changing the frame of reference by drawing all the characters into the web of intrigue. At the same time, she inverts the usual renaissance/restoration comedy of errors that occurs when the heroine takes on a transvestite disguise in order to pursue her own desires. Traditionally this androgynous figure inevitably attracts the transgressive affections of another female character who mistakenly believes her to be male. In *Swollen Tongues*, there is no mistake in the protagonist Catherine's sexual attraction to Sonja. Having set up Catherine as the desiring lesbian subject, Oliver then shows us the kinds of obstacles she finds herself up against in a man's world.

Thus Act One is devoted mainly to the intrigues that occur when Catherine's desire for Sonja leads her to try to emulate her brother Thomas by plagiarizing his poetry. Encouraged by the new tutor Alex to write her own sonnets instead of serving as her brother Thomas's secretary, Catherine avails herself of the only model available to her. Referencing the actual historical conditions which prioritized male education, Oliver uses Catherine's subservient position to legitimize her dishonest actions in imitating his very bad sonnets in an effort to compete with him for the love of Sonja. When Thomas recites his very bad sonnet to Sonja, she returns the favour by reading him a slightly better version that she has found in a collection of verses by a certain Sir Overripe.

What we soon discover, along with Sonja is that Sir Overripe is the male pen name that Catherine has invented to conceal her identity. In an unexpected reversal, Sonja now favours the imaginary Overripe over Thomas whom she believes is an imposter. When Catherine learns of the plan to invite the imaginary Overripe to the house for a poetry improvisation contest, she worries aloud what will happen when Sonja finds out that she is Overripe. Sonja who has listened to everything from her concealed down stage hiding place, decides that she will help her win the contest against Thomas.

The spectators' delight in watching these endless complications derives in large measure from the unabashed celebration of lesbian desire which would normally be completely submerged under the cross-dressed disguise. Sonja's decision to go along with the discovery that Catherine loves her, uttered in an aside to the audience (*She might indeed… though I'm a little shocked! This is all new to me, but hey… why not?)* invites us to share in her sexual experimentation and prepares us for her decision to impersonate the fictitious Overripe in order to save Catherine. With Alex helping Thomas to cheat, Thomas convinced that his honour has been impugned by a poetry thief, and Catherine worried about getting caught, the next poetry contest begins when Sonja arrives in male disguise. Drawing attention to Sonja's transvestite appeal by having Alex fall all over her, Oliver successfully reverses the traditional use of male disguise as a means for a woman to pursue her male lover, by having Sonja adopt it for the opposite reason. Unrecognized by the rest of the characters, Sonja openly courts Catherine, who slowly cues in to her passionate kisses. While Thomas uses his rhyme to ask for Overripe's confession of his guilt, Overripe surprises everyone by asking for Catherine if he wins the contest.

In Act Two, the setting moves to an imaginary space where the drawing-room conventions of Act One no longer apply. Presided over by a giant statue of a woman, fragments of Sapphic poems, and a sign that reads "Women Only Land," we find ourselves in the mansion that the tutor Alex (now revealed as a woman) had abandoned years ago. It is in this fantasy space that the final poetry competitions will take place, only now the male aesthetic of Act One will be pitted against the Sapphic aesthetic of ancient Greece. As all the characters reassemble here, each of them will be forced to compete anew, but this time it will no longer be possible to be merely formulaic. As Sonja wanders away with Catherine in pursuit, Alex arrives on site to reclaim her property and renew her vows to Sappho and to Catherine. Possibly the biggest reversal of all occurs when Thomas arrives and is forced to take on a female disguise. Sonja who is unable to penetrate his "Amanda" commandeers "him" to enter the poetry contest that she has set for Catherine. In this complete overthrow of traditional gender roles, Thomas finds himself uttering the central question posed by the play: "How does a woman play a woman's suitor?" (306), as he agrees to compete for her even though she's in love with his sister. When his lessons in humility pay off in producing a poem full of deep yearning for the secrets he has to keep, the poetry contest itself becomes a testimonial to the restrained power of womanly love. Having won the fickle Sonja in his womanly guise, Thomas's revelation of his true identity signals the acceptance of a male presence into the Sapphic space. To bring the motif of the poetry contest to a close, Catherine is now urged on by her exposure to the yearning in Alex's haunting Sapphic fragments to improvise an inspired version of her own. As Catherine and Alex swear their love to one another, they also raise the vision of resurrecting Alex's old home into their dreamed-for school for Lesbian poets.

To bring this spiralling *tour de force* excursion into the gender politics of poetry and desire to its close, Sonja's epilogue, which urges everyone to enter the contest to vie for her favours, leaves the audience with a final reminder that practice makes perfect and that genius knows no gender.

photo by Kate Battle

Kathleen Oliver

Bio and Artist's Statement

Kathleen Oliver completed her BA and MA in English Literature at the University of Western Ontario, and moved to Vancouver in 1991, where she works as a playwright, critic, teacher and arts administrator. Her plays include *Swollen Tongues*, which won the 1997 National Playwriting Competition and has been produced in Vancouver, Toronto, and London; *Carol's Christmas*, which premiered at the Arts Club Theatre in 2002; and *The Family Way*, which Touchstone Theatre and the Vancouver East Cultural Centre premiered in May 2003. She has worked for at least a dozen Vancouver arts organizations and is a regular contributor to *The Georgia Straight*.

•

Swollen Tongues didn't start out as a lesbian play. The first draft was all about Thomas, an aspiring poet who feared that his words would amount to nothing. His fears were a thinly disguised projection of my own; for years I had been planning to write something, someday. *Swollen Tongues* began to become that something when Catherine—an extremely minor character in the first draft—emerged as the central figure in the play. Tormented by her desire for another woman, she hides her feelings behind her craft, afraid that her love will not be reciprocated.

The script evolved, through countless rewrites, into an elaborately playful coming-out story. Writing the play in verse and setting it in a distant, artificial past gave me a safe container for the emotional truth of my own experiences of unexpressed and unrequited love. I had read a lot of very earnest lesbian scripts, and I wanted to write one that didn't take things so terribly seriously. In *Swollen Tongues*, the characters indulge in outrageously exaggerated versions of the romantic dramas that many of us experience as part of our coming-out process. It was, perhaps paradoxically, the very outlandishness of these characters that allowed me to treat them with real generosity.

The play pokes fun at patriarchal oppression as well as lesbian separatism; it's feminist and queer and mostly it's meant to be a fun ride. In this world, language is alternately tortured and caressed, and gender is fluid: a woman dressed as a man ends up falling in love with a man dressed as a woman. Basically, nothing is sacred. That's an approach I hope to bring to all my plays.

Production Information

Swollen Tongues was first produced by View, the Performing Arts Society at the Vancouver East Cultural Centre as part of the Women in View Festival, in February 1998, with the following company:

CATHERINE	Laara Sadiq
SONJA	Sonia Norris
THOMAS	Bob Frazer
ALEX	Suzie Payne

Directed by Kathleen Weiss
Set and Costume Design by Kate King
Lighting Design by Heidi Lindgren
Stage Managed by Allan Clement

•

Swollen Tongues was the winner in the Full-length Category of the 9th Annual National Playwriting Competition in 1997 sponsored by Theatre BC.

Characters

Thomas, 20s. A committed but not very talented poet. Brother to Catherine. In love with Sonja.

Catherine, 20s. Sister to Thomas. A talented but recalcitrant poet. Secretly in love with Sonja.

Sonja, 20s. Catherine's dressmaker and friend. Has a passionate, expressive, and playful nature. A free spirit.

Alex, aka Dr. Wise. Catherine and Thomas's tutor. Secretly in love with Catherine. Older than the others, and possessor of a mysterious history.

A Note on the Text

In order that the verse flow as freely as possible on the page, I have attempted to minimize stage directions and use typographic shorthand where possible. Asides are generally denoted by (text in parentheses), except in cases where one character's aside is addressed only to one other character, in which case a stage direction in italics *(aside, to THOMAS)* appears at the beginning of a speech. Italics without parentheses are used to indicate poetry that is being read or recited; while poetry that is being composed or improvised is set apart by quotation marks.

SWOLLEN TONGUES

ACT ONE

scene one

A well-appointed room in the family estate. CATHERINE is sitting at a table strewn with papers. Enter ALEX. Catherine, startled, tries to conceal the papers.

ALEX   Ah, Catherine, glad I caught you. Hard at work?
I am impressed—you never seem to shirk.
Tell me, what sort of progress have you made?

CATHERINE   You mean the sonnet? Oh. Well, I'm afraid
I still don't have a lot to show. I fear
I'm simply not a poet.

ALEX   I won't hear
another word to that effect as long
as I'm your tutor! Now, there's nothing wrong
with being shy at first about the form—
a certain shyness is, in fact, the norm.
But practice, Catherine! For I know that rhyme
will help you find your honest voice in time.
Don't say you've failed before you even try!

CATHERINE   Who has had time for trying? Well, not I
with all this work for Thomas. You've been quite
demanding, it appears, for no respite
could he have taken from his pen and book
to pile up such a heap of words. Just look!

ALEX   But his assignment was the same as yours:
a single sonnet.

CATHERINE   Ha! In threes and fours
and sixes, eights and dozens, he has writ.

ALEX   My, he's prolific!

CATHERINE   Yes. (Too bad it's shit.)
I've noticed, ever since you came to teach,
Thomas has grown in his poetic reach
(if not his grasp) beyond his wildest dreams.
You are an inspiration, it would seem.

ALEX   And have I not inspired his sister, too?
I have not seen a sonnet yet from you.
What business have you writing out his dozens,
playing handmaid to your own creations' cousins,
before completing your assignments first?

CATHERINE   Are teachers always trained to think the worst
of their poor students' motives? If you mean
to dare suggest that I would thus demean
myself by copying the work of Thomas—

ALEX   I'm sorry, Catherine—please, relax. I promise
I meant to suggest nothing of the sort.
C'mon, cheer up. There, there. That's a good sport.
But I will not permit you to neglect
your own work for the sake of his. Subject
your deepest feelings to the closest scrutiny:
perhaps the blank page will succumb to mutiny.
For don't forget you have the seeds in you
to create works as beautiful and true.

CATHERINE   (More beautiful and truer, I would hope!)
I have not yet fine-tuned the microscope
with which a poet peers into her soul.
Thomas has had more practice, for my role
with all the other tutors we have had
was that of secretary. I am glad
you think me worthy of my own expression,
but give me time! This is a new profession.

ALEX   It will take time, but you must try to nurture
the tiny voice inside you, the researcher
who stares into that microscope and sees
her truth at last, and turns them into these.

> *ALEX holds up the poems.*

CATHERINE   (Or something better.)

> *Enter THOMAS carrying a sheet of paper, reading it over critically, making revisions.*

ALEX   Here's our poet now.
Good morning, friend. We were just saying how
prolific you have been in versifying.

THOMAS   Oh, well, a man can't help but keep on trying.
Shall I use "moon" again?

CATHERINE   What rhymes with moon?

THOMAS   "My heart is like a bug in its cocoon"—

ALEX   Thomas, you never rest! Your dedication
should to your sister be an inspiration
when she gets down to work on her assignments.

THOMAS   What, practicing her womanly refinements
like needlecraft and elocution? Yes,
I daresay dedication would be best.

ALEX   I meant her writing.

THOMAS   Writing? Oh, how jolly!
A woman write a poem? Outlandish folly!

ALEX   You think your sister not a worthy writer?

THOMAS   Uh, no; indeed, I know that words delight her.
And she's a secretary past compare...
but should be glad that her fair sex is spared
the grief that comes with writing, and revealing
your every innermost and secret feeling;
and wondering if your words will meet their mark
or be more futile shots into the dark.

ALEX   What do you mean? shots in the dark? If they
are true in their intent, and do convey
the honest aspirations of your heart,
then no one can deny that they are art.

CATHERINE   (Until they read them.)

THOMAS   I do not deny
that they are honest, but until their cry
is answered by the one that I adore,
I fear my greatest efforts will be poor.

ALEX   Now that you mention it, I did detect
a subtle thread of longing. I expect
you've made your feelings known to her? Who is it?

THOMAS   Heaven to let my parched lips pay a visit
to those sweet syllables that spell her name!
"Sonja!" My love, my fantasy, my pain!

ALEX   The dressmaker. How can I not have met her?

THOMAS   Believe me, if you had, you'd not forget her!

CATHERINE   Yes, that is certain. Sonja has a way...

ALEX   Then, Thomas, it is up to you to pay
her compliments: and nothing has the power
to bring a tender bud into full flower
like poetry, with all its sweet caresses
for mouth and mind, the feelings it expresses…

CATHERINE   I'll leave you to your little man-to-man.

ALEX   If you must go…. But don't forget, I plan
to check on how your homework's coming later.

THOMAS   Me, too! To see my secretary as creator!
That sight for all the world I would not miss!

ALEX   Thomas, be more supportive, I insist!

CATHERINE   Don't worry, Dr. Wise, it's nothing new.

CATHERINE goes to exit.

ALEX   You'll overcome it—I have faith in you!
Some gentle muse is waiting for your call,
so get to work!

CATHERINE   I thank you.

ALEX   Not at all.

Exit CATHERINE. ALEX turns to THOMAS.

And once the words are written, you must share them.
Oh Thomas, women! We think we will scare them!
You've got a stack of poems that sings her praises;
why not just let her hear some of those phrases?
Just tell her, Thomas! You can best intuit
what might unfreeze her heart. Go on. Just do it!

THOMAS   I know, I know. I feel like such a coward.

ALEX   Just tell her! You are bound to be empowered!
Thomas, I think I know what you are feeling.
Without embarrassing you by revealing
the gory details of my younger life…
you may have wondered why I have no wife.

THOMAS   I never questioned—

ALEX   No, it's quite all right:
perhaps my past can give you some insight.
You won't want to regret this when you're older.
I loved a woman once, but never told her.

THOMAS   You loved a woman?

ALEX   Once upon a time.
And though I tried to honour her in rhyme,
my lines remained vexingly incomplete,
and so I dared not lay them at her feet:
I stayed my tongue, and loved her from afar.
My poetry became a mocking scar!
This heart was never put to proper test,
for love's not love until it is expressed.
But you, my friend, have heaps of words to share.
So simply screw your courage up, and dare
to let your Sonja hear what you have writ!
The time is now, so make good use of it!
You take my lesson?

THOMAS   Yes, though I'm still fearful.

ALEX   Thomas, I know my story isn't cheerful,
    but I must spare you the same wretched fate.

THOMAS   This woman… are you certain it's too late?

ALEX   Too late for me. That was a different life,
    and so I've carried on without a wife,
    and into teaching have my passion poured,
    for education is its own reward.
    But if there were a girl who stopped my heart
    I'd find the nerve to dedicate my art,
    however rough, however incomplete,
    to her who made my poor heart skip that beat.

> *ALEX and THOMAS both look off, dreamily.*

SONJA   *(off, calling)* Catherine!

> *ALEX and THOMAS both start.*

THOMAS   Sonja! She's here! My sister has a fitting!

ALEX   It's now or never, Thomas.

THOMAS   Oh, I'm shitting!
    Um, sir, if you don't mind…

ALEX   I'll disappear.
    I wouldn't dare intrude or interfere.
    I know you lovebirds need your privacy,
    so I'll excuse myself and leave you be.

THOMAS   Thanks, Dr. Wise, I knew you'd understand.

ALEX   Be brave! And she'll be putty in your hand!

> *Exit ALEX. Enter SONJA, opposite, carrying a measuring tape, some pins, and a book.*

SONJA   Thomas, hello. Is your sister about?

THOMAS   Oh, hello, Sonja! No, I rather doubt
that she's around just now—well, do you see her?
So she's not here, no, it's just you and me here.

SONJA   Thanks for that helpful bit of information.

THOMAS   Oh, Sonja! Fairest one of all creation!
More heavenly than heaven's lofty pillows,
more swishy than a field of weeping willows!
More sparkly than the magic fairy dust!
Please! May I read you something?

SONJA   If you must.

THOMAS   I'm sorry to detain you, but I think
you'll be delighted with these drops of ink.
Let me, my dear, read you what I have writ
of Sonja's grace, your beauty and your wit,
the spell your eyes have cast upon my heart,
the music of your tongue, its golden art...

SONJA   Get on with it! I haven't got all day.

THOMAS   Of course, my princess. Whatever you say.
Please, darling Sonja, give ear to this sonnet
for I spent much of last month working on it.
I have a tongue too long to go on biting it.
Besides, I really cannot stand the taste.
I have a secret, there's no sense in fighting it.
But I'm afraid to put my tongue to waste
on all these words I'm stuffing down my throat.
I swallow them and keep them in the dark,
and in my stomach, they take on a coat
that helps me to digest the silent spark
that cracks my heart a little. I won't tell
because I am afraid that I might say
a truth that you don't think is quite as swell
as I do. But I'll say it anyway:
and that is that I love you. There, I've said it.
I only hope I don't live to regret it.

SONJA   I hope it won't be long till I forget it!
If I could put this moment in a bottle
I'd smash it, making sure I spared your model,

which I must now recite, to clear the air.
Of your base imitation I despair!

    SONJA clutches the book to her chest, closes her eyes and recites:

How long my tortured tongue has longed to tell
I cannot tell you, only bite my tongue;
which bitten, tastes the longing twice as strong
and would against my better sense rebel.
The words rise from my throat; I push them back,
back to the darkness of their secret place,
where they contrive new longings to embrace
while silently my heart begins to crack.
I ask myself what harm could come from telling?
But overwhelmed by fears, I dare not speak;
and so my silent heart and tongue are swelling,
afraid to burst, and let my secret leak
from rain and sun and clouds and sky above you—
the secret that I cannot say: I love you.

    THOMAS throws himself at her feet.

THOMAS   There is a god in heaven after all!
At last the angels there have heard my call
for Sonja loves me, loves me, loves me, yes!
My efforts have at last paid off! Success!

SONJA   Thomas, get up, and when you do, get real!
You know that this is not the way I feel.

THOMAS   And how did I not know you were a poet?
I am ashamed to say I did not know it!

SONJA   Please! Stop pretending you don't understand;
you know these verses are not from my hand.
What nerve you have, to be the imitator
of this seductive music's great creator!

THOMAS   What do you mean? Who do I imitate?

SONJA   Only Sir Overripe, one of the great
inspiring lyric poets of our time.
And you thought I would not see through your crime
of pilfering your own library shelf!

THOMAS   But I wrote every word of that myself!

    SONJA shows him the book.

SONJA   Thomas, these are the words I was reciting,
and I admit they can be most inviting

of imitation, as are all great voices;
but you have made some less than brilliant choices.

> *THOMAS takes the book from SONJA, and flips through it, with growing anger and hurt.*

THOMAS   What is this book? Who is this Overripe?
What! Page by page he manages to swipe
my inmost thoughts…. Who is this wicked swine?
These are my poems! Reworked, it's true, but mine!
Where did you get this?

SONJA   Like you have to ask!
I found it on your sister's writing desk
beside a sheaf of your own cramped handwriting.
I guess this model was just too inviting…
I must get going. May I have that, please?

THOMAS   Sonja, I swear to you, on bended knees,
I did not steal these words. *I* have been thieved!

SONJA   Your desperation's not to be believed!
Please, get up. I will take that, thanks. Farewell.
Remember, those who steal will burn in hell.

> *SONJA takes the book and exits.*

THOMAS   What! Can this be? How have I been so conned?
I feel I am misunderstood beyond
my own pathetic means of comprehension.
To be betrayed by this, my own invention!

> *THOMAS collapses on his desk. Enter ALEX.*

ALEX   Why, Thomas, what's the matter? Are you ill?

THOMAS   Indeed, I choke upon a bitter pill!

ALEX   Can I assume you did not win her heart?
But don't give up! You've only made a start—

THOMAS   A start—ha! And an end to all my dreams!
She does not just reject me—no, it seems
another poet makes her spirit tremble.
Do you know Overripe?

ALEX   No.

THOMAS   You don't dissemble?

ALEX   I've never heard of Overripe. Who is he?

THOMAS Only the one whose words make Sonja dizzy.
  I read her my most recent song of love,
  and she recited back a hand-in-glove
  adulteration of my very verse,
  said it was Overripe's, and then, what's worse,
  accused me of embezzling words from him!

ALEX This Overripe... must be a pseudonym
  for someone with the nerve to plagiarize.

THOMAS And not just once, but many times disguise
  my work as his; for Sonja had a book,
  and page by page this crook had undertook
  to rob my images right from my brain!
  Oh, Dr. Wise! I've never known such pain!

ALEX Now, Thomas, can you think of anyone
  whose sick idea this might be of fun?
  Think hard now, Thomas. Who would wish you ill?

THOMAS I cannot think... such cruelty and such skill...
  No hands but mine and Catherine's ever touch
  my private papers... oh, this is too much!

ALEX Does Catherine keep them under lock and key?

THOMAS Under her pillow, probably, for she
  is more devoted to my verse than I!
  I know no one who'd wish me ill. And why
  would anyone devise such a cruel game,
  one calculated only to bring shame?

ALEX Well, let's find out. Why not invite him here?

THOMAS To torture me? I think not.

ALEX   Have no fear;
  I mean, to show him for the fraud he is.
  Why not request that he exhibit his
  poetic prowess right here on the spot?

THOMAS You mean a challenge? I like that... a lot...

ALEX I thought you might.

THOMAS   Yes, I can see it now!
  A challenge to compose! He'll not know how
  without the crutch of my verses before him.
  There'd be no way that Sonja could adore him!
  But what if he possesses greater skill?

If he defeats me, she will think more ill
of me than she already seems inclined to.

ALEX   Just put those insecurities behind you!
You have some time to get prepared, *n'est-ce pas?*

THOMAS   What do you mean?

ALEX mimes writing.

ALEX   I mean... you know...

THOMAS   Aha!
If I've already writ and memorized,
then only Overripe will be surprised
by the configuration of our game.

ALEX   Precisely.

THOMAS   Dr. Wise, have you no shame
suggesting that I cheat a proven cheater?

ALEX   He won't be proven till you're his defeater.
So I suggest you take whatever measures
are necessary to protect your treasures.
I will apprise your sister of our plan,
for she will help.

THOMAS   I am a lucky man!

ALEX   I'll ask her to send Overripe a letter
with all due haste.

THOMAS   Yes, but... it would be better
if she did not tell Sonja! I'd prefer
that these arrangements should be kept from her,
for I would rather it were a surprise
when I crush Overripe before her eyes!

ALEX   I'll ask your sister for utmost discretion
in helping you extract the thief's confession.

THOMAS   And now I must get to the work of writing!

ALEX   Yes, that's the spirit, Thomas! Keep on fighting!

Exit THOMAS and ALEX together.

scene two

CATHERINE is sitting at a table, surrounded by papers. She is reading dreamily, with a book in one hand and a pen in the other.

CATHERINE *"You know the place: ...cold*
streams murmur through the
apple branches, a young
rose thicket shades the ground
and quivering leaves pour
down deep sleep.... Come,
fill our gold cups with love
stirred into clear nectar."

> *She closes the book and looks up, dreamily.*

Oh, Sappho's syllables are such a treasure:
imagine tasting such exquisite pleasure!
I dream, oh Sappho, of a distant land,
wherein your spirit leads me by the hand
and tickles words from my reluctant throat...
Whole founts of love spring up! I would devote
my every word to honouring your face,
if only you could find me such a place,
where women take each other as their lovers...
Do I dream this alone? There must be others!
Were I a man, and not an aberration—
were I a man, or some approximation,
like Thomas, then I might hope to compete.
There was a woman once, just down the street,
who held a woman's name upon her tongue...
or so the story goes, for I was young,
and never understood quite what was said—
but when the truth got out, away she fled,
for everybody said she was a witch.
No wonder I do not dare scratch the itch
of my desire for Sonja! Oh, the torment!
To keep my passions locked up, silent, dormant!
I long to sing my loved one's praise in verse
but still my voice refuses. How I curse
in jealous rage at Muses's honeyed throats,
my dumb tongue swollen with unuttered notes,
while Thomas carols day and night off-key,
and leaves his love-stained lyric sheets for me.
And so I take the trouble to improve
my brother's tributes, hoping they might move
their object to some sense of her own worth;

for if she is not heaven, there's no earth.
With brother dear's rapt bleatings as my base,
my poems have incalculable grace:
I wring whole symphonies from one shrill note—
but my own words of love catch in my throat.
I wonder if dear Dr. Wise suspects
that I'm a member of the twilight sex,
for he encourages, while never chiding—
it's almost like he knows the love I'm hiding.
And he reveres this book, while others burn it,
whose words so thrill me that I can't return it!
Please, Sappho! Let your words my pen infuse!
Great lyricist of Lesbos, be my Muse!

> CATHERINE *clutches the book to her chest, closes her eyes and waits for inspiration. Enter* SONJA, *who sneaks up behind* CATHERINE *and puts her hand over* CATHERINE's *eyes. She examines* CATHERINE's *papers mock-critically.*

SONJA   Well, well, your artistry is undeniable;
though I confess I'm not the most reliable
of judges, but I can't say that I've seen
a page so blank as this—what can it mean?

> CATHERINE *immediately hides the* Sappho *book, but* SONJA *notices.* CATHERINE *tries to act casual.* SONJA *makes the occasional grab for the book throughout the following speeches, but is repeatedly thwarted by* CATHERINE.

CATHERINE   Unhand me, Sonja! Let me take a look...
Indeed, it's blank—

SONJA   Hey, Catherine... what's the book?

CATHERINE   It's nothing, just some homework that I missed.

SONJA   Then let me see! Perhaps I can assist.
Besides, what sort of homework makes you blush?
Don't tell me Catherine has a little crush?

CATHERINE   A crush? What do you mean? Are you suggesting—

SONJA   Oh, you protest! How very interesting!
Then I would have to guess that it's your teacher.
Is Dr. Wise a roguish handsome creature?

CATHERINE   Quit teasing, Sonja. You don't have a clue.

SONJA   And does he also have a crush on you?

CATHERINE   I mean it. Cut it out right now, okay?

SONJA   When do I get to meet him?

CATHERINE   Not today!

SONJA   Don't be so testy! Can't a girl have fun?
I can't believe how earnest you've become!
But I swear I see stars there in your eyes...

CATHERINE   Sonja! I'm not in love—with Dr. Wise.

SONJA   I'm not convinced.

CATHERINE   Look, I don't have much time.
This homework's due tomorrow, and if I'm
not finished, then I'll really have to pay.
Well, you can see I'm busy—

SONJA   You don't say.
Well, this is quite a switch. You, in a hurry!
You really make me wonder... but don't worry,
it's fine, we'll get to work. But while we measure
please lend your lips to this delicious treasure.
Restore its wounded music for my pleasure!

> *She hands the Overripe book to CATHERINE.*

CATHERINE   What? You want me to read you this?

SONJA   Oh, yes!
while I take measurements for your new dress.
And while you read, I'll dream that you are he
who penned these gorgeous syllables to me!

> *Throughout the following speeches, SONJA is taking measurements and fitting a dress for CATHERINE, who is increasingly uncomfortable with the physical intimacy.*

CATHERINE   (How near to truth her blithe fantasy hits!)

SONJA   Hold still, Catherine! I can't tell if this fits...
The bust is much too big. It needs a dart...

CATHERINE   (Her hands upon my breast! Be still my heart!)

SONJA   Why aren't you reading? Please, don't make me wait!
I love the fantasies these words create!

> *CATHERINE reads nervously.*

CATHERINE   *How long my tortured tongue has longed to tell*
I cannot tell you, only bite my tongue;
which bitten, tastes the longing twice as strong
and would against my better sense rebel.

The words rise from my throat; I push them back,
back to the darkness of their secret place,
where they contrive new longings to embrace
while silently my heart begins to crack.
I ask myself what harm could come from telling?
But overwhelmed by fears, I dare not speak;
and so my silent heart and tongue are swelling,
afraid to burst, and let my secret leak
from rain and sun and clouds and sky above you—
the secret that I cannot say: I love you.

SONJA   Oh, Catherine! That was quite simply the best!
I mean, I've never felt quite so... *caressed*
by words—you read that with such feeling!

CATHERINE   (I only hope I wasn't too revealing!)

SONJA   I wonder who he wrote these verses for?
And why was he so scared to try and score?
If I were the recipient of this,
my lips would ache for Overripe's sweet kiss!
How ever could he fear that she would not
reciprocate?

CATHERINE   My God, this dress is hot!

> *SONJA gives CATHERINE a puzzled look, then returns to her reverie.*

SONJA   I can't imagine what he'd fear.... Unless
some higher powers would refuse to bless
their sacred union.... I can barely guess
what fatal flaw, or gap in age, class, race
had meant he could not tell her to her face...

CATHERINE   Perhaps he feared rejection...

SONJA   What a skill
to write such words! If once I felt the thrill
of having verses in my honour spill
from lover's pen—my God, it would be glory!
But certain poets I must say I'm sorry
to have inspired. Your brother, for example,
has seen fit on these very words to trample,
and worse, to try to woo me with his vile
approximation of a master's style,
though he denied that this had been his source!

CATHERINE   What do you mean?

SONJA   Your brother's cute, of course,
   but he needs to learn how to give due credit!
   He offered me a clumsy little edit
   of these delicious lines you've just recited
   as his own work!—need I add, uninvited.

CATHERINE   You mean you think that Thomas—that he's stolen?

SONJA   Oh, he protests! I swear, his tongue is swollen
   from swearing up one side of me and down
   that he invented every verb and noun
   of every poem that he ever wrote.
   What does he take me for? He said—I quote—
   "But I wrote every word of that myself."
   As if this book were not from his own shelf!

CATHERINE   Wait, Sonja—let me get this straight. Did you
   show this to Thomas?

SONJA   What else could I do?
   I had to wrest it back from him, the crook!
   He gladly would have burned my favourite book!

CATHERINE   (So it has come to this. Not how I'd planned.)
   Sonja— (No, there's no way she'd understand!)
   Sonja— (How can I tell her *I'm* the thief?)
   Sonja—

SONJA   What?! Spit it out! Don't give me grief!

ALEX   *(off)* Catherine!

CATHERINE   (Thank God!) One moment, Dr. Wise!
   Sonja, I need some time to organize
   my thoughts before our lesson. I'm behind
   in my work, so if you would be so kind…

          SONJA unpins CATHERINE and gathers up her sewing kit.

SONJA   Oh, I can take a hint. I'm on my way.
   (Though curiosity would have me stay.)
   You'll have to introduce me someday, though…

CATHERINE   Another time.

SONJA   You promise? Then I'll go.
   (But not so far that I can't watch the show…)

          *Exit SONJA, to a corner of the room where she remains, unseen by
          CATHERINE, but able to observe everything that follows. Enter ALEX,
          opposite.*

ALEX   Oh, Catherine, there you are!

SONJA   (So that's the tutor!
He's older than I thought—but also cuter!)

ALEX   I've come to speak to you on pressing matters.
Your brother's confidence would be in tatters
if not for a small scheme I have devised.

CATHERINE   What do you mean?

ALEX   Well, Thomas was surprised
to learn, not half an hour ago, that he
has been the victim of a forgery—
or, more properly, plagiarism.

CATHERINE   No!

ALEX   I am afraid to say it seems as though
someone has somehow snatched your brother's words,
and, like the cruellest of mockingbirds,
has tossed them back in his astonished face.

CATHERINE   How horrible!

ALEX   Indeed, it's a disgrace.
Worse yet, it was the object of his dreams
who made him know the plagiarizer's schemes;
for Sonja praised the plagiarist and said
that Thomas must have been the thief instead!
Well, you can well imagine his distress.

> *CATHERINE nods nervously.*

But I've a plan for Thomas to impress
your Sonja with his skill, and win her back;
and make the criminal's hard armour crack,
so he'll admit that he has done the thieving,
and never sink again to such deceiving.

CATHERINE   What is the plan?

ALEX   It's simple, as things go,
but rather clever, if I may say so.
This Overripe—no doubt a phony name—
will be invited here to play a game.

CATHERINE   What? Croquet? Billiards? Darts? A round of chess?

ALEX   A far more intellectual prowess
is needed for the match I am proposing.
The game will be a contest of composing,

extempore, some verses for our pleasure.
And Overripe, without the private leisure
to plunder Thomas's poetic store,
is bound to come up lacking in his score.

SONJA   (If I were judging, there's no doubt who'd win!
Bring on the poets! Let the games begin!)

CATHERINE   I'd ask that I might send the invitation—
to spare my brother further indignation.

ALEX   Of course you may.

CATHERINE   When will the match take place?

ALEX   This Friday. I can't wait to see his face!
And now I must see how your brother's faring.
I do love the excitement of preparing!
Perhaps this story will inspire a sonnet?
Farewell. I'll let you get back to work on it.
I'm anxious, dear, to see what you create!
I've no doubt you'll impress me—I can't wait!

> *Exit ALEX.*

CATHERINE   A sonnet? Ha! My number's up for sure!
I never thought my plot would thus mature!
What choice have I, if they must play this game
than to reveal myself—reveal my shame!
And lose forever any shred of hope
that someday Sonja might…. How will I cope
with knowing that I've guaranteed my doom?
When not ten moments past, right in this room
she opened wide the door for my confession…
but I'm too much a victim of repression!
Would she love Overripe if she knew he
were not some lonely poet-man… but me?

SONJA   (She might indeed… though I'm a little shocked!
This is all new to me, but hey… why not?)

CATHERINE   If only I'd a co-conspirator;
one with a certain flair for theatre,
who'd play the poet and belittle Thomas…

SONJA   (Now that idea certainly shows promise!)

CATHERINE   What hope is there for Friday? That's the question!
Dear higher powers, got any suggestions?

> *She collapses on the table.*

SONJA (No need in higher powers faith to posit;
I've got your answer hanging in my closet.
The truth is out, though you dared not declare it.
I've got the costume. I can't wait to wear it.)

> *Blackout.*

scene three

> *Friday. ALEX and CATHERINE are tidying the parlour.*

ALEX And that is done… and that… and that's another.
Good. Everything's in place. Where is your brother?
When he gets here, I will explain the game
whereby he'll have revenge on what's-his-name.

CATHERINE Good heavens, Dr. Wise, in all the haste
of preparation, I somehow misplaced
this letter for you. It came yesterday.

ALEX Please open it, my dear. What does it say?

CATHERINE But it's addressed to you.

ALEX   That's quite alright.

CATHERINE Well, I'd prefer you opened it—it might
be private.

ALEX   Nonsense, I've no secrets!
On second thought, perhaps I will just read it.
My goodness, it's from our intended guest!
"Dear Dr. Wise, while I was quite impressed
with your most eloquent of invitations,
I am afraid that other obligations
prevent me from accepting, so with sorrow
I fear that I cannot attend tomorrow."
And it is indecipherably signed…
Oh, well, he obviously changed his mind
for look at what arrived here just this morning.

> *He takes a letter from his pocket and hands it to CATHERINE.*

CATHERINE "I hope this will provide sufficient warning
of my intended visit; I must say
I'm very eager to meet you today.
I cannot say enough how I'm delighted;
it's been a while since anyone invited
my humble self to such a test of skill.

I hope we all discover it's a thrill!"
Well, fancy that. So he is on his way.

ALEX   Yes, I can't wait to meet him.

CATHERINE   I must say,
  it seems surprising that you do not know him...

ALEX   I'll know him soon enough. And then we'll show him!
  He's nowhere near as clever as he thinks!
  Where is your brother? I must fetch some drinks.

> *Exit ALEX.*

CATHERINE   A drink to cool the fever in my brain!
  Who dares to try outwit me in my game?

> *Enter THOMAS, extremely agitated.*

THOMAS   Oh, Catherine, there you are! Is Sonja here?
  How do I look? How do I smell? I fear
  I give off a strong whiff of agitation!

CATHERINE   You're fine. Relax.

THOMAS   Oh, what humiliation
  if I should be defeated by this thief!
  Thank goodness you are here! What a relief
  to have my secretary at my side!
  Without your help I'm not sure I'd abide...

> *Enter SONJA, carrying the Overripe book and a suitcase; looking very rushed.*

SONJA   I can't believe my rotten luck today!
  Oh Catherine, Thomas—sorry I can't stay.
  Of all the luck! I have been called away.
  I so wanted to meet him—Overripe!—
  and find out if he lives up to the hype
  that I know I've had a hand in creating...
  Alas, I cannot stay. My cousin's waiting.

CATHERINE   What cousin, Sonja?

SONJA   Just my little cousin.
  If I have one, I swear, I have a dozen,
  and I can't keep them straight sometimes, you know!
  But anyway, I really have to go.
  I'm deeply sorry I won't meet the man
  whose words so thrill me! Thomas, if you can,

please ask him if he'll write a dedication
in my beloved book.

> *She hands him the book.*

Your education
will no doubt be enhanced by the mere meeting.
And please convey to him my warmest greeting.
And Catherine, if you're bold enough to try
to get a little closer to the guy,
please give him one of these on my behalf.

> *She gives CATHERINE a big long kiss, which leaves the latter reeling.*
> *THOMAS watches, at once envious and hurt.*

Now Thomas, don't forget that autograph!

> *She starts to leave but comes back for her suitcase.*

Take care, you two. Oops, can't forget my bag!
I can't believe I'll miss him. What a drag!

> *Exit SONJA. Stunned silence from both CATHERINE and THOMAS.*

THOMAS   She's gone.

CATHERINE   (And so am I!)

CATHERINE & THOMAS   I can't believe it!

THOMAS   What cruelty!

CATHERINE   (What sweetness!)

THOMAS   Who'd conceive it?
And after all the care I took preparing…

> *Enter ALEX.*

I swear, there is no justice!

ALEX   Why the swearing?

THOMAS   Sonja has dashed my hopes. She's gone away,
and will not see my prowess on display!
So what's the point, I ask you, in defeating
the cheater, if the one who loves his cheating
is not around to see him take the fall?

ALEX   Oh, Thomas, all is not lost, after all.
This is your chance to set the record straight.
Are you all set?

THOMAS   I was. Here.

THOMAS glumly hands some papers to ALEX, who looks them over.

ALEX   These are great!
Chin up, my friend! Do not waste time with sorrow.
We'll boast about your victory tomorrow!

THOMAS   And Sonja?

ALEX   She'll regret not having witnessed
your great display of true poetic fitness!
And when we tell how brilliantly you fared,
she'll realize all at once how much she's cared,
and will return your love with twice the fire
that you profess her looks in you inspire.

THOMAS   Well, I suppose that is some consolation…

ALEX   Don't let dull spirits dampen your creation!
Now Catherine, dear, the game we're going to play
is called—the name is French, dear—*bouts-rimés*,
which means, of course, end-rhymes, and as a rule—
I sometimes played it as a boy at school—
the players draw out random sets of rhyme
and each compose a verse within the time
they are allotted. Follow me so far?

CATHERINE   I think so.

ALEX   Good. Now, in this little jar
are slips of paper. These are just a prop.
The words I'm placing now, right here on top,
you'll offer to the players when requested.
Your brother has an awful lot invested
in coming out victorious in this game
and putting Mr. Overripe to shame.

THOMAS   So I've ensured that I've the upper hand
by memorizing these. You understand?

CATHERINE   I do. But is that fair?

THOMAS   I don't expect
I need to show a morsel of respect
to such a thief. I'd like to wring his neck!

SONJA   *(off)* Hello? Anyone home?

THOMAS   He's here, he's here!

ALEX   Thomas, stay calm. You have nothing to fear.
We'll welcome him and let the match begin!
Catherine, if you don't mind…

CATHERINE   I'll show him in.
(I want to be the first to meet the fiction
who plans to play my part with such conviction.)

> *As CATHERINE goes to exit, enter SONJA, disguised as a man.
> Somewhat androgynous; very attractive. THOMAS is subtly hostile,
> CATHERINE curious, ALEX immediately smitten, in spite of himself.*

SONJA   I beg your pardon, barging in like this.
I knocked, but…

ALEX   Nonsense, we have been remiss!

SONJA   I am surmising, Sir, that you must be
the Dr. Wise who has invited me.

ALEX   I am indeed. An excellent surmise.

> *Awkward silence while ALEX fixes drinks, looking appreciatively at
> SONJA. Finally:*

CATHERINE   The other introductions, Dr. Wise?

ALEX   Oh, yes! My manners! Mister Overripe,
meet Thomas Barren, also of the stripe
that makes his mark in verse.

CATHERINE   (Or so he thinks!)

SONJA   I'm pleased to meet you.

ALEX   And here are your drinks…

THOMAS   I'm pleased to meet you, too. It's quite a treat,
for since I read your work I've hoped we'd meet.

SONJA   It's always nice to meet another fan.
So you're a poet, too, my little man?

THOMAS   A poet, yes. A fan, I never said.
(*aside, to ALEX*) He's over-ripe indeed! What a swelled head!

ALEX   (A more attractive head than I expected,
which seems to stir up passions long neglected!)

> *CATHERINE clears her throat. ALEX snaps to.*

And this is Catherine, my other student.
Catherine will write verse, too, but she is prudent,
and hesitates before the daunting task.

SONJA   What is so daunting, Miss, if I may ask?
　　For if your words be worth but half your looks,
　　I daresay there'd be mountains of your books.

　　　　SONJA kisses CATHERINE's hand.

CATHERINE   Oh, my! You flatter!

THOMAS　　　　　　　*(aside, to ALEX)* How dare he presume!
　　To court my sister while I'm in the room!

ALEX   *(aside, to THOMAS)* Indeed, he has a most seductive art—
　　but we will show him up! Just play your part.
　　(to SONJA) I didn't think you'd be quite so attractive—
　　so young, I mean, so young!

SONJA　　　　　　　　Well, I keep active.
　　And I must say I'm truly *enchanté*
　　to be here with the three of you today.
　　But was there not to be a "Sonja" here?
　　Your note said there'd be four of you.

ALEX　　　　　　　　　I fear
　　that Sonja had some business to attend to.

CATHERINE   But she requested of us that we send you
　　her warmest greetings. Didn't she, now, Thomas?

THOMAS   Indeed she did.

CATHERINE　　　　　In fact, you made a promise
　　that you'd ask Mister Overripe to sign
　　her cherished volume, did you not?

SONJA　　　　　　　　Well, fine!

　　　　She takes the book from THOMAS, signs it, and gives it back.

　　You sure that's not for you now? I'm just kidding!
　　Now Catherine, did this Sonja deem it fitting
　　to call on you to seek some favour from me?

CATHERINE   She did... but I fear it would not become me
　　to do as she requested.

SONJA　　　　　　I'm not shy!
　　Please go ahead! Come on! Give me a try!

　　　　CATHERINE reluctantly offers a very quick kiss. SONJA prolongs it;
　　　　CATHERINE begins to clue in.

ALEX   *(aside, to THOMAS)* How boldly he presumes!

THOMAS *(aside, to ALEX)* I swear, that does it!

> *SONJA and CATHERINE disengage.*

SONJA Now, Catherine, that wasn't so scary, was it?
I like this Sonja! Any more requests?
Or should we get down to our round of tests?

> *CATHERINE, who has been a little woozy since the kiss, faints. SONJA catches CATHERINE in her arms. THOMAS and ALEX gather around very close.*

Bring water, quickly! Help me to revive her!
Stand back! She needs more air! Do not deprive her!

> *ALEX hands a glass of water to SONJA, who throws it in CATHERINE's face. CATHERINE moans a little as she regains consciousness.*

CATHERINE Where am I? Oh, I had the strangest dream…
there was a man… a woman… no, they seem
within one single body both to dwell…

ALEX Catherine, it's Dr. Wise. You've had a spell.
You're having visions. There's no woman here,
except yourself. You're dreaming. Is that clear?

CATHERINE *(dreamy)* I swear, the air in here has gotten thinner…
(coming around) Where were we? Don't we have to pick a winner?

> *Sighs of relief from the other three.*

THOMAS We haven't even started on the match!

SONJA What made you faint?

ALEX And please do not attach
too much significance to woozy visions!

SONJA Unless, of course, they answer with precision
a pesky mystery or a nagging question.
And don't ignore the power of suggestion.

CATHERINE *(aside, to SONJA)* Sonja? How did you know?

SONJA *(aside to CATHERINE)* I have my ways.

THOMAS Well, now that Catherine's come out of her daze—

ALEX Thank goodness, for you gave us quite a fright—

THOMAS Let's start this contest of poetic might.

ALEX You know the rules, then. We'll draw *random* pairs
of rhyme words for you, and whoever bears

up best under the pressure to compose
will be the winner.

SONJA Well, I don't suppose
there's any more straightforward test of skill.
I'm ready. Get us started, if you will.
(aside, to Catherine) I came prepared for this important game.
Here, use these words.

She hands CATHERINE some slips of paper.

CATHERINE *(aside, to SONJA)* Sonja, have you no shame?

THOMAS Why don't we up the stakes ere we begin,
and let each player name what he might win?

SONJA Why should we name them ere the match commence?
Why not keep one another in suspense
and state our wishes in poetic form?
Let's see if Catherine's rhymes our needs inform.

CATHERINE Here are your rhymes; I hope you find them just.
There's "fraud, God"; "wise, eyes, prize"; then "must" and "trust."

THOMAS Are you sure, Catherine? Did you read those right?

SONJA Why? I see nothing wrong with her eyesight.

THOMAS No, I just wondered…

SONJA I think they'll work fine.

THOMAS *(aside, to ALEX)* These words she offered—why were they not mine?

ALEX *(aside, to THOMAS)* Perhaps her little spell made her forget.
But keep on writing, Thomas! Please don't fret.

THOMAS Uh, Catherine! I could use your help, my dear…

SONJA Nonsense! She is my Muse! She'll stay right here!
I'm almost ready! How're you making out?

THOMAS Not quite yet. *(aside, to ALEX)* I am lost! I am without
a single verse inside my troubled head.

ALEX *(aside, to THOMAS)* Just write your truth. You will not be misled.

SONJA Okay, time's up. Have you got something now?

THOMAS I scribbled something, though I'm not sure how.
I'll let you have this, my most naked plea.
Here is what I request: verse speaks for me.
Stop doing this. It's torture. You're a fraud.
Words fail me. Please, if you are wise,

give it up now, and make your peace with God.
All that I ask for as my prize
is that you give me, in front of my own eyes,
a confession of your crimes. You must
if there is good in you, I trust.

SONJA   How interesting. Your style is—I don't know.
Well, here's what I wrote. Does my passion show?
In naming what I seek, I know I must
humbly beseech the honoured Dr. Wise,
in whose esteemed discretion I most trust.
If I'm the victor in his honest eyes,
I'll claim… the lovely Catherine as my prize,
and run away with her this night, by God—
for if I do not love her, I'm a fraud.

THOMAS   You can't be serious.

SONJA   I'm quite sincere.

ALEX   Now, let us just hold on a moment here!
Whether you win this contest or you lose,
dear Catherine's fate will be her own to choose.
My students are not chattel to be won!

THOMAS   Don't you realize the sole reason you've come
is to admit you stole from me? Confess!

SONJA   Confession's not my style, as you might guess.
But any game I play, I play to win.
Let's have the verdict! Judges, please begin!

ALEX   Well, were I to ignore all that's at stake
and let your verses my decision make,
I would be torn. You've both borne up so well,
the judge in me makes motions to rebel
against the obligation to decide:
and thus I must declare the contest… tied.

SONJA   If we're to have a winner in this game,
it must be up to Catherine, then, to name
the victor, and unknot this little snag.
What do you say?

THOMAS   (I've got it in the bag!)
Yes, tell us, Catherine, what's the verdict, then?

CATHERINE   To let a woman judge the work of men
is such outlandish folly, I'm compelled
to play the judge who in you, sir, rebelled.

And thus I declare… Overripe the winner.

THOMAS   And you his prize?

CATHERINE   His breakfast, lunch and dinner.

SONJA   A wise choice, Catherine! We'll at once away.
Our life together will begin today.

CATHERINE   *(aside to SONJA)* The joke's gone far enough. Shed the disguise.

SONJA   *(aside to CATHERINE)* Who's joking? I intend to claim my prize.

> *SONJA escorts CATHERINE toward the door.*

CATHERINE   *(aside, to SONJA)* Wherever you will lead me, I will go.

SONJA   We must be leaving now, and though I know
this may seem sudden to you, have no fear.
Together we shall forge a new frontier.

> *Exit SONJA with CATHERINE.*

THOMAS   Does Catherine really love this roguish cheat?
I can't believe the depth of my defeat!
For though his pen delivered some fine jabs,
my sister's hand was never up for grabs.
Thus, though it grieves me to depart from you,
the path is clear. I know what I must do.
For if I give in to this charlatan
and let him take her, I am not a man.
Tell Sonja I have had to leave, to save
my loving sister; tell her I am brave
and that I will return to do her honour,
and if you will, please plant a kiss upon her
delicious little lips—here, just like this.

> *THOMAS kisses ALEX.*

Farewell, I must be off!

ALEX   Farewell!

> *Exit THOMAS. ALEX puts his hand to his lips, closes his eyes.*

That kiss,
had it come from a certain other student,
might have been far more welcome, if imprudent…
How can I have been blind to my own heart
while claiming to instruct them in its art?
I know such scruples well become a tutor,
but damn that dashing Overripened suitor!

How easily his fancy he expressed,
while I've choked back these feelings in my breast,
without my even knowing they were there!
How could I let him take her? It's not fair!
But why give up now? No! I won't play nice,
for I can't make that fatal error twice!

> *ALEX begins to take off some of her clothes, revealing that she is actually a woman.*

If Catherine wants a poet, I've a mission,
and know just where to find my ammunition!
Enough repression! Damn this old disguise!
No more concealing! Farewell, Dr. Wise!

> *Exit ALEX.*

ACT TWO

scene one

Sound of rain. Darkness, a creaking door.

CATHERINE   *(off)* What? Sonja, don't go in! This place is haunted!

SONJA   *(off)* I thought you said a shelter's what you wanted.
Besides, it looks okay. It's warm, it's dry…

> *Enter SONJA, still wearing the Overripe disguise, somewhat disheveled
> and a little wet from the rain. She strikes a match. We see her, but not
> much else, in its light. She looks around. The match goes out.*

CATHERINE   *(off)* Did I ever say "haunted house?" Did I?
Sonja, I don't think you quite realize—

SONJA   Catherine, come here! You won't believe your eyes!

> *Enter CATHERINE. SONJA lights a candle. Lights up gradually on
> a decaying house. Everything is overgrown with moss, cobwebs, dirt. The
> decay has a distinctly vegetative quality; what appears to be a couch could
> be decomposing upholstery or an overgrown log. There is a prominently
> posted sign that reads "Women Only Land," and the room is dominated
> by a giant statue of a woman, so overgrown now that it looks more like
> a tree.*

CATHERINE   My God, it's beautiful! I never dreamed…

SONJA   I guess it's not as haunted as it seemed…
What gave you that idea, anyway?

CATHERINE   Some years ago—well, in my mother's day
there was a woman here who lived alone
whose looks were said to have turned men to stone,
so no man dared to venture in her trap.

SONJA   I can't believe you'd buy that sexist crap!
It's obvious what sort of girl she was!

CATHERINE   What do you mean?

> *SONJA points to the "Women Only Land" sign.*

SONJA   Look! She was one of us!

CATHERINE   A Women Only Land! Land of my dreams!
I can't believe…. Do you know what this means?
A place where our true love can be expressed
no matter who we are, or how we're dressed!
It's time to let you know what I've been feeling!
No more disguises and no more concealing!

> *CATHERINE kisses SONJA, gently at first, then with growing passion.*
> *SONJA disengages.*

SONJA   Aren't you afraid that someone might have followed?

CATHERINE   Who, Thomas? Do you think he could have swallowed
his wounded pride that quickly?

SONJA   Dr. Wise?

CATHERINE   He'd never know you out of that disguise.
So let's transform you back to the real you…

> *She begins to make a move on SONJA, who squirms out of it.*

SONJA   I must be certain they would not pursue!

CATHERINE   Sonja, I can't imagine they would miss me
enough to try. So just relax and kiss me!

> *They kiss. SONJA disengages.*

SONJA   I still feel somehow like we're not alone.

CATHERINE   I hardly think we need a chaperone!
All right. One kiss, then we'll search high and low,
but if it's just us…

> *They kiss. CATHERINE tries to prolong it but SONJA breaks away.*

SONJA   Catherine, let me go!

CATHERINE   You were all eagerness in front of Thomas,
but now that we're alone…

SONJA   Catherine, I promise,
it's nothing about you that makes me shy.
It's just that—well, it's really just that I—
am scared—that we might not have privacy!

CATHERINE   Well, fine. On with the search, and you will see
there's no one here to ravish you but me!

> *SONJA exits. CATHERINE pursues. Enter ALEX.*

ALEX   Oh, how I've missed these simple floors and walls!
And how I've stopped my ears against your calls
for all these years, reminding me of home:
My Women Only Land! At last I've come!

> *She approaches the statue.*

Oh, Sappho! Will your blessings still rain down
upon a poet of such poor renown

who's left your fires untended all these years?
Please help me make new music for your ears!

> *She pulls out a stack of papers, curled with age, from a hiding place*
> *under the statue, and as she looks through them, scatters them around*
> *the statue's base.*

These hymns to you I started as a girl,
in search of the poetic, perfect pearl
that would convey my longings fittingly
to my beloved…. But unwittingly
I'd set my sights too high, and never could
complete a paean worthy of your good.
And so I forfeited my declaration,
and never knew my love's reciprocation.
But now, with love fresh-stirred within my heart,
I've come at last to realize my art,
and to reclaim, in technicolour pride,
the passions that for years I have denied!
Let Catherine choose the poet she prefers:
she holds my heart; I hope I can win hers!
But first, I must make peace with every nook:
My heart is full enough to write a book!

> *Exit ALEX. Enter CATHERINE and SONJA, opposite.*

CATHERINE   We've searched in every cranny of this home!
I hope you're satisfied that we're alone.

> *She notices the statue.*

Except for this bold figure, and I doubt
that she'd object to our going about
our business; no, she seems to look approving!
So let us get down to the work of loving.

> *CATHERINE kisses SONJA. SONJA disengages, approaches the statue,*
> *finds the poems ALEX has scattered around it.*

SONJA   Why Catherine, look! Here's poem after poem!

> *CATHERINE comes over, picks up some of the pages, marvels at them.*

CATHERINE   My God! This must have been a poet's home!
"*Imagining my lips upon your face*
unstrings the orchestra of my desire:
and now, mere splinters of their former grace
these broken bows cavort within the fire
that turns their love to smoke." It's incomplete…
nothing but fragments at this statue's feet.

And fragments of desire, not consummation,
for longing seems to be their inspiration.

SONJA   What lover could resist such poetry?

CATHERINE   Indeed, I wonder… certainly not me!
Perhaps they're offerings in this statue's honour.

     She notices an inscription at the base of the statue.

And praise of praises be rained down upon her!

SONJA   What is it?

CATHERINE   I have found a kindred spirit!
This poet's inspiration—I can't bear it!
This figure represents my very Muse,
great Sappho! Sonja, how can you refuse
your favours in such noble company?

SONJA   Now, Catherine, wait—

CATHERINE   Her ghost will live through me!
The author of these great unfinished songs
will find at last the love for which she longs,
and you will be the vessel to receive it!

SONJA   I will? Right now? What?

CATHERINE   You'd better believe it!

    CATHERINE embraces SONJA. SONJA pulls back.

SONJA   But Catherine, this is too intimidating!

CATHERINE   What is your problem? Please don't keep me waiting!

SONJA   Please, Catherine, stop! I'm not what I appear!

CATHERINE   Well, Sonja, duh! What, did you really fear
I thought you were a man?

SONJA   No, no! I mean
you probably think that I… well, that I've been
around the block a couple times, you know?

CATHERINE   Yes, and…

SONJA   Well, no. I haven't.

CATHERINE   Never?

SONJA   No.

CATHERINE   You sure know how to fake it with bravado.
 You carry on like an aficionado!

SONJA   I guess sometimes I overact a bit.
 It makes things more exciting…

CATHERINE   Yeah, no shit!
 Look, Sonja, I'm no expert here myself,
 but I think I am ready now to delve
 into the mysteries that your disguise
 has too long hidden from my eager eyes.

SONJA   Whoa, Catherine, please! I need to take it slowly;
 for love, like poetry, is something holy,
 and I need you to worship me some more.
 How about a poem to her whom you adore?

CATHERINE   Is poetry the only form of praise?
 I'd like to worship you in other ways…

SONJA   A poem is a fitting place to start.

CATHERINE   But I am ill-equipped now for that art!
 Without my brother's doggerel to improve,
 I have no verses to express my love.

SONJA   You mean to say you stole your poems from Thomas?

CATHERINE   I never meant to! Sonja, please, I promise!
 I couldn't bear to see you so debased,
 to see your features praised with such poor taste!
 And so, I played the part of his improver,
 but love for you was always my prime mover.
 And I can't wait for my own words of praise
 to finally cry out in our loving ways!

   She makes a move on SONJA, who keeps her at bay.

SONJA   Then Catherine, if you want to earn my trust,
 I'll need some confirmation that your lust
 is genuine, and is inspired by me,
 and not some twisted sibling rivalry.

CATHERINE   Sonja, I swear, I did it all for you!

SONJA   A simple protestation will not do.
 No, no. I need a poem, fresh and new.

CATHERINE   Of course, my love! But nothing could inspire
 my passionate, fierce, poeticizing fire
 like making love with you right here and now!

SONJA Too bad. I've set my terms. I won't allow
for any clever new negotiations,
and so I hope you've other inspirations—
like Sappho here, and this old poet's ghost;
I'm sure she'll prove a stimulating host!
And in the meantime, while you write your poem,
I'll make myself acquainted with our home.

Exit SONJA.

CATHERINE What sort of muse plays such outlandish games?
Sonja, come back! Sonja! Have you no shame?

CATHERINE follows. Exit.

scene two

Sound of rain. Enter THOMAS.

THOMAS What's this decaying floor on which I stand?
What means this sign? This "Women only land?"
Only land where? The thought seems incomplete.
I know that cats only land on their feet,
but women… sometimes land in someone's lap,
or sometimes they might fall into a trap…
like my beloved sister! Help me save her!
Don't let that nasty Overripe enslave her!
Who knows how low that rotten scum might sink?
Or float… yes, scum would float… I cannot think!
Oh, Catherine! Catherine! Catherine! Are you here?
They must be somewhere relatively near.
I swear I followed them into this place…

THOMAS looks around and realizes where he is.

The haunted house! I dare not show my face!
For it is said no man dare hope survive
a visit here; none has come out alive!

He finds SONJA's suitcase and CATHERINE's unfinished dress from Act One. Enter ALEX, unseen by THOMAS.

This suitcase looks familiar… and this dress!
My sister! She is here! Oh, who could guess
my plan for rescue would hit such a glitch?
God help me, I must save her from the witch!

ALEX   (Alas, the witch has not yet found her prize.
    Let's hope her brother will not recognize
    his old beloved tutor, Dr. Wise.)

       ALEX approaches THOMAS. THOMAS is startled, then terrified.

    Good afternoon, young man. How came you here?

THOMAS   I'm sorry, please forgive me, but I fear
    I've taken a wrong turn. I will be going.
    I would not want to trouble you, and knowing
    how women like you love your privacy,
    I'll take myself away and leave you be.

       THOMAS begins to leave. ALEX stops him.

ALEX   (No hint of our acquaintance on his face.
    Then I am free! And can pursue the chase!)
    A wrong turn, did you say? What were you seeking?

THOMAS   Please! Don't prolong my agony with speaking!
    If you must kill me, please just do it now,
    as quickly as your cruelty will allow!
    At least I'll know that I did what I could
    to rescue Catherine from that ne'er-do-good!
    And if you have a heart, let Sonja know
    that with me die, in wordless embryo,
    a hundred thousand poems that sing her praise!
    Oh, cruel, silencing fate! Such unjust ways!

ALEX   Relax, my friend. I won't kill you today.
    You think a "Catherine" might have passed this way?

THOMAS   I swear I saw her duck into this door!

ALEX   But I've just combed the first and second floor
    and there is no one here.

THOMAS   Then I will go.

ALEX   Wait. Not so fast. Why do you hurry so?

THOMAS   Well, with all due respect, I have heard rumours
    that women here fall into vicious humours
    and do the most appalling things to men.
    I would protect myself from you—from them.

ALEX   (I see my reputation still exceeds me.
    But if I can convince him that he needs me,
    then he can help direct me to my prize,

and learn about the value of disguise.)
You think you are in danger?

THOMAS   Am I not?

ALEX   Well, that depends on what you have been taught.

THOMAS   What do you mean?

ALEX   Well, it is safe for me,
as I'm a woman. But to men, you see,
this neighbourhood is not entirely warm.
Those rumours—well, some men have come to harm.

THOMAS   Then I must leave!

ALEX   No! Even that's unwise!
Your scent has surely been picked up by spies,
and once they have your scent—well, that's the end.

THOMAS   I have no hope!

ALEX   There's one way to defend
yourself against the amazonic threat,
but it's a little out there—oh, forget it…

THOMAS   No, tell me! I'll do anything you say!

ALEX   Become a woman.

THOMAS   What?

ALEX   Just for today.

> *ALEX takes CATHERINE's unfinished dress from the suitcase and gives it
> an appraising look. THOMAS looks dubious.*

THOMAS   What do you have in mind?

ALEX   Oh, nothing drastic.
I think there's enough give in the elastic…

> *She helps a reluctant THOMAS into the dress. It is not quite finished, and
> keeps falling off one shoulder, so that THOMAS is continually fussing
> with it.*

THOMAS   You're sure that this is necessary?

ALEX   Yes,
and just our luck! This is a lovely dress!

THOMAS   It is my sister's…

ALEX   Does that mean she's here?
Why then, you have more reason still to fear,

for women tend to turn against their brothers.
Do not reveal yourself to any others
you might encounter here, for news might spread!
Let's get to work on that exquisite head…

> *ALEX begins to apply makeup, occasionally backing up to give THOMAS an appraising look, throughout the following.*

Your secret's safe with me, if you've the wit
to make a most convincing counterfeit.
There's nothing like the safety of disguise—
I think a little more around the eyes…
and pucker for me now, there, that's a dear—
oh, lovely! Yes, you'll have nothing to fear!
Exhibit some conviction while you fake it,
and you just might discover that you like it!

THOMAS   I don't think I'm the type…

ALEX   Don't speak too soon!
You never know who might be in the room,
for walls have ears, and floorboards might have eyes—
I'd hate for this to get back to the spies!
Let's see now… here's some shoes that you can wear…
and we'll have to do something with that hair…

> *She produces a wig.*

Wear this for now. And stand up like a girl!
Here, let me give you just a little curl…

THOMAS   How long must I endure this? Ow! My feet!

SONJA   *(off)* How is the writing going there, my sweet?

ALEX   There's someone here! Well, now's the perfect test
to see just how convincingly you're dressed!

> *ALEX begins to leave. THOMAS hobbles after her.*

THOMAS   No, please! You can't just leave me here alone!

ALEX   Now be a woman! Show us some backbone!
I will stand over there, just out of sight,
and if her bark suggests she has a bite,
I'll quickly rescue you from any danger.
Good luck, my friend!

> *Exit ALEX before THOMAS can reply. Enter SONJA, opposite. She initially mistakes THOMAS for CATHERINE.*

SONJA   Well now, don't be a stranger!

> *THOMAS sees SONJA and is too shocked to move. SONJA immediately
> realizes that he is not CATHERINE. Throughout their conversation,
> THOMAS is continually pulling at the dress to cover his shoulder.*

I'm sorry! I mistook you for my friend.
Where did you get that dress? And don't pretend
you haven't stolen it, for I did sew
each stitch of it with my own hands, and though
it's not quite finished yet, it does become you
so well that I can't repossess it from you.
I'm sure you'll find some way to make amends.
My name is Sonja. I hope we'll be friends.
Are you the "witch" who fled this place in shame?

THOMAS   I am a man—Amanda is my name!

> *SONJA offers a handshake. THOMAS limply accepts.*

SONJA   Is something wrong? You're staring. Oh, my clothes!
You're probably wondering if I'm one of those
who moves about the world as something other…
I only dressed like this for Catherine's brother.

THOMAS   Catherine?

SONJA   My lover.

THOMAS   Lover?

SONJA   Yes! My lover!
We had a contest… that was just a cover;
for I learned that she loved me, and I thought,
well, this is kind of new, but hell, why not?
Besides, I got to dress up as a man!
You ever tried it?

THOMAS   Me? No…

SONJA   It began
as just a means to a delightful end,
but now there's something… these clothes seem to send
an unexpected surge of power through me…
I mean, you'd be astonished if you knew me!
Where is your lover?

THOMAS   Lover?

SONJA   You're alone?
A pretty girl like you? Look, since I own
the dress that you have on, won't you permit
a quick adjustment from my sewing kit?

She takes out a needle and thread and comes over, starts sewing up the
loose shoulder. THOMAS looks very uncomfortable.

As you can see, it wasn't quite completed.
But you are just the wearer that it needed!
On Catherine, it was lovely, but on you—
such radiance! The colour suits you, too!

THOMAS   Where's Catherine now?

SONJA   Well, I should hope she's writing.
I made a deal with her: before requiting
her passionate advances, I must hear
a fresh verse from her pen. For it is clear
there's talent in her fingers, but I must
have confirmation that her newfound lust
is meant for me, the one she calls her lover
and not just retribution on her brother.

THOMAS   Her brother...

SONJA   It's too tawdry to relate.
You'll thank me sparing you. Really, I hate
to dwell on trivia... but here's a thought!
You're awfully cute, Amanda! Have you got
poetic aspirations?

THOMAS   I'm not sure...

SONJA   Oh, don't be shy! I think I might secure
a better verse from Catherine if she had
some competition—ooh, I'm such a cad!
It's only fair to put you to the test
as payment for your lovely purloined dress.
Amanda, if you write a poem superior
to Catherine's efforts, then my sweet interior
will be your land in which to pioneer.
I daresay you've the hands for it, my dear.

She takes THOMAS's hand and licks his fingers very seductively. He
makes a move to kiss her. She pushes him away.

Don't rush things now! You've got a little time.
So I suggest those lips caress a rhyme.
If it's most pleasing to my ear, I'm yours.
Farewell, and may your words open new doors!

Exit SONJA. Enter ALEX, opposite. At every turn in the following speech,
ALEX tries to respond, but THOMAS's train of thought is unstoppable.

THOMAS   I can't believe the nightmare I've stepped into!
  I'm mute, dumbstruck, I can't even begin to
  articulate the horror that I feel!
  That Sonja, woman of my dreams, did steal
  my heart, and then my sister, and now barters
  the honour of dishevelling her garters
  for lines of verse—oh, fates! you are too savage!
  What of my faith remains for you to ravage?
  I feel the very ground beneath my feet
  has thoroughly betrayed me! Oh, deceit!
  And yet, there's some small comfort in the fact
  that Sonja so lasciviously snacked
  upon my manly digits... what a tease!
  But still, her lips can bring me to my knees,
  regardless of her loving my own sister...
  a painful truth, but how can I resist her?
  If all I have to do is write a verse
  to taste her favours... well, it could be worse!
  But she thinks I'm a woman. Does that mean
  that Sonja's tastes fall somewhere in between
  forbidden fruit and normal fleshly pleasures?
  How can I satisfy her in those measures?
  No doubt in verse I'll manage to outstrip
  my sister; but this new relationship
  might well capsize if Sonja should discover
  that I'm a man, and worse yet, Catherine's brother!
  How does a woman play a woman's suitor?
  Now, more than ever, I could use a tutor!

ALEX   You could not be in better hands, my dear;
  or better placed, for this statue, right here,
  pays tribute to the memory of her
  to whom all lyric lovers must defer:
  great Sappho, in whose merest fragment flickers
  the pulse of love's intoxicating liquors.

THOMAS   A woman poet?

ALEX   Yes, one of the oldest,
  and in the ways of love, one of the boldest!
  She has inspired my pen a thousand times,
  as you can see by these unworthy rhymes.
  Still, one might prove a starting place for you.
  Ah, here is something. I think this will do.

        She hands him one of the papers.

THOMAS   *"My broken instruments can hardly scrape*
   a tune less eloquent than all my wanting.
   Then hush their strings, and let their notes escape;
   those unheard melodies are far more haunting."
   You never finished it?

ALEX   I never could,
   but as a model it will do you good.
   You see, a woman's poetry is humble:
   it's rare for unconsidered words to tumble
   too freely from her lips in songs of love.
   And though that costume fits you like a glove,
   if as a woman you would seek to date,
   restraint's the hallmark you must emulate.

THOMAS   Restraint? Where will that get me?

ALEX   Wait and see.
   If you rehearse this poem, it just might free
   a new voice that you haven't yet discovered
   within you—and that might impress your lover.
   She might even forget about your sister.
   (Though I'm not sure how any could resist her!)
   I will do everything within my power
   to see you triumph in this fateful hour!
   Now you must go. I have some work to do.

THOMAS   But I can't be alone here without you!

ALEX   Relax. You will be safe in your disguise.

THOMAS   But Sonja—

ALEX   You're a woman in her eyes.
   Now be the woman that her heart desires,
   and see what magic poetry inspires.

            ALEX ushers THOMAS from the room, then turns to the statue.

   It will take magic for that boy to win,
   but I will throw my every effort in
   upon his side: his victory would free
   his most bewitching sister up for me!
   Her absence these few hours but fans my fires
   with ever more articulate desires!
   But would she have me? For her love inclines
   to most unworthy, fickle Valentines
   if Sonja here is any indication—
   oh, how I've failed her in her education,

insisting only that she speak her passion,
not teaching her to choose with some discretion!
No wonder Overripe was such a dish,
for Sonja is attractive; but I wish,
while nursing Catherine in expression's art,
I might have shown her this more faithful heart.
It's not too late. I'll give it one last shot:
if there's a contest, I will stir the pot!

> *Exit.*

scene three

> *CATHERINE is sitting in front of the statue, desperately trying to write.*

CATHERINE   "My bones are jelly
and my brain is vermicelli… "
I must have quite a hunger in my belly!
Not half the hunger that for Sonja craves!
But I won't let my verses here be slaves
to fleshly longings; these poor metaphors
are not about to open any doors.
"My bones are moaning and my brain's in pain;
without your love I'm going to go insane."
No. Far too coarse! For Sonja is ethereal;
my images must not be too material.
"My bones are shaken and my brain is rattled,
for ever since the moment we skedaddled
from brother's house, I've felt a burning passion
on which I hope so very soon to cash in."
No! Sonja likes some mystery in her verse,
and this is too direct. It's getting worse!
How come my lines all come out sounding shoddy?
And time's-a-wasting! And I want her body!
I know the labour-saving thing to do:
I'll aim for brevity with a haiku!
"so much bone shaking
so much rattling of the brain
my adoration…"
But so few words can scarce begin conveying
the magnitude of what I hope I'm saying.
"You shake my bones and you rattle my brain…"
A fitting epic opening, to gain
admission to the gates of Paradise…
but how can I give it a bit more spice?

I never second-guessed myself this much
when I had Thomas's doggerel to retouch!

> *She picks up some of the papers scattered around the statue.*

This gifted ghost might well unlock my heart
if I had but a fraction of her art...
but Sonja will not tolerate more stealing.
Why can't she just believe in what I'm feeling?
I find my paucity of words surprising...
If only Dr. Wise were here advising!
For he had faith in my ability,
despite my brother's imbecility,
when even I was doubtful of my skill.
Oh, help me, Dr. Wise! I know the drill:
just write my truth. Oh, Sappho, loose my tongue!
Great Muse, infuse me with what must be sung!

> *She resumes trying to write, eyes closed, concentrating. Enter THOMAS,
> unseen by CATHERINE, rehearsing the poem ALEX has given him.
> CATHERINE writes down his words, as if the Muse is dictating to her.*

THOMAS *My broken instruments can hardly scrape*
a tune less eloquent than all my wanting.
Then hush their strings, and let their notes escape;
those unheard melodies are far more haunting.

> *THOMAS walks straight into CATHERINE, who opens her eyes and
> gasps. They are equally startled.*

CATHERINE Sorry! I didn't hear you. Are you new?
My name is Catherine. I just got here, too.
I love your dress! I have one just the same,
though not quite finished yet, which is a shame...
You've quite a way with words. Are you a writer?

THOMAS Well, yes, but—

CATHERINE Well! I'm pulling an all-nighter,
and I could use some help with it. You see,
I've done my share of work with poetry,
but most of it has been—well, underhanded.
But now my darling Sonja has demanded
that I supply a brand-new verse before
she'll let me hold her whom I most adore!
(Or most adored until I heard you speak!
Why am I babbling? Why this hot-flushed cheek?)

THOMAS She makes you write?

CATHERINE   I try, but there's a catch:
my brother's rotten eggs aren't here to hatch!
Have you a brother?

THOMAS   No.

CATHERINE   You should be grateful.
It's possible there's not a thing more hateful!
My brother never gave me any credit,
and never dreamed how cleverly I'd edit
his tuneless songs into a symphony
to win his cherished prize away with me.

THOMAS   You stole your brother's poems?

CATHERINE   It served him right.
Besides, his images were awfully trite.
But now that Sonja knows of how I borrowed,
she's happy to put off until tomorrow
what I can hardly wait to do today!
And I'm discovering, to my dismay,
that thus bereft of raw material,
my stabs at poetry are far inferior
to my improvements on what brother puled.
Somehow my rage at his injustice fuelled
a passion in my poems that made them sing;
where now they barely hint at whistling.
But your tongue has a gift, I understand.
Would you consider lending me a hand?

THOMAS   I must be going.

CATHERINE   Please! Linger awhile.
If you don't mind, I'll fortify my style
by trying out my first attempts on you.
Pretend you're Sonja.

THOMAS   No! I don't want to—

CATHERINE   Relax! Just listen. Imagine I'm your lover.

THOMAS   (Oh, Catherine, please stop torturing your brother!)

> *She gives him her paper and pen, flirtatiously touching his hand.*

CATHERINE   Here. Write this down, while I extemporize
a tribute to the one I idolize…
"You shake my bones and you rattle my brain;
my limbs are all akimbo with desire.
If we don't do it soon I'll go insane:

so hotly burns my something something fire."
What do you think?

THOMAS   I don't think I could tell you…

CATHERINE   But would these lines attract you or repel you?
Be honest!

THOMAS   I have no critique for you.
You'd not want my opinion if you knew!

> *Enter SONJA. CATHERINE and THOMAS are both flustered.*

SONJA   Well, well, contestants. I can see you've met.
I hope you're both prepared for your first sweat.

CATHERINE   Contestants? Sweat? Whatever do you mean?
And I was missing you! Where have you been?

> *CATHERINE goes to embrace SONJA. SONJA keeps her at bay.*

SONJA   I thought you might enjoy some competition,
and so I made a little proposition
to my new friend, Amanda, to engage
her pen in making love to a clean page.
Whichever of you writes the sweetest lines
will pop the cork on my untasted wines.

CATHERINE   A contest? Very funny.

THOMAS   Not at all.

SONJA   And I've no doubt you've got the wherewithal
to set the little hairs on my neck rising.
I won you in a game of man's devising,
so why not win me back on my own terms?

CATHERINE   Sonja, my every breath just reaffirms
that I adore you! Must I play a game?
My heart beats in the rhythm of your name!
(Or did, until a few short breaths ago…
Is Sonja still my prize? I do not know!)

> *Enter ALEX, unseen at first by the others.*

ALEX   (At last the sight of Catherine burns my eyes,
whose virtues I can scarcely itemize…
Oh, how I yearn to let these arms enclose her!
But patience! I must not lose my composure,
for words will have a more effective reach…
Let's see if I can practice what I preach!)

ALEX joins the group.

Hello, young women! Welcome to my home!
I just came in to fetch one of my poems.

CATHERINE You wrote these verses?

ALEX   Oh, they're nothing much.
I try to, but I fear I've lost my touch.

CATHERINE I beg to differ! These are words of gold!
But what's your name, if I may be so bold?

ALEX You may. My name is Alex, and I see
I'm blessed with rather charming company.

CATHERINE I'm Catherine. This is Sonja, and Amanda.

ALEX Why yes, we met just now on the veranda.

CATHERINE Your poems are so rich…

ALEX   But incomplete,
and though I lay them here at Sappho's feet,
I fear they are not worthy, for my art
is stifled by my complicated heart.

CATHERINE I know the feeling…

ALEX   Please, do carry on.
When I came in you seemed intent upon
some business, no?

SONJA   Well, these two are competing.

CATHERINE Sonja!

ALEX   For what?

SONJA   The privilege of eating
Some succulent and yet untasted fruit,
that ripens even now beneath this suit.

ALEX Well, well! That's quite a prize. What must they do?

SONJA One poem each: original and new.

ALEX How clever! Words of beauty never fade.
And I've seen unexpected matches made
when games of rhyme and reason have been played.
So I would love to help adjudicate
and even, if it isn't yet too late,
sweeten the pot a little.

SONJA   How is that?

ALEX   Well now, a contest can be somewhat flat
    if there's no second prize; and so I'll be
    the consolation. Loser's prize is me!

SONJA   You obviously have a way with verse:
    as second prizes go, they could do worse.
    Let's start, then. Catherine, you've been working hard.
    What can you offer me, my little bard?

CATHERINE   I'm sorry, I have been far too distracted
    and so my verse is somewhat—well, compacted:
    I've only four lines, but they are sincere!
    It's called: "I Go All Crazy When You're Near."

ALEX   (At last she writes! I cannot wait to hear!)

CATHERINE   *You shake my bones and you rattle my brain;*
    my limbs are all akimbo with desire.
    If we don't do it soon I'll go insane:
    so hotly burns my— burning— something—fire.
    You see, I didn't have a chance to finish
    but don't think that my passion is diminished!

SONJA   That's all you could come up with on your own?

CATHERINE   I barely started!

SONJA   Still! "You shake my bones?"

ALEX   I like the bit about the limbs akimbo.

SONJA   What do you take me for? Some kind of bimbo?
    My God, isn't there more to how you feel
    than getting me in bed? I mean, get real!
    Amanda. Perhaps you are more romantic?

CATHERINE   Sonja, this isn't fair! You make me frantic!

SONJA   Go on, Amanda.

THOMAS   I have nothing written.
    But from my heart these words are somehow bidden:
    "What violence has the truth done to our love,
    to what I knew of you, and you of me?
    What further secrets lurk there, poised to glove
    the naked hand that sought to reach out, free?
    Oh, never will I trust in truth again
    if it is only shattering illusion
    and leaving broken hearts and sorrow's pain

and lost souls wandering in their confusion.
Yet, doomed to wander in my own disguise,
I find the painful truths in women's eyes."

ALEX   I think we have a winner!

SONJA   Undisputed!
Such depth, and so divinely executed!
But so much sadness in Amanda dwells...
What are her secrets that she never tells?

> *SONJA cups THOMAS's chin in her hand and looks deep into his eyes.*
> *They kiss for a long time.*

CATHERINE   I'm sorry, Sonja, but I really must
hereby retract my longing and my lust:
I cannot love you, for I do not trust
your fickle heart as far as I can throw it.
This has all been a game for you. You know it.

> *SONJA and THOMAS finally disengage.*

SONJA   But, Cath...

CATHERINE   You can't deny that it's the case.
Your willingness to suck Amanda's face
so readily, when you had only met her
convinced me that she's won you... and I'll let her.

SONJA   Oh, Catherine, please! You were the one who started
the games we've played! Don't act all broken-hearted
and righteously indignant! It won't do.
Your brother was more trustworthy than you!

THOMAS   I was?

> *Beat. Bewildered stares from the other three.*

You may be shocked by what I must uncover,
for I am not a woman, but... her brother.

> *He takes off part of the disguise and everyone gasps when they realize he*
> *is:*

CATHERINE   Thomas!

SONJA   Thomas?

ALEX   Thomas.

THOMAS   I came here with the purest of intentions:
to rescue Catherine from her cruel inventions—
for I assumed that Overripe was real.

I knew not that in this guise I'd appeal
with unaccustomed strength to fairer sex:
to whom I've been unfair in most respects,
as I now realize, being thus attired...
Forgive me, Catherine. These clothes have rewired
my sensibilities, and now I see
your silencing was largely due to me.

CATHERINE   Oh, Thomas! If you'd then shown but a fraction
of this compassion... heavens! My reaction
would have been to abet you in your quest
to win sweet Sonja's love! I can attest
that since you followed us onto this land
you are a very different sort of man.

THOMAS   Your absolution, Catherine, is most sweet;
but my apology is incomplete
until I turn to her whose merest glance
can put my smitten heart into a trance.
I won you, Sonja, in a false disguise;
and so I'll understand if in your eyes
I am unworthy to retain my prize.

SONJA   You've won my heart, regardless of the game;
for Catherine's right: you really aren't the same
annoying little man you used to be.
Now that I know your sensitivity,
and trust that you will keep it past the time
you shed this costume—however sublime
it looks on you, and oh, it does! believe me;
I'm grateful that you managed to deceive me.
But if you hope to keep me in your heart,
you must commit to me and to your art:
your poetry reached new heights in this game.
I will expect a lot more of the same.

THOMAS   My darling, I shall keep you well supplied,
for now that I have shed some of my pride,
I'll trust my words to find angelic grace
in honouring the charms of Sonja's face.
And Alex, for your coaching you've my gratitude:
this costume has done wonders for my attitude.

ALEX   In honour of your thanks, please let me offer
these humble words from my poetic coffer.
My heart is with you, though the poem is poor
and incomplete—I wish it could be more.

*She takes one of the papers from around the statue and reads, mostly to
CATHERINE:*

*Imagining my lips upon your face
unstrings the orchestra of my desire:
and now, mere splinters of their former grace
these broken bows cavort within the fire
that turns their love to smoke.*

CATHERINE improvises, directing her words to ALEX.

CATHERINE "And in the haze
of ghostly melodies that they have haunted,
my eyes are blinded by the sudden blaze
of you, bright vision I have always wanted.
This vision stirs me into silent song,
afraid to make a ripple you might hear,
whose notes cried out inside me for so long,
cried out and yet were silent in my fear.
But face to face with you I'm left no choice:
so let my orchestra reclaim its voice!"

ALEX Catherine, bravo! The Muse has heard your call!

CATHERINE looks at ALEX, cluing in.

THOMAS (My sister can write poems after all!)

SONJA Oh, Catherine! Overripe was just a shadow
of your true voice, held incommunicado,
for so long—but your music is so sweet!

ALEX At last my favourite fragment is complete!

CATHERINE Now all I need to make my world completer,
and make my happiness just that much sweeter
would be if Dr. Wise were here to see
the words that have come tumbling out of me!
I wish that I could tell him to his face
his confidence in me was not misplaced!

ALEX Your wish is not an idle one, my dear.
Where else would Dr. Wise be but right here?

SONJA The tutor?

ALEX Yes, that's me. The very same.
And both my students I am proud to claim!

THOMAS You're Dr. Wise?

ALEX I am.

THOMAS   Aren't you a man?

ALEX   I'm not sure if you'll really understand.

SONJA   I think *I* might… but tell us if you can.

ALEX   In younger days, I had a reputation
that caused my premature evacuation
from this, my home. I donned a mannish guise;
and the poetic tutor, Dr. Wise,
became my alter ego fixed and sure,
for teaching was my passion and my cure.
How could I ever guess my teaching would
lead me right back to my old neighbourhood?
But when I met you as prospective pupils,
I put aside my past, my fears, my scruples,
for I could see you both had the potential
to craft your words into something substantial.
And I am thrilled to see how well you've learned!
Thomas, your lovely prize has been well-earned!

CATHERINE   As has my consolation in the game,
which I am happy now, at last, to claim,
for you have opened up my heart to verse.
As second prizes go, I could do worse.

CATHERINE kisses ALEX.

ALEX   Oh, Catherine! This is more than consolation!
To hear your voice complete my old creation,
and then to top it off with such a kiss!
Do you sincerely offer me such bliss?

CATHERINE   Of poetry I still have much to learn,
but other subjects more urgently burn
at my deep thirst for knowing. Will you slake it?

ALEX   If love is ours to make, then let us make it!

They kiss again.

And when our thirst returns to poetry,
we might decide to use our expertise
to cash in on this wave of Sappho-mania,
and start a school here, and call it…

CATHERINE   Lesbania!
Oh, yes! A place where women find Love's voice!
And have no need to camouflage their choice

behind elaborate games and webs of lies.
Lesbania! Let's do it, Dr. Wise!

SONJA   And when you tire of your poetic labours,
you'll not forget to call upon your neighbours…

THOMAS   For we're all family now! And I'm delighted!

ALEX   Indeed, my long-dead fires are fresh ignited!
A whole new life that I can't wait to start!

CATHERINE   And I've found words for what was in my heart…

THOMAS   I've grown by leaps and bounds within my art…

SONJA   And I am still a shameless little tart!

Blackout. Beat. Spotlight up. SONJA steps into it.

This ending's not entirely satisfying,
for I've not had my fill of poets vying
to taste my favours. Would a wider field
provide a more intoxicating yield?
And so the floor is open, ladies, gents…
Mine is the most straightforward of intents,
for poetry delights the tender Muse:
its best practitioners she'll not refuse.
So if you find this little game inviting,
get out your pens, my friends, and get to writing!

Spotlight out.

The end.

Life and
A Lover

Natalie Meisner

Introduction:
Life and a Lover

Life and A Lover (2000) by Natalie Meisner uses letters and other historical documentation to tell a version of the story of Virginia Woolf's love affair with Vita Sackville-West. Focused on Virginia's perspective, Meisner chooses to bring her literary creation, Orlando, to life as her buffer. The other characters: her brother-in-law Clive Bell and the two socialites, Lady Patricia Compton, and Lady Edith Malgrove, are included for the purposes of offering an ongoing commentary on the affair. As such, they frequently act as a framing device to direct our attention to the dangers that they feel Virginia will be exposed to if she falls into Vita's clutches. It is through their relaying of the standard gossip before Vita even arrives for her impromptu visit at Virginia's new home in Tavistock Square that we are prepared to watch their first private exchange.

It is the occasion of this encounter that brings about the arrival on stage of Orlando, "*a dashing young man dressed in Elizabethan clothing, and wearing a sword*" (329) who materializes from the "*large, framed portrait*" (339) from which he has been watching everything that has gone on. Mirroring the trance that Virginia is in, and the indelible effect that Vita has had on her, he replays all of Vita's moves, repeating her enticing invitation: "We don't live long, when you really look at it. And when we meet someone we truly admire, why not say so?" (338). Less "real" than the other characters who are based on historical figures, his presence reminds us that we are witnessing an imaginative recreation of an actual historical event. At the same time, we are privileged to share in watching Woolf's creative process take a tangible shape. Only visible to our eyes, we are put in the position of not only sharing Woolf's secret invention, but also in watching him attain increasing independence from her.[1]

To mark his coming into existence as Virginia's imaginative reconfiguration of Vita, Meisner includes a moment where a letter addressed to him flutters down from the flies. By having him look back to the frame he has stepped out of as if to inquire if he is Orlando, we witness the fragility of his conception in Virginia's mind. As she speaks aloud the words, "Dear Vita," while writing to her, we see Orlando walking stealthily behind her, without her yet being fully aware of his presence. Each time, she turns to look for him, he hides in the shadows. The staging of their tender and tentative recognition of each other progresses slowly to the place where Virginia acknowledges him by asking how he got in. His answer, twice from off stage, and once from the frame (340), both locates him in stage space and signals that he is now real to her. When he bends over to kiss her neck as she tries to resume writing, we know that she has fallen under Vita's spell.

By the next scene, he is in full evidence, shown reclining on the edge of the picture frame as if he is a very comfortable acquaintance. Since he can only be seen by Virginia, her awkward efforts to conceal him by first stuffing him into a cabinet when Vita appears, and then dragging him off stage by his ear, playfully stage her confusion at their encroachment upon her. When we arrive at the pivotal scene six, Orlando has transformed into a petulant and impulsive Elizabethan courtier brandishing his quill and sword. Watching Virginia wrestle with his irritating requests to understand how he came into existence keeps us deeply engaged in processing the ways in which he, as her creation, experiences being transferred from the page to the stage. As he makes affectionate moves towards her, she reasserts her ultimate artistic control over him by writing him off the stage as a result of a terrible headache. The second half of the scene with Vita recalls the same delicate moments that mark the growing intimacy between them. Vita's bold declaration of love, ending with a stolen kiss and an invitation to share "an evening of complete hedonism, total abandon" (353), leaves no doubt that the love affair is on.

In scene eight, Orlando's official existence as the subject of Virginia's latest work, *Orlando, A Biography*, which gives him a new stature, is marked by his increasing ability to fight with Virginia over what kind of character he should be. Now that he has become the aggressively daring and somewhat dangerous adventurer and lover, she imagines him as, she finds it impossible to wrestle him out of the room in time to compose herself for the visit with Clive. The staging of her struggles to hide the traces of his existence from Clive who has come to warn her away from Vita, dramatizes her inability to resist Vita's charms. Resolute in defending Vita when Clive tries to warn her off, Virginia's obvious distraction, coupled with the evidence that all the biscuits have been partially eaten, leads him to predict that she is already falling into madness. Act One culminates in the scene where Virginia uses Orlando as her go-between to woo Vita. The masculine embodiment of Virginia's literary love letter to Vita, he carries the letter to Vita, passes the words between them and reacts as he learns that he is going to be transformed into a woman himself.

Orlando's existence as the embodiment of the love that Virginia is unable to shower directly on Vita reaches its climax in the lovemaking scene that takes place at Knole in Act Two, when Orlando, hidden in the bed sheets, joins in to make it a threesome.

After these moments of joy orchestrated by Orlando, everything begins to fall away between them. Orlando, now transformed into a woman, no longer seems to interest her creator, since the biography has been completed. For the rest of Act Two, as Virginia's relationship with Vita deteriorates, she will try to punish the now freewheeling female Orlando in Vita's stead. In the climactic scene eight when Virginia and Vita have their quarrel, Orlando is shown, wrapped in sheets, being yanked back and forth between them. As the manuscript of Orlando is destroyed by Virginia, Orlando falls lifeless to the ground. Having destroyed her own creation, Virginia is now able to speak of the intense suffering that her writing requires.

In the coda that follows, we are given a glimpse not only of the real bond that Virginia and Vita shared, but also of a reawakened Orlando who begins to climb up out of the theatrical frame towards a new future.

Note

¹ A considerable body of critical material exists connecting Woolf's *Orlando* to the theory of the androgynous mind she later developed in the essay, *A Room of One's Own* (London: Hogarth P, 1929). In articulating her theory of androgyny Woolf states, "[I]t is fatal for anyone who writes to think of their sex. It is fatal to be a man or woman pure and simple; one must be woman-manly or man-womanly" (Woolf 156-57). The construction of the character Orlando in the first act of Meisner's play can be interpreted as the dramatization of this theory designed to express the co-existence of the other (gender) within the self. (Note supplied by Janine Plummer.)

Natalie Meisner

Bio and Artist's Statement

Natalie Meisner is an award-winning playwright, poet, and fiction writer whose plays have been produced across Canada by Playwright's Theatre Centre (Vancouver), Lunchbox Theatre (Calgary), On The Verge Festival (Ottawa), Mulgrave Road Theatre, Chestnut Tree Theatre (Nova Scotia), and Nightwood/ Buddies in Bad Times's "Hysteria" Festival (Toronto). Her plays have won the Canadian National Playwriting Competition, been featured in the International Women's Playwriting Conference in Athens, Greece, shortlisted for the Herman Voaden Award, and been produced by CBC Radio. She has edited both the esteemed literary magazines *PRISM International* and *Dandelion*.

Publications include her book *Growing Up Salty & Other Plays*, *Oral Fixations*, *Lady Driven: More Writing By the Seven Sisters*, *Grain* Magazine, *Pottersfield Portfolio*, and *Love Poems for the Media Age*.

•

The word lesbian has been one of the most contentious of the twentieth century, running a close second only to that beleaguered term: "woman." At this theoretical moment it is a word that many run away from like scalded rabbits and I have to ask myself why this might be. Is it to avoid being labelled "essentialist" that many theorists, writers and activists eschew the term? Signifying chains that I do not fully understand have attempted to de-sexualize the word lesbian, to cordon it off from playfulness and pleasure while laminating it onto politics… as if politics were somehow boring. As if politics could ever be separated from sex! Perhaps the word lesbian, with the way it forthrightly lays claim to literary history—to a classical, canonical history no less—is simply too offensive to mainstream culture.

Woolf has been both claimed by lesbians, and has taken a lot of guff for not labelling herself one. She was willing to take the stand to defend Radclyffe Hall's right to publish *The Well of Loneliness* when Sir Archibald Bodkin was poised to declare the work obscene. When Hall insisted that Woolf swear under oath that the book was not only a work of art, but a work of genius… well that Woolf respectfully declined to do. Woolf also made the censor a figure of fun in *A Room of One's Own*, asking the women's society she was addressing to make sure he was not hiding in the china cabinet spying on them.

For my part, I find *Orlando* to be a hotter lesbian book by far than *The Well of Loneliness*, which after I read it sucked the fun out of my love life for a good… okay, week. But still, I was an undergraduate and it was traumatic.

Woolf was critical of the traps of essentialism, illustrated the performativity of gender, and reassigned the term queer a positive value in much the same way as "queer theorists," claim it in the second half of the Twentieth century. Far from the prudish asexual representation of Woolf in Cunningham's *The Hours*, Woolf's works reveal a writer animated by lesbian desire and fond of "the society of buggers" as she put it, for the opportunity this society provided her to publicly interrogate matters of the body. She had a Rabelaisian appreciation for plumbing and a good-natured respect for bodily functions. At the same time, however, as a historical materialist, Woolf could not overlook the ramifications of hundreds of years of platonic conceptions of women as "the dark continent."

A few years ago at the International Federation of Theatre Research in Amsterdam, Sue Ellen Case said she was puzzled by the way that recent theorists presumed that the lesbian feminists of the second wave were all prudes. "It is as if they're assuming that all we've had is vanilla, missionary position, I'm okay, you're okay type sex." She said. "Oh well I guess they don't frequent the same leather bars as me."

Can we afford to vacate the term lesbian, with its attachments to poetry, history, politics and above all, to the women who came before us? It is more useful to acknowledge the shifting meanings and contentions that have gathered around the word. After all, vacations are nice, but if, when you come back to your place everything is flattened… it might be time to rethink the logic of vacation.

Production Information

Life and A Lover was first produced at the Brave New Play Rites Festival in February, 1998, with the following company:

VIRGINIA WOOLF	Jen Covert
VITA SACKVILLE-WEST	Melanie Skehar
ORLANDO	Karen Ounpuu

Directed by Sheila James

•

A longer version of *Life and A Lover* was subsequently produced by Playwrights Theatre Centre, PTC Festival House in September, 1999, and also by Theatre @ UBC, Frederick Wood Theatre in March, 2000.

Life and A Lover won the Canadian National Playwriting Award and garnered the Playwright Theatre Centre's Best Emerging Playwright at the Jessie Richardson Theatre Awards for its author. Selections from the play have been staged at The Brave New Play Rites Festival, the Belfry, and The Women's International Playwright's conference in Athens, Greece.

Characters

Virginia Woolf
Vita Sackville-West
Orlando
Clive Bell
Lady Patricia Compton
Lady Edith Malgrove

Playwright's Note—About The Play

Life and A Lover was inspired by the literary lives and love of Virginia Woolf and Vita Sackville-West. The play does not attempt to be a comprehensive biography, but rather, tries to imagine the private scenes between the two that are implied by their lifetime of correspondence. The famous novel/biography, *Orlando* by Woolf, was modelled on Vita Sackville-West and remained a connection between the women for their entire lives. In the play, Orlando is brought to life as a character. This allows for an exploration of how s/he served as the confidante and foil of these two complex and extraordinary women, as well as a conduit between them.

Life and A Lover

ACT ONE

prologue

The lights come up in two pools. In one sits VIRGINIA WOOLF, at her desk writing. The other one, in the middle and closest to the audience is empty.

ORLANDO suddenly catapults into the empty pool of light, almost as if he'd been pushed. He is, to all appearances, a dashing young man dressed in Elizabethan clothing, and wearing a sword.

He stumbles forward and drops his sword with clatter. VIRGINIA looks up from her work, toward the source of the noise. She sees the ghostly, if rather clumsy vision of ORLANDO and a look of fascination crosses her face.

Blackout.

scene one

In darkness, music, muffled speech and laughter can be heard as the lights come up to reveal the end of a dinner party. VIRGINIA, her brother in law, CLIVE BELL, LADY PATRICIA COMPTON and LADY EDITH MALGROVE are discussing the success of Mrs. Dalloway.

VIRGINIA, in spite of being the centre of attention seems subdued, as though her mind were elsewhere. She is attentive and pleasant, but does not seem truly engaged by the company or conversation. The others vie for her attention, often cutting each other off, or speaking over one another.

CLIVE   Congratulations are certainly in order, Virginia, on your second printing.

LADY M   I think it can simply be said that *Mrs. Dalloway* is the most moving book written in the English language. It's a credit to you, Mrs. Woolf.

VIRGINIA   How very kind.

LADY C   Yes, I thought it was simply—

LADY M   ...and as I read of Clarissa's struggles I felt I knew just what she was going through.

LADY C   You know what it made me think of?

CLIVE   Your instinct for the poetic is, of course right on the mark, but what is truly amazing about this book is—

LADY M   Many's the time, in fact, that it's crossed my mind someone should make a book out of my life.

LADY C   I couldn't help thinking of—

CLIVE finally lets her have the floor.

CLIVE   Yes?

LADY C   Well it made me think of… of… *The Mill on The Floss.*

VIRGINIA   Really?

LADY C   I can't decide which of the two I like more. Why don't you tell us where you got the idea for *The Mill?*

VIRGINIA   I'm sure I'd love to… had I written that particular book.

LADY C wilts.

CLIVE   What is truly amazing and different about this book is the depth of character development, how you delve into Clarissa's mind. That's why there's this extraordinary response to it. *(pause)* From the refined reader.

LADY C   Is someone at the door?

CLIVE   It's taken a while to go into a fresh printing, but we all know that the general public resists innovation. That's what separates you from all these merchants and tradesmen who have turned to the inkwell of late.

LADY C gets up and goes to the door.

LADY M   Our lives aren't that dissimilar after all. Clarissa Dalloway is such a stately name. I hold it as a truth that names make all the difference in life.

VITA breezes in, greets LADY C.

VITA   Patricia, what a lovely frock, it has a sort of simple, animal appeal…

LADY C   *(hesitant)* Animal…?

VITA   It shows off your best attributes, which between you and me just can't be purchased in a shop.

LADY C   Vita, shh! Honestly, someone will hear you.

VITA   I should have thought six months of married life would have been sufficient to take that out of you.

LADY C   What?

VITA   That pinkness, that inclination to blush.

VIRGINIA   But I disagree. It's all very workmanlike. What does a writer do that a carpenter can't, after all? Nail two words together and hope they hold in the middle.

VITA   *(looks up, sees VIRGINIA)* Who's that?

CLIVE   Following your analogy, there is a great deal of recent novels that should be condemned and torn down.

LADY C   *(to VITA)* Vita, really! I thought you prided yourself in keeping abreast of these things. That is Virginia Woolf.

> *VITA makes a beeline for the table.*

She has a terrifying intellect, and yet poor health plagues her.... Where are you going?

> *VITA sits down. Silence.*

CLIVE   Well... Vita. What a surprise.

VITA   I was passing by and so I thought I'd see what Clive was doing with himself.

CLIVE   I'm flattered. It imparts such a feeling of security to know that someone takes an interest in my life. And such a surprise.

LADY M   Indeed. *(barely glances at VITA)* Speaking of unlooked for surprises, we were at tea with Miss Bowen last Tuesday and she told us the most amusing story it was... what was it about dear?

LADY C   *(thinks she has the floor, but LADY M cuts her off)* It was—

LADY M   Oh yes, she was telling us about a fish that fell out of the sky—

CLIVE   *(clearing his throat)* I say, Virginia—

LADY M   ...Said it would have hit her fair square in the head, if she hadn't ducked.

VIRGINIA   Oh my.

LADY M   Yes, I know. Can you imagine her arriving with a herring caught in her hat? I would have paid to see that!

CLIVE   *(raising his voice)* Virginia, I'd been meaning to ask you—have you read that scandalous little pamphlet that claims to have discovered the existence of a third sex. You know the fellow... calls them Urnings or Yernings or Awnings or some such.

VIRGINIA   Yes.

CLIVE   Fancies himself a poet too...

> *VIRGINIA is caught between the two of them, trying to follow both conversations.*

The name of Carpenter, I believe. Perhaps that would have been a better vocation for him. What did you think?

VITA   I see no one will give the celebrated Mrs. Woolf a moments peace. *(jokingly)* Do you think fishes ought to fall from the sky, Mrs. Woolf? Do you think So and So ought to write boring old tropes? Do you or don't you? What's the price of tea in China and let us know if you think books ought to be written about flying fishes, bad poets and Chinese tea… Mrs. Woolf.

> *CLIVE, leaning back in his chair gives her a small, mocking and nearly silent round of applause for the speech. VITA ignores him.*

CLIVE   How you adore prodding the coals.

LADY M   I'm sure I meant no offense.

VIRGINIA   None taken. No doubt this *complete stranger*—who seems to know me although I haven't had the pleasure—is only pulling your leg.

> *CLIVE and LADY C overlap while making the introductions.*

LADY C   Mrs. Nicolson.

CLIVE   *(wryly)* Oh, that's Vita.

LADY C   Excuse me.

CLIVE   Sackville-West.

> *Pause.*

VIRGINIA   Well, your name remains a complete mystery after all of that. You must be a spy.

VITA   A spy?

VIRGINIA   The collection of so many aliases can only point to scurrilous activities.

VITA   Well, if we needn't bother about standing on custom—

VIRGINIA   Which we shan't.

VITA   Very well, as no one else seems up to the task. I had better introduce myself.

LADY C   *(aside, to LADY M)* Quite the to-do.

VIRGINIA   By all means.

VITA   *(uncertain of the word's meaning)* And clear myself of all charges of…?

VIRGINIA   Scurrilous: shameful or indecent.

VITA   Thank you. Scurrilous, shameful, *and* indecent behavior.

CLIVE   That, I'd like to hear.

VITA *(shoots him a dirty look)* You see, Sackville-West belongs to my father and mother, respectively, and Nicolson to my husband. I am obliged to take on the second, but can't bear to give up the first, so I sit on the fence.

CLIVE As you make it your practice in so many aspects of your life, Vita.

VITA *(sharply)* Ah yes, now I had heard you, on the other hand, had given up fence sitting altogether. Had fallen over the other side completely. Or so I heard.

LADY C *(aside to LADY M)* Now what in the name of heaven are they talking about?

LADY M I know I haven't the foggiest idea.

VITA And perhaps this isn't the best conversation to be having in company. Oh my goodness, I interrupted Mrs. Woolf in mid sentence. And there is no one in His Majesty's England.... Nay, in the civilized world who ought to be doing that. I am such an ardent admirer of your work, Mrs. Woolf. I have never been met, between the covers of a book, with such skill, such brilliance...

VIRGINIA There's no need for... for...

VITA For what?

VIRGINIA The trumpets and confetti. You needn't go on so.

VITA On the contrary, I feel that no one's gone on enough. Here we sit with a genius in our midst and we've barely let you get a word in edgeways.

LADY M It seems difficult for anyone to get a word in edgeways.

LADY C Mrs. Woolf, I heard you are moving to Tavistock Square.

LADY M You'll like that. It's infinitely better for society. So hard to visit people who live in such a... rustic fashion. But then you writers are used to hardship, sitting alone for days and days at a stretch. I think I'd go out of my wits—

CLIVE Lady Malgrove—

LADY M *(pause)* But then, you're a breed apart, Mrs. Woolf, a genius does not get lonely. *(emphatically)* No, the mind of a genius is enough comfort and company for itself.

> *VIRGINIA considers this statement, her gaze drops into her lap. Everyone falls quiet, suddenly. The conversation has dropped into matters too severe for a dinner party. VIRGINIA tries to relieve the pressure with a small joke.*

VIRGINIA Ah. Perhaps you're right. We'll have to find one and ask him.

> *They all titter, thankfully. LADY M smiles at VIRGINIA. She really means no harm by these comments, it is simply what she believes.*

VITA   *(to VIRGINIA)* Tavistock Square? That's exciting news. I should love to see your new abode.

VIRGINIA   The house itself is not worth even the trip across town for a look, I'm afraid.

VITA   If you need things transported or toted I'm your woman, for what I lack in social graces I make up with a strong back.

CLIVE   Not much out of your way, since you're roaring about London in that yellow monster day and night anyway.

LADY C   At night? You don't go alone do you?

CLIVE   You know, they ought to pass some sort of law to keep them out of town.

LADY M   *(Nodding, she seizes on this as if it were a stroke of brilliance that she had just thought of.)* Yes, I am of the opinion that motorcars should not be allowed in London!

VITA   I'll keep a special eye out, to ensure that you don't wind up on the nose of mine.

LADY M   *(nearly speechless with rage)* Well!

VITA   So, after all that, a visit or no? If you say yes, of course it could only be from politeness. But then again if you say no, you wouldn't be perceived in *present* company to show a lack of it.

VIRGINIA   I barely know what to say, but I do know this; You, Mrs. Nicolson, are having a bit of fun with us.

    Pause, as everyone looks at VITA.

VITA   Yes, just a bit of fun… *(quietly, to VIRGINIA)* But won't you call me Vita?

    Lights fade.

scene two

    CLIVE, LADY M and LADY C enter wearing winter coats, and mufflers. The sounds of a busy street can be heard, as the trio near a park bench.

LADY M   I just don't know how you could abide it, Clive.

LADY C   I thought you'd invited her.

CLIVE   Not on that occasion, but that's seldom an impediment for Vita.

LADY M   Wherever did you make the acquaintance of such a…

CLIVE   Let's not descend to name-calling.

LADY M   Such a… *forward* woman.

CLIVE (*offhand*) A mutual acquaintance, I suppose.

LADY M You mean to say you can't remember?

CLIVE Ah… let me see…. Yes, her husband the diplomat. But don't pretend you haven't heard of her, Lady Malgrove. Her books are in every corner shop.

LADY M You use that term loosely, Clive. Perhaps keeping up with the latest stacks of penny dreadfuls has made you go soft in the head.

CLIVE I was remarking on their existence, not their merit.

LADY C You know Harold Nicolson?

CLIVE I met him only briefly.

LADY M Well let us hope he has a trifle more decorum, if he's a diplomat.

CLIVE Yes, a good sort… as far as I can recall. But really, making a mountain out of a molehill in this way will only delight Vita. It's grist for her mill.

LADY M You wouldn't take this whole affair so lightly if you knew some of the things that I know about that woman.

CLIVE How things change, only a moment ago you didn't even know her name…

LADY C (*whispering*) What have you heard?

CLIVE …and now you seem to know her entire past history.

LADY M Not much, only that she passes herself off as a poet and writes off-colour lyrics under the guise of it. Only that she's responsible for the tearing asunder of many a husband and wife.

LADY C Why would she wish to do that?

LADY M I have it on good authority. A close friend of mine is an aunt to one of the parties involved… who shall remain nameless—

LADY C Who?

CLIVE Have a care, Lady Malgrove.

LADY M I am under oath not to say. (*pause*) Would you mind running over to the shop and getting me an ice?

LADY C But—

LADY M Lemon, if you please and take care he doesn't cheat you.

> *LADY C gets up to go, but unbeknownst to the other two she stands just a short distance off eavesdropping.*

CLIVE You know telling something to Patricia is much the same as running it front page of the paper. (*LADY C fumes silently.*) Who?

LADY M Violet and Denys Trefusis.

CLIVE   Ah yes, the Trefusis'.

LADY M   You know them?

CLIVE   Yes, the husband.

> *LADY M looks at him sharply—as if to say "Not him too!" He squirms, and denies it vehemently.*

(clears his throat) I met him briefly. Don't waste another thought on Vita. As I said, she'd be pleased to know that we're even discussing it.

LADY M   It wouldn't surprise me, in a weak moment, if Mrs. Woolf were drawn to that creature. After all, who knows what people are capable of in their secret heart of hearts.

CLIVE   It's nothing more than Vita's brash manner. Nothing to concern ourselves with, surely.

> *LADY C clears her throat to warn them of her approach.*

LADY M   But what if you're wrong, Clive? Virginia has too trusting a nature—

CLIVE   Shh! No sense broadcasting it prematurely.

LADY M   It pays to keep one's wits, when there are venomous creatures about.

> *They get up from the bench, meet LADY C halfway. They exit.*

LADY C   They were out of lemon.

> *Lights fade.*

scene three

> *VIRGINIA's sitting room. The furniture is covered with cloth, there are boxes and trunks everywhere. The room has now (and manages to retain throughout the play) a transient or "not yet unpacked" feel. The lights come up on VIRGINIA who is seated at her desk absorbed in books and notes.*
>
> *VITA enters, taking off a scarf and hat. She sees that VIRGINIA is working and rather than announce her presence, she creeps forward quietly. Presently, however she trips over a crate. VIRGINIA leaps up.*

VIRGINIA   Oh!

VITA   Blast! Here I was trying to glide in like a seraph and I up and trip over a crate. I'm sorry.

VIRGINIA   Don't give it a thought, you gave me a turn, is all.

VITA *(pointing at the stacks on the desk)* You're in the midst of something, I should have rung first—

VIRGINIA No—

VITA You were working, I'll go.

VIRGINIA No, no—

VITA You weren't working?

VIRGINIA No, that is to say, I was working, but I could use a break and your visit will provide a welcome distraction.

VITA Because if I'm keeping you from something and you won't tell me, I'd never forgive myself.

VIRGINIA I'm pleased you could make it. I half thought you wouldn't come.

VITA Why is that, when I practically begged for the invite?

VIRGINIA Maybe it was all just a prank—charging in that way—to scandalize Edith.

VITA Edith...?

VIRGINIA Malgrove. Excuse me, Lady Edith Malgrove, if you please.

VITA To think you're on a first-name basis with that formidable creature.

VIRGINIA Yes, well that's after twelve years and only when she's in good humour. When one hasn't neglected her invites twice in a row.

VITA Of which you've been guilty?

VIRGINIA On occasion. My health is always a factor. We have a doctor come through every so often to tell me what I ought not do.

VITA Which must be quite convenient at times.

VIRGINIA If one accepted every invitation that turned up in the post, one would be quite bewildered. No chance to pull a cohesive thought together and just forget about getting any of it down on paper. Besides, no one expects it. If you turned up every time you were invited, you'd be a dreadful bore.

VITA Thanks for the lesson in Bloomsbury etiquette. I expect it will come in handy. So it's rather fruitless to extend an invitation to you, Virginia, I suppose.

VIRGINIA Am I to consider that one?

VITA Yes. And two and three if that's the magic number that fetches you. Only the house is not the place for quiet beatitude, I'm afraid. I no sooner sit down to write and it's *Mummy may we catch fish in the pond?* Yes, I say only don't fall in. *Mummy, may we go and see the horses?* Yes, only don't get behind the gelding, he'll kick you. And *Mummy, Nigel's got a thrashing from Elliot and Jim!*—and

I'm off and running to fix whatever is broken, salve whomever is hurt. On the way back I am waylaid by the cook who wants to know the number and size of turnip he ought to buy at the market a week Tuesday. After a ten minute conversation he goes off saying the very number he planned on buying in the first place and so I conclude that the entire household is against me ever completing a few sparse poems, let alone a work of fiction.

VIRGINIA   It's easy to picture you at the hub of all that, somehow. You look a person who could control anything. Balance and bandage an indignant child on one hip, toss out orders to a host of servants, all the while juggling turnips and shoeing the gelding.

VITA   They are darlings and I'd never do without them, or without Harold. But how I envy your peaceful, scholarly life.

VIRGINIA   See that stack there? All to be read—with commentary by Friday. That shambles of notepaper and henscratch must become a cohesive article in less than a week, and that pile has not yet decided what shape it wants to take and yet *still* contrives to give me headaches strong enough to make me take to my bed.

VITA   Oh. Are you feeling fine now? Do you want me to leave? You should get to work.

VIRGINIA   No, not at all.

VITA   If I'm keeping you from something, and you won't tell me, I simply couldn't bear it. I only asked to come—and I know it was forward of me—because we don't live long, when you really look at it. And when we meet someone we truly admire, why not say so?

VIRGINIA   Why yes I suppose…

VITA   Oh, I know that's not the rules of Bloomsbury, obviously. I know that I chaff them at times.

VIRGINIA   Sometimes I think they could use some chaffing.

VITA   I thought I saw something in your eye, a glimmer, when I was raising the devil with—shall *I* call her Edith, now?

VIRGINIA   By all means, at risk of giving her an apoplectic fit.

VITA   EDITH! I'll say. THAT'S A LOVELY PEACOCK VEST YOU'RE WEARING NOW GET OFF THE HOOD OF MY CAR!!

VIRGINIA   *(amused)* If we needn't stand on convention—

VITA   Which we shan't.

VIRGINIA   Very well, I'll accept your invitation without bothering to reject the first two.

VITA   Well I consider myself lucky. That's so very kind of you, as I do enjoy your company… *(hesitates)* Virginia.

> *There is a pause, the women look at each other. In the distance, a dog barks. The intimacy of the moment is broken.*

VIRGINIA   That'll be Leonard and the dog.

VITA   I had better go and see what a ruin the house has fallen into in my absence. Now don't forget you've promised to come. Write and tell me which day is best.

> *VITA stands and steps forward. She puts out her hand and VIRGINIA shakes it, awkwardly. VITA keeps her hand for a second longer than is strictly necessary.*

VIRGINIA   What a powerful grip you have.

> *VITA moves toward the door and exits. VIRGINIA walks with her and stands watching her retreat through the window, with her back to the audience.*
>
> *The light shifts subtly, and the large, framed portrait is revealed to contain ORLANDO, who has been watching and listening all this time.*

VITA   *(off)* Don't forget.

> *ORLANDO carefully extricates himself from the frame and stands on the floor. He extends his arms and legs, opens and shuts one hand, to see that it is working properly.*

VIRGINIA   My memory, thankfully is still quite intact.

> *VIRGINIA stands, almost motionless, watching VITA's retreat. The lights shift further, and only her silhouette at the window is seen. ORLANDO imitates VITA thoughtfully, as if he were trying to puzzle out the meaning of the phrase and learn how to speak at the same time.*

ORLANDO   That's a lovely peacock vest you're wearing, now get off the hood of my car.

> *VITA's car starts with a roar. ORLANDO drops to the ground as though in an air raid. After a couple seconds, he unfolds himself cautiously.*

(tries to imitate VITA's tone and inflections, though quietly) We don't live long, when you really look at it. And when we meet someone we truly admire, why not say so?

> *A letter flutters from the flies down to ORLANDO. He picks it up.*

(reads) Orlando…Orlando?

> *He looks back toward the frame.*

Is that you?

VIRGINIA returns to her desk, and begins to write. ORLANDO steps back into the shadows.

VIRGINIA   *(She writes and speaks aloud.)* Dear Vita…

ORLANDO walks behind VIRGINIA stealthily. Several times, she looks up and turns around, as if she felt a presence in the room, but he manages to hide each time. He moves closer and puts a hand on her shoulder from behind. She looks up as if she has heard something, and stares out over the audience.

Each time VIRGINIA is about to say something, ORLANDO speaks. This often has the effect of his answering her questions a split second before she asks them. The effect is eerie.

ORLANDO   You should get to work.

VIRGINIA   *(almost as if she heard him, or as if she heard a voice in her head)* I should get to work.

ORLANDO steps forward, as he does, he trips over the same crate that VITA did. VIRGINIA sees him. She stares for a moment, and then looks down and shakes her head, as if to clear it. She looks up again, ORLANDO is still there

ORLANDO   Who am I?/

VIRGINIA   Who are you?

ORLANDO   *(holding up the paper)* Orlando… but—

ORLANDO extends his hand to shake, VIRGINIA raises hers in the air, in a gesture to keep him back.

VIRGINIA   Who?

ORLANDO   Orlando?

VIRGINIA   How did you get in?

ORLANDO   Twice from there. *(points off stage)* Once from there. *(points to the window)* and just now from up there. *(points to the frame)*

VIRGINIA circles him, warily. He stands still and watches her.

(confesses) I don't know.

VIRGINIA   *(quietly)* Oh no. *(to herself)* Go back to work, it will pass.

VIRGINIA sits down at her desk, picks up a pen and tries to dip it. Her hand is shaking. ORLANDO goes behind her, places his hands on her shoulders as before. He bends down and kisses her neck. She drops her pen.

ORLANDO   Do you want me to leave?

What shall I do?/

VIRGINIA   What shall I do?

VIRGINIA squeezes her eyes shut. When she opens them, ORLANDO is moving back toward the picture frame, almost as if being drawn there magnetically. VIRGINIA stares after him, amazed, as the lights fade.

scene four

VIRGINIA is at her desk. ORLANDO, quite at home now, reclines against the edge of the picture frame, reading a book. He puts the book down and lets out a big, audible sigh.

ORLANDO   Wouldn't you like to go outside?

VIRGINIA   Shh.

ORLANDO   I can see blue sky from here, and oh! A bird.

VITA is heard offstage.

VITA   *(off)* Oh, Leonard it's lovely, perfectly lovely, thank you.

VIRGINIA jumps up and motions ORLANDO away. He does not want to go.

VIRGINIA   Go, quickly!

VITA is heard approaching. VIRGINIA stuffs ORLANDO in a cabinet and spins around to see VITA who enters, wearing a scarf.

VITA   Hello Virginia. Look at what Leonard gave me.

She sees VIRGINIA leaning against the cabinet in a rather awkward position.

He's such a dear…. Are you all right, Virginia you seem a touch distracted.

VIRGINIA   Not at all. *(moves away from the cabinet carefully)* Oh, yes, he likes you immensely. The last time you visited we sat for an hour saying how nice you were and how much we enjoyed the visit. Which is something one can't do after the departure of every guest.

ORLANDO gets out of the cabinet, and begins to walk toward VITA. Perhaps extending his hand.

VITA   I like him too, although at first I confess I thought he was a bit what's the word… stoic?

VIRGINIA darts forward and grabs ORLANDO by the ear.

VIRGINIA You'll excuse me for one moment?

VITA Oh?

VIRGINIA Just for one moment, I'll be back directly.

VITA Certainly.

> *VIRGINIA exits, with ORLANDO by the ear.*
>
> *Left alone, VITA looks around VIRGINIA's room. She looks over the bookshelf, maybe even sneaks a glance at the papers on the desk. She spies a small, potted plant on a table in the corner. It is brown and withered. It is, in fact the only one clinging to life although there are several pots. VITA bends over and examines it. She dumps out the small dry clump of soil into a larger pot, and begins to repot the plant.*
>
> *VIRGINIA comes back in, and sees her working away busily. She is rather taken aback.*

VIRGINIA Rude of me to rush off…

VITA No trouble. Sorry for leaping in *(indicates the plant)* but really, the poor little thing was not much longer for this world.

VIRGINIA No, I was not gifted with a green thumb. Hopeless in that department, I'm afraid.

VITA Rootbound is all. Just give it a little water, when you think of it. In between fits of brilliance… and it should come around in no time at all.

VIRGINIA Yes, yes I'll be sure to.

> *There is a pause. VITA notices her hands are dirty, and since she has no place else to clean them, she wipes them on her skirt. VIRGINIA wants to laugh, but turns her face away.*

VITA Where were we…. Ah yes, we were discussing Leonard. And how much I like him. So very different from Harold. But he does take your work to heart so, puts it before his own, even. Anyway, do pass on my kindest regards.

VIRGINIA I will. And give my warmest greetings to Harold.

VITA Of course. When I write to him. *(pause)* You know he's gone to Teheran?

VIRGINIA Oh. Yes, you must have mentioned that… and what about the children are they—

VITA On holiday at his mother's. I'm completely yours for the moment.

That reminds me, I've been re-reading *To the Lighthouse*… and I have to say it's not been an entirely enjoyable experience.

VIRGINIA Oh?

VITA   Reading your books provokes in me the most curious sensation. Ramsay drives his wife from the room with a single word, and since I know you personally, I can't help but ascribe his actions to you, to a degree. How could she have thought of it, I think. It's so minutely accurate, and so monstrous at the same time. And yet here you sit, lovely and kind and such wonderful company. It's a mystery.

VIRGINIA   I'm flattered that you find me mysterious, but I'm afraid you can't blame me for Ramsay's shabby behavior. I'd tried to warn him all the while I was writing him, that he was in grave danger of losing his wife.

VITA   I should hate to lose my wife… had I one.

VIRGINIA   Well, what an odd thing to… to say. So, I expect, would I. *(pause)* So tell me. What is it you're working on now?

VITA   The gardening column of course, that's such a regular feature of my life… aphids and loam, moisture and drainage… I half-wish I had never begun. But for serious work, not much. Why do you ask?

VIRGINIA   Two reasons. The first being, I'm so ill used to company I've forgotten how to talk about anything except books, and the second is that, as the publisher of Hogarth Press I must keep my ear to the ground constantly for material.

VITA   Well, I have started a novel, but it's all in tatters. Only a phrase here and there that's any good.

VIRGINIA   If you keep up that steady drone about it, you might just convince me.

VITA   I only say that because I don't think you'd care for the subject—

VIRGINIA   No, my dear Vita. You only say that by way of fishing. Well you've caught a big silver fish. What it amounts to is this; I'm asking to take a look at your novel. How soon can you get it to us?

VITA   *(draws herself up for the challenge)* When you put it like that. I think I could have it done when I get back from my trip.

VIRGINIA   Your trip?

VITA   Oh yes, I'm going to join Harold in Teheran. Didn't I mention it in my letters?

VIRGINIA   No, my dear, I don't believe you did.

VITA   Yes, and I'll have to play the diplomat's wife. Dinners and ceremonies and presidings. Everything so grave and so very very—oh, I mean you simply wouldn't believe it—long. But I'll endure somehow. I know, I'll tell them I simply can't go to the ribbon cutting or the beast roasting, since *I* have a book to write.

VIRGINIA   When do you plan to come back?

VITA   In May.

VIRGINIA   Even if you keep your nose down the entire time, I don't see how that's enough time to haul together a book.

VITA   Well never let it be said that there was a glove thrown down that Vita didn't pick up!

VIRGINIA   We'll take a look at it in May, then.

VITA   Shall we shake on it?

VIRGINIA   Certainly. Shake on it, like men.

VITA   Spit and shake?

VIRGINIA   Not that much like men.

> *They shake hands. VITA extends the handshake for a split second longer than is usual. The lights fade on VIRGINIA as she watches VITA exit.*

scene five

> *The park. VITA walks by the bench and CLIVE pops up, almost as if he had been lying in wait. He guides her by the elbow for a couple steps before VITA shakes him off.*

CLIVE   Hello, Vita, I've caught you alone at last.

VITA   Yes Clive, alone at last. Did you… want to propose to me?

CLIVE   Propose, right. Very funny.

VITA   Or did you want me to speak to Harold on your behalf. I'm always telling him he'd make a beautiful bride.

> *CLIVE laughs in the way that someone does when they don't think the joke is funny.*

CLIVE   I must speak with you about…. Well you see everybody's talking—

VITA   *Are* they? How unusual.

CLIVE   We must discuss the matter of Virginia—

VITA   Yes, on to the inquisition. You're so predictable Clive, you head straight for it with no preamble, whatsoever.

CLIVE   Very well, my dear.

VITA   A lady likes a bit of a build up… but then you wouldn't know that.

CLIVE   *(icily)* Quite. How are Ben and Nigel?

VITA   Robust and healthy. Don't you want to know where Harold is?

CLIVE   Fine. *(beat)* And Harold, where is he?

VITA   Now, this isn't so hard, is it? Harold is in Teheran and since it's evening there, he's probably off hunting ibex's with Nelson.

CLIVE   Nelson?

VITA   A strapping young American Ambassador.

CLIVE   Well they won't catch many ibex in the dark.

VITA   I think that's rather the point.

CLIVE   I dare say you two are a perfect match.

VITA   Of course we are, we've recognized it long ago. Yet I love him dearly! These other friendships and so on simply have nothing whatsoever to do with he and I.

CLIVE   Indeed. About Virginia.... You likely haven't made plans to see her again…

VITA   Oh but I have! We're becoming great friends and we've so much in common.

CLIVE   So much in common…

VITA   And it's an absolute oversight on your part that you haven't introduced us before.

CLIVE   As you may be aware emotions are a delicate subject with Virginia. You, for instance, are tough, you're like a man.

VITA   *(drily)* Flatterer. She's a grown woman and you fuss and cluck over her like an old mother hen!

CLIVE   Well let us be frank, Vita, you were aiming your considerable and lethal charm in her direction, and you've got someone else on the side, rather others on the side. Tell me if you've not.

VITA   What a thing for you, of all people to scold me for, Clive.

CLIVE   I'm not judging you, understand, it's just that Virginia is different. You can't be thinking of going to bed with her. And for heavens sake don't give her that impression.

VITA   That's lovely, Clive. "Going to bed" you make it sound like "going to the lavatory." Really, you have such a way with words.

CLIVE   Heavens knows someone should take the plunge, but not you. You'd treat the matter more seriously, if you'd been around when she was in a bad way. Ask Leonard. Really you must watch what you're doing, Vita. You're smoking over the petrol tank.

VITA   You've nothing to fear from me, I'm off to join Harold until May and I've plenty to keep me busy, not the slightest of which is a book… which Virginia and Leonard may publish.

CLIVE   A book? *(horrified)* Of yours?

VITA   Yes, as a matter of fact. Close your mouth Clive, you're catching flies.

> *VITA chucks him under the chin, exits as the lights fade.*

scene six

> *VIRGINIA sits, writing. The sun filters through the window and birds can be heard chirping outside. The plant that VITA repotted is now sitting on her desk and is not only flourishing but has produced a huge glistening flower.*
>
> *ORLANDO is draped over VIRGINIA's desk, holding a book in front of his face. He has stacks of books around him, some open and some not as though he had tried to read them all at once.*

ORLANDO   Virginia?

VIRGINIA   Shh. I'm working.

ORLANDO   Ohhhh. Working.

> *He nods as though he knows what that's all about and places a finger to his lips. He tiptoes back to his pile of books, in an exaggerated fashion, which is actually more distracting. He goes back to his book. Briefly.*

You say it's 1924? And here I have four hundred years of literature and not one thing that suits my tastes.

VIRGINIA   You've only read one page of each, so how on earth would you know?

ORLANDO   What are you writing? *(She ignores him.)* Is it a letter? In my day if a woman even touched a quill, she'd get a thrashing.

> *VIRGINIA whirls around to face him, angrily.*

VIRGINIA   Do be quiet, Orlando!

ORLANDO   I can't bear to be ignored. Tell me what you're working on.

VIRGINIA   It's a novel. Rather, it's meant to be a novel.

ORLANDO   Ah!

VIRGINIA   But I am vexed by the pedestrian. Everyday things: the moving from one room to another; keeping run of the days in a week, take up such a great lot of space.

ORLANDO *(nodding, seriously)* Yes, yes, I see.

VIRGINIA People must go out to market, and they must come home for tea. People naturally grow older, become over-fond of dogs in old age and spend more time in the lavatory than in the library. But what one really wants to be writing about are the important parts.

ORLANDO What *are* the important parts?

VIRGINIA Why, births, deaths… falling in love.

ORLANDO I've an idea! Why don't you write my life story?

VIRGINIA You little beast, you weren't even listening.

> *VIRGINIA goes back to her work. Ignores ORLANDO. He tries to do the same but can only keep still for a matter of seconds.*

ORLANDO Then I'll just write a tale of my own. A long narrative poem, in the style of of… *(He fumbles about in his stack of books.)* Keats! No, of Byron! No, Baudelaire!

> *VIRGINIA is amused and watches him. He has the floor, but he can't think what to say.*

And it's about… it's about… *(Pause, he looks at VIRGINIA who has gone back to her work.)* Hey! Don't you want to know what it's about?

VIRGINIA Very well.

ORLANDO It's set in a pasture, no in a wood. On a riverboat steamer and it's about you! But I'm afraid I can't show it to you until it's finished.

> *ORLANDO turns away from her, shielding the phantom poem. VIRGINIA shrugs and goes back to work.*

(wailing) But don't you want to see?

> *She holds out her hand. He stalls.*

Well… it's not finished. *(whispering)* I only work on it at night, when it's quiet. *(pause)* But tell me what you're writing about. Is it a love story? Am I in it?

VIRGINIA Why? I suppose you're in love?

ORLANDO Yes!

VIRGINIA With whom?

ORLANDO *(points out the window)* I am in love with that oak tree. Isn't it glorious?

VIRGINIA Don't be ridiculous. One may appreciate its beauty, or draw comfort from its shade, but one cannot be in love with a tree.

ORLANDO   Then how is it that most of these poems you've given me are written for trees, for flowers, for entire fields!

VIRGINIA   They're being metaphorical. *(Pause. ORLANDO's brow furrows.)* They seem to be written to objects, but it's… well, a disguise I suppose. They are usually written for a person. By a man when he loves a woman.

ORLANDO   Why doesn't he simply come out and say what he means?

VIRGINIA   Well that's a very good question. But then I guess we wouldn't have any poems. *(pause)* Perhaps I'll use you for a protagonist, after all. You seem to have all the faculties needed to fall in love…

ORLANDO   *(cheering up, preening)* Really, do you think so?

VIRGINIA   …of which it takes very few. Only a lovely face, a bit of charm… and a talent for running down walls.

ORLANDO   Running down walls?

VIRGINIA   One needs a bit of clumsiness to help with the falling part.

ORLANDO   *(fuming)* Then you're only having a joke on me. A very mean one. I'm afraid I am forced to challenge you to a duel.

VIRGINIA   A duel?

ORLANDO   *(gravely)* Yes, I have no choice. It's a point of honour. I'll ask you to draw your… sword.

VIRGINIA   Yes? You want to kill me, Orlando? Do you think you could?

ORLANDO   That won't be necessary, we'll go just to the first fall. Ready? Oh no. This won't do. One should not fight with women.

VIRGINIA   In any case, you'd be cutting off your nose to spite your face. *(ORLANDO looks at his sword, touches his nose uncertainly.)* Biting the hand that feeds you. *(looks from his hand to VIRGINIA helplessly)* Or putting your own mother to the sword before you were ever born.

ORLANDO   *(drops the sword with a clatter and sinks to the ground)* I give up.

VIRGINIA   What's the matter, monkey?

ORLANDO   I can't tell mad dogs from mothers or see my own nose in front of my face. *(bats at his nose helplessly, then stops and regards VIRGINIA shrewdly)* Are you my mother?

VIRGINIA   Not strictly speaking.

ORLANDO   *(fascinated)* Where did I come from? *(VIRGINIA is at a loss, he stamps his foot.)* Tell me!

VIRGINIA   You're driving me to distraction.

ORLANDO   Where is that?

VIRGINIA   It's not a place. The long and the short of it is that you're some sort of apparition I suppose.

ORLANDO   Am I an Apparition? Where is Apparitia? Am I the King?

VIRGINIA, in frustration, throws a dictionary to/at ORLANDO.

VIRGINIA   Look it up.

He reads aloud, walking as he does so. He is not looking where he is going, and nearly walks into a mirror.

ORLANDO   Apparition: A spectre, spirit, shade, haunt, phantasm or ghost. An eerie or startlingly unusual sight.

ORLANDO looks up, apparently sees himself in the now reflective surface of the frame. His face changes, it is almost as if he were to age 20 years in an instant.

Oh!

He takes out his feather quill and creeps up behind VIRGINIA. Standing behind her, he tickles her neck. She brushes the feather away. He tickles the other side.

VIRGINIA   Go away.

As she reaches up to brush him away, he grabs her hand and holds it.

ORLANDO   It seems everyone in modern times has perfectly horrid manners.

Still holding her arm, ORLANDO leans over her and kisses her neck. She sits, frozen—a deer in the headlights. VITA's car is heard outside.

VIRGINIA   Orlando, you must let me go. I've a guest coming—

ORLANDO   A guest! I'm exceptionally fond of guests and so… you're in luck, I'll most definitely stay.

VIRGINIA   Very well, you're forcing my hand.

With an effort, she takes a pen with her free hand and scribbles something on a paper. ORLANDO lets her go, picks it up and reads aloud.

ORLANDO   "Orlando suddenly was wracked by pains in his head and had to take to his bed for the rest of the day."

He grasps his head as the pain hits him.

Hardly fair.

He retreats groaning, a split second before VITA enters.

VITA   *(enters carrying a large satchel)* Oh, Virginia how well you look.

VIRGINIA Ha! I've been hunched over a grubby printing press all morning, my fingers are stained and my hair is a fright. If I look anything different than a scullery maid, I'll eat my hat, Mrs. Nicolson.

VITA *(feigns hurt)* I see I've come all that way for nothing.

VIRGINIA What do you mean?

VITA If you won't call me by my first name when you see me in person, as well as in your letters, I'm going straight back to Teheran and wait for your next letter.

VIRGINIA Goose!

VITA Goose, I might well be. Here's hoping that I've laid you a golden egg. *(drops the satchel on the table)* My book. It's finished.

> VITA opens the satchel and takes out a large, unbound manuscript. She drops it on the table and it lands with a thud. VIRGINIA looks at it, rather alarmed and does not move to take it.

VIRGINIA Finished?

VITA Its called *Seducers in Equador*.

> VIRGINIA tries not to grimace. She thinks the title is horrid, but doesn't want VITA to know.

VIRGINIA A… romantic title, one that's sure to be a cause of perturbation to the old gents down at the bookshop. *(pause)*

VITA Aren't you going to look at it?

VIRGINIA To finish such a bulky thing when you're on holiday!

VITA That's the story, not much of one, I'm afraid.

VIRGINIA I only meant that if we wanted a chance to get it into print this year, you had better hurry. I never meant to steal away your life.

VITA Virginia calls and Vita obeys, but I enjoyed every minute. Just the thought that you would read my drivel made it deliciously exciting.

VIRGINIA Drivel? Oh come now, Vita.

VITA Just the thought that you would read it drove me into wild fits. Of course I don't expect you'll like it…

VIRGINIA You're like a whirlwind, Vita. A force of nature. *(She takes the manuscript gingerly and opens it.)* You've dedicated it to me.

VITA Yes, I could think of no one else I would rather dedicate it to.

But you mustn't feel bound to take it, because really, I have the feeling that it's not the sort of book that best suits Hogarth…

VIRGINIA   Here it is, freshly dropped from its mother and you're set to hobble it already? I'll read it as soon as you're gone. I'm delighted and touched... Vita. *(takes her hand for a moment, then lets it go)* So, other than the writing of an entire novel, what did you get up to in Teheran? England's certainly been the duller for your absence. Was it very savage and beautiful?

VITA   The sunsets were like a spilled palate, and countryside was beautiful, but I barely ventured out into it. It's a testament to the perverse nature of man that one should crave a splendid view and solitude when one is in the city, and society when one is in on holiday in the mountains. But I've just had the best idea! You must come with me next time.

VIRGINIA   I couldn't possibly keep up with you, I'm not hearty enough.

VITA   Oh nonsense!

VIRGINIA   To hear you tell it, you dash from country to country, galloping across deserts and plains—merely pulling riders off their mounts when you need a fresh one.

VITA   Well I would certainly pull any rider from any mount that dear Mrs. Woolf required. ONE SIDE! I would say. MAKE WAY FOR VIRGINIA WOOLF!

VIRGINIA   Oh, Vita!

VITA   Doff your caps to the great Lady of English Letters! I would yell it to the four corners of the earth... Virginia.

VIRGINIA   One doesn't know whether to believe a word that comes out of your mouth.

VITA   Rest assured, I mean every word I speak and I speak only a small part of what I feel. If you would doubt my sincerity on this count, perhaps you would call me a liar on another as well.

VIRGINIA   On what other?

VITA   With my husband, with Harold. I told him just before I left that I dared think I might be able to claim some small part of your affection.

VIRGINIA   *(carefully)* You told your husband...?

VITA   Oh yes, and told him too, that I was terribly in love with you.

> *VIRGINIA is brought up short.*

That I was utterly knocked over, completely smitten. He warned me off, of course. He told me you'd have nothing to do with me. That I'd have to look elsewhere.

VIRGINIA   That's what he said?

VITA   Well, not exactly. He laughed at me first.

VIRGINIA   He did.

VITA   Yes, until I let him know that I was perfectly serious and that I held you in the highest esteem—

VIRGINIA   *(somewhat relieved)* Esteem, yes. I see. That is very kind of you to say. You certainly have a way of putting things.

VITA   And that I thought of you night and day.

VIRGINIA   Oh…

VITA   Night more than day.

VIRGINIA   Oh!

VITA   In short, that I was at the mercy of very, very wicked thoughts… about you, Virginia.

VIRGINIA   I believe I'm starting to get your line, Mrs. Nicolson.

VITA   I should hope so, I thought I'd wear myself out. But why back to Mrs. N now?

VIRGINIA   The formality will have to do, at least until you quit making your fun by teasing an old woman.

VITA   *(moves closer)* Oh, Virginia, I assure you there are no old women in my view. And I doubly assure you that I'm not having as much fun as I would like to be. It would be lovely to travel together, wouldn't it? The train ride itself with you would be a dream. I would throw a blanket down and hold your hand under it, in secret.

VIRGINIA   You certainly are a marvel…

VITA   We could gamble, go to taverns, dress as men, drink and smoke… fall in love.

VIRGINIA   Your husband must be a saint.

VITA   *(laughing)* Well, I've never seen a saint chasing the young men up the back stairs with as much energy as Harold's been known to. But no matter, he is a dear, dear man and that's close enough to a saint for me.

VIRGINIA   Surely you don't mean to say—

VITA   Oh dear prude! For the last time, Harold does just as he likes in these matters and so do I. I don't say that to shock you, but I was under the impression that your husband did the same.

VIRGINIA   *(flustered)* In the first place, what Leonard does with his—Well he would never get into scrapes such as you're implying.

VITA   Aha! There, you see you were only pretending to be naïve. I wonder why?

VIRGINIA   One does what one can to stay out of the clutches of the most notorious sapphist in His Majesty's Empire.

VITA   Oh my! *The* most notorious? How you flatter me. You could come and sit over here you know. We had better, after all, huddle together to escape that terrible draught.

VIRGINIA   Strange... I don't feel a draught.

VITA   Well you would feel it if you'd come and sit down here. Unless, of course, you're afraid.

VIRGINIA   What a.... Oh nonsense. *(She sits beside VITA.)* The only reason I should have to be afraid of you is if you want a go at fisticuffs. There you might have me. Otherwise—

VITA   So how are you scoring?

VIRGINIA   Scoring?

VITA   Staying out of clutches or no? Twelve for Virginia and maybe one little point, say just the tiniest one for Vita's side?

VIRGINIA   You just march into a person's house, do you, and tell them where to sit? Vita, I...

> *VITA leans in and steals a kiss, quickly, then stands up and begins to gather her things.*

VITA   I suppose I've taken up enough of your time for one day.

VIRGINIA   You're going?

VITA   Yes, I have an appointment, but ring me up next week, and we'll celebrate. I've had my nose to the grindstone all spring, after all. I propose an evening of complete hedonism, total abandon.

VIRGINIA   Complete hedonism and total abandon are not my strongest suits...

VITA   That's all right dearest, they are mine.

> *VITA blows her a kiss from the door. VIRGINIA waves, puts one had up to her lips where VITA kissed her.*
>
> *Lights fade.*

scene seven

> *LADY C stands, with a basket of fruit. Birds sing, the sunlight ripples down through the leaves. She closes her eyes for a moment and takes a deep breath in. VITA enters approaches quietly.*

VITA   What a rare treat to find you alone, Patricia.

LADY C   Vita! How was Teheran?

VITA   Dull, as dishwater, I'm afraid. Visits to castles, viewing of treasure rooms, decadent feasts with round after round of toasts to the health of the king, to which we were called upon to reply with rounds of toasts to obscure deities, and wishes for the health of each and every crop in the land. In a word—Yawn.

LADY C   But that sounds exciting!

> *LADY M enters, with a basket on her arm as well. She cannot believe her eyes, her hand comes up to her heart.*

VITA   However the women there were captivating in the extreme. Looking at one from behind yards of bright cloth… tinkling with silver coins about the ankle…

LADY M   Lady Compton, we had better make our way indoor, I feel an ill wind blowing.

VITA   But how can you say that, Lady Malgrove? It's simply gorgeous out.

LADY M   *(plucks LADY C aside by the sleeve)* Just keep looking straight ahead and take long steps. She'll be gone before you know it.

LADY C   But, Lady Malgrove…

LADY M   It's the only way. Anything you say to her opens the door a crack. The only safe road is silence.

> *VITA walks around in front of them, blocking LADY M's path, enjoying her discomfort.*

VITA   You've been to market, I see.

LADY M   We've other stops to make.

VITA   Like a lift somewhere? *(looking at the fruit)* Those look heavenly.

> *LADY C looks tempted, but LADY M is horrified. She will not look directly at VITA, but addresses her comment to the air a few feet over her head.*

LADY M   When pigs fly.

VITA   Suit yourself. I think they're taking flight as we speak.

LADY M   I'd mind what enemies I made, if I were you my girl.

VITA   Is that right?

> *VITA examines the fruit in each of the ladies baskets, wrinkling her nose at the ones in LADY M's basket.*

Those are a little too dried out for my taste. *(reaches into LADY C's basket)* These, however, look just right. May I?

VITA takes a piece of fruit and bites into it sensuously, giving LADY C a last glance as she exits. LADY M glares balefully. Offstage we hear the purr as VITA's car roars to life... then takes off.

CLIVE approaches, coughing from the fumes and wiping the front of his trousers as if he had been sprayed with mud. LADY M spies him and beckons imperiously.

LADY M   CLIVE! What did I tell you—that woman has been back on English soil for a matter of hours and already she's been at Tavistock square, wrecking the peace of mind of our dear Mrs. Woolf.

CLIVE   I know—

LADY C   Vita didn't say that's where she'd been.

LADY M   She didn't have to—that sordid glow she was broadcasting told the whole story. She had the audacity to suggest we ride in that public menace of hers.

LADY C   I might have liked to.

CLIVE   It is not being maimed by her motorcar that we need fear.

LADY M   *(to CLIVE)* Speak for yourself. *(to LADY C)* No you wouldn't, my dear, trust me.

LADY C   But how could you say that? Motorcars have given women a freedom of movement, and an independence that just wasn't possible before. And Vita handles hers with such a... sure hand...

CLIVE   Nor is it her sapphism.

LADY M   Should be shot. That'd be an end on it. That woman, and those like her are completely ludicrous and laughable, running around in trousers and work gloves. Dress like that and you can bet your last farthing that someone will ask you to do work they don't want to do themselves. It does not grant you equality to drive your own car and muck out your own barns my girl, it makes you a servant. That's what all these brash young women will find out one of these days. The advantage of a skirt will become evident to them.

LADY C   But Lady Malgrove, surely—

LADY M   It seems that we have somehow birthed a generation of singularly bullheaded and stupid girls. I blame the petrol, it gets into the water and stunts the growth of their brains. There's your problem, but there is no antidote for stupidity.

CLIVE   Vita's chief crime against humanity is that turgid and antiquated prose she insists on inflicting on the reading public. *(shakes himself, as if he had cold chills)* And all the sensibilities that go along with it. It's very likely catching.

LADY M She casts a sort of venomous spell over people—they become addled as though they were in love.

LADY C In Love? Mrs. Woolf?

CLIVE No, it's far worse than that.

LADY M How could it be worse? *(with an air of a prophetic declaration)* Passionate relationships of any sort are not good for the constitution of a genius, and falling in love is its scourge.

CLIVE She's going to publish one of Vita's books.

LADY C What?

CLIVE I'd thought it was some sort of monstrous joke, but I've had a confabulation with Leonard and it seems she's bent on it.

LADY M Well there's your proof. She must be besotted, even to consider the prospect. I suppose it will be left to we, concerned citizens to put a stop to it.

LADY C Mrs. Woolf seems far too sensible and serious a person.

LADY M Don't be fooled, it can happen to anyone where this love business is concerned. And women are more susceptible to it than men. She must have taken leave of her senses, as any sensible person would as likely let a Tasmanian Devil in the house as let... Mrs. Nicolson in.

LADY C But this is silly, I'll just ask Vita myself.

LADY M Just as useful to ask the cat whether it ate the mouse. I would never ordinarily involve myself... but any sacrifice for the safety and preservation of our dear Mrs. Woolf.

CLIVE Of course every precaution must be taken to ensure that Virginia is not put in a precarious state of mind. Given Vita's reputation... I would speak to Virginia, but I feel this is very delicate and feminine matter, best handled by women—

LADY C Oh no! I couldn't.

LADY M As her brother-in-law, it's your responsibility to shield her from the attention of undesirables.

LADY C Yes, Clive, you do it.

CLIVE There's only one fair way to settle this.

> *He reaches into his jacket pocket and pulls out a pound note, tears it into three strips, two short and one long.*

LADY C You're not suggesting, surely—

CLIVE *(to LADY C)* Draw.

LADY M (*a wicked gleam in her eye*) Very well, Clive if you insist.

> *LADY C draws a short piece and lets out a sigh of relief. LADY M glares at CLIVE and then draws. She too draws a short piece and becomes animated for the first time in living memory.*

LADY M Ha ha! You lose! One thing I should have told you, Clive, in games of chance I never lose.

CLIVE How delightful of you to impart that information now.

> *Lights fade.*

scene eight

> *VIRGINIA is setting out tea. She hums to herself and moves around the room, exhibiting a great physical vigour. On a small table in the corner of her room she has set two spots for tea.*

> *ORLANDO enters, in a dressing gown, holding an enormous ice pack on his head and looking very martyred. He sits at one of the spots.*

ORLANDO I suppose the least you could do is get me some tea, after bringing me to death's door.

VIRGINIA You do have a gift for hyperbole.

ORLANDO (*still sulking*) I'm afraid I don't. Is that a friend of yours?

VIRGINIA Never mind. You'll have to go back upstairs. Clive's coming.

ORLANDO I thought Hyperbole was coming.

> *He picks up a biscuit and munches it morosely.*

VIRGINIA No, not for you, Orlando.

> *He puts it down on the plate, with one bite out.*

ORLANDO Can't I have a title? At least a Lord?

VIRGINIA Certainly, certainly. Remove yourself upstairs, *Lord* Orlando.

ORLANDO You have to write it down.

VIRGINIA (*writes*) There. Now will you go?

> *ORLANDO takes another biscuit, takes a bite, and grimacing replaces it. He repeats this several more times throughout the scene, until most of them have a bite taken out.*

ORLANDO But where shall I go? If I am a bore, then the blame lies squarely with you. I have exactly nowhere to go and exactly nothing to do since you haven't written a single word for me all day. Not one word.

VIRGINIA   Fine, fine. *(writes) Orlando, A Biography.* Now how would you like it to go? Hurry, I don't have much time. I'm having my dear brother-in-law over for tea and it will look bad if the lady of the house is muttering to herself like a raving lunatic.

ORLANDO   Yes, I suppose it would. *(jumps up)* I've just had an idea. You could make me King.

VIRGINIA   *(amused)* I don't think there's a vacancy at present.

ORLANDO   Even better, a general! *(slicing at the air with his sword)* EN GARDE! HUZZAH, HUZZAH!

> *He fights off an imaginary opponent, and striking a fatal blow finishes him off.*

TAKE THAT, KNAVE!

VIRGINIA   *(imitates a gruff soldier)* I say, there goes a little whippet wearing white taffeta and riding at the head of the Calvary. What would you do in a battle?

ORLANDO   *(slashing at the air with his sword)* I would ride out on a horse 45-hand high—a gift from the Prince of Arabia…

VIRGINIA   I suppose you're an intimate friend of the *Prince* of Arabia?

ORLANDO   …give orders to my faithful legion from her back. I would—

VIRGINIA   Be killed, in a battle You would be dispatched very shortly and without much fanfare. No more Orlando, poof.

> *Holds her pen poised.*

ORLANDO   Would not! Would not!

VIRGINIA   *(pretends to write)* The young Lord Orlando had a short and inauspicious career in the military—

ORLANDO   NO!!! Stop, I beg you!

> *Pause. VIRGINIA removes her pen from the paper.*

I'm not demanding, you know. Any little adventure at all will do.

> *ORLANDO takes out a dagger and tests the edge against his thumb. He tosses it from hand to hand. VIRGINIA suddenly has an idea. She starts writing in earnest, it takes a while for ORLANDO to realize she is no longer listening to him.*

Personally I'm in favour of conquering, battles, pillaging and capture, of course just on principle.

> *ORLANDO keeps talking, as he walks casually behind her. He reads some of what she is writing, over her shoulder and his face becomes more serious. His tone is light, but his hands come to rest around her neck.*

In the company of ladies, though I admit to a penchant for strolling in gardens and looking at birds, so you pick something that suits your constitution.

> *ORLANDO allows one hand to slide forward slightly, a caress that has the shade of a threat. VIRGINIA is frozen, torn between enjoying the caress and throwing him off.*

I'm completely yours, for the moment.

> *These are VITA's words, and ORLANDO even gives them a similar intonation. VIRGINIA is taken aback.*

VIRGINIA   What did you say?

> *ORLANDO runs his hands forward, over her shoulders, and kisses her neck.*

ORLANDO   I'm completely yours… for the moment.

VIRGINIA   Vita…

> *CLIVE is heard entering, offstage. VIRGINIA begins to make excited, frantic notes.*

(*suddenly*) I know who you are, Orlando. You'll give me no more trouble, I know who you are.

CLIVE   (*entering*) I should hope you'd at least have an inkling, after an acquaintance of nearly three decades.

> *VIRGINIA motions frantically for ORLANDO to go away. He puts a finger to his lips and sits in a chair hugging his knees and grinning mischievously.*

VIRGINIA   Clive, I…

> *She flaps her hand angrily at ORLANDO. CLIVE, of course does not see ORLANDO and takes a step back, alarmed.*

CLIVE   Virginia are you feeling quite well?

VIRGINIA   Clive! Oh, dear Clive, I'm so glad you've come. (*pause*) You'll have to go.

CLIVE   Who were you talking to just now?

> *CLIVE picks up a biscuit, and is about to begin eating it. He notices that a bite has been taken out. Revolted, he replaces it. Picking up another, he sees that they all have bites taken out. He is shaken by this, but tries to ignore it.*

I heard you call out. It sounded like... Orlando?

VIRGINIA   Yes, that's it. That's the next book I'll write. Oh Clive, I'm in a rapture—I can see the whole novel hovering before me in the air... as if it were a crystalline structure.

CLIVE   You don't say... now that interests me very much, because you see it is quite the opposite, when I write—

> *He moves to sit on the chair that ORLANDO is seated on. ORLANDO doesn't move.*

VIRGINIA   *(crying out)* No!

> *ORLANDO slips out of the way at the last minute and crosses the floor on tiptoe, waving to VIRGINIA as he exits. She breathes a sigh of relief and turns to the task of showing CLIVE the door.*

CLIVE   Is Leonard at home?

VIRGINIA   Leonard? How should I know? Go and ask him yourself if you like, you can find his study.

CLIVE   Are you feeling quite well? Perhaps I should ring the doctor?

VIRGINIA   On the contrary! I am feeling like I have never felt before. Until now, I've had a husk over my head, a cowl over my eyes—lived in a hole in the ground and am suddenly let out into the day...

CLIVE   Virginia... I came to speak with you about a small matter—

VIRGINIA   As if I were sitting on the rooftop and looking out over the landscape, only the landscape were history and all its events and they aren't stacked in order as books on the shelves...

> *CLIVE tries to butt in, but VIRGINIA takes no notice.*

CLIVE   A rumour that you were going to publish a certain book. A romance... *Seducers in Equador.*

VIRGINIA   ...Each has a shape and a texture, to each a color and form and the relations to each other are as the oceans currents...

CLIVE   See here, Virginia.

VIRGINIA   I can see, Clive and do!

CLIVE   I'd heard a ridiculous rumour that you were going to publish a book by Mrs. Nicolson.

VIRGINIA   Who?

CLIVE   Vita.

VIRGINIA Oh, Vita… Vita! That's the Latin for life, isn't it? Funny how I'd never thought of it before.

CLIVE Her writing is primitive and sentimental!

VIRGINIA Yes, isn't it wonderful?

CLIVE Not to mention clumsy.

VIRGINIA Yes, but people simply adore it… for this very reason. Which fascinates me. Now Clive, I must ask you to leave me. I've got to start afresh.

CLIVE But we depend upon you to provide some standards. What will people, people of substance, think when they see "Hogarth Press" stamped on the spine of a common romance?

VIRGINIA People of substance might well conclude that literature is dead, that the sky has fallen, or that we need to settle our account books, I can't say I care. Now you really must go.

CLIVE But our tea!

VIRGINIA There's tea to be found all over town.

CLIVE Your interest in her is, of course understandable.

VIRGINIA Is it?

CLIVE She is… exciting, I suppose. She excites wild… violent passions in people. But what shall I say…. What she is to you, Virginia, you are not to her.

VIRGINIA See here, Clive, must you speak in riddles? Do you think I'm a schoolgirl? And I don't need *your* council on affairs of the heart—

CLIVE Of course you're aware how much one's writing can be affected by the company we keep.

VIRGINIA —nor on the subject of writing.

> *This stings. CLIVE takes a moment to gather himself, it seems as if he will leave, but swallows his indignation and makes a final appeal.*

CLIVE I came out of concern, Virginia. I've only seen you behave in such a fashion once before.

VIRGINIA Ah, yes. The time in my life that I try hardest to forget, and which those around me insist on remembering.

> *VIRGINIA turns away from him.*

CLIVE Neither Leonard nor I… none of us want you have another dark time. I know it's difficult. You're so used to depending on your mind—it's your greatest tool but Virginia what I'm telling you is that, on some occasions you can't trust it. It is then, that you must lean on your loved ones. Your trusted colleagues.

VIRGINIA   I must lean... on you, for instance?

> *CLIVE realizes that he may have gone too far.*

You can go and take tea with Leonard, or you can go to tea with any number of ladies, who will be glad to have you for the pleasure of your company alone, *(She starts to push him through the door.)* but go you must.

> *She hustles him out still protesting.*

CLIVE   But, Virginia, wait. I insist on having a word with you.

VIRGINIA   Yes Clive, any time but now.

> *She closes the door on him, leans on it.*
>
> *Lights fade.*

scene nine

> *The park, a short time later. CLIVE and LADY M confer beneath some shrubbery.*

LADY M   Talking of Virginia, what did you accomplish?

CLIVE   Truthfully not a lot. When I arrived, she was distracted in the extreme and she next to tossed me out on my ear!

LADY M   Ah!

CLIVE   I'm sure it's just the strain of her work...

LADY M   Come, Clive, what did you see?

> *He glances around furtively, to be sure no one is listening in.*

CLIVE   When I arrived, she appeared to be talking to herself.

LADY M   There, there you have it!

CLIVE   And when I questioned her about undertaking to publish Vita's... "book" she did not deny it. She instead... *(He hesitates, not wanting to paint VIRGINIA in a negative light.)*

LADY M   Yes, yes?

CLIVE   *(admits, reluctantly)* She rather cried out that Vita was latin for life, and how strange it was that she'd never noticed it before and then pushed me bodily out of the room.

> *LADY M considers the symptoms gravely, and shakes her head.*

LADY M   Poor Virginia is afflicted much more seriously than I thought. *(She makes a sudden decision.)* Now Clive, what is coming is not going to pleasant. Virginia must be purged of this infatuation, and the cure will not come easily.

CLIVE   What are you proposing?

LADY M   You'll plan a party at your cottage, on the day of the upcoming solar eclipse, to view it, as it were. You'll invite the Woolfs, the Nicolsons and all of us. If you have the reach of intellect that you claim—

CLIVE   I don't see how that's called for.

> *LADY M is warming to the task, nearly rubbing her hands with glee.*

LADY M   Then it should be no great task for you to simply expose her in a battle of wits. Humiliate her, publicly.

CLIVE   Oh but Lady Malgrove, surely there's another way. That's so… why that's so…

LADY M   You see, it is her illusions that Virginia must be divested of. She has wrapped that woman in a shroud of mystery. When that is stripped away, Mrs. Nicolson will hold no lure for her.

CLIVE   But it's so… *(wrinkling his nose disdainfully)* straightforward.

LADY M   Clive. We do agree that Virginia is perhaps one of the greatest minds of our time.

CLIVE   Yes, yes of course.

LADY M   Most unnatural in a woman, and for this reason it is to be protected and nurtured like an orchid in a glass box. Nobody said it's an easy task to be the steward of a genius. And Mrs. Nicolson is turning out to be a much more treacherous foe than I ever imagined. But we're up for the challenge, aren't we?

CLIVE   The challenge?

LADY M   I'd lay odds on you, Clive!

CLIVE   Please, this isn't a day at the races, Lady Malgrove. I know Virginia and once she's romantically attached to something or someone it's in her nature to cling to it…

LADY M   That's it exactly. Virginia must be made to see that horrid woman for what she is. A flatterer, a hanger-on!

CLIVE   …much as a child will cling to an old doll, or a bad habit, which if ripped away quickly can cause great harm.

LADY M   Of course if you're not up to it, I'll have to find another man for the job.

CLIVE   It's not a matter of being unfit for the job, I care only that Virginia's feelings are spared at all cost.

LADY M But of course, if it's done properly, no one but you, I and our opponent will know what's transpiring.

CLIVE Tactfully, Lady M.

LADY M Don't you worry! If there's one thing that I am known for it is discretion and tact.

Lights fade.

scene ten

VITA and LADY C sit at a small table in a café, having tea. In the background the low hum of conversation can be heard.

LADY C I am so glad we're becoming closer, Vita. It would be simply lovely if you could come and stay with me for a night next week. What do you say?

VITA Now Patricia, you know very well that an evening's conversation around the fire with your husband—and I mean no offense—would bore me to tears.

LADY C That's just it, Reginald will be away.

VITA Well you'd better not have me visit, or everyone will be abuzz. It's hard enough to live in the shadow of one's past scrapes, without giving everyone leave to talk about me for something I haven't done.

LADY C Perhaps there is a reason, after all Vita. I have heard a rumour…

VITA Given the company you keep, I'd wager you've heard them all.

LADY C I had heard that you'd given up all of your other engagements and weren't taking calls at all unless they were from a certain someone. That your days of carefree adventure were over.

VITA Don't be ridiculous, Patricia. Now who would have given you that idea?

LADY C It gets even better. I had heard, in fact, that you were in love.

VITA Is that so?

LADY C With a mutual acquaintance of ours. I defended you of course.

VITA Chivalry is not dead… alas.

LADY C I also have my own selfish reasons for thinking your attentions might lie elsewhere.

LADY C meets VITA's gaze and leans toward her over the table.

VITA If I didn't know better, I'd think you were suggesting—

LADY C And what if I were, Vita? Reggie has affairs after all, and I believe that women should have equal right to…

VITA *(amused)* To…? Tell how you think women should be emancipated, exactly.

LADY C Well I—Vita, you're teasing me.

VITA I am rather intrigued. To my mind you've hit upon the best argument for the suffragists yet. Let's go, then.

LADY C Go?

VITA Yes, I'm won over. Take me home so we can see if you make as bold a usage of that sharp tongue of yours behind closed doors as you're able to do in a café, my dear.

> *LADY C is nearly speechless. VITA enjoys this, smiles.*

LADY C Now, I hadn't thought you would be quite so… forward. If you'll excuse me for one moment, I think I must… I must powder my nose.

> *VITA watches LADY C's retreat.*
>
> *The lights come up on VIRGINIA at her desk, she picks up ORLANDO's red feather quill and writes. ORLANDO sits on the floor, near her desk. As she finishes a page she lays it aside, where she thinks there is a table, but there is not. The page drifts down into ORLANDO's lap.*

VIRGINIA Dearest Vita, enjoyed your visit of Sunday last more completely than I have enjoyed anything in quite some time… Teheran seemed like the ends of the earth and the stretch without seeing you was so long that you must promise not to do it again.

ORLANDO Why, this sounds like a love letter.

VIRGINIA Don't be ridiculous.

> *Another page drifts down to him. He reads out loud.*

VIRGINIA & ORLANDO I'm inconsolable tonight. Distracted and nervous. I look out the window into the rain and there see your face etched in lithograph as the drops hit the tin roof. Leonard rocks in his chair. The springs complain: Vi-ta, Vi-ta.

> *Lights begin to fade on VIRGINIA. ORLANDO stands up and crosses to VITA. He puts the page in her hands, and leans over her shoulder. She feels the caress as they read.*

ORLANDO I look into the fire and still your dark body flits around the logs. This afternoon, I was ecstatic and I'll tell you why… I've a new book in mind called *Orlando* and it's your biography.

ORLANDO & VITA You must tell me honestly if you mind and I won't do it. You see I've taken a few liberties. Orlando starts out as a man and about mid the way through suddenly becomes a woman.

ORLANDO   NO!

> *He slowly checks the front of his pants.*

VITA   Just say the word and I'll toss the whole thing in the fire. Only I make it up on cold, wet nights when there is no possibility of seeing the real Vita, and it consoles me.

ORLANDO   *(incredulous)* I think… I'm going to faint.

VITA   If I were to ring you up to ask, would you say that you were fond of me? Let's see now… yes, I'm almost certain that I would. If I saw you, would you kiss me? If I were in bed with you…

> *ORLANDO totters, reaches out toward VITA…*

VITA & ORLANDO   …would you?

> *And faints.*

VITA   Yes. Virginia, you wretch, you've captured me.

> *VITA gets up, and exits, the letter clutched to her chest. LADY C returns to the table, to find no one.*

LADY C   I have composed myself finally and what I wish to tell you is—Vita?

> *Lights fade, as LADY C looks around first in disbelief, then outrage.*
>
> *End of Act One.*

ACT TWO

scene one

VIRGINIA and VITA are in a bedroom at Knole. VIRGINIA sits on the edge of the bed, nearly engulfed by the pillows and clouds of blankets. The bed itself is bathed in light, but the stage immediately around is left dark, giving the impression of a huge room.

VIRGINIA   So finally I am permitted to visit your beloved Knole.

VITA   Beloved, yes, but not mine. My cousin Eddy is the heir, even though I can count the number of times he's been here on one hand. If only I could wake up a man, as easily as you have it happen in your book.

VIRGINIA   Yes, it would simplify a great many things for you, Vita. The question remains… would you like them so?

VITA formulates a quick retort, then changes her mind, remains silent.

It must have been lonely, growing up here?

VITA   Oh, it's musty and stern and the stones tumble around your ears when you bang the door shut, but it's the only place I've ever felt at home. Some rooms haven't been opened for generations, and there are unopened trunks bursting with letters and diaries—you could crack a new one like an egg each day and spill out the lives inside.

VIRGINIA   It suits you, then. A room to hide each new rapscallion personality as it springs up. Well you needn't worry about losing this place, I'll net it for you.

VITA   Even you, Virginia, cannot uproot centuries of English law on my behalf.

VIRGINIA   Between the covers of a book, I mean. When I'm finished *Orlando*. Knole will be yours forever. For long after your cousin, or you, or I for that matter, are food for the worms.

VITA   Perhaps it was a mistake to bring you here.

VIRGINIA   Why?

VITA   I can't tell whether you're actually in the room with me, or off somewhere writing your book.

VIRGINIA smiles, says nothing. She is enjoying all this, completely in her element.

You know, you'll have to do rather a lot of sweeping over your tracks to keep people from guessing Orlando's true identity.

VIRGINIA   There won't be any room for guess work. Especially with the photographs.

VITA   Photographs? Of me? You can't be thinking of putting them in? But everyone will be scandalized!

VIRGINIA   Aha! It's all been worth it to live to see this day! I have shocked Vita Sackville-West, and who would have guessed I had it in my power to do that?

>   *VITA ponders this, VIRGINIA watches her, smiling.*

VITA   I'm feeling strangely taken advantage of—

VIRGINIA   It would not, I suspect, be a feeling that you are overly familiar with and so I say enjoy it. But there is one catch…. You'll have to let me in on every clandestine meeting in your checkered past, tell me every secret whispered in each and every ear.

VITA   Ah, but you won't care for me any longer, if I do that.

VIRGINIA   No… I'll care for you more.

VITA   Is it possible? If I told you everything?

VIRGINIA   Oh yes, it will test your mettle. I want to hear even the parts you barely let yourself think about. But be warned, I won't hold back, I'll display you in full regalia, all flags flying for the whole world to see. *(pause)* Are you afraid?

>   *VITA looks off into space, thinking. Trying to maintain her composure.*

I'll call a halt to the whole thing, if you want me to, Vita.

VITA   I would be a fool to refuse you.

VIRGINIA   Then it's a deal. *(pause)* So how is it with you and other women? What do you do together in bed?

VITA   Do you ask now on behalf of Orlando, or for your own interest?

VIRGINIA   My own.

VITA   Wouldn't you like to know?

VIRGINIA   That's rather the point. I don't make it my practice to ask questions I don't want an answer to. I leave that to you and your kind.

VITA   My kind?

VIRGINIA   The poets. That's what you're on about, isn't it?

VITA   I suppose it is, though I don't think that one published poem will do to admit me into the ranks—

VIRGINIA   But surely a poem of such prodigious length must count for two or three.

>   *Pause.*

VITA   Well it varies you see…

VIRGINIA   Is there a scoring card of some kind or do you have to petition the king—

VITA   Let me see now... making love with Violet, it was very much the same as with a man.

> *VIRGINIA falls silent, drops her eyes. VITA sneaks a sidelong glance to see the effect her words are having.*

But with Dottie, not at all. One must sit up and play word games with her afterward so that she doesn't get maudlin. *(pause)* Your turn.

VIRGINIA   What on earth...?

VITA   Fair is only fair, after all. Tell me, what is it like with Leonard?

VIRGINIA   Drag Leonard into it, will you? You have no limits.

VITA   You're the one who asked the question first. As you're always the one to ask the questions, you could at least tell one tiny detail—

VIRGINIA   Well we don't...

VITA   Of course not *now*, but back when you got married you must have—

VIRGINIA   We never did.

VITA   Oh come now, surely you—

VIRGINIA   Never. Not once.

> *VITA is shocked, and genuinely concerned for them both.*

VITA   Oh poor dear! And poor Leonard, what is to be done?!

VIRGINIA   You needn't pity us, Vita. You with your browned arms and your curls. You needn't pity me!

VITA   I don't!

VIRGINIA   I expect it's a blessing—my poor health. It's at least given me the time to write seriously.

> *Pause. VITA becomes abruptly chilly.*

VITA   Yes, perhaps I'm disturbing you now. You've brought along some work, I suppose. I won't keep you from it. *(moves to leave)* If you need anything, ring the bell.

> *VIRGINIA stalls.*

VIRGINIA   Am I meant to sleep in here?

VITA   But of course. It's the best room we have.

VIRGINIA   I don't think I can—

VITA   If it's the chill you mind, I'll stoke the fire.

VIRGINIA   Oh no, the room itself is not the problem it's me. If I sleep here and then have to go home, I shall go the way of the stray cat fed cream.

VITA   Don't worry stray tabby, I'll fetch your cream at once.

VIRGINIA   But then, after you've spoilt him, poor cat, he can't bear to go back to the dust bin for his dinner and so…

VITA   And so?

VIRGINIA   You finish by killing him with kindness.

VITA approaches VIRGINIA and takes her hand, looks directly into her eyes.

VITA   Virginia, Virginia Woolf, I am enraptured with you. Do you not know?

VIRGINIA tries faintly to get her hand back, VITA hangs on.

VIRGINIA   So you say…. But just you neglect me to go gamboling about the lanes with Mary Campbell, or Marlene Dietrich or whatever herring-cooker it is that you do gambol with and you may find Virginia's soft crevices lined with hooks.

VITA takes VIRGINIA's other hand, grips it and drops onto her knees, her head in VIRGINIA's lap, she kisses her legs through her skirt. VIRGINIA's hand slowly disentangles itself from VITA's and winds its way through her hair at the nape of her neck.

VITA   I care for you as I care for no one else. Do you want to get into bed?

VITA sits beside her on the bed.

VIRGINIA   Have you brought others here? Have you slept with Dottie… here?

VITA is caught a bit off guard, freezes for an instant. From the mound of pillows and blanket, a hand comes out softly and begins to find it's way up VIRGINIA's shoulder. It caresses her, gently.

VITA   I thought you said you didn't make it your practice to ask questions you don't want the answer to.

VIRGINIA   Quite right. Come here.

The hand belongs to ORLANDO who emerges from under the blankets, and sits behind VITA. VIRGINIA reaches for VITA, strokes the side of her face.

You're like a Roman… a sea nymph… damn your lovely mouth…

VITA   Ha! I've made you one.

VIRGINIA   One what?

VITA   A poet.

VIRGINIA   Or besotted. But why split hairs.

Pause. VIRGINIA, still touching VITA's face, becomes suddenly serious.

Close your eyes. Are you mine? Mine only?

ORLANDO   *(overlapping)* Mine only?

VITA opens her eyes looks at VIRGINIA questioningly. Nods yes.

VIRGINIA   Close them.

VITA closes her eyes. VIRGINIA makes a couple false starts toward her. ORLANDO reaches around VITA and takes her hands, he pulls them toward him, so that she is held against him and cannot move. With one hand he reaches forward, and pulls her chin to one side, exposing her throat. VITA is taken aback by the strength of the grip she thinks is VIRGINIA's and she makes a surprised, but pleased sound in her throat, but does not open her eyes. VIRGINIA leans forward and kisses VITA. She lowers her dress a few inches, exposing her shoulder. VIRGINIA pauses.

(gives a small, light laugh) I don't know what to do.

VITA laughs. It is a sensuous laugh, with an edge of hardness.

Show me. I don't know what to do.

VITA opens her eyes, breaks free from ORLANDO's grip and suddenly lowers VIRGINIA onto the bed. ORLANDO curls on the foot of the bed, watching.

VITA   *(in near darkness)* You'll just have to trust me then, won't you?

Lights fade.

scene two

Lights come up on the bed. VITA and VIRGINIA have left, although the bedclothes are still rumpled. There is a rustle from underneath them and ORLANDO crawls out wearing a huge frilly white nightgown, with a sleeping cap slightly askew. She wakes up, stretches and yawns.

ORLANDO   Another day, another glorious day! I have had the strangest of dreams. I thought I was… that is to say, I thought I had…

She catches sight of an outfit of clothing, carefully laid out. Crinolines, a dress, boots, hat. A look of comprehension and horror crosses her face. Slowly, very slowly she peeks down the front of her nightgown, and… shrieks!

(clutching her head) O, O, O, I feel faint! *(looking at the clothes)* My word, what plumage! Bulky things these dresses are. If there were an emergency of some kind, I'd be no help to myself. Come a hurricane, or a robber or a pack of wolves, I couldn't run away, I'd have to call for help. *(She holds the dress up in front of her and looks in the mirror.)* On the other hand, displayed to such advantage, I'm almost certain to get it. Do I mind that? Do I mind it, I wonder?

> *She hauls the dress over her head, and judges the result in the mirror. Walks the length of the room, then suddenly whirls around upon her reflection in the mirror and questions it severely.*

Orlando? Is that you? No battles from now on, no horseback riding, no solitary walks, no adventures abroad! No taking a wife! Oh my word, how does one endure? No travel—or none to speak of—all closed up in a carriage—No lovers, no… life. And yet suddenly it occurs to me: Why not? Why not indeed!

> *Lights fade.*

scene three

> *The background sounds of a noisy pub. VIRGINIA stands, facing outward, looking around her. VITA, dressed as a man, stands facing VIRGINIA with her back to the audience.*

VIRGINIA   In such a raucous establishment, I'd be afraid if I weren't in the company of a man. Still, this is real life, I suppose. Bring me a pint of ale!

> *VITA leaves, VIRGINIA sits down.*

> *ORLANDO enters, dressed in her finery. VIRGINIA catches sight of her and tries to hide behind a menu. ORLANDO spots her.*

ORLANDO   Hello Virginia! *(holds out a fold of her dress)* What do you think? Restricts movement to a certain degree, but people are so kind, and men hold the doors wide for one. Do you think it suits me?

> *VIRGINIA tries to take as little notice of ORLANDO as possible.*

VIRGINIA   Quite fetching. Haven't you somewhere to go…?

ORLANDO   No place to put a sword, but then one hardly ever has time for a duel anyway, what with the rush of modern life. *(indicates the music)* Are they making those sounds on purpose?

VIRGINIA   It's a new kind of music, it breaks all the rules.

ORLANDO   Looks as if they'll break all their instruments instead.

> *VITA returns, holding a pint of ale and a drink in a tiny delicate glass. VIRGINIA reaches for the pint. VITA gives her the glass.*

VITA   Here you are, my dear.

ORLANDO   Nothing for me, thank you.

> *VITA takes her arm and guides her toward a table. ORLANDO falls in step and sits down with them. VITA, of course is not aware of ORLANDO and VIRGINIA is able to take her presence in stride, and for the most part ignore her. ORLANDO doesn't seem to notice.*

VIRGINIA   What is it?

VITA   Lime Cordial. A suitable drink for a lady.

> *Tastes it and grimaces.*

VIRGINIA   Suitable for a lady to rinse her stockings perhaps, but not to drink. Oh no matter, I'll just drink out of yours. It will be a loving cup.

> *She takes a drink, wipes her mouth with the back of her hand.*

VITA   You'll have to behave, or else risk drawing attention to us.

VIRGINIA   Why this isn't enough to put in a bird's eye.

VITA   The illusion will only hold if people don't look too closely.

VIRGINIA   *(points offstage)* You seem to have fooled that girl, at least. Or perhaps she's waving because you know her Vita.

> *VITA does recognize her, but pretends not to.*

VITA   I don't know her.

VIRGINIA   She's looking right at you.

VITA   No, she's looking past me, for certain.

ORLANDO   I... I think she's looking at me.

VIRGINIA   *(to VITA)* No, no, she's not. She thinks you're a man.

ORLANDO   It's no wonder! Up until recently, so did I. Well what should I do?

VIRGINIA   *(to VITA)* Perhaps you ought to go and ask her to dance.

ORLANDO   But hadn't I better wait for her…

VITA   There, you see? She's going.

VIRGINIA   Reluctantly. Although I can't say I blame her, for you do look dashing.

ORLANDO   But then… we'll both be waiting all day.

VIRGINIA   Imagine, a pair of trousers and a little velvet on the cheek admit you to a secret world…

VITA It's not just a change of attire, but an adjustment of the body. Feet planted firmly on the ground and chin and eyes up in anticipation of the privileges and boons that are coming your way.

VIRGINIA Yes, the illusion is remarkable and nearly complete. Unless one looks closely. As I do…

ORLANDO I'll go and speak to her. Wish me luck!

ORLANDO exits.

VIRGINIA As I have done since I first laid eyes on you and will continue to do, no matter what comes.

VITA Is that a promise?

VIRGINIA I haven't a choice. No matter what twists and turns you put me through, no matter if I don't see you for weeks on end. All I need do is think "Vita" and there you are on the inside of my eyelids, fixing a fence, dressing down a servant, astride a horse in full gallop, all in exquisite detail like a moving picture. *(Pause, as she sits back and looks at VITA.)* Can our lives weather it? I'm afraid I'm going to want to be with you every moment.

VITA And I with you. We'll long to, but of course we won't. Things are infinitely better this way.

VIRGINIA Are they?

VITA Of course! Everyone knows a lover is a far better thing to have than a wife. One can have both a life and a lover, but never a life and a wife.

VIRGINIA You've a neophyte poet's weakness for rhyme, Vita—

VITA After all, why would we want to settle down in a wretched little cottage when you've got Leonard at home already, and I've got Harold and the children? Isn't it better, to remain adventurous, to meet secretly…

VIRGINIA And when the intrigue grows tiresome?

Pause. VITA tries to read VIRGINIA's expression.

VITA I need the intrigue. It's all the rest that grows tiresome with me. *(quietly)* Now let me ask you something. Just what would you—no, rather what *wouldn't* you do for your writing.

VIRGINIA I don't quite take your meaning.

VITA Is there anything you wouldn't do, in service of the book you're working on?

VIRGINIA No, I suppose there isn't.

VITA There's your wife, then, and so why pretend otherwise? We're alike in that respect. I, too would go to great lengths… to further your writing.

VIRGINIA   Vita, no—

VITA   *(playfully)* Lie, cheat, steal. Anything for the perfect book. After all, without Orlando in common, I doubt whether we'd have become more than acquaintances to each other.

VIRGINIA   How can you say that? You have stolen my heart.

VITA   We are two thieves, then. Perhaps we deserve each other. You've stolen my past.

VIRGINIA   Vita, my writing is something that I do completely alone.

VITA   And so all those questions about Knole, about my past… I wasn't in the room then at all, I suppose?

VIRGINIA   Truly significant writing is nonetheless done from a place of solitude. Or so it has always been with me.

VITA   I only meant that we had ground in common. Perhaps I'd the wrong impression.

VIRGINIA   *(lightly)* Perhaps you've taken a bluestocking as a lover for the good of her mind alone?

VITA   OH, VIRGINIA! To even think such a thing. You have a monstrous imagination, it's going to do you some harm one of these days. I'll go and get us another drink, and then we'll move on to more pleasant topics, shall we?

> *VITA exits. ORLANDO comes back to the table, happily flushed and excited.*

ORLANDO   We agreed, between us two that neither should lead. Instead we let it be decided, moment by moment. And the result was most thrilling. Love is not determined by shapes and angles, it is not as precise a science as geometry. It must, after all be admitted that even the terms themselves, "man" "woman" are laughably out of date! She has invited me to go on an extended holiday on a steamship… and I think I will accept.

VIRGINIA   Yes, yes. Off you go. Don't forget to write.

> *Lights fade.*

scene four

> *The lights come up in two pools. In one, VIRGINIA sits at her desk, writing. In the other VITA sits on her bed with a small lap desk.*

VIRGINIA   Dearest Vita, I can only surmise that you've taken off again for Teheran, or a walking tour of Borneo as I haven't heard from you—

> *She tears the sheet off and lets it fall onto the floor.*

VITA   Dear Dottie… *(She rubs it out, begins again.)* Dear Edna *(She crumples the page and begins again.)* Dear Mary,

Of course you're only too aware of the effect you have on me and I won't deny that I have been irresistibly drawn to you since first we met—

VIRGINIA   *(with forced levity)* Since you've not darkened my door for a week, I suppose I'll have to get on without you.

VITA   But I feel I must warn you. You see, I've promised myself not to have any of the recriminations, squabbling and jealousies that people seem, perversely almost, to enjoy.

VIRGINIA   Luckily I've finally dispatched Orlando. I wonder if you felt a little tug, wherever you were last night as I made the last penstroke… and you died.

VITA   After all, my dear, physical love is the only fleeting respite we have from the gloomy, dreary routine of daily life. It takes a person of uncommon depth of soul to enjoy it to the fullest, to avoid sullying it with hateful feelings, with harsh words.

VIRGINIA   In fact, you needn't even bother coming round, for if you did I'd be much too busy to see you. Yes, it's a constant stream of luncheons and parties, on my end… and I've bought a new hat…

VITA   So we'll see then. Until next Tuesday, I remain,

Yours Vita

VIRGINIA   *(faltering)* Yes, I've bought a new hat and I'm told it looks quite fetching.

> *VIRGINIA lets her head fall forward onto her hand.*
>
> *Lights fade.*

scene five

> *LADY M, LADY C and CLIVE are on the front porch of CLIVE's cottage in Northumberland. They are gathered, ostensibly to watch the total eclipse of the sun. Sitting on the rail are specially made devices to view the eclipse. CLIVE fiddles with the devices, and paces nervously.*

LADY M   Clive, do you need something to fortify you?

LADY C   The Woolfs are coming, and the Nicolsons? What's going on? It vexes me so that you won't tell me what you've got planned.

LADY M   We've no time to explain. When they arrive, just follow our lead—

CLIVE   And say nothing.

LADY C   You don't think that would look a trifle odd, if I were to sit, completely dumb.

CLIVE   You're right, an event so unprecedented would no doubt arouse suspicion. Just make idle chit-chat as usual.

> *LADY C shoots a murderous look at CLIVE, and goes nearer to LADY M.*

LADY C   I warn you, I will not be kept in the dark.

> *VITA arrives suddenly, giving CLIVE a scare. He is tense about the task he is supposed to undertake, and his nervousness makes it appear as though he were coming slightly unhinged.*

CLIVE   Ah! Vita we were just talking about… that is to say…

LADY C   *(icily)* How do you do, Vita? As Clive was saying, we feared we might not have the pleasure of your company, prone as you are to sudden departures— which would have been such a pity. *(to CLIVE)* How long until the eclipse? I'm dying to see one.

LADY M   I heard tell of a woman who was so proud, she watched the whole eclipse and told all her friends. Next day she woke up and there was a hole burned in her eye.

LADY C   How disgusting!

> *VITA attempts to joke with LADY C, who ignores her completely.*

VITA   A hole burned in her eye? Extraordinary. She didn't notice it before she went to bed?

LADY M   What I meant was, there was a hole burned on the inside so that everything she looked at after that had a great gaping black spot in the middle. It's nothing to scoff at, my dear.

CLIVE   That's what these boxes are for. So we can watch without harm.

LADY C   Are you sure?

CLIVE   I followed the instructions to the letter. You see, they've mirrors on the inside and you look through here… *(points)*

LADY M   I wonder what's keeping the Woolfs?

> *CLIVE is chattering now, from nervousness.*

CLIVE   …and everything appears just the reverse of what it is. And ah… therefore it can't hurt you. Ha ha. Maybe they've changed their minds after all.

VITA   I think they'll be along.

CLIVE   Virginia's been kept exceptionally busy of late, with the final edits of her new book.

LADY C   Oh? What's it called?

CLIVE   *Orlando.* A new twist on biography, apparently.

LADY C   A biography? Of whom?

CLIVE   A young Lord in the court of Elizabeth—

VITA   Isn't that funny, now I had thought it was a woman.

LADY C   Well which is it, Clive?

CLIVE   I am almost entirely certain that Virginia's book is about a man, or at least when she discussed it with me on several occasions—

VITA   Ah yes, you would know best, after all.

CLIVE   *(aside to VITA)* Tread softly, Vita.

VITA   *(loudly)* Oh, Clive. Harold sends his love by the way.

CLIVE   Harold? Oh yes, your husband, I remember him. He seemed a good... good diplomat.

VITA   He said he was ever so sorry to miss this little gathering as he so wanted to see your cottage... again.

CLIVE   Quite.

> *Sound of a car pulling up and the engine turns off. LADY C spots the car.*

LADY C   The Woolfs, here come The Woolfs!

CLIVE   Sound the alarm, the Wolves are here.

> *CLIVE stands up and shouts to LEONARD. VIRGINIA continues onto the balcony. She enters, attempting bravado... wearing a hat with some odd things on top.*

(exiting) Leonard, there is a splendid view of the water from the back. Let me show you the stonework, I've had workmen up to finish it off...

LADY M   Clive?

CLIVE   I'm sure you ladies have plenty to discuss. I leave you to it.

> *He exits.*

LADY M   Clive! *(sees he is gone, turns to greet VIRGINIA)* We're so happy you could make it, we feared maybe your health would keep you away—

VIRGINIA   No, I feel strong as an ox these days, and rather as though I could eat one. And your own health, how has it been of late?

> *VIRGINIA grabs a fruit from the tray and bites into it. LADY M winces.*

LADY M   I can't complain...

VITA   I'm so happy you made it Mrs. Woolf.

LADY M   …but now that you mention it, my back has been plaguing me…

VIRGINIA   I wouldn't miss it and I've heard that this is the superlative place for viewing the eclipse. But certainly, in these intimate circles, your conscience will permit you to use my given name.

VITA   As you wish, Virginia.

LADY C is not pleased. Neither is LADY M.

LADY M   What's keeping Clive? Patricia, perhaps you'd better go round and get the men.

LADY M plucks at her sleeve, but LADY C shakes her off and approaches VIRGINIA.

LADY C   We've just been talking about your book. I'm positively on pins and needles to read it. Do tell us, what's it about?

VIRGINIA   If I went round telling that, we'd never sell a copy. *(slyly, for VITA's benefit)* It's about an imp named Orlando… whose character you might be familiar with. And that's all I can say.

LADY M   There seemed to be some confusion about the protagonist. Clive was of the opinion that it was a man, while… others seemed to contend that it was a woman.

VIRGINIA   *(deadpan)* I guess you would have to conclude that it was a mixture of the two, Edith.

There is a pause. The others sense the change in VIRGINIA and are uncomfortable.

LADY C   Yes, perhaps we should call them back—

VIRGINIA   I think the eclipse will be happening in the back yard as well as the front, Lady Compton.

LADY C   Clive went to all the trouble of making these clever little boxes…

LADY M   *(looking off, in the direction of CLIVE's disappearance)* Though I wouldn't bet my eyes on a gadget that Clive built.

LADY C   We'll be fine if we only look in little bursts, don't you think?

VIRGINIA is gazing at VITA.

VIRGINIA   To be sure.

LADY C is uncomfortable, tries to engage VIRGINIA in conversation.

LADY C   In another day, if the sun winked out for no reason, they might have thought it was the end of the world.

> *CLIVE comes back in, dusting off his hands and the knees of his trousers.*

CLIVE   Good thing we're enlightened.

> *LADY M motions to CLIVE. He pretends not to see her.*

LADY M   Hsssstt!

LADY C   If it were, if today were the end of the world, what would you do?

CLIVE   That's a question that requires some—

LADY M   *(to CLIVE)* HSSSTTT!

> *VIRGINIA looks, concerned toward LADY M. She stops hissing, immediately and puts on her best benevolent smile.*

I, for one would hurry right up the steps of Buckingham Palace and demand an audience and a good dinner.

LADY C   What about you? I'm sure *you* have an engaging answer Mrs. Nicolson?

VITA   March straight up to the pearly gates, demand an audience with God and tell him that it is a damned inconvenient time to end the world, as I have several pressing engagements, the Hawthornden Prize to accept and a book very close to being forced into its seventh edition.

VIRGINIA   I don't doubt but what you'd get his attention, Vita.

LADY M   *(aside, to LADY C)* He, like the rest of us, wouldn't have a choice.

> *Pause. They all peer out at the sky.*

LADY C   And what about you Mrs. Woolf? What would you do if this were your last day on earth?

VIRGINIA   I guess you expect me to say something grand, or ambitious or clever. But what I would like is to spend the day by the sea on a shabby old blanket, with a basket of food, a bottle of wine… and Vita.

> *Pause, everyone is absolutely dead silent, LADY M's hand comes up to her heart involuntarily. She chokes on her tea and coughs.*

LADY M   Clive! I think I've got something caught—be so kind as to get me a glass of water.

> *CLIVE, all too glad to have something to do, rushes over to a tray and pours a glass of water, brings it to LADY M.*
>
> *VIRGINIA drops the public façade, entirely and speaks to VITA intimately, as if they were alone.*

VIRGINIA   Circumstances being as they are, I suppose I can just proceed as if it were the last day of the world and ask you directly…

VITA   Absolutely anything your heart desires on any day of the year.

> *LADY C steps forward and drops the bombshell.*

LADY C   Except tonight of course. Correct me if I'm wrong, Vita, but didn't Mary tell me you were collecting her for a walking tour this evening?

> *LADY M mouths something silently to CLIVE, like "What is she doing?"*
> *CLIVE shrugs, helplessly.*
>
> *VITA turns away.*

VITA   It was… we discussed it. It was one idea among many.

LADY C   Isn't that strange, as she seemed to be looking so energetically forward to it. Packed and everything, so she said.

> *CLIVE looks as if he wants to step forward and put a stop to LADY C's drastic measures, but he can't quite bring himself to intervene.*

VIRGINIA   Ah yes, well I expect you've other things to fill your time aside from a picnic at the seaside with an invalid.

> *VIRGINIA quietly takes off her hat and puts it in her lap.*

VITA   This is only a diversion, an idea for a way to spend a week, Virginia. I can call it off.

LADY C   Or was it Dottie?

VIRGINIA   That won't be necessary.

LADY C   Or silly me, was it Violet?

VITA   Do shut up, Patricia.

LADY C   I had heard she was back from Paris. I have such a time keeping up, I don't know how you do it, Vita.

VITA   I'll ring her up right now and cancel.

> *A pause. Everyone holds their breath. VITA would like to throttle LADY C, but she keeps her eyes on VIRGINIA.*

VIRGINIA   Don't alter your plans for me.

VITA   It's nothing.

VIRGINIA   No I, unlike your friend Mary, am unfit for a walking tour. But enjoy yourself all the same. I expect you find it useful to be on intimate terms with—with a great number of people… if one wishes to write for the common masses, one must, after all, know them intimately.

> *VIRGINIA is quiet through this next bit, but she grips her hat so tightly she crushes it.*

CLIVE   Too true, Virginia, too true. You've put your finger on the fatal flaw of contemporary writing: Writers fascinated by woodcutters and gardeners who try and write.

VITA   Perhaps I'll take your good advice and remove myself to the society of those who would appreciate it?

CLIVE   I am speaking metaphorically of course.

VITA   Yes, I see.

LADY M   A glimmer of light dawns at last!

> *VITA waits for another signal from VIRGINIA. VIRGINIA sits and clutches her hat tightly, wrecking it. VITA hesitates, then spins on her heel and leaves.*

LADY C   Rather dramatic... isn't she?

VIRGINIA   Horrible!

> *An uncomfortable pause, no one asks VIRGINIA to explain what she means. CLIVE very gently takes the twisted hat out of her hand and places it aside. They all pick up just as if nothing has happened.*

CLIVE   Now settle an argument for me. Is your book about a man or a woman?

VIRGINIA   Please don't bring up *Orlando*, I'm sick to death of it.

CLIVE   Of course, it's at that stage where—

VIRGINIA   It is the worst thing I've ever written, I can't wait to get clear of it.

LADY C   Oh look! Look, it's starting.

> *An intense bright white, filtered light falls on the party.*

LADY M   I'm shutting my eyes and if I were you, I'd do the same.

> *The light begins to be shut out, casting shadows on their faces.*

LADY C   This is exciting, isn't it?

LADY M   It's the only way to be safe.

LADY C   It's so dark.

VIRGINIA   Yes... the darkest day in living memory.

> *VIRGINIA jumps to her feet with an odd cry—something between a laugh and a cry and rushes off. The others look after her as the sun is shut out completely.*

scene six

Several weeks later, VIRGINIA sits at her desk. The plant that VITA had re-potted has shrivelled up to a brown husk. Unable to concentrate, she gets up and sprinkles some powder into a glass of water, stirs and drinks it quickly, grimacing.

She sits back down, and picks up her pen. She presses too hard, and breaks the nib. Ink flows all over her work, she jumps up trying to contain the mess. In the process she gets ink on her hands, which transfers to her face in streaks when she rubs her brow.

ORLANDO suddenly appears at the door, tosses down a valise with travelling stickers pasted all over it.

ORLANDO   Virginia, I've had the most wonderful adventures! I've gone and gotten married twice! Once to a Duchess who turned out to be a Duke and once to a hard eyed Muscovite Princess. Well thrice really albeit this last one was an informal ceremony… performed at sunset… by the Chieftain of a pack of Gypsies. As, you see, she herself claimed gypsy heritage, and although we shall love each other forever, we have realized it will never work and said our goodbyes albeit reluctantly. I don't mind telling you it literally wrenched my heart from my chest…

ORLANDO mimes ripping her own heart from her chest and holds it out, then suddenly looks around, taking in the room and drops comfortably into a big stuffed chair.

But it's wonderful to be back. Everything is just as I remembered it. I expect you'll want to hear everything, while it's all fresh in my mind.

VIRGINIA   What on earth for?

ORLANDO   Why, for your book of course.

VIRGINIA   No. It's finished and I won't need anything further from you.

ORLANDO   Finished…?

VIRGINIA   Yes, you're finished, you're done.

ORLANDO   Dead, you mean. Well this is hardly a fortuitous change in circumstances. You've awakened me, juggled my plumbing, used me to woo another woman, sent me scurrying around the globe like a mad person, scolded me, moulded me, shaped me and mocked me, and finally mashed every drop of life out of me between the pages of this book, this now hated and scornful object.

VIRGINIA   Oh, Orlando.

ORLANDO   Pardon my temerity... but this is a rather abrupt way to find out about your own demise. You didn't think of dropping me a letter? No? Perhaps sending a telegram.

VIRGINIA   You're not dead for everyone. Just for me. Others will open your cover, peel off your clothes and you'll leap out... full of colour, and breath and life.

ORLANDO   There will be no others.

VIRGINIA   Many, many, others.

ORLANDO   *(looks at her shoes)* Never.

VIRGINIA   *(VIRGINIA pulls her chin up, gently.)* If you care to see how you've been received, there's a stack of reviews on the table. You may read them, then leave quietly.

ORLANDO   How exciting! *(reads) New York Evening Post.* "Orlando is a poetic masterpiece of the first rank." *(sniffs)* Though they've run it in small type... at the bottom of the page...

VIRGINIA   If ever I start setting the *New York Post* as my guiding star, all hands abandon ship—for there's no one at the helm.

ORLANDO   "Sometimes dull and drear under the fog of words and sensitively realized redundancies." Walter Yust. Mr. Yust obviously wouldn't know a good book if it came up and bit him.

> *ORLANDO gnashes her teeth, experimentally as if she were contemplating doing just that. She goes to the mail tray, sees a pile of unopened letters and snatches them up.*

Hello, what are all these? You haven't opened them. Lady Colefax, Vita Sackville-West... E.M. Forester... Vita Sackville-West again... T.S. Eliot... Vita Sackville-West. An invitation, engraved with gold lettering... *(reads)* A gathering to celebrate the publication of *Orlando* by Virginia Woolf. A party for me! How lovely. Oh bother. *(notes date)* It's passed. Was there champagne and taffeta? Fireworks or sculptures in ice? Tell me everything.

VIRGINIA   I did not attend.

ORLANDO   And Vita?

VIRGINIA   Don't mention her to me.

ORLANDO   But whyever not? Virginia. Virginia?

> *Pause, VIRGINIA goes back to her work, ignoring ORLANDO.*

Oh why did I ever come back here then? *(She suddenly gets an idea.)* All right, if you'll have nothing further to do with me, I shall simply throw myself out the window. *(pause)* Here I go, don't try to stop me.

VIRGINIA   Mind the rosebush, will you? We're on the ground floor.

ORLANDO   Very well. *(spies her sword under the desk, and picks it up thoughtfully)* Good-bye faithless and cruel world. *(Pause, as she gets ready again and places the tip of the sword at her breast, trying to figure out how to fall on it.)* How does one… how is this done, anyway?

VIRGINIA   I believe the standard practice is to place the tip at the heart, the hilt on the floor and using the body weight for leverage, drive the blade home.

ORLANDO   Oh. Yes, thank you. *(places the blade as instructed and shuts her eyes, concentrating)*

VIRGINIA   Orlando, you're becoming a bore.

ORLANDO   Why that's your fault! You must write me a sequel—

VIRGINIA   I can't think of a single thing that I have less of a taste for right now.

ORLANDO   *(snatches up a review)* According to Rebecca West, I'm your greatest triumph. She said—

VIRGINIA   I know what Rebecca said, Rebecca's a humbug. The truth of the matter, Orlando, is that you are a freak. I never before, nor will I again work on something with as little depth, as little substance as you have. I should never have turned my hand to biography.

> *Going to the bookshelf.*

ORLANDO   Why here, what about *The Life Of Flush*?

VIRGINIA   Ah yes, Miss Barett Browning's spaniel. I shouldn't think you'd be flattered to be lumped in with a cur.

ORLANDO   Perhaps you had better check your account books before you condemn poor Flush and I.

VIRGINIA   I can thank him at least for providing a steadfast and noble character, of the two of you, I truly think the spaniel was the better subject.

ORLANDO   I will not allow you to speak to me in that fashion.

VIRGINIA   That's the problem there is no you to speak of. You're a copy, of her, of Vita. But you're worse again than she ever was. I've caught only the flaws faithfully and in the reproduction, they magnify and magnify. Oh, I can't bear to look at you!

> *VIRGINIA rushes at ORLANDO, gives her a series of small pushes and tugs. In the process she notices that she has dirtied herself and ORLANDO with smears of ink. ORLANDO backs off a few paces, uncertain what to do.*

ORLANDO   I… I'll go, then.

VIRGINIA   Yes, yes! That's the idea. I assure you, my sigh of relief will provide a tailwind to speed you on your journey.

> *VIRGINIA snaps a sheet of paper into her typewriter and begins to type rapidly. ORLANDO picks up her few things, her quill and long roll of blank manuscript paper and stands in the doorway. She fights back tears.*

ORLANDO   *(gravely)* I suppose this is goodbye.

VIRGINIA   Goodbye, Orlando.

ORLANDO   Fare you well, Virginia

> *ORLANDO curtseys and exits. VIRGINIA keeps typing, listening for ORLANDO to change her mind and come back. She looks carefully around, when she is sure ORLANDO is gone, she allows herself to stop typing and lets her head fall forward into one hand. She sees the ink on her hands and scrubs at it, as the lights fade.*

scene seven

> *VITA's room. She sits writing at her desk. Opposite her, there is an oblong freestanding dressing mirror, the pane has been removed. VITA is dressed in breeches, riding boots and a linen shirt. She holds a flower loosely in her hand. For a moment, she has the poise and look of a statue.*

VITA   Artemisia abrotanum. Artemesia ludoviciana…

> *In a split second the spell is broken and she stoops to pick up a pencil and pulls the flower apart at the stem.*

Sage. Why plant sage in a rock wall anyway? Even if the soil is bad, there must be something else…

> *She opens an illustrated volume of perennials.*

Stonecrop. *(writes)* A hardy perennial that will grow in almost any soil. Dragons Blood will give you some colour, unless, like myself, you prefer the virtue of restraint…

> *She trails off and gets up. She dusts off her hands and goes to the manuscript of* Orlando *which is sitting on its own wooden rack. She picks it up, opens it. ORLANDO enters.*
>
> *VITA does not hear ORLANDO. When she speaks aloud, it has the effect of an argument with her conscience or inner voice.*

ORLANDO   Hello Vita.

> *VITA reads silently, smiles.*

I don't mean to impose… but you see Virginia's thrown me out on my ear. Could I stay here?

VITA No…

ORLANDO She's acting very peculiarly. I think she misses you.

VITA I will not be the one to call her. She's made her feelings quite clear.

ORLANDO Virginia once said that when people are in love, they wear a disguise. But I confess it is hard to see her through this new one.

VITA Still, in spite of her faults, she's the finest individual you've encountered, Vita. The finest mind, the finest spirit and if she holds the slightest regard for you…. No! I will not go crawling back like a lap dog.

> *ORLANDO circles around behind the clear glass frame of the mirror, speaks to VITA through it. VITA looks up, sees ORLANDO in the mirror, as if she is seeing/hearing a warped reflection of herself.*

ORLANDO Yes, perhaps you're right. One day she'll realize what she has lost. Virginia must be taught a lesson, this time. After all, how dare she besmirch the reputation, insult the writing of the great Vita Sackville-West!

> *VITA starts back from the mirror as if she'd seen a ghost. Runs out of the room.*

Vita, where are you going? Wait for me!

> *VITA leaves, closely followed by ORLANDO. Lights fade.*

scene eight

> *CLIVE, LADY M and LADY C cower behind a shrub, outside of VIRGINIA's. CLIVE has a black eye.*

LADY C I think I can see a lamp, in her rooms.

CLIVE Keep your head down, or you may get one of these for your troubles.

LADY C I can't believe it, she struck you?

CLIVE She launched something out of her window. I don't know that she intended to strike me.

LADY C What was it?

> *CLIVE holds up a heavy volume.*

CLIVE *Hard Times.*

> *LADY C smothers a giggle.*

I'm glad my injury should provide you with an occasion for mirth, Patricia. *(peers up toward VIRGINIA's window)* Virginia won't see me, and has even gone to the trouble to return my letters unopened. I fear she suspected that we'd a plan afoot.

LADY M   *(stepping out of the shrub)* Suspected? My dear boy, there's absolutely no way she could have missed it. I don't know if 1 have ever been party to such a poorly executed plan in my life.

LADY C   If you'd only told me what you were planning, this wouldn't have happened.

LADY M   If you hadn't rushed off 'round the back with Leonard…

CLIVE   I was coming back directly.

LADY M   You lost your nerve.

CLIVE   No, I was choosing my moment, when our bull in the china shop charged in—

LADY C   If we'd waited for you to choose your moment, we would have been there until the next eclipse!

CLIVE   Yes, better we should charge forward like the light brigade, then call in the cleaners to sweep up the shattered remains.

LADY C   I got the job done, anyhow.

CLIVE   Where did you dig up all that business with Dottie and the others?

LADY C   You might think that I am completely helpless, Clive but I keep my ear to the ground.

CLIVE   Yes, so I'm learning.

LADY C   Being informed is one of the greatest tools a woman can employ.

LADY M   Tools? Women? My dear girl, how many times have I told you, you must avoid contact with them at all costs!

CLIVE   A tool in the wrong hands becomes a weapon, Patricia. Leonard says Virginia can't sleep, won't work and won't let anyone in the room. I can't help but feel that our ruse was, to some degree, responsible.

LADY C   We were only trying to help. If anyone is to be held responsible for Virginia's condition, I say it's Vita.

CLIVE   If I didn't know better, I'd say you had some personal grudge against her.

LADY C   I, like yourself and Lady Malgrove, want only what's best for Mrs. Woolf.

LADY M   *(quietly)* You're a bungler, and you're a gossip. I ought to wash my hands of the both of you.

CLIVE   Please, this isn't the time.

LADY C   What should we do?

LADY M   The most expedient solution would be to go and get a firearm, and be done with Mrs. Nicolson once and for all, but failing that—

> *Another book comes whizzing toward the trio. CLIVE, seeing it, grabs LADY M and moves her out of the way.*

Clive, Unhand me! What has come over you?

> *CLIVE picks up the book.*

CLIVE   *War And Peace*, Lady Malgrove. Mind your head.

> *CLIVE looks up toward the window.*

I... think she's beckoning for me to come inside. *(points to himself, questioningly)* Very well, I'll go in.

> *He draws himself up bravely, and looks toward VIRGINIA's room as the lights fade. A pause, they watch to see if he is ejected.*

LADY C   If Clive should be admitted, then I don't see why we...

LADY M   He's family.

LADY C   Only by marriage. I should think the company of women would be more welcome.

> *VITA's car is heard approaching. The door slams shut.*

LADY M   You spoke too soon. Not the company of every sort of woman.

LADY C   You cannot go in. Mrs. Woolf is not to be disturbed particularly by the likes of you.

VITA   I warn you I'm not in the mood for pleasantries.

LADY C   *(calling out)* Clive, Clive! Come out at once.

VITA   Oh yes, by all means let's call Clive. What on earth do you think he's going to do?

> *CLIVE comes outside.*

CLIVE   Vita! I've found out the truth—

LADY C   You're exposed, Vita!

CLIVE   Hush, Patricia!—the truth about *Orlando*, and you must forgive me—

LADY M   What in the name of heaven are you apologizing for?

CLIVE   The book was based on Vita, that's why Virginia had to spend so much time with her, she was only a model.

LADY M   What?

CLIVE   *Orlando* is a kind of farcical biography of Vita.

LADY C   That doesn't change the fact that she's a common—

VITA   Hold your tongue. What a lot of hypocrites you are! You hover around Virginia to "protect" her from me, meanwhile Clive has chased my husband halfway around the globe in order to bed him—

> *LADY C moves away from CLIVE, and closer to LADY M.*

LADY C   Oh Clive, for shame!

VITA   You, Patricia invited me to your house with the intention to do the same.

> *LADY M boxes LADY C's ear, just once. She is indignant, but in light of this new revelation keeps quiet.*

LADY M   *(eyeing CLIVE and LADY C)* You don't say. *(turns to VITA)* A model for a book. That's it, is it? You might have let us in on the matter sooner, my dear. It would have saved a lot of trouble.

> *LADY M meets VITA's eye for the first time. She seems almost impressed.*

VITA   And you, Lady Malgrove, are not kept clear of affairs by virtue, as you would have us think but by the very fact of your rotten company and miserable disposition!

> *VIRGINIA has come outside during the course of the exchange.*

VIRGINIA   I don't need your care. I'll thank you all to take yourselves off home, now.

CLIVE   But Virginia—

VIRGINIA   No, Clive. Do as I say and take your watchdogs with you. I would like to speak to Vita alone.

LADY C   *(aside to LADY M)* Such ingratitude. How can she dismiss us? We who have done so much for her.

LADY M   I have no other explanation than that these artists and writers are compelled to court disaster and hardship. She wouldn't write brilliant books if she were a happy person. Come, Patricia, come, Clive.

> *CLIVE, LADY M and LADY C exit.*

VIRGINIA   There you are—

VITA   Yes, here I am.

VIRGINIA   *(VIRGINIA takes her in, not having seen her for some time then speaks fondly.)* Look at you, all full of earth.

VITA   I've been gardening.

VIRGINIA   Of course. Come a hurricane or a flood or a war, you'd be out gardening, though the shells may whiz by your head. Come here, you great bloody ruffian.

> *VITA goes to her and kneels down. Puts her head in VIRGINIA's lap.*

VITA   How I've wanted to see you, Virginia. How the zest has gone out of my life since you've left it.

VIRGINIA   I wonder at your mind.

VITA   Well I spend the largest part of my days wondering about yours, so that's only fair. About *Orlando*...

> *ORLANDO enters. She is wrapped in a long white sheet whose ends disappear offstage in both directions. At times she winds it around her legs and arms.*

VIRGINIA   I know, the book is trite, facile, sentimental. In short the worst thing I've ever written.

> *The sheet pulls tight on ORLANDO. She gives a little cry.*

VITA   But what are you saying, Virginia? I really think it's your best work. I was dazzled, bewitched, enchanted.

ORLANDO   *(to VITA)* I like you. You I like very much.

VITA   In fact, *Orlando* seems to me the loveliest, wisest, richest book I have ever read.

ORLANDO   *(gravely)* I would have to agree.

VITA   And yet you've made him pompous, full of air, and a bad poet.

ORLANDO   I beg your pardon!

> *ORLANDO is suddenly yanked offstage by the sheets, in the opposite direction from which she entered. When she comes back on, there are sheets attached to her from both directions, and they are all pulling her. She may even be raised off the ground. This continues throughout the scene, as an underscore to VIRGINIA and VITA's argument.*

VITA   I should have to shut myself away from the world and never write again if I thought everything you wrote were true. You've made him wondrously clever in parts, lovely and full of hope...

VIRGINIA   Like you.

VITA   Yes, a womanizer, and a great bloody fool sometimes... like me.

VIRGINIA   What shall we do?

VITA   Let's go abroad for a holiday. Let me take you to Italy or Greece.

VIRGINIA   And when we come back?

VITA   Yes, there's Leonard. There's the Press, and there's your health, your work…

VIRGINIA   To wake up together, Vita. To sit at nights by the fire, peeping at each other over the top of books, eat together and take walks…

VITA   …and my writing, and Harold and the children.

VIRGINIA   Yes. You see I… I don't want a holiday, I can't bear a holiday.

> *VIRGINIA has turned away, so VITA cannot see her face, which contains a hope that is almost terrible to see.*

VITA   Would we uproot everything?

VIRGINIA   One has to do drastic things sometimes, Vita. I'd never known you to be adverse to them.

VITA   No, but you are. It's only because I care for you that I won't take you out of your place here. That is to say I… even if I could conscience doing that, taking you away selfishly just to be with me, why then you wouldn't be the same. You wouldn't be the Virginia I love.

> *VIRGINIA turns to face VITA, slowly. A change has come over her, she speaks carefully, deliberately.*

VIRGINIA   Why did you force me—If I hadn't spoken… I could have stood it. There is something in you that… doesn't vibrate. Whether it's an accident or whether you don't let it, I don't know. But you keep everything at a certain distance. You don't feel it all the way in.

> *VITA gets up and moves away from her, stung.*

It shows in your work, too by the way.

VITA   If you don't like my writing then why did you publish it?

VIRGINIA   Oh the novels are fine for what they are—

VITA   They sold, they sold very well.

VIRGINIA   Yes, well a glance at the daily paper will tell you that atrocity turns a steady profit. And when it comes to poetry, you write with a pen of brass.

VITA   You may say I can't write worth a damn and tell it to all of Bloomsbury. But at least I don't stick my brass pen into the hearts of those I love and twist!

(pause) I told you everything, my past, my dreams and now you've turned them against me. And because I love you, I let you.

VIRGINIA   You say you loved me?

VITA Yes!

VIRGINIA And yet you don't love Mary. Dottie… Edna… Violet…

VITA I care for them, but I don't—Virginia, please…

VIRGINIA You don't love them?

VITA No.

VIRGINIA But yet they love *you*, and you let them. Then you must enjoy being cruel. To them as well as to me.

VITA Yes, I had a dalliance with Edna! And yes I went on a trip with Mary! Who are you to judge me? You, a married woman sitting there like some old priest—doling out your God-given rights and wrongs. But the truth is, you needed to use me for copy, as I'm sure you use every situation and the people who surround you, anyway.

VIRGINIA You flatter yourself to think I needed you at all. You can burn *Orlando* for all I care!

ORLANDO has wound herself up in the sheet, trying not to hear.

ORLANDO Noo…

VITA You want every last bit of a person, Virginia. Every last drop and yet you give nothing in return.

VIRGINIA You will go down in history as a gardener, not a poet.

VITA And you'll go down in history as a surgeon. After all, the way you render people on the page must call for a great deal of… what can I say, cold-blooded dissection? You huddle in your room amongst the tomes of the dead, but you've no real attachment to living, breathing people. Unless, that is, they interest you and you can haul them apart and dissect them, as raw material for a book.

VIRGINIA Anyone, Vita Sackville-West, who undertakes friendship or intimate relationships for the purposes of writing a more interesting book, FIRSTLY is a beast and SECONDLY must be so dull that they will only succeed in writing a ghastly book anyway.

VITA And yet, what is to be done, since you've made such a lovely job of me with your surgeon's hands.

VIRGINIA If that is what you think of me, then I see no reason for you would burden yourself with my friendship and so I will relieve you of the obligation. *(Pause. Vita holds her gaze, doesn't move.)* Well? Did you not hear me? Go!

VITA takes the original copy of Orlando *out of her bag, and pushes it into VIRGINIA's arms.*

VITA   Here! I hope you're happy with the portrait you've painted in *Orlando*, for that's all you'll see of me from now on.

> *She turns to go.*

VIRGINIA   *(softly)* One last thing, Vita…

> *VITA turns, and as she does, VIRGINIA slaps her—a short, stinging blow across the cheek that comes so quickly, they are both shocked. At that instant, the sheets come unknotted and detach themselves from ORLANDO, who slumps, lifeless to the floor as VIRGINIA picks up the manuscript copy of* Orlando.

In thirty years, this book will be the only record of you. In fifty years no one will even know who you are.

> *VITA is stunned for a moment, then advances toward VIRGINIA in what seems a menacing fashion. She pulls VIRGINIA toward her and kisses her passionately.*
>
> *There is the smallest sound from ORLANDO, a very tiny moan.*
>
> *VIRGINIA lets the manuscript of ORLANDO fall from her hands. As she does, many sheets are dropped from the flies and flutter down. VITA exits as the sheets fall around VIRGINIA and the lifeless body of ORLANDO. VIRGINIA holds herself stiffly until she is sure VITA is gone.*

But you're right, Vita. I can't look at anything now, not even you, Orlando without this horrid yellow pall.

> *VIRGINIA kneels over the body of ORLANDO. She may stroke her, touch her hair.*

Everything I have ever written—every word is the rambling of a diseased mind or an injured spirit. Nothing better than a lame dog licking its wound. I stare at the page and nothing comes. First nothing, a low pain and then… a flood, a glut of words so foul and with so little sense that I can't bear to put them down…. And so I snatch up a book like starving child will snatch at food. I cling to the sides of the book like gunwales on a boat. I pitch and I roll through the centuries, the lurch and stretch of history tosses me up onto its wake, down into the undertow. And then, the chimes strike 1… 2… 3… 4—it is after tea and I've not even looked out the window. I run then, and throw open the shutter. The fresh outside air burns my lungs and I see a bird on a patch of sky and there is more real joy in the motion of that bird and in the flossy stretch of cloud behind it than I will ever have.

> *Lights fade.*

scene nine

The sound of a river, and of birds singing. Two pools of light. In one, stands VIRGINIA, her face and body criss-crossed with the shadows of branches that sway in the wind. In the other stands VITA. In the middle, and barely lit is the shrouded body of ORLANDO. As the scene progresses, the light gradually changes to a refractive blue wash, as if reflected off water.

VIRGINIA   Dearest Vita, the other day I received a letter that was clearly to you, all about how to feed and care for budgerigars. And yet it's addressed to me.

What a queer thought transference! No, I'm not you. No, I don't keep budgerigars… we've scarcely food for ourselves what with the war, let alone birds. They say they'll survive if you feed them on scraps…. If we come over, may I bring back a pair, if any live? When shall we come, Lord knows. Do they all die in an instant? [1]

(She breaks off, turns toward VITA.) Vita?

VIRGINIA disappears. The birds stop singing abruptly. The sounds of the river fade as VITA looks over toward VIRGINIA.

VITA   Orlando…?

VITA collapses onto her knees, lets her head fall into her hands.

That lovely mind, that lovely spirit.

Lights fade on VITA, and the stage is empty, except for the body of ORLANDO under the sheet. Then, we see a stirring. ORLANDO extricates herself, rubbing her eyes. She looks around the stage… no one. She looks out over the audience, and then back at the sheet that was covering her, thoughtfully.

She winds the sheet into a cord and throws it up over her head. It snags the bottom rung of a ladder that we haven't noticed before. She pulls the ladder down toward her and begins to climb it. Almost as an afterthought she turns back, over her shoulder and speaks to the audience.

ORLANDO   If I haven't occurred to you… I will.

The End.

---

[1] Excerpt from Virginia's last letter to Vita.

Random Acts

Diane Flacks

Introduction:
Random Acts

Diane Flacks's virtuosic *Random Acts* (1997) in which she plays multiple characters can best be categorized as what Michael Peterson has labelled a "monopolylogue."[1] Resembling Jane Wagner's and Lily Tomlin's Broadway hit, *The Search for Signs of Intelligent Life in the Universe*, Flacks's out status as a lesbian writer and performer helps to inform the transformational message she brings to us. Although written before the events of 9/11, the text brings to mind the angst-ridden climate of uncertainty in which we all live. Using the persona of the Oprah-like feminist talk-show guru, Antonella Bergman, Flacks invites us to engage with her in the search for meaning in a random universe. To suggest Antonella's prophetic qualities, Flacks opens the play with an apocalyptic appearance of the Jewish matriarch Sarah who became pregnant at the age of ninety. As she morphs into a pre-accident Antonella, we are invited to listen in on one of her inspirational talks and thus become directly implicated in participating in her journey.

While the particular question that is posed to us is whether the now wheelchair-bound Antonella will ever return to the Toronto-New York talk-show circuit after her accident, the answers that we are asked to come up with embrace the larger questions of our own responsibility for making sense of our lives. Paralyzed after she was pushed in front of a bus over a year ago, Antonella has been in hiding ever since, unable to cope with the fact that all her positive self-help messages seem totally empty now that she has to deal with life from a wheelchair. As a disgruntled Antonella struggles with the cruel blow that fate has dealt her, Flacks moves in and out of her disabled body, bringing to life a host of other characters whose lives have been affected by her. Each of them brings to light some piece of the puzzle as they voice their responses to the random injustices they have fallen prey to. Through them we come to understand why Antonella's recovery is so crucial in itself. As one peripheral character, Sasha, "a tense looking" divorcée describes it, Antonella's tapes and books have helped her face her rage by putting it in perspective with the lives of "garbage pickers in India, the girl prostitutes in Bangkok, the street children in Brazil" (409). Observing that Antonella is now living through the lesson of having to face her own rage, Sasha sets up the expectation that Antonella's message will be even more meaningful now that she has to take her own advice.

Since Antonella has isolated herself in her home office, Flacks spends most of the play trying to reach her through the other characters, most notably her assistant, the much maligned Brenda MacDonald, who runs the office as her still optimistic stand-in. As we watch Flacks transform herself back and forth between all these characters, they come to be seen as aspects of herself. The impact of watching her virtuosic rapid switches back and forth sets up a powerful stage metaphor that enacts the interconnectedness of us all to each other. As we enjoy the "dynamic oscillation between corporeality and signification in th[ese] embodied images," we come to share in accepting the reality of their different lives.[2] To further heighten our involvement with her creation, Flacks has several of her characters talk both to the audience and to each other. And if her message is intentionally feminist, she also includes as silent but appreciative male witness in the form of Stephen the good-looking repairman who comes to the office. His supportive responses to Brenda's rants help to focus attention on the importance of restoring Antonella to her former prominence as a modern sage.

While Flacks's monopolylogue is intended to speak to the whole spectrum of female experience, she gives a special voice to one of Antonella's former fans, the lovelorn lesbian Lisa is still able to get through to Brenda. Flacks's sympathetic detailing of Lisa as she suffers through her breakup brings Lisa into sharp focus. In her first transformation, she embodies her as drunk and crying as she leafs through one of Bergman's books citing and rewriting the canned affirmations she finds there. Mumbling scrambled versions of "Forgiveness is letting go of the right to hurt someone for having hurt you" (407), her resolve is completely shattered by the inevitable phone call from her ex-girlfriend Lizzie. Ostensibly calling her to get back her alarm clock, Lizzie's call from her new lover Margaret's home becomes increasingly tortuous for Lisa who can't resist telling her she loves her. She then delivers a long crazed eulogy to love before crumpling to pieces and making another call to Antonella's office to ask how much time it will take to get over her loss.

Through her iconic incursions into Lisa's body, Flacks sets up a dynamic whereby Lisa's reaction to her breakup will operate as a parallel to Antonella's journey through her disbelief and rage. Back in the wheelchair, a bitchy Antonella muses on the irony of her fate and her reluctance to go to New York "to be wheeled out in front of an audience of weeping voyeurs and get a standing ovation just for not dying" (411). Accelerating the very randomness on which the action is premised, Flacks now builds the chaos to its inevitable climax. As Brenda tries to keep the lines of communication open while Antonella concentrates only on sneezing herself into orgasm, everything threatens to fall apart. Antonella's decision to reject the New York offer is parallelled by Lisa's angry phone call to Margaret, the so-called straight friend who stole Lizzie. Trotting out every stereotype of the straight woman who uses her straightness to take advantage of her lesbian friend's vulnerability, she lapses into a vindictive rant, followed up by a phone call to Brenda to find her the chapter on hate. The stream of abuse that comes out of Lisa's mouth, is then reinforced by Flacks's next transformation into the butchy tow-truck operator, Trash Talker. Recycling the rumour that Antonella might have engineered her own accident to help her career, Trash Talker's parting threat that she's going to tow the guy's lexus, shows us that Antonella's message may indeed have backfired completely by unleashing even more hatred into the world.

In the showdowns that follow, Flacks takes the characters' rage to the point of explosion by having Antonella launch a personal attack on Brenda when she questions her decision to not go to New York. In this moment, Flacks lets us in on the fact that while she understands Antonella's right to despair, she can now allow Brenda, her more optimistic side to surface. As Brenda comes fully alive in her "shit happens"

(420) monologue, Lisa also finds the strength to stick up for herself when Lizzie phones to complain about her call to Margaret. The action keeps building to its frenzied close as Brenda, the latter-day prophet side of Antonella, takes over and dictates solutions to Mindi, the New York agent, Antonella, and Lisa. Keeping them all on the line, she puts them on hold one by one as she orders them to take charge of their lives. Mindi is forced to offer a better contract, Antonella is ordered to accept the booking, and Lisa is counselled to make peace with Lizzie. Brenda orders Lisa to "be proud and loud and here and queer and out and about and whatnot" (422), thus including the lesbian presence in her brave new world. The show ends with Antonella's call to New York with this apocryphal message: "Hello, New York. Sarah the biblical matriarch came to visit me in Toronto. She was 103 years old and rangy. It was the end of the millennium, and anything is possible" (423).

Notes

[1] Michael Peterson, *Straight White Male: Performance Art Monologues* (Jackson: University of Michigan P, 1997) 12.

[2] Bruce McConachie, "Approaching the 'Structure of Feeling' in Grassroots Theatre," *Theatre Topics* 8, no.1 (March 1998) 40.

photo by Tim Leyes

Diane Flacks

Bio and Artist's Statement

Diane Flacks is a writer/actor who enjoys talking about herself in the third person. Recently, McClelland & Stewart published her first book, *Bear With Me—What They Don't Tell You About Pregnancy and New Motherhood*. Subsequently, Diane developed a solo play based on the material, and will be touring it. She has acted and written for theatre, TV series, and films across Canada, including the series "Moose TV," "PR," "Delicious," "The Broad Side," "Listen Missy," and the "Kids in The Hall" show (for which she was nominated for a writing Emmy). Other published work includes her critically acclaimed solo show, *By A Thread* (adapted for CBC TV) and her hit play *Sibs* (written and performed with Richard Greenblatt—which was also adapted for a CBC film). *Random Acts* was produced by Nightwood Theatre, directed by Alisa Palmer. It has toured in Canada, and was developed for a CBC TV special. Diane lives in Toronto with her partner and son. Visit <www.dianeflacks.com>

•

Although this was written on the eve of the millennium, unfortunately, we are all still "rangy." Tragedy and random joy are as inexplicable and mysterious as ever. We still might consider following the example of Sarah, the biblical matriarch, who became pregnant at age 90; and laugh, since we have no other choice. As for the lesbian nature of the material, the only thing I might say is that the character of Lisa was one of many who were dealing with seemingly random, sometimes banal, and terribly painful loss. She is a lesbian whose partner has left her for someone who was supposed to be "safe," a formerly straight friend (sound familiar?). As in most of my work, I have attempted to present Lisa as a humane, complex individual who happens to be, like me, proudly out.

Production Information

Random Acts was first produced by Nightwood Theatre in association with Buddies in Bad Times Theatre and Mything Inc. at Buddies in Bad Times Theatre Mainspace, Toronto, in 1997, with the following company:

ALL CHARACTERS   Diane Flacks

Directed by Alisa Palmer
Designed by Vikki Anderson
Lighting design by Lesley Wilkinson
Original music and sound design by Cathy Nosaty
Stage Management by Kathryn Davies

•

Random Acts toured to One Yellow Rabbit's High Performance Rodeo in Calgary and the Neptune Theatre in Halifax, as a co-production with Jest In Time, in 2000. The material was adapted by Diane Flacks for a TV special for CBC.

Characters

Sarah
Antonella
Brenda
Lisa
Sasha
Jen
Gina

Set Note

For this premiere production we had a centre platform with a raked triangular platform on it. The triangular platform looked like a forced perspective room, with a window. Antonella's wheelchair sat counter-raked off centre. At each side of the chair were two computer keyboards: Antonella's and Brenda's. They both used this space—Antonella from her chair, and Brenda using the wheelchair as an office chair and also she used the rest of the platform area. There was a headset part of a headset phone that the two characters both used in their office/home. A large white cyclorama was behind the platform and three long, white towers of varying heights stood to each side of the platform. Other characters performed around, in front of and on these towers. There was also a raked ramp that lead up to the platforms from the stage floor.

RANDOM ACTS

*Biblical lighting! Wild Klezhmer-like clarinets. The figure of SARAH,
90 years old and pregnant, appears and walks toward the audience,
mumbling in Hebrew—at the height of the music, SARAH climbs the
ramp and platforms to ANTONELLA's wheelchair, removes her long talit
(prayer shawl), hat, purse, and cane, and transforms into ANTONELLA
BERGMAN, modern spiritual adviser (pre-accident, in flashback). She is
revealed in the middle of a speech to an audience. We hear their laughter
and applause.*

ANTONELLA So there she was, Sarah the biblical matriarch, the original Jewish
mother, the first person to coin the phrase, "you could call," there she was 90
years old, shaped like a question mark, and still waiting for a miracle. According
to the old testament, Sarah was promised by God that her and her husband
Abraham's offspring would be as numerous as the stars in the sky and the sand
on the beach, yet here she was, 90 years old, and barren as a bucket.

And one day, some handsome angels came to her tent, and as she washed
their butter-soft feet they revealed to her that she was now pregnant. What?!
At 90?! Hysterical! Her breasts were two figs, her womb curled in unto itself in
loneliness, her nether lips pursed together so tightly that when she ran, the wind
made them whistle! "Get out of here God!"

So what did she do? Run? Beg? Scream? Tear her hair and rend her garments in
true biblical fashion? No. It is recorded in biblical history: Sarah laughed. Don't
you love that? Screaming howling gut-splitting gales of laughter spreading out
all over the desert like a midnight wind. Because God's timing is a little funny.

But we aren't all as patient as Sarah. It is the end of the millenium and everyone
is rangy. Face it. Say it. I am rangy. And I would like to blame someone for it.

I don't care that nobody knows what year it is really—it is the end of the
millennium as far as I am concerned, because even though my intentions are
good, they keep pinwheeling off in the wrong direction as my world is tilted
and spun like a Rubik's Cube in the hands of a pimply-faced prodigy god!

Okay. But the guy in the oversized lexus who, in your "road rage," you gave the
finger to, because he deserved it—he'll probably pass that finger on to the
Danish woman in the Volvo who doesn't know you can turn right on a red in
Toronto. And she'll give a big up yers to the couple on the tandem bike who are
trying just a bit too hard to salvage something a little bit too late. And they'll
bang on the hood of a kid in his father's new jeep because it is their right of way
they own it, and they're doing good things for the environment, and this kid

will be so afraid of his dad seeing the dent on the jeep he will cruise right through the 4-way stop, almost hitting an off-duty police officer, walking her Rottweiler/Sharpe cross after another frustrating day of inability to make a difference and Sunshine girls slipped into her "to do" box by her brothers in blue, and she will throw a finger up in the air that will remarkably wind it's way back to *you*! Stop the pay back! Court the Calm! Do it yourself first! We are all part of one body. You are the man in the lexus! You are your own Rubik's Cube! You are Sarah and you're stuck with your fertility, so laugh, and get on with the loving!

> *At the top of the speech, to wild applause, we hear the sound of the bus crash.*

> *Lights cross fade and ANTONELLA's face contorts as she tries to sneeze. She turns from the audience, sits in the wheelchair. It is now the present.*

ANTONELLA   (*She is wearing a headset phone and facing the audience. She is still trying to sneeze, she can't.*) Damn. (*almost sneezes again*) Shitdamnfuckshit damncrap. Damn it. (*She dials her phone.*) Brenda? Hi. (*responding to a "how are you" question with irritation*) Fine.

> *To Tom Jones's "She's a Lady", she transforms into a middle-aged maritime woman, BRENDA MACDONALD, ANTONELLA's assistant. She sprays a plant and dances. The phone rings.*

BRENDA   Antonella Bergman's office, Brenda MacDonald speaking. Oh, hello, Ms. Bergman. (*very maternally*) And how are you? Good. What can I do you for? Oh my gosh! This is terrific! This is a beautiful thing! This is just...! No I don't think I am able to contain myself, if I could do that I'd be a size 10 again. This is a beautiful and sacred thing!

Alright, now, which of your past speeches would you like me to e-mail you, all of them? No, you see Ms. Bergman what I've done is I've organized all of your speeches in a little separate file, according to subject, so—Oh... the Sarah speech! Oh that's a favourite of mine. "Sarah the biblical mother, chosen by God to be pregnant at 90, what in the world kind of a choice is that?!" Oh that's a good one! "You are your own darn Rubik's Cube, now what I want you to do is—" sorry yes, leave it to you alright. Oh my this is a beautiful thing! You've broken through! You're working you're not brooding.... So, this is like a come-back in a way isn't it? Yes, I would call it that. So, then this might be the perfect exact time to talk about the New York comeback lecture again, especially since they just made an even more lucrative offer, including a suite at the Plaza Hotel! Pardon? Oh, well, no, but that is my job, to um noodge you. That's part of my job description. So, alrighty no, we can talk about it a little later like within the hour. Alrighty no, why don't we see how your speechwriting goes, and then— sorry not speechwriting, um creating, um channelling? protheslisizing, prothesizing, prophecising, process—proces?... sorry? Leave that to you as well. pardon? "B.S.-ing?" NO Ms. Bergman don't say that about yourself! Did Mother

Teresa B.S.? Alright, maybe that's a bad example. What about Oprah? Oh don't say that about Oprah, she's so fond of you and she's looking so slim and fresh. And you're in the Book Club—uh oh wait a minute, Ms. B. you're heading down that spiral again aren't you? I can tell. Now um now don't do that.... Don't you go there, girl, um—Don't you get down now! You can do it! Yes you can! You can do a speech! You can go to New York! You can face the public! You can get a big cheque, you—Sorry. Do I? Funny you should compare me to a cheerleader. I've always had a terrible fear of cheerleaders. Yes. Well, exactly, who doesn't? "Give me a V give me an I give me a C T O. "Wait a minute, what was it you wanted? Because I can get you a V but the rest is a blur!" *(She laughs for a second.)* Oh I haven't laughed like this in—

Alright back to Sarah. Is it on your screen yet? No? Oh, hang on. Well, let's see what else is going on then, oh! There is this young woman who's been calling fairly regularly. Now I know you don't like to return calls from fans but I was wondering if you might make an exception in this case. No, she's not ill, she's been dumped, and she thinks you're the only person who can—no she's not suicidal, but just a word from you might—alright, I'll tell her you're busy. No problem sorry to bother you with that.

Okay. There, is it through now? Oh good—

(She starts, as if someone has just entered her office unexpectedly.) Oh! Antonella I'm sorry could you hold, because that guy is here now about the thing. *(to the guy)* Have a seat, I'll be right with you. Can you turn that camera off? *(to the phone)* —the thing. The whacahcull thing attached to the thingamebob makes the whosits go? Yeah, it's been broken all week. Okay yes I will, yes I'll get an invoice. I always do. Bye bye for now.

> *She hangs up and fixes her hair.*

Hello. You must be Stephen. Bit early.

> *Music change, "Strong Enough" by Sheryl Crowe. She crumples and puts her hair up and becomes LISA, a distraught young woman.*

> *LISA is drunk. She cries and looks through a book by Antonella Bergman called* The Calm.

LISA *(reading)* "Affirmation number one: Love is not a butterfly to pin to your wall."

No.

Love is not a butterfly. It's a vampire bat!

> *Music. She imagines and acts out the image of a bat sucking her blood out and getting caught in her hair. She then imagines she's being pinned to the wall like a butterfly. Finally she returns to the book.*

"Forgiveness is letting go of the right to hurt someone for having hurt you."

Trying to recite from memory

Forgiveness is letting of the right of someone to… forgiveness is the right to… forgiveness, forgiveness is hurting the—start again—Forgiveness is letting go of someone who hurt you… because they don't love you any more!

Music again. Suddenly a phone rings. She rushes to answer it.

Hello? *(She almost starts to cry.)* Hi. Um. Hi…… How are you? F-fine. *(She just cries.)* How are you?… Why are you calling me? I thought we weren't supposed to speak during our separation. Why are you calling me anyhow!—Oh. No I don't have it. Sure, I'll look. *(She doesn't.)* Nope. I guess you'll have to buy a new alarm clock. You'll have to get your *own* alarm clock! Oh Lizzie! Can you come over? What? What is that? Margaret?! What is Margaret doing at your house?!… What?! Why are you calling me from Margaret's house?! Don't call me from Margaret's house!! Can you come over? I can't sleep. I have a headache. Okay well, I love you. What?! Why can't I say that I love you?! Don't you love me? What kind of a person—no—I—you—… Okay. Okay. Can you call me later, when Margaret's not there? Okay. Bye bye Lizzie. I love you…. Sorry.

She cries.

I love you. I still love you! I do! I love you. Oh I loooooove YOU! I love you, I looove you.

Your skin is so smooth! It's like it's not even solid. It's like it's between solid and liquid?! It's so smooth I could go crazy! I love you so much I'm in a constant state of fear! "Drive safely! Wear your helmet! Don't talk to… anyone!" I want to lock you in a room and cover you in bubble wrap and follow you around and basically, just stalk you. Our love is perfect! Our love has no issues! Our love is big! Our love is a Clydesdale horse. Big, bold, enormous hairy feet, used for carrying Persian princes and virgins—and now Carlsberg beer. Oh, well. Our love can evolve. Our love is a city teeming with life—and loneliness and strange secrets kept in dark alleys. Our love…. Our love is a naked leaping stellar constellation! Orion the hunter! Look at him one way and he is a symbol of strength and power, look at him another way and he's a million little lonely specks randomly floating through time desperately shrinking to nothingness.

She crumples and rolls to the book.

Love. Love.

Picks it up and the phone.

Hello Antonella Bergman's office? Can I speak to her please? Oh. Oh hello, Brenda MacDonald? Yes, it's Lisa… again. Um, yes I have a question for her. Yes, I was just looking through her book at the chapter on loss and um at the part where it says the only thing that can alleviate the heat of a crisis is time? I was just wondering, How much time?

Lights. Whale music plays. She straightens into a very tense looking woman, SASHA, she smiles and speaks as if to a camera. She has a tray of tea.

SASHA   How's this? Is this alright over here? Here?

Yes, well, I'm a real believer in Antonella Bergman. I read all her books? and I listen to her tapes and I did her workbook? and I joined her reike circle? laying on of hands? and I feel I have a very open channel? I'm divorced? And I was having trouble letting go of a very deep rage.

Antonella Bergman says that people that say they've let go of their rage and just feel love are usually the angriest people around. *(laughs oddly—like the Mona Lisa, her eyes show nothing).*

Oh, sorry, that's not an ashtray? that's a drum.

Yes, well, that night, Antonella Bergman talked about… the garbage pickers in India, the girl-prostitutes in Bangkok, the street children in Brazil, abattoirs—things that when you think about them seriously? they can really make you feel sick. And suddenly I felt better. All my problems shrunk to the size of a bean. And in my silent prayer at the end of the lecture, I popped that bean in my mouth. I ate my bean.

Oh sorry, that's not an ashtray. That's ash. It's an installation.

Yes. I believe that I witnessed what happened to her for a reason. So that I could be saved from following in the path of the person who pushed her? Some days last year, after the divorce "arbitration," I just felt so mad at my ex, I wanted to push people. Not to punch, to push. But when you imagine doing something violent like that, you romanticize it, you know? You don't think about the 4-year-old screaming because her mother is screaming in terror. Or a bus driver hunched over sobbing into the arms of a street person.

Yes, but you see, Stephen, it is the people who have suffered the most who are the truly inspirational people. And now, she has really suffered, something completely tragic and meaningless—can you imagine the incredible insight she has to offer? We are capable of magic and mercy and miracles. And alliteration. I can't wait to see her speak again!… I mean when she's ready, done gestating. Who are we to say NOW! You know—be well NOW! You can't push the river. You're program is not going to try to push the river, is it? Hmm? Oh. That chair's not for sitting in it's a birthing chair! No that's alright. I can get another one.

Lights. Whale music. She walks up and sits in the wheelchair becoming ANTONELLA BERGMAN.

ANTONELLA   *(in mid-sneeze)* Hello. Hello New York.

Forgiveness is letting go of the right to hurt someone for having hurt you. *(typing)* Forgiveness is… well, it's a little waspy.

(yelling to someone offstage) Excuse me! Don't come in here! I am working! Can I have some privacy please?

> She dials a number on a computer keypad.

Brenda. Hi. *(more irritated)* Fine. Listen. Brenda, my new homecare worker has shitty breath. It smells like shit. Not like stale danish and a coffee. Like actual shit. What has she been eating? Shit?! You have to fire her.

(yelling to offstage) I'm not hungry, Susie! I will tell you when I'm hungry. Don't touch my food with your hands!

(back to the phone) Well, I don't want her making me a shit burger or a shit shake or something. You have to fire her. Thank you.

> She hangs up and immediately is overcome by the urge to sneeze. She can't. Speaks to the audience.

We have 90% dormant big baluga brains. People bend spoons with their minds. Sneezing should be a snap! It's like trying to make yourself have an orgasm—mentally—oh, everyone's tried it. I know it is possible because it happens in dreams and the literature surrounding people with this kind of disability suggests it can be done, but the minute I consciously focus on becoming aroused—*try and fail*—see you have to get to a state of calm—but then images come in that—that just kill the mood.

There she is… Sarah, ancient, pregnant, filthy, laughing… at me? For what? You think I deserve this? For being so arrogant as to think I could help people? People who secretly I began to think were a little stupid for believing in me when I clearly had it a lot better than they did—and the reason they believed in me is they are stupid—so why do I get punished?

Maybe the joke is that this was completely random. I was in the wrong place at the wrong time. It could have been anyone. There was no motive. ha ha ha?! I refuse to believe in that, it is horrible to contemplate.

Or maybe I was chosen. I was chosen for this because I can handle it and I am supposed to learn and evolve into something greater that will be inspirational to everyone who meets me. I am becoming the wounded healer. The crippled shaman. The twisted witch. It's the blind seer syndrome. And you get chosen for it because nobody volunteers. Sarah didn't want to have a baby at age 90. But she did it and she became the mother of the Jewish people. A people who've had their ass kicked in every country they wandered into, been besieged, persecuted, and ridiculed for 5000 years. Congratulations Sarah!

So the reason for this, the silver lining behind this is: I will have new insight to share with the world.

Well, here's some insight: It's not worth it! I don't forgive this. This sucks. That'll be $28.00.

The phone rings. She clicks her computer keys.

Uh huh. Fine. Yes I'm reading it. Looking back on what I was saying a year ago, it's no wonder someone pushed me in front of a bus. No, I haven't made up my mind yet about New York. Because. Because I'm not sure I want to be wheeled out in front of an audience of weeping voyeurs and get a standing ovation just for not dying. They need an answer do they? Well, so do I!

How is the office? Just as I left it? Really. Where are you now?—At the desk. Okay. Stand up. Just "up," Brenda. Because I asked you to. You are my assistant so assist me. If I could get up in my own office I would but I can't so I want you to…. It's alright. It's alright, Brenda, don't sigh. Thank you. Now turn to your left. Okay. What are you facing? The plant? The plant? What's the plant doing there? The plant shouldn't be there. Well, I don't want it to have more sunlight. I want it to have the measly shitty little crappy sliver of sunlight I put it in. That would make me happy, Brenda. Please try not to rescue everything at all times, it's annoying. Now turn to the left. What are you facing? The window okay. I thought the window. What do you see out there? The sky. Okay. What colour is it? Grey. What kind of grey?… Is it dryer lint grey? Is it filing cabinet grey? Is it dark circles under your eyes grey? Is it street ice grey? Is it—dryer lint grey? Okay all of it? Really? All of it? The whole sky? Well, I didn't think so. No I do not think so. That's meteorologically improbable. Oh come on! I'm sitting here incompletely paralyzed and you think you can pass off on me that the whole sky is suddenly able to be all one single colour of grey because Brenda MacDonald…. Swirls of white? Oh.

Are you still at the window? Do me a favour and touch the glass. Is it cold? What else? Moist on the inside? What else? Don't move! You were so! Oh. Oh. You're uncomfortable with this, are you? Okay no you're right. You have a point. No that's fair. Just work-related orders then okay. Brenda, go to the window. It is for work. Now open it. Now jump out.

She smiles at herself, and hangs up.

Drum-heavy music. She jumps out of her chair and becomes JEN, the squeegee girl being interviewed by "Current Affairs." She is a soft-spoken, slightly twitchy little rocker.

JEN *(makes little faces and gestures, as if into a camera)* Hey. Hey. Hey. Hey. Hey. Put me on TV. Hey put me on TV. *(to the car she was squeegying)* It's okay it's free. *(under her breath)* Fucking asshole. Hey! If I do your windshield will you put me on TV? No? Okay. So what are you doing, making a movie? Oh a TV show? Right on. What's it about? Oh yeah? That lady who was pushed? Right here? hey hey hey hey hey put me on TV I seen it! Me and Denny seen it. Put me on TV! We were supposed to go to Vancouver, but we didn't, and I'm not supposed to fly now, 'cause of the baby— *(She touches her stomach.)* 4 months. Yeah, well it shows to me. I feel fatter.

So anyway, yeah that was a weird night. This lady I'm doin' her windshield right and she's like, "Do you know about feminism?" And I'm like yeah, sure, okay. Because I don't have a lot of time to chat right. No, because of the lights. No her light was red, but the other light was yellow and then it turns red and then they're both red, double red, for a second, and then this one's green! It may seem like it happens fast to you, but I live there. To me it's like suspended animation, like in space, like the road runner when the coyote steps off the cliff and he's like *(steps out, looks out as if frozen, holds up an imaginary sign)* "Mother." Ahh. *(steps back)* Double red. Denny says the coyote is an idiot. And a loser because he keeps letting these things happen to him: a locomotive, a bomb, cliffs. Denny says he should fight it. I says, "well, shit happens. Not much you can do. Sometimes fighting makes it worse." Besides, it's not really happening. The coyote's not really hanging in mid-air. That's in his mind. Like his life flashing before his eyes, like when you think you're gonna die, time stops, and you can think about things. Double red's like that sometimes to me.

So anyway with this lady, feminism, lady, she's like "would you like to come to a lecture," and I'm like yeah sure yeah whatever okay yeah, and then she starts to go, so I grab her, well not her but her seatbelt and I go "Excuse me, Ma'am, but don't you like your windshield?" So she gave me forty bucks. So it was a good night.

But then the lady got pushed, and we took off, because the cops came and if I get one more ticket for squeegying, cops can throw me up against the wall, put me in jail it happened to a friend of Denny's we seen it.

What do you mean? I don't get it. What are you after? What are you trying to say? Who what? Oh, I don't know. I think it was the demons that did it. Denny says the demons are after us to split us up, and sometimes they tell him to do things like jump off a bridge and he did once and he landed on his face—it was a low bridge but still. And sometimes when we're sleeping, I can hear them laughing, but they just help me, like if I can't breathe I hear a low voice "Jen, sit up" and I do and I can breathe so.

A lot of people got a lot of anger in them like Denny, but he's working on it. He just is so angry all the time I think cause of his Mom died in September. He says "I don't know what to do with my anger" I says, "I already told you you can beat up Eddie." Well, he's such a scumbag. He stole our ID when Denny was in the shelter. So now I'll never get a health card, even if we wanted one which we don't, but because of the baby.

So maybe someone was angry about something and they just fucking pushed her. I'm surprised it doesn't happen more often. But like I said, we took off because we finally got an apartment—landlord said we could stay as long as the baby doesn't cry. So, hey hey hey maybe anyone that's watching this on TV has an apartment could call you because I don't know how you get a baby not to cry. *(sees light change)* Oh. Excuse me.

> *She runs off. The music changes to "Help Yourself" by Tom Jones. She becomes BRENDA, rushes back up to the chair and puts on the headset, dancing a little, as she seems to be talking to someone, looks out the window, then wheels around gasping, music stops.*

BRENDA Jump?! Oh! Oh. Oh ho ha ha ha Ms. B. Alright now I've got to go. I have a million lines ringing and a very handsome young uh mechanic standing here with a wrench and a new thing in his hands. Alrighty.

Sorry about that, Stephen. Oh no no I wouldn't do it. Oh no she's a riot that way! One time she had me run up and down a flight of stairs 15 times "because I could." Well, I could, but then I couldn't do anything else for the rest of the day.

But that's why I love working for Ms. Bergman. There's always something. And she's got a dental plan. *(She taps on her front teeth.)* I don't even feel that. All fake. All free.

Well, I prefer these long hours. When I worked downtown I had to get on the subway with everyone else and leave with everyone else. I don't know why they call it rush hour, no one goes anywhere, you just sit there in the subway breathing in each others' aggravation. Oh, it was the worst work, well maybe mining is worse, but not by much. We used to complain about how much we had to do and then everyone got laid off. Just as well, my eyebrows were plucked within an inch of their life by then. And that did not work on my moon face I can tell you. It's alright, now, I know—you stop that. Stephen, it's a moon face. Moon face. It's just that once I started plucking I couldn't stop, and pretty soon the whole floor was plucking—looking for that perfect arch—and let me tell you, it does not exist. We all looked like pot bellied pigs, or those hairless Mexican dogs that everyone feels sorry for—or Queen Victoria.

But here it's just me and the phones, so I can let my eyebrows become a jungle! And I have I guess, in a way, so,—Pardon me? Well, yes, I love her—as an assistant though, not as a person. I mean I do as a person, but my goal is to make her life smooth, not happy.

Oh, you know by answering the phones and dealing with her correspondence, and—oh yes people are very enthusiastic. They all want her to get back out there, I'll tell you. There's even talk of a comeback show, I shouldn't tell you where, but New York city—but it's not confirmed yet. Yes, letters, stuffed animals, someone even once sent her the tip of his index finger, which was puzzling. Well, exactly—what DO you do with it? I didn't want to put it in the garbage where a dog could get at it. So I popped it in the composter. Exactly reduce reuse recycle— *(little chuckle)* Oh I haven't laughed like this in—

> *Phone rings.*

Excuse me for a moment, Stephen. Antonella Bergman's office, Brenda MacDonald speaking. Oh Hello Mindi! How's New York? Great. Yes, I relayed your latest offer and she is very positive about it! Yes, we love the Plaza Hotel. We especially love a corner suite. I'm sorry, Mindi, are you eating something right now? Do you mind not eating it into the phone dear it's making me sick. Yes I promise, I'll get back to you within the—by the end of the day within the—soon. Bye bye.

Antonella Bergman's office Brenda MacDonald speaking. Hello? Who is this? Can you speak up please?... Ohhh Lisa.... Yes, I know my dear, well I did. I mentioned that to Antonella and she asked me to offer you love and light and hope on her behalf in this crisis, and to send you an 8X10 ASAP what is your address? Lisa, I know, yes, I am truly sorry to hear about your Lezzie, Lizzie, Lizard, lovie partnie partno spousie wife husba—your ex—yes, but I've done all I can. Of course she "gives a shit," but my honey, put yourself in her shoes. Oh for the love of Mike, Lisa there's the other line—now listen—you, uh go take a shower and a walk and meet some other nice young lady wherever it is you people meet each other! Okay. Good luck. Bye bye.

Sorry about that. Well, yes it is a bit, but the fun outweighs the stress. You see, Stephen, I believe there are certain people that attract love and hope, and then become a target for people's disappointments; people like Richard Simmons— John Lennon, Antonella Bergman. They're targets. Exactly, because she has a light, of understanding—! Oh Stephen this is wonderful.

Have you ever seen a hummingbird? They are so beautiful, aren't they? They move so fast in a straight line and just hover in front of your face, hello. Everyone loves them. I'm simple. I don't understand why someone would do what they did to Antonella Bergman and I certainly can't understand why anyone would kill a hummingbird, put it in a box, mail it, wrapped as a gift. Cruel joke. "Birds of a feather." Its little neck twisted to one side.

Maybe there is no reason why bad things happen—maybe it's about what you make from it. Ms. Bergman would say well God gave us all the books of rules and stories to sort things through, the Bible new and old, the Koran, the Bagavavita, bagagavita bagavaviva, bagavita, bagavitava, just a minute... Baga Baba.... But you know I think God should keep some people sacred.

You know what I would say to that person, should I ever meet them: don't you know that beauty wins out? Nature keeps on. Whatever we try to do to stop her. There's always another hummingbird, or a breathtaking sunset, or lovely gasoline rainbow in a puddle.

Oh no no I don't think that she'd want to be interviewed. I don't mind talking to you, if it will help motivate her. Sometimes we all need a little push.

No, she's very eager. She's tripping all over her own feet to—. She's practically jumping out of her—she's—you know what? Maybe this wasn't such a good idea. I've got a lot of work to do.

You'll have to see your own way out. Left down the hall left left right at the green elevator left right under the awning left.

> *She rapidly types and sneaks a look to see if he's gone. She becomes ANTONELLA.*

ANTONELLA *(continuous, a sexual fantasy)* Jump!… the wind rushing past, blue sky above. No sound but that rush of air all around. And then impact as skin and bones spread aside in deference to the pavement. Exposing long hidden nerves and tendons to the AIR the open AIR, more more until I sink into a thin puddle around myself, wink at life and just ooze away…

Feeling. Not feeling. Recalling: like a dream, like a wet dream.

> *She almost sneezes again.*

Dreams should not be dependent on the spinal chord.

Okay. Okay let's look at the 5 phases of acceptance by that peppy Elisabeth Kubler-Ross.

1) Denial—I have no idea what you're talking about. Deny what? There's nothing to deny. That must be a mistake.

2) Anger—oh please like that's a phase, like we're not always in anger all the time anyway—I hate it when those bastards call anger a phase!

3) Bargaining—I promised God that if I could just have an explanation, or an orgasm, I would be nicer to Brenda. Thankfully neither has happened yet because Brenda is too fun a target.

4) Depression—you know, it's not bad—as long as no one is lurking around trying to cheer you up.

5) Acceptance—well that's a made up phase. They mean, "too tired to fight anymore."

So the phases actually are: denial—skipped it, anger—not a phase, bargaining—doesn't work, depression—still in it, and acceptance—doesn't exist!

When Sarah was 103 years old, with a 13-year-old son, God came to her husband Abraham and asked him to sacrifice their son on an altar like an animal in some ridiculous macho wager God had going on with Satan, and Abraham said, "okay." *(to SARAH)* I bet you weren't laughing then.

My first outing like this was to Canada's Wonderland. It was Brenda, me, and Brenda's frighteningly precocious 9-year-old niece, Sky. They parked me under an ice cream umbrella and went off to do the rides. The unfortunate kid hocking popsicles beside me broke into a sweat when he realized I was there to stay. I really could see he just did not know what to do. I tried not to torture him. I did. First he tried very hard to entertain me and to look at my eyes not the chair. I used to have that same problem but with my breasts. Then he tried being cool, like strong enough to look my disability in the face and just be totally up front with me about it. I love that from a complete stranger. "What happened to you?" "What happened to you, when did you become such a pig?" He was so relieved by the time Brenda and Sky came back, he gave me a free ice cream cone. Which I of course fellated, which caused him to explode.

So I was in a good mood. Sky and Brenda were literally spinning like dogs, all covered in sticky cotton candy. Sky immediately started telling me about all the rides she went on and how she was upside down! She always loved being upside down! Ever since she was little. She jumped onto my lap and tried to wiggle herself upside down. She was so happy! It was infectious! All of a sudden we started to tip. "Get off me! I'm not a ride! I'm not a fucking go-cart!" I hit the ground, and they hit the ground running.

A helpful crowd of 7-foot stuffed animals gathered, and hoisted me into the chair and escorted me out of Hanna Barbara Land, removing their big laughing stuffed heads as we got to the parking lot in a pathetic display of dreamlike absurdity.

(She calls BRENDA.) Brenda—Fine. I've made up my mind about New York. Get a pen. Tell them I said, "No. No, you sycophantic loonies." Yes those exact words. Thank you.

> *She hangs up.*

Get out! Get out! I can smell you from here! You are fired! Yes. Get out. Just go.

> *She almost sneezes again but stops it on her own.*

> *She is now LISA, stumbles to her spot and plunks down. She sits cross-legged doing yoga breathing. Suddenly she leans over like she's going to barf, puts her head in her hands, music out.*

LISA   Forgiveness is letting go of the right to fucking kill them!

> *Crosses to platform. Leans against it. She dials a number. She gets a machine and reacts to it.*

Hello, Margaret, it's me Lisa. I just wanted to ask you something. So, maybe when you get this message, you can call me back. Yeah, um, I was just wondering: I thought you were straight! You're supposed to be straight! I thought you were straight! Hello you're straight! You said you were straight! You're supposed to be straight! Don't say you're straight if you're not STRAIGHT!

I used to blame myself every time I fell in love with a straight woman. But now I know! It's a ruse! It's a ploy! To get your little Lesbian lackey. "You're such a good listener." Straight! "I'm so tense, could you give me a back rub?" Straight! "I've never felt this way about a woman before it's so weird." Straight! "Could you help me move?" Straight! Straight! Well just you wait. You think we had lesbian bed death, I give you three months and then pffff! Oh and wait till Lizzie gets laid off from Federal Express again, then you'll see the real person! She probably told you I was the co-dependent one, well she keeps you on a little string, so you always have to focus on her needs and her problems and oh my God wait until she gets a cold! Waahhhwahh. I have a cold. So good luck, with the love of my life!

She hangs up.

Hello Brenda? It's Lisa. No no wait wait. No, it's about the book! I have a question. Where's the chapter on *hate*?

Music, very rude hip hop. She turns around and starts talking to imaginary people around her. She is GINA, the Trash Talker

GINA is a young pissed off "neighbourhood" girl. She is being interviewed by "Current Affairs."

GINA What are you lookin' at? What are you lookin' at? You are not my type cottonelle wipe… Tina Tina whats up whats up how you doin'?

She dances suggestively.

(to someone offstage) What? What are you lookin' at? Va funkulo, eh! Hey ugly, quit playin' with your dick, aiight. What are you lookin at we're talkin' her aiight! Whatever…

So, yeah, I didn't think I would like her show. I only went because my cousin the little bitch putana asked me to and she got free tickets. And at first it was nasty, people gettin' up and talkin about like their lives and shit—shutup! you marry a fucker he's gonna fuck you up, you loser.

But I liked what she said about women. How like for 7 generations women were burned at the stake as witches. Did you know that? 7 generations?! So now we got like this psychic scar on our DNA chromosomes that we carry with us. So get out of my way motherfucker, this is not PMS, I got witchy genes! HA ha ha ha! Tina.

And like you should walk around in my shoes for a day. Because I got a mediterranean ass right, so guys are always callin' out—my ass. It's mediterranean. I don't know…. It moves with the tides alright. Mm. Yeah.

Like one time one time one time hold up hold up hold up hold up. One time, in my own neighbourhood. Bunch a dickheads sitting around on a porch start yelling shit at me right. "Sit on my face etc. and whatnot?" So I go up to them to do the mother sister speech right? You know the mother sister speech? You don't know that? Oh this would be very informative for your viewers at home. It's like "you got a mother? You got a sister? I bet you wouldn't like anyone talkin' to them like that." It works 'cause sometimes they just doin' it cause their friends are doin' it and really they're a nice guy, like my brother. So I go up there to do mother sister and what do I see? Sittin' on the porch with them the whole time is… their mother! Lookin' at me like I'M some putana, right! And then I see a sister cowerin' in the corner all in black, and the butt-ugly, cow-eyed, arrested development, Deliverance motherfucker brothers are smackin' each other on the arms and shit, and I'm thinking "holy shit there's some weird pathetic shit going on here" like I feel sorry for her? So I can't do mother sister right, because obviously they got one but they don't care, so I go like this I go like this, hold up, hold up: "very nice very nice excuse me, You don't know how to treat me? How about you treat me like you'd treat yourself. Just because I'm a girl doesn't mean I'm not a person. We're all in a global village, aiight? So stop bein' so aggressive and—"

WHAT are you lookin' at? I'll tow your fuckin Lexus man, I fuckin will. So don't fucking fuck with me. Fuck you.

Yeah, I drive a tow truck.

So, yeah, well, I heard a rumour that the person who pushed Antonella Bergman was someone she hired to push her because her career wasn't going that well, uh huh. I also heard maybe it was a fan who listened to her and did what she said and it didn't work out. People just wanna believe you know, in something—

Look no one should go through what she's gone through aiight, *but*—like maybe if there is a God and not the catholic God, but like a cool kind of funky God *(dancing)* this God has dreads—long fuckin' dreads—and big cazzo and big boobs and real smart and real gentle? You'd let him brush your hair? This God sees all the little injustices and the little kind moments and adds them up in a big ledger. Like a abacus? Abacus. You never heard of that? It's like a chinese uh calculator. Whatever. This God maybe knows when you gotta raise people up and when you gotta take them *down*, for their own fucking good.

Okay that's IT man your Lexus is history you illiterate motherfucker!

> *She turns around and stomps over to the wheelchair, sits, becomes ANTONELLA.*

ANTONELLA If only I had gone out the other exit door, if only I had been hit half an inch to the right, if only the bus had taken a little longer at the last stop, if only I had gone for a drink with Brenda. If only it had been Brenda.

If only I had done more. If only I'd had that menage à trois that night in Jasper national park when there was no moon. If only I'd done more drugs, and learned latin dancing and Tai Chi like I said I would.

Lifting your foot up and feeling the cold porcelain smoothness of the toilet seat against it as you click away at your wild toenails. Or lying under a duvet and that urge you get to kick your legs and twist around and then be perfectly still and let the feathers settle all around you. Or dropping to my knees in long grass, so a dog can stand on my thighs and lick my face. Chasing him running after him running running hiding in a man's closet, with his smell, leaping out at him! His chest pounding against my hand. Oh… oh…

> *The phone interrupts her. She answers it slowly.*

What? Fine. No. I told you "no." "No you sycophantic loonies," is that clear? I wasn't kidding. No one takes me seriously anymore. Brenda, It takes 40 minutes to hoist myself out of this chair, as the sweat pours into my eyes and I can't wipe it away, and I have to focus, Brenda, and swallow the rising panic that screams "this is it. This is your life." It will not get better, and though everyone is pulling for me to recover, to fight and beat this, I know that I will never "beat" this, and I will never accept it, Brenda, never. No no! I used to believe anything was possible. "Used to," Brenda, don't you listen to me?! I don't want you to help me, I want to be myself—who I was. By myself. No no no! I said "no you sycophantic loonies." Stop it, stop everything you fat awkward Newfie! You would be nothing without me, nothing, do you know that, you pain in the ass! You healthy, toothless, lucky pain in the ass! You have nothing to regret! Just go! You are fired, Brenda! Just leave!

> *She removes her phone. Suddenly she looks up, as if seeing an apparition. We hear the SARAH clarinets.*

Sarah! What? What?! What is so funny?

> *The clarinets seem to laugh at her. She is shocked. She becomes BRENDA, also in shock.*

BRENDA   She doesn't mean that. She's just upset.

I have worked tirelessly for Ms. Bergman. I have put up with things you wouldn't—hoo.

> *She takes a joint out of a cigarette case in her purse.*

Hydroponic. *(She licks it.)* My son taught me this. My son "smoke the reefer." He "smoke the reefer."

He was always so handsome. Derek. Had lots of girlfriends. Blonde on the inside is what I'd call them. They stuck to him like shit to a wool blanket pardon my French. He thinks I'm a pain too. Is there anything wrong with trying to see the sunny side?! It was hard for him, I know, there was no work. He's not super bright, I wouldn't say that to his face, but it's true. So when he wanted to go off to Asia, I said fine. Not a word about mosquitos and dyptheriah, dypth, dyptheria! Not a word.

But then not to call me for 3 months! What was I supposed to do. "Derek, you had me so upset! You could call… collect?"

"Shit happens, Mum."

"Then don't bother calling when you get home!"

I didn't think he'd take it literally. Oh well, if someone doesn't want to talk to you, there's not much you can do. You just have to leave them be.

>   *Has a "super toke."*

The truth is she's turned down everything that's come our way in the last year. What am I supposed to do? I have a feeling this is it. The longer you stay off the horse the harder it is to get back on, and one day there's no more horses left, just buses.

I'll tell you something right now. If that woman thinks she could function one day without me—and I'm from Nova Scotia I am not a Newfie!—And I'd like to see her get someone else to go to the window for her?! You big bully! Oh I hate a bully, don't you? Little bastards making the smaller ones eat rocks and doggy doo and whatnot.

"Shit happens." Well I don't think so. Sometimes I think God is just a big old bully needs his ears boxed for him! What are you thinking?! Wars, and disease and famine and rogue waves sucking people to their doom off Peggy's cove, and poor Buster humped to death at the lake!

Poor Buster. Buster was our dog. Little runt. Derek and I were at the cottage. Derek's dad was off at some air force thing. We were just passing time playing Yahtzee, when another dog got on top of Buster and just you know, started humping him, for a bit. Well I never know what to do in those situations. Do I explain or ignore? Derek was just ten at the time so I chose ignore. But what we didn't realize was that the whole time he was being humped, Buster's head was under the dock, and he drowned. Humped to death at the lake!! Shit happens!

>   *Toke. The phone rings.*

Nope. Nope.

>   *Finally she gets it.*

Antonella Bergman's office Brenda Madonie smoking spoking speaking. Oh, yes, hello Mindi Mindi Mindi. Yes, in fact Ms. Bergman does have an answer for you. Do you have a pen? She says "No, you sycophantic loonies!" (*giggle*) Oops could you hold?

Antonella Bergman's office Brenda Mac—hoo! hoo! calm down. Who is this? Oh. She what? She fired her already! Well, I'm sure she had a good reason— what?! Bad breath? Hoo! Well, now there's no reason to get all—sue us?! What for? Abusive behaviour—I could tell you stories that'd curl your curlies!—So what? so you—Well, you tell her she does have shitty breath! She should have a gum!

(hits the previous line) That's right sycophantic. That's your problem. You look it up! Will she change her mind? I don't know. She might! In the meantime: you people stop noodging me!

> *She hangs up. She turns the music LOUD ("Daughter of Darkness" by Tom Jones) and dances around a bit. She takes off her headset, glasses, and jacket, and suddenly slumps over and becomes LISA.*
>
> *LISA throws the book away. The phone rings.*

LISA   Hello? Lizzie! Oh Lizzie, I knew you would call. I knew you would call!… Yes I, I might have given Margaret a call. Forgive who? Margaret? No, I don't think she's totally responsible—but—Yes, I know what my responsibility is in this whole thing oh yes I do: I forget to flush the toilet, I'm shaped like an egg, I tend to repeat a nonsense phrase all day "a baluga baluga…," I faked it the first time—I fake it all my first times—it's just easier. I didn't tell you because I didn't want to hurt your feelings! I chew the tops of pens and leave them on the dining room table, I watched you sleep—your back rising and falling and sometimes it seemed like your back wasn't moving at all so I'd nudge you to see if you were dead. And then you wouldn't be dead and I'd fall back asleep, and you'd be awake. I hate your sister's kids—and lets face it you hate your sister's kids too. Yes! See! I accept my share of the responsibility!

But what about your responsibility? No not to me oh no no! God forbid. To God! You have a responsibility to God, to the Goddess! To be a nicer person! To make this world better and not more wounded! You have a responsibility to be nice! What do you mean so do I? Fuck you! I am nice.

> *She hangs up. She dials BRENDA.*

Hello Brenda. No, don't put me on hold! I have a new book for Antonella Bergman. It goes like this: Forgiveness… don't do it. Hold on to it. And if someone tries to hurt you, fuck 'em! Fuck 'em first.

> *She drops down. The phone rings.*

BRENDA   Hold please, Lisa.

Well, Mindi, I meant sycophantic in the nicest way. What?! No. Oh my honey, you can't do that. Hold please.

> *She hits the key for ANTONELLA.*

Ms. Bergman, Ms. Bergman, Ms. Bergman! Fine. Listen, I just spoke with New York and they are chomping mad. Well I told them no you sycophantic loonies and now they're saying they're going to book Doctor Phil, God save us. Hold on.

Hello, Mindi? Lisa? Oh hold on.

Mindi? Hold on, we're having a breakthrough!

Ms. Bergman? Ms. Bergman it's now or never. The horses have left the building! Hold on.

Mindi—Lisa?! Do you have redial?

> *She yells at the phone.*

Enough of this ALL of you!! It's like dealing with little children!

(She hits a line.) Ms. Bergman, you have an obligation to go out there and help all the people you can help!

(She hits a line.) Lisa, you go over to Lezzie's house with a Bundt cake and forgive her! It's the decent thing to do and you'll feel much better!

(She hits a line.) Antonella, I just told Lisa to go over to Lezzie's with a Bundt cake and you should call her before she does. She's clearly having a hard time too. Pain is pain.

(She hits a line.) Now Lisa, you be proud and loud and here and queer and out and about and whatnot. I am very busy holding up my end and I don't need you dragging that end down.

(She hits a line.) I don't need you dragging that end down, Mindi!

(She hits a line.) Ms. Bergman, we have lives to lead and they're small enough and short enough without this nonsense! If you can help another being in this lonely shuffle, by God why would you hesitate?!

(She hits a line.) By God why would you hesitate, Mindi?!

(She hits a line.) Antonella, I'm booking the New York lecture, and you better plan on being ready!

(She hits a line.) Mindi, Ms. Bergman has had it with your pestering. I want a signing bonus for all you've put us through! Now she'll do it but on my terms!

(She hits a line.) Antonella, you will do it but on my terms!

(She hits a line.) Lisa, Antonella is doing the New York lecture but on my terms and if she can do it SO CAN YOU! Questions? Comments? GOOD.

(She hits a line.) Mindi, questions comments good!

(She hits a line.) Antonella, Questions? Comments? Good.

> *She falls back in the chair.*
>
> *Music—clarinets.*

ANTONELLA   *(breathing hard)* No oh no oh no oh God oh no oh Jesus oh God oh ohoh…

> *She sneezes. Again. Again. She laughs, orgasms, looks to SARAH.*
>
> *Klezhmer clarinet music, and she becomes SARAH again. She gives the audience a knowing look.*

SARAH   Vatizhak Sarah Bekirbah, and Sarah laughed inside. Deep inside. At God. With God. Same difference. What would you do? I was 90 years old, my breasts were two figs, my womb had curled up into itself like a dead squirrel! God sends angels to tell me I was pregnant, at 90. Hysterical. And to be the mother of the Jewish people, God help me.

When I was 103, getting on a bit, one day my husband Abraham comes up to me with this bad little boy glint in his eyes—"Sarahleh. I was thinkin of takin our precious son Yizhak on a stroll in the mountains." Who strolls in the mountains? I smelled a desert rat. But I let him go. I let my son go. To be sacrificed like an animal in some game of chicken God had going on with Abraham. And at the last minute God provided a ram to be sacrificed in little Yizhak's stead yada yada so on so forth. Testing testing always testing. For me, it's I love you, shoin already!

What you gonna do? Does it make sense I should have a baby at age 90? *(She unlocks the wheelchair and rolls it off it's ramp to downstage centre and sits in it.)* Was I being punished? Believe me I've gone through everything. I decided no. I was being chosen for a reason I can not understand because I'm just a pisher. That is my faith.

The people said to God "we need help, why don't you send someone?" God said to the people, "I did. I sent you."

There are times when you just have to take the gift, painful as hell as it is, laugh, and get on with your pregnancy. *(laughs)* You got no choice.

> *Lighting and the same kind of music as we heard at the top of the show for ANTONELLA's first speech. Applause.*
>
> *ANTONELLA, in the wheelchair, looks out at her audience.*

ANTONELLA   Hello, New York. Sarah the biblical matriarch came to visit me in Toronto. She was 103 years old and rangy. It was the end of the millennium, and anything is possible.

> *The end.*

Smudge

Alex Bulmer

Introduction:
Smudge

Alex Bulmer's *Smudge* (2000), developed in collaboration with Kate Lynch, Diane Flacks and Alisa Palmer, charts the journey of the central character Freddie into blindness. Set on an empty stage with only a scrim to divide the up and down stage areas, the stage area itself created a powerful visual metaphor for Freddie's condition. Freddie herself never crosses behind the scrim where the character Blindness first begins to lurk. Having the actor who plays Blindness also take all the other peripheral roles of the characters who come in and out of Freddie's world adds another very powerful visual dimension to the piece since it emphasizes Freddie's increasing inability to distinguish one face from another. It is also of huge importance to have the same actor play her lover Katherine, the one stable presence in Freddie's world.

The juxtaposition of their hopeful journey towards a loving lesbian relationship against Freddie's tragic progression towards Blindness sets up the parallel trajectories that drive the plot forward. Much of the poetic resonance of this beautifully articulated meditation on the gift of sight, is intimately tied to the gift of love. Just as Freddie finds herself increasingly pushed more and more to the margins of society by her inability to see, she is also forced to find news ways to negotiate even the simplest of activities. The marginalization that her blindness brings echoes the marginalization that her alternative sexuality automatically carries. The precariousness of her state as she wanders the streets of her downtown Toronto neighborhood highlights both her vulnerability as a person with limited vision, and as a single lesbian woman trying to make it on her own. The short scenes that flash by in rapid succession put the spectator in the position of having to decipher their heavily compacted meanings in much the same way that Freddie is forced to do as her field of vision narrows.

Thus Freddie opens the show by introducing us to the world of her imagination where she compares herself to a silent screen star who suddenly loses her sight and with it her ability to enthrall her audiences with her trademark acting gimmick—that of constantly introducing the unexpected. In signalling that this play is more about artistic process than blindness, Freddie invites us to frame everything through her distorting lenses. In each of the next four scenes, she takes us through the stages of her progressive sight loss as her diagnosis of Retinitis Pigmentosa begins to manifest itself. Picking up chicks at the Dyke Club turns into a comedy of error; visiting a library brings on the first appearance of Blindness who casts her shadow on the screen as she holds up a page of print for Freddie to read. As Blindness taunts her by moving the page around so that the words appear and disappear, we experience the disappearance of written words from Freddie's life. In her own words, she sees the world through: "Foggy Jello. Like looking through a straw. Mud splattered on a windshield" (443).

Offsetting Freddie's descent into blindness are the scenes which trace her entry into a relationship with Katherine who takes her at face value and enters into her limited field of vision. At the movies, at the dyke club, at the restaurant, she gives Freddie back a place in the world. With her, Freddie resists being turned into the empty cipher that she becomes for everyone she meets in the outside world. The safety that she feels with Katherine becomes more and more intensified by the build up of scenes showing what life is like for Freddie as she tries to operate without her sight. The Toronto landscape near College and Euclid now appears through her defamiliarizing experience of negotiating the traffic, the crowds, the cafes and bus stops with only the benefit of a cane.

The impossibility of keeping the dangerous outside world from infringing on the safe harbour that the relationship offers becomes evident in the scene where Freddie is regaling Katherine with the story of trying to buy Tampax in the gas station. Katherine's anger at Freddie for going out without her cane overshadows any humour she might feel. This time the imbalance between them is saved by Freddie's joke equating carrying a cane with wearing a big cashew on her head to say she was allergic to peanut oil. However, as these dinner dates get repeated, Freddie's increasing difficulties in negotiating her life begin to loom over them.

The mounting evidence that Freddie is less and less able to participate equally in the relationship comes to a head in the climactic scene with Katherine when their weekend escape plans fall apart. With Blindness now in front of the scrim, shadowing Freddie as she hides under her duvet, the scene is set for Freddie's slow confession of her humiliating experience trying to bring home the special groceries that she buys for the occasion. Whether or not her alleged tormentor is real, or only a figment of her paranoid mind, the chain of events whereby she drops the groceries and flees home believing that he is pursuing her, marks a turning point in her relationship. As Katherine patiently listens to her recount how she threatened to beat him up with her cane, her tenderness towards Freddie surfaces, but is offset by the impression that no more plans will be made for country escapes.

In the few remaining scenes, we witness the final stages whereby Freddie enters into her state of total Blindness. In her final scene with Katherine, Freddie traces the stages by which she is erasing Katherine from her life. When Katherine asks Freddie if she knows that she is crying, Freddie responds:

> No, it's not in your voice. In the dark, I don't even know if you're still there. In fact, maybe you've quietly slipped away. *(pause)* You see, you didn't say anything just now and I don't even know if you're there. *(pause)* Is your face all squished up in horror. It is, isn't it. *(pause)* It would be nice if you would tell me. I can't see, you know! (462)

The victory of Blindness over the relationship carries enormous symbolic resonance as it reminds us of the precarious nature of both life and love. In this particular case, the terrible poignancy that we feel is intensified by the knowledge that the irreparable loss of losing one's ability to see is also accompanied by the loss of the ability to love.

Alex Bulmer

Bio and Artist's Statement

Alex Bulmer is a Canadian writer currently working in the UK. She has written for CBC radio's OutFront and her radio play *Criminally Sighted* was part of CBC's New Voices Festival in 2003. *SMUDGE* was Alex's first full length play and has been produced in Toronto and London, England. It earned an Ontario Dora and Chalmers nomination as Best Play and was selected as Critics Choice by London's *Time Out* Magazine. Current literary work in progress includes *Minutes Pass* with Polka Theatre, UK and development of a new radio drama with the BBC.

•

How do you know what you can't see? A question I asked myself for many years and perhaps continue to ask metaphorically with reference to things I find difficult to understand. I wrote *SMUDGE* during the first six years of my gradual sight loss. The solitary act of writing gave me some order and perspective within an experience that entirely disrupted, disoriented and displaced me. The world around me was disappearing, but more significant was the feeling that, in public, I was disappearing. At the core of this was an ongoing conflict between my sense of self and the degenerative social and economic standing that society offered a woman who functioned without eyesight.

Production Information

Smudge was first produced by Nightwood Theatre in association with S.N.I.F.F. Inc. at the Tarragon Back Space, in November 2000, with the following company:

FREDDIE   Diane Flacks
KATHERINE / OTHERS   Kate Lynch
THE ENTITY / OTHERS   Sherry Lee Hunter

Directed by Alisa Palmer
Set and Costume Design by Carolyn M. Smith
Lighting Design by Andrea Lundy
Sound Design by John Gzowski and Deb Sinha
Stage Managed by Fiona Jones

·

Smudge was nominated for a Chalmers Award for Best New Play, and a Dora Mavor Moore Award for Best Play, Best Production and Lighting Design.

Smudge was also produced in the UK by In Tandem TC and earned a *Time Out* Magazine Critics Choice Award.

Characters

Freddie, A young woman who is losing her sight
Katherine, Her girlfriend
The Entity, An inextricable presence, a facet of Freddie's mind and soul
Others, who come and go in Freddie's darkening world

Set

The stage is bare, except for a single chair with a white cane resting on it. A scrim divides upstage from downstage and beyond that is a mirrored wall. The reflection of the chair is seen through the murky scrim in the upstage mirror. Throughout the play, Freddie appears in front of the scrim. The Entity begins behind the scrim, appearing as a shadow, a ghost, a memory of sight, a fantasy of vision. As the play progresses, the Entity moves closer and closer to Freddie, finally entering Freddie's world.

SMUDGE

ACT ONE

scene one

Imagination

FREDDIE, with her cane and glasses, stands alone on stage.

During the course of the opening monologue, the Silent Screen Star becomes visible upstage of the scrim.

FREDDIE   I imagine myself a wild and crazy Silent Screen Star who has had an unfortunate accident and is suddenly left blind. She insists upon continuing with her career despite everyone's disapproval. She demands tighter shots and less movement on set. She never moans, grieves, or complains. A cutting moment occurs during a break. A young girl innocently asks Estelle—we'll call her Estelle—"Estelle, what's it like to be blind?" Estelle turns and says quite matter-of-factly,

FREDDIE & THE ENTITY   "Boring. Dead, outright boring.

THE ENTITY   My life as a Silent Screen Star is based on the unexpected. Shocks, tricks, escape. I give people what they don't expect, can't predict and walk away with a tremendous grin. But this my dear, this is the ultimate humdrum, anti-drama. This unfortunate addition to me is my disaster. Boring, boring, and I refuse to be boring."

The word "Smudge" appears from the darkness as the Silent Screen Star's light fades. The word slowly disappears.

scene two

Hospital #1

A HOSPITAL TECHNICIAN stands beside FREDDIE.

FREDDIE   E   M   P

TECHNICIAN   Anything? Anything else?

FREDDIE   A fuzzy worm?

FREDDIE looks at the TECHNICIAN, puzzled.

Blackout.

Hospital #2

TECHNICIAN Okay, "Fingers or Fist." Fingers or fist?

> *The TECHNICIAN moves her hand to the left, and to the right, top and bottom alternating between fingers and fist at each position.*

FREDDIE Fist. Fingers. Fingers. Fist. Fingers.

> *The TECHNICIAN moves her hand towards the centre*

Fist. Fisht—fishters—sishticks—shingers

scissors!

TECHNICIAN What?

FREDDIE Rock, paper, scissors.

> *FREDDIE demonstrates with her hand.*

Ready? One, two, three.

> *They play.*

TECHNICIAN Dynamite! I win!

> *Blackout.*

Hospital #3

TECHNICIAN Follow my finger.

> *The TECHNICIAN traces her finger from right to left in front of FREDDIE's face. FREDDIE is able to follow to the centre, and then stops. The TECHNICIAN continues with her finger to the left. FREDDIE is frozen, looking straight ahead. Her eyes then jump to the far left, catching a glimpse of the finger tracing left of her face.*

> *The TECHNICIAN's hand then moves right, and then to the centre, and up. FREDDIE follows, and assuming the hand will go straight to the right, she looks that way. Realizing it's not there, FREDDIE searches with her peripheral vision to find the TECHNICIAN's hand. When she does:*

Are you following my fingers or are you guessing?

FREDDIE I'm not sure there's a difference.

> *The TECHNICIAN touches FREDDIE's nose. FREDDIE doesn't see it— she's startled.*

> *Blackout.*

Hospital #4

TECHNICIAN   Look at this picture. What do you see?

FREDDIE   A bunch of dots.

TECHNICIAN   In the dots what do you see?

FREDDIE   Um in the dots—in the dots?

TECHNICIAN   There's a picture in the dots. You can't see it?

FREDDIE   Wait, in the dots! Two people having sex. Three people having sex? Oh! A star!

TECHNICIAN   I suspect that you're guessing. Look right into the dots. Would you say it looks like a dolphin?

FREDDIE   No.

TECHNICIAN   No? Are you sure?

FREDDIE   No, I do not see a dolphin.

TECHNICIAN   You don't see a dolphin?

FREDDIE   Yes, that is what I said.

TECHNICIAN   No dolphin.

FREDDIE   That is what I've always said! No dolphin!

> *Enter FREDDIE's mind's eye. The TECHNICIAN is suddenly transformed to S.S. Gestapo Officer.*

TECHNICIAN   And yet we have on record as you seeing a dolphin several times. In fact, I believe you saw a dolphin yesterday in the Soviet Embassy!

FREDDIE   That is a lie!

TECHNICIAN   Is it? Look at the next picture!

FREDDIE   No! No! No!

TECHNICIAN   Do you by any chance see the code number 786 XRP?

FREDDIE   No! You will never get away with this! I'll never tell you anything. No matter what you do to me. You will never break me! I'll tell nothing! I see nothing!

> *We return to reality. The TECHNICIAN watches FREDDIE with mild concern.*

Nothing!

TECHNICIAN   I think we'll stop here.

FREDDIE   I thought you said we were going to do a couple more.

TECHNICIAN   We did. You didn't see them. We'll rest your eyes now.

The TECHNICIAN places a blindfold over FREDDIE's eyes and exits.

scene three

Doctor's Office

DR. DUVALL enters carrying a clipboard.

DR. DUVALL   Hello Freddie, I'm Dr Duvall. This must be very difficult for you.

FREDDIE   I'm alright. Can you tell me some results?

DR. DUVALL   The technicians say you're quite a pleasure to work with.

FREDDIE   Yeah. I like them too. So what did you find?

DR. DUVALL   Just wait one moment.

DR. DUVALL writes notes on her file.

FREDDIE   I know I bombed the colour test.

DR. DUVALL is still writing.

DR. DUVALL   Just wait one moment.

FREDDIE   And the field test was a big bust.

DR. DUVALL   Just a moment.

DR. DUVALL finishes writing.

FREDDIE   The red dye stuff made me barf.

DR. DUVALL   It did, yes. That's a reaction that can happen.

FREDDIE   I barfed three times.

DR. DUVALL   You're probably allergic to the red fluorescence. It can make some patients' heartbeats race and it can be a cause of nausea. I'm sorry you had to go through that. We won't need to do that test again for a few years.

FREDDIE   So, I'm coming back then?

DR. DUVALL   Yes. What I'm seeing appears to be an atypical dystrophy of the rods and cones, pigmenting of the cells. It looks like spider webs in the back of the eye.

FREDDIE   Oh. What does yours look like?

DR. DUVALL   In a healthy eye, the cells regenerate and the back of the eye is clear. Yours are scarred.

FREDDIE   So, how bad does it get, the scars?

DR. DUVALL   As far as we know the scarring progresses and eventually leaves the eye with light and shadow perception. It is a genetic blindness. In your case you have what is called Recessive Retinitis Pigmentosa Inversa.

FREDDIE   Sorry, retinisis…

DR. DUVALL   Retinitis Pigmentosa. We call it R.P. for short.

FREDDIE   We do.

DR. DUVALL   In normal Retinitis Pigmentosa, the loss of vision begins at the periphery and gradually moves to the centre. In your case, Retinitis Pigmentosa Inversa, the loss of sight begins in the centre and moves towards the periphery. You can see the doughnut but not the hole, as it were. On the other hand, that's a very good definition of an optimist, isn't it?

FREDDIE   Okay, so what are we gonna do about it?

DR. DUVALL   I can't tell you that.

FREDDIE   Do you mean, I can't tell you that because it's a doctor's secret and we're not sharing, or I can't tell you that because you don't know?

DR. DUVALL   Because we don't know. I will know more each time I see what stage the vision is at. Your condition has no cure, at present. No cure.

> THE ENTITY, *appearing behind the scrim, raises arms to heaven, slowly lowers them to sides and looks at FREDDIE.*

FREDDIE   This is a jolly moment. And you do this for a living?

DR. DUVALL   It's very difficult telling people that they're going to lose something so precious, so vital.

FREDDIE   Well, people must survive, otherwise there wouldn't be a CIBC.

DR. DUVALL   CNIB. Yes. We'll get you signed up. I just signed up a little baby this morning. It was very sad. I understand what it is to lose something so precious, so necessary. I spent eight months in bed as a child with polio and I learned the hard way how valuable things are. How much I thanked God I could see, since I wasn't able to do much of anything else. I couldn't go to school or play with anyone. I know how quickly things change and how painful that can be. Just the other night I came home from school, Christina's school, a parent teacher meeting, and when I got home, the car was gone from the garage, and Barry had just suddenly left me.

> DR. DUVALL *breaks down.*

FREDDIE   Oh, I'm sorry.

DR. DUVALL   Thank you. We can take the blindfold off shortly. *(in tears)* Would you like a cup of coffee?

She starts to rush off.

FREDDIE   Sure. And sorry about—

DR. DUVALL   *(exiting, tears again)* Thank you.

FREDDIE   —Barry!

> *THE ENTITY approaches FREDDIE and gently touches her on the shoulder. FREDDIE reacts to the touch. Then, THE ENTITY removes the blindfold. FREDDIE reacts to the light.*

scene four

Outside

FREDDIE   How do you know what you can't see?

> *FREDDIE looks and sees.*

Red car. Royal Bank. Old man. Blue sky.

I like to think the next few years will be just like always. I'll still see and when it comes, it comes.

Look… at the… pigeons!

> *FREDDIE waves her arms at them.*
>
> *THE ENTITY mirrors the pigeon's flight behind the scrim.*

scene five

The Dyke Club

> *Dance music blares. FREDDIE is alone, centre in a tight pool of light, with a cigarette in her hand and a lighter. She puts the cigarette in her mouth, backwards, and tries to light it. As she vainly attempts to light her smoke, a BAR BABE crosses down to FREDDIE and turns her cigarette around for her.*

BAR BABE   It's backwards.

> *The BAR BABE crosses left of FREDDIE and bends over to tie her shoe. A WAITRESS crosses down to FREDDIE with a beer.*

WAITRESS   Coming through, coming through, here's your beer, lady.

> *She hands it to FREDDIE, and crosses upstage. FREDDIE tries to drink her beer, but there is a cup over the bottle. FREDDIE removes the cup and drinks.*

Mistaking the back of the BAR BABE on her left for a table, she places the unwanted cup on the BAR BABE's back. The BAR BABE stands, and the cup falls.

The BAR BABE bends to tie her other shoe facing downstage. FREDDIE touches her back—or table—again to make sure it's still there. The BAR BABE is annoyed by the touch, and crosses upstage of FREDDIE. FREDDIE tries to put her beer on the "table," but it is gone, and she bobs up and down to the music with her beer, to cover her faux pas.

The WAITRESS enters again. She asks FREDDIE to pick up the fallen cup.

Would you pick that up.

FREDDIE bends over to pick it up, but cannot see it.

All the while, a Patron noisily orders drinks from the WAITRESS. The WAITRESS is frustrated by FREDDIE's inability to help.

Don't bother, I'll get it myself.

The WAITRESS crosses downstage of FREDDIE to retrieve the cup, barely missing stepping on her hand.

Dancer 1 wildly flails over the top of a still crouching FREDDIE, who would be hit if she stood up, which she does, but Dancer 1 regains her composure in time. DANCER 2 dances up to FREDDIE and the flailing Dancer 1 at centre.

DANCER 2   You are so sexy. You are so hot. Come here and give me a big kiss.

FREDDIE puckers up and moves downstage but DANCER 2 has grabbed Dancer 1 and plants a huge kiss on her. They embrace, and Dancer 1 carries DANCER 2 away.

FREDDIE is left alone with her cigarette and beer bottle.

Dancer 3 dances up to FREDDIE, silently. FREDDIE is lighting her smoke inadvertently in Dancer 3's face. Dancer 3 waves the smoke away. FREDDIE doesn't notice. Dancer 3 coughs loudly in FREDDIE's face. The cigarette is still not lit.

FREDDIE   Can you cover your mouth when you do that!

Dancer 3 crosses upstage of FREDDIE in disgust.

The WAITRESS crosses down to FREDDIE.

WAITRESS   Coming through, coming through. Empties, got any empties?

FREDDIE holds her bottle in the air, afraid of being bumped again. The WAITRESS takes her beer away and crosses right.

*From both left and right people start yelling: "Freddie!" "Freddie!"
Confused as to where the voices are coming from, FREDDIE reluctantly
raises her arm to wave.*

scene six

Library

*FREDDIE stands centre. The LIBRARIAN is to her right with her back to
FREDDIE.*

A LIBRARY PATRON behind the scrim looks for a book.

FREDDIE   Hello?

LIBRARIAN   Ssssh!

FREDDIE approaches the desk.

How can I help you?

FREDDIE   Ah, yes. I'm looking for a journal.

LIBRARIAN   Yes, a journal?

FREDDIE   Yes. A journal. A medical kind of journal.

LIBRARIAN   Yes, a medical journal.

FREDDIE   Yes.

LIBRARIAN   That would be in the Medical Section. Just over there.

The LIBRARIAN nods her head in a direction that FREDDIE cannot see.

FREDDIE   Where?

LIBRARIAN   Just over there to the left.

FREDDIE   The left?

The LIBRARIAN turns to face FREDDIE.

LIBRARIAN   Yes, just over there to the right.

FREDDIE   To the right?

The LIBRARIAN turns back.

LIBRARIAN   To the left.

FREDDIE   To the left or right? Which is it?

LIBRARIAN   Well it's to your left if you're standing this way, but to the right if
you're facing—

FREDDIE   Right. Uhm, I'm looking for something specific.

LIBRARIAN   Yes?

FREDDIE   About eyes and conditions.

LIBRARIAN   Eyes and conditions. Yes.

FREDDIE   For a friend of mine.

LIBRARIAN   A friend. Yes.

FREDDIE   She, uh, has dyslexia.

LIBRARIAN   Oh, dyslexia, that's neurology. That's just over there.

The LIBRARIAN points in the opposite direction.

FREDDIE   No, no it's eyes. I'm sure it's eyes.

LIBRARIAN   No, no my dear it's neurology—

FREDDIE   It's eyes.

LIBRARIAN   Neurology.

FREDDIE   No, it's eyes. I know it's eyes because I have it.

LIBRARIAN   Oh, my dear girl. Never be ashamed of your disability. Just say, "I have dyslexia!"

FREDDIE   I have dyslexia!

LIBRARIAN   Shhhh! That's right.

FREDDIE   I have trouble reading things from left to right. So could you take me to the medical section?

LIBRARIAN   Of course I can. Now, how would you read that? Section medical?

FREDDIE   No.

LIBRARIAN   I would be happy to get your book for you and read it to you.

FREDDIE   No, no, that's okay.

LIBRARIAN   Oh I'd be happy to—

FREDDIE   It's okay, I'll read it.

LIBRARIAN   No, no because how will you read it forward? Backwards?

FREDDIE   You don't have to. I'll—

LIBRARIAN   I want to, it's no trouble—

FREDDIE   No. Look I don't even have dyslexia.

LIBRARIAN   Oh?

FREDDIE   I have RP.

LIBRARIAN   Received Pronunciation. Linguistics, that's downstairs...

The LIBRARIAN starts to direct her in another direction.

FREDDIE   No, it's Retini, retinisis—

LIBRARIAN   Retinisis?

FREDDIE   Retinisis—

LIBRARIAN   Retinisiss—

FREDDIE   Resinissin—

LIBRARIAN   Resisin—

FREDDIE   Pigmenso, pigisis—

LIBRARIAN   Pigmesis—

FREDDIE   Pig, pig, pig—

In her effort FREDDIE is suddenly, momentarily, transformed into a pig. She squeals, then stops suddenly with—

Retinitis Pigmentosa!

LIBRARY PATRON   Shhhhh!

LIBRARIAN   Oh! Retinitis Pigmentosa! That's in the Medical Section. Just over there.

The LIBRARIAN points but FREDDIE can't see where.

scene seven

Reading

FREDDIE holds a sheet of paper, trying to read the information she retrieved at the library. FREDDIE reads only from small spots of vision available to her from the outside corner of each eye. Reading for FREDDIE at this stage in her blindness means holding the page close to the outside of each eye and moving it as her vision shifts each moment. It is an elaborate, time consuming and fatiguing activity.

THE ENTITY, upstage of the scrim, physicalizes and expands on FREDDIE's efforts. Both hold a piece of paper.

FREDDIE   *(slowly and with increasing difficulty)* Retinitis Pigmentosa is a series of hereditary eye diseases affecting the eye. Retinitis Pigmentosa is a series of heredit.... The vision de... gen... er.... The vision degenerates, leaving the eye with light and shadow perception. Total blindness may occur. It may affect one in 13,000. Those affected complain of disjointed images, fogginess and difficulty adjusting to changes of light.

> *FREDDIE stops reading, stands and describes what she sees.*

Foggy Jello.
Like looking through a straw.
Mud splattered on a windshield.
The world looks filthy.
Slash of light!
Flashing Picassos.
It's wild.
It's a picture party.
It's a mess.

scene eight

Sitting

> *FREDDIE enters a café. People bump into her, leaving her disoriented. We hear: "Excuse me" and "Hey!" from the bumpers. "Sorry!" from FREDDIE. She sees something. FREDDIE makes her way towards a chair. We hear her thoughts.*

> *THE ENTITY, behind the scrim, playfully accompanies FREDDIE's imagination with movement.*

FREDDIE   The light catches the edge of the chair and gleams its existence into my eyes. My hand rests on my left thigh preparing for an unknown reach. I'm expecting six inches and make contact far sooner. My fingers find the cold hard steel of a frame. Exploding out of its hardness is a soft bulge. My palm widens, my mind goes to my hand. Feels like leather. Feels like red. This is the chair. My right knee guides me toward the 90 degree angle. My knee leads me across the frame. Reaching down, I give myself the assurance that I have found the centre. Go. Down with butt. Impact. When both hands are at equal distance from my hips I know I have achieved optimum sitting position. My legs cross one over the other. I lean seductively forward, I smile with a twinkle, hoping to divert my audience from recognizing the efforts invested in such a simple action.

> *FREDDIE is smiling with self congratulation. She doesn't realize that she is staring straight at another woman in the café.*

KATHERINE   Hi.

FREDDIE   *(startled)* Hi. Who are you?

KATHERINE   I'm Katherine.

> *FREDDIE's smile broadens.*

scene nine

Café Sightings

FREDDIE and KATHERINE sit facing each other. FREDDIE stares straight ahead, never moving her eyes. KATHERINE waves her fingers up to her left, then up to her right, down at centre, down left, and down right. Each time FREDDIE nods in affirmative.

Then KATHERINE waves her fingers at FREDDIE in the left corner of FREDDIE's vision. FREDDIE sees this too. KATHERINE then brings her face towards her own hand until FREDDIE can catch a glimpse of her. FREDDIE, seeing KATHERINE's face, waves back at KATHERINE, smiles gently, and says:

FREDDIE   Hi.

scene ten

The Movies

KATHERINE whispers a description of the movie into FREDDIE's ear.

SOME GUY is eating popcorn behind them.

KATHERINE   She just threw her head back and—close up shot of her face—she groans—I guess you know that—oh, he's making a move, yup, there goes the hand.

FREDDIE   Where?

KATHERINE   Right up her shirt—Inside—

FREDDIE   Inside? Where?

KATHERINE   Inside. You know. Okay, she's quivering her lips again, there's a shot of the leftovers by the sink, he's carrying her to the sink—

FREDDIE   Is he putting her on the leftovers?

KATHERINE   No—he just propped her right in the sink—well, in front of it—her shirt's off now, she has perfect round breasts, of course.

FREDDIE   Of course.

KATHERINE   He's kissing her neck.

FREDDIE   How?

KATHERINE   It looks like a bit of tongue sliding—

FREDDIE   How?

KATHERINE   —and now he's nibbling her ear—

FREDDIE   How, nibbling?

KATHERINE   Well, it looks like lip nibbling—no, pulling maybe. And he's—oh no they're going into the bedroom—he's moving down her leg with his face—

FREDDIE   Moving where?

KATHERINE   Down to her feet and she's—you can hear that—

FREDDIE   I heard that.

KATHERINE   He's staring at her feet, oh okay now, now he's sucking your toes—

FREDDIE   My toes? What about my toes?

KATHERINE   Her toes. He's sucking her toes.

FREDDIE   He's sucking your toes.

KATHERINE   He's sucking your toes.

FREDDIE   Ohhhh.

KATHERINE   Now, he's sliding his hands down her pants—

FREDDIE   She's bearing down waiting—holding back—

KATHERINE   He's taking his time, feeling every inch of her as he moves down—

FREDDIE   She's hot.

KATHERINE   She's on fire.

FREDDIE   She says—

SOME GUY   Will you shut up!

FREDDIE & **KATHERINE**   Oh, sorry.

> *Pause. They laugh.*

FREDDIE   God, this is a really boring movie, eh?

KATHERINE   Yeah. I'm really bored.

> *They look at each other.*

FREDDIE & KATHERINE   Let's go!

scene eleven

The Dyke Club

> *Dance music blares. FREDDIE and KATHERINE slow dance at centre.*
>
> *The WAITRESS enters from left with two beers, and crosses centre and hands them to KATHERINE, who hands one to FREDDIE.*

FREDDIE begins to search for her money, but KATHERINE has beaten her to the punch and pays.

The WAITRESS exits off left.

FREDDIE and KATHERINE dance.

scene twelve

The Second Cup

FREDDIE describes what she sees.

During the text, two figures upstage of the scrim transform from coffee shop patrons to flamboyant flamenco dancers, flashes of FREDDIE's fantasy.

FREDDIE   I'm sitting at the Second Cup. *(FREDDIE goes to lean her chin on her hand and notices—)* My fingers are sticky. I have cream cheese all over my face. I have to get a serviette. It's a big decision, it means getting up and moving across the table-cluttered room to the stuff stand. It's dire. I'm covered in goo. I go. I see the east/west parameters of this café-minefield. I find my markers and place myself between them. Hey! I see the piled up stuff. This would be the serviette centre—or someone's piley-up hairdo. I stop, I stare. I focus. Ah Hah! I see something. It could be a serviette holder. Hold it, I stare at it. I stare it down like a matador. I won't be fooled. I won't reach out expecting paper wipes and make surprising contact with plastic forks. I stare with indignation. Nothing I perceive bears resemblance to anything other than the serviette holder. The white contrasting the dark shiny thing gives all my suspicions the assurance to reach out. I'm convinced. I reach out a little more to the left, now down, over, yes! Serviettes! *Fucking ace! I rule!*

> *FREDDIE waves her arms in triumph, and bashes a WOMAN next to her.*

WOMAN   Oh my God, you got it all over my sweater—

FREDDIE   Oh, I'm so sorry.

> *FREDDIE goes to wipe the sweater, but instead accidentally brushes the woman's breast.*

WOMAN   Oh!

FREDDIE   Oh, sorry. Very nice!

scene thirteen

The Great Outdoors

FREDDIE on the street.

PEDESTRIAN 1 and 2 play a bevy of characters, an urban whirlwind around FREDDIE.

PEDESTRIAN 1   Excuse me—

PEDESTRIAN 2   Taxi, taxi—

PEDESTRIAN 1 speaks into a cellphone.

PEDESTRIAN 1   I want that delivered by 3. Are you listening to me? Are you listening to me?

FREDDIE   What?

PEDESTRIAN 2   Hey lady, got any spare change?

FREDDIE takes off her knapsack to look for change.

PEDESTRIAN 1   Would you like to buy some flowers?

FREDDIE turns and inadvertently bashes the flower lady in the gut with the knapsack. Flowers go everywhere.

PEDESTRIAN 2   Watch out for the doggy doo!

They all high step over it.

PEDESTRIAN 2 taps FREDDIE on the shoulder, indicates she is deaf and tries to sell FREDDIE an ASL alphabet.

FREDDIE   What?

PEDESTRIAN 1   Excuse me.

PEDESTRIAN 1 is trying to pass by FREDDIE and the deaf woman.

FREDDIE   Just a second.

The deaf woman signs again.

What!!

PEDESTRIAN 1   Excuse me!

FREDDIE   *(turns to PEDESTRIAN 1)* Just a second!!

The deaf woman taps FREDDIE on the shoulder again.

(turns to PEDESTRIAN 2) What!!!

PEDESTRIAN 1   What are you, blind?!

PEDESTRIAN 1 pushes past FREDDIE, spinning her around.

scene fourteen

Elevator Music

FREDDIE ends up in a crowded elevator.

ELEVATOR PASSENGER 1   Press three please.

Beat.

ELEVATOR PASSENGER 2   Press three, please.

FREDDIE is oblivious.

ELEVATOR PASSENGER 1   Could you press three, please?

ELEVATOR PASSENGER 2   Press three! For chrissakes!

ELEVATOR PASSENGER 2 pushes past FREDDIE to push the button herself.

ELEVATOR PASSENGER 1   Excuse me, I have to get out! This is my floor!

ELEVATOR PASSENGERS 1 & 2 exit the elevator, shoving FREDDIE out.

A WOMAN comes up to FREDDIE.

WOMAN   Freddie!! Freddie! Freddie, Freddie !!! Guess who. Guess! come on, guess, guess, guess who, guess who, come on, come on, guess!!!

FREDDIE freezes as we hear her name distort into a high pitched confusion.

scene fifteen

Denise's Cane Lesson

FREDDIE is standing with her cane instructor.

DENISE   Using a cane requires a whole new focus for movement than you used as a sighted person. The focus is lower, you gather information with your kinaesthetic sense, your ears, and your residual vision. To start, can I see your current technique with the cane?

FREDDIE tries to walk with the cane.

Okay, so you've got no technique. Don't even bother with the ID cane. I'm thinking a 48-inch Louis Hebert, with a roller tip and a golf club grip.

FREDDIE   I'm thinking the same thing, Denise.

DENISE   Good. Okay. Starting with your grip. Hold the cane in front of you and shake hands with it. Shake hands with your cane.

scene sixteen

Outdoors Again

FREDDIE walks down the street with her sunglasses on, tapping her cane rhythmically from side to side.

FREDDIE   Legally blind, criminally sighted. Blind, blind drunk, blind faith, blind as a bat, blindfold, Venetian blinds, Helen Keller, Stevie Wonder, John Milton, Oedipus, Three Mice, professional German Shepherds, piano tuners, piano tuners, piano tuners.

FREDDIE bumps into someone on the street.

GOTH GIRL   Watch it crap face.

FREDDIE   Sorry, I—

GOTH GIRL   I didn't know!

FREDDIE   What?

GOTH GIRL   You don't see?

FREDDIE   A bit.

GOTH GIRL   Are you blind?

FREDDIE   Partially. Mostly.

GOTH GIRL   *(to her FRIEND)* Is she blind?

FRIEND   She just told you. She should know.

GOTH GIRL   I didn't know! Here, have some cigarettes.

FREDDIE   No, thank you.

GOTH GIRL   Here's three. I'm sorry. I didn't know. I'm not a bad person.

FREDDIE   I'm sure you're not.

GOTH GIRL   I'm sorry. You're nice.

A MAN comes up to FREDDIE.

MAN   Giss yer blind, eh.

FREDDIE   Partially.

MAN   I'd help the blind. Honestly I would. Honestly.

FREDDIE   I'm sure you would.

MAN   Sorry. *(The MAN describes the building across the street.)* Eeet's a brownish beeeelding witz layters on eet. *(as they cross the street)* Green now.

They walk.

Streetcar tracks—streetcar tracks. *(describing the building as they approach)*
Eet has white layters… gold treem and eeet say: Star Boooo—Star Buck. For
coffee—

> *FREDDIE turns to elude the man.*

—tea and things like donut—

> *At the corner, HEROINE WOMAN approaches FREDDIE at the crossing.*

HEROINE WOMAN   Oh, I'll tell you when you can cross.

FREDDIE   That's okay, I can handle traffic.

HEROINE WOMAN   It's still red, still red, still reeeeeeeeeeeed—GREEN! Here,
I'll take you.

FREDDIE   No, it's okay, I'm fine.

HEROINE WOMAN   I can't see very well, either. There's a haematoma in my left
eye. My boyfriend Jerry hit me upside the head. Okay about five feet from the
curb, ready, two three one, STEP!

FREDDIE   Okay, I'm stopping for the streetcar now so I'll just say 'bye.

HEROINE WOMAN   How did you know it was a streetcar stop?

FREDDIE   I can see sort of.

HEROINE WOMAN   Can you see colour? My boyfriend says he's colour blind,
says he can't do the laundry cause he'll mix it up.

FREDDIE   I think he's lying.

HEROINE WOMAN   Can you tell what I look like?

FREDDIE   Nooo, because I can just sense auras.

HEROINE WOMAN   What's mine?

FREDDIE   Lime green. Take care of that eye.

> *An OLD MAN approaches.*

OLD MAN   *(loud)* God bless you.

FREDDIE   Thank you. God bless you.

OLD MAN   I delivered boxes to the CNIB for 49 years.

FREDDIE   Goodness.

OLD MAN   Wife worked there. Taught making fridge magnets.

FREDDIE   Well, goodness me.

OLD MAN   Couldn't think of anything worse than what you've got.

FREDDIE   Well, maybe you're not thinking hard enough.

OLD MAN   Eh?

FREDDIE   There's death.

OLD MAN   Eh? God bless you.

FREDDIE   And bless God you and thank God this is my stop.

scene seventeen

Dining with My Girl

FREDDIE and KATHERINE are at a restaurant.

THE ENTITY appears behind the scrim, FREDDIE's private shadow.

FREDDIE   So I'm walking here and some guy walks by and I ask him if there's a variety store nearby. I don't have my cane with me but of course there's a store right behind me. So the guy probably thought I was a lunkhead. So I wander my way into the store and there's all these tough gas station men in there and they're wanting to help me. I kept saying no, then blankly staring in hopes of any toiletry section or Kleenex. Eventually I knew I had to ask the guy behind the counter. "Excuse me, do you have Tampax?" Dead silence. "Tampax, do you carry Tampax?" "What's Tampax?" "Tampax, Tampax tampons, in a small box?" "Oh no, we don't carry that sort of thing, but, um, we do have Certs!" *(She starts laughing.)*

KATHERINE   They've finally got spicy Thai bundles on the menu.

FREDDIE   What am I gonna do with a packet of Certs? I'm not sure they'll work very well.

KATHERINE   Do you want a salad? I think I'm going to have a salad tonight.

FREDDIE   Ah, yeah, I'll have the unscented breath mints with the flushable applicator, please?

KATHERINE   The goat cheese salad is $6.50 and the pear salad is $6.25.

FREDDIE   Ha ha ha. *(pause)* Well, I thought it was funny.

KATHERINE   Oh rats, the Thai Bundles are made with peanut oil. I can't have that. Oh and they've taken my favourite bean dip off the menu.

FREDDIE   Well, that's just terrible. Does it devastate you?

KATHERINE   No, I'll find an alternative. It wouldn't be very smart if I didn't. It would be senseless not to eat just because what I wanted was no longer available.

FREDDIE   I think I'll have the Thai Bundles.

KATHERINE   That's nice of you to order something that would put me into surgery.

FREDDIE   Since when did you have your sense of humour surgically removed?

KATHERINE   I did not have my sense of humour surgically removed.

FREDDIE   Well, you're a real Thai bundle of laughs tonight.

KATHERINE   You know, strangely enough, hearing stories about you wandering around without your cane somehow doesn't strike my funny bone.

FREDDIE   Well, that wasn't the point of my story.

KATHERINE   Well, that's what I got out of it.

FREDDIE   It's a funny story about buying Tampax!

KATHERINE   Yeah, it's especially funny that you didn't have your cane. Ha! Maybe next time you go out for toilet paper, you'll get hit by a bus. That'll be hilarious!

FREDDIE   Well, I guess I'm just a big suck. Why would I want to leave my cane behind? I should love using it, it's just a big white stick. I'm sure everyone has one! Sure! Hey, why don't you go out with a big cashew on your head and a sign that says "I'm allergic to peanut oil"?!

KATHERINE   That is so ridiculous. *(They begin to laugh together.)*

FREDDIE   I just have this clear image of you with a big nut coming out of your head.

KATHERINE   Yeah, I could hang around with coconut and I'd be trail mix.

FREDDIE   Ha!

KATHERINE   Wipe your right arm, you've just got a bit of butter smeared on it.

scene eighteen

Encore Diner

In the restaurant. KATHERINE and FREDDIE are at a table.

THE ENTITY is still with them.

KATHERINE   Feel like salad or entrée?

FREDDIE   I'm kind of hungry. Do they have that noodle thing?

KATHERINE   Think so.

FREDDIE   I'll have that. How was your day?

KATHERINE   Hard. I'm tired.

FREDDIE   Wait. What's the soup?

KATHERINE   Black bean.

FREDDIE   I'll have that.

KATHERINE   Did you go to the library today and get signed up?

FREDDIE   No. I went, but I can't just sign up. I have to get a medical form filled out.

KATHERINE   Oh, did you bring it with you?

FREDDIE   No. Look, it doesn't matter. I need a doctor to sign it anyway, so it's going to take a while.

KATHERINE   Well, I can help you if you want.

FREDDIE   No, there's really nothing you can do. I just have to put the date on it or something.

KATHERINE   Oh.

Pause.

FREDDIE   I wiped out on the steps when I was leaving. Can you see a bruise here?

KATHERINE   Yeah.

FREDDIE   Is it bad?

KATHERINE   Yeah.

FREDDIE   You didn't say anything.

KATHERINE   No.

FREDDIE   Okay.

KATHERINE   What am I going to say?

FREDDIE   Oh, I don't know. How about; "Why don't you use your cane?" "Why don't you be more careful?" "Why don't you get a guide dog?" "Why don't you get a little volunteer from the CNIB?" Why don't YOU finish your thesis?

KATHERINE   Do you want wine?

FREDDIE   Yeah.

KATHERINE   Red?

FREDDIE   Sure.

KATHERINE   A half litre, then, cause I'll have some too.

KATHERINE turns to find a waiter.

scene nineteen

Shrink

In the psychiatrist's office with DR. SONDRA.

THE ENTITY appears behind the scrim and mirrors DR. SONDRA.

FREDDIE I, ah, thought it was time to get some support, and deal with some of the, um, inside stuff. I guess, I, well, there's not a lot of, I mean, you know, my mother, and um… I do swim a lot.

DR. SONDRA You'd like to have an appointment.

FREDDIE Yeah, that would be good. I'd like to come weekly.

DR. SONDRA Or more if necessary. Mondays and Wednesdays at 3?

FREDDIE Good, fine.

scene twenty

Dining, Wining and Running

At the restaurant.

THE ENTITY watches KATHERINE and FREDDIE at the table.

KATHERINE Aren't you going to eat something?

FREDDIE No.

Pause.

KATHERINE Has the library called you yet with the books?

FREDDIE Yup. This wine tastes funny. Here, taste it.

She gives it to KATHERINE.

KATHERINE Tastes all right to me. It's not like it's a twelve dollar glass.

FREDDIE Hmmm. Tastes funny to me.

KATHERINE Do you want to send it back?

FREDDIE No.

KATHERINE Would you like my beer instead?

FREDDIE No, keep your beer. Why should you drink skanky wine?

KATHERINE I don't find it skanky.

FREDDIE It's skanky.

KATHERINE What books did you order?

FREDDIE   One Charles Dickens, a children's book. Some Canadian plays.

KATHERINE   That's great. When do you get them?

FREDDIE   I've got them already.

KATHERINE   Are they good?

FREDDIE   I don't know. Not really, I mean, it's someone else's voice. It's not like it's reading.

KATHERINE   Maybe you'll get used to it.

FREDDIE   I think there's cork in my glass.

KATHERINE   Let's see—no, I don't see anything.

FREDDIE   How was your baseball game?

KATHERINE   It was fun. We lost, of course, but it didn't matter. I hit a homer.

FREDDIE   Great. And you had your film class last night?

KATHERINE   Yeah, we watched "Bringing Up Baby."

FREDDIE   Great! I hear that's funny.

KATHERINE   It's so funny! I'm not sure if you'd like it though, it's quite visual.

FREDDIE   Well, I'm sure I would like it if I could see it. I'm not sure I'm going to come over Sunday.

KATHERINE   I bought large print cards so you could play.

FREDDIE   Oh, well, that was kind. Thank you. I just don't think I'm going to feel like playing cards on Sunday.

KATHERINE   How do you know? It's Tuesday.

FREDDIE   Um, I think I'll feel like, um, maybe taking a bus somewhere out of town for the day.

KATHERINE   Where are you going to go?

FREDDIE   Wawa, I think, Wawa, maybe, or Puslinch. I like Puslinch.

KATHERINE   Do you know the place?

FREDDIE   I've driven through it years ago. It's small, historical.

KATHERINE   And the bus goes there.

FREDDIE   I think there's a Go train.

KATHERINE   Even better.

scene twenty-one

Shrink II

At DR. SONDRA's office.

THE ENTITY appears behind the scrim and mirrors DR. SONDRA.

FREDDIE   It has nothing to do with my sight.

DR. SONDRA   Well, you seem quite anxious about something.

FREDDIE   I'm just thinking I have a hard time with commitment. I like things to be what they are, not some contract, you know, sign here on the dotted line.

DR. SONDRA   That sounds like a trap.

FREDDIE   Yes, yes I guess so.

DR. SONDRA   Is it possible that someone might be in that position with you without feeling trapped?

FREDDIE   They can always leave if they want to. I don't expect anyone to commit to me, not now anyway.

DR. SONDRA   Why not now?

FREDDIE   Because I'm going blind. Someday I won't be going blind, I'll just be blind and then it'll be okay.

DR. SONDRA   What will be okay?

FREDDIE   To commit to me. Once I'm blind, it'll be over.

DR. SONDRA   What will be over?

scene twenty-two

In a Diner

FREDDIE sits and listens.

FREDDIE   The waitress clanks down ashtrays. Clicking lighter behind to my left. Busy eaters and, "there you go." Not much talking in here. A radio blares. Shuffling of feet. An elderly man—homeless, maybe? Money crunches. It even sounds cold. How many times can one person sniffle during one meal? How many sniffles can you detect in one room? Velcro. The Cadillac of goofy sounds. The older ladies are gathering for tea in the upper left corner. I decide to take a peek. Silhouettes. Shapes blurring the window light and nothing more. The world is becoming an old photograph right before my eyes. The ladies' voices are so full, so rich with history and detail. "I'm schtarvin' Edna, just schtarvt." Beauty basks in the comfy schmoosh of these overly-soft leather benches. Mid afternoon. My favourite muffin. Ecstasy lives.

The lights fade.

scene twenty-three

A Hospital Room

FREDDIE sits in the middle of the space. A TECHNICIAN stands behind her.

TECHNICIAN   Look at this picture. Tell me what you see.

FREDDIE does not look.

FREDDIE   Oh no. A bunch of dots?

TECHNICIAN   Look at the picture.

Pause. FREDDIE looks.

FREDDIE   Smudge. I don't even really see the dots any more.

scene twenty-four

Shrink III

At the DR. SONDRA's office.

THE ENTITY appears behind the scrim and mirrors DR. SONDRA.

DR. SONDRA   How did you make out with the anti-depressants?

FREDDIE   Not very well.

DR. SONDRA   What happened?

FREDDIE   Well, you gave me drugs for the sadness and drugs to make me sleep.

DR. SONDRA   The anti-depressants can give you sleep disorders.

FREDDIE   Yes, and at the same time I was taking antibiotics for an infection.

DR. SONDRA   Well, that shouldn't be a problem.

FREDDIE   No, except when you mix them all up and take the wrong dosage of everything when you think it's something else!

DR. SONDRA   Well, why would you do that?

FREDDIE   Because I can't see! *(THE ENTITY now crosses upstage of the scrim, she is blinded.)* I overdosed on Prozac, I underdosed on the sleeping pills. I completely forgot to take the antibiotics at all! I landed in emergency after collapsing in a big twitching sweat! As for the infection, well, let's not even go there!

DR. SONDRA   I suppose now you're going to think drugs are bad, won't try any more. *(THE ENTITY returns mirroring DR. SONDRA.)*

FREDDIE   Yeah, right, forget it.

DR. SONDRA   You had a bad experience because you didn't take the time to organize yourself. You didn't have to mix up your pills.

FREDDIE   No, I didn't have to mix up my pills but I did.

DR. SONDRA   You can't help yourself until you're feeling better.

FREDDIE   I don't want them, for fuck's sake! Ooops. For heaven's sake.

> *Speaking simultaneously.*

DR. SONDRA   You can swear in here./

THE ENTITY   You can say Fuck./

FREDDIE   Oh. Thank you. Fuck.

scene twenty-five

Hi There. Fuck You.

FREDDIE is at home on the phone, leaving a voicemail.

FREDDIE   Hello, doctor? I am leaving you a message and I would prefer that you don't return my call. Thank you for the time you've given me. I've decided that our therapy relationship has come to an impasse and I don't see the point in continuous conflict over what is best for me. I'm cancelling my next week's appointment and I will not be making any more. Goodbye. *(pause)* She told me I could swear in her office. Maybe I should have said "Hi there. Fuck you."

scene twenty-six

Positive Thinking

THE ENTITY lifts FREDDIE up onto one shoulder.

FREDDIE   Ladies and Gentlemen of the House and Garden Positive Thinking Society, how honoured I am that you have asked me here today to speak on the power of positive thinking and how it has affected my journey of loss. I'd like to begin by saying that losing your sight positively sucks. I think this. I'm positive about it. It's absolute, positive shite. Thank you. Any questions? Good.

> *Blackout.*

> *In the dark we hear loud "Look out."*

scene twenty-seven

In Freddie's Room

KATHERINE stands.

FREDDIE lies in bed, under the duvet.

THE ENTITY crouches behind her, holding onto the bed which she moves for FREDDIE throughout the scene.

KATHERINE $300. I just spent $300 on this weekend and now you don't want to go!

FREDDIE   Sorry.

KATHERINE   What is wrong with you?! You wanted to get out of the city for weeks. We picked this weekend. I go. I get a car. I take time off work and now you've changed your mind!

FREDDIE   I didn't change my mind.

KATHERINE   Last week you wanted to go, today you don't. I would say that's changing your mind.

FREDDIE   It's not my mind! I think you should go without me.

KATHERINE   Okay, just get out of bed, put your shoes on. Right there. Right there!

FREDDIE puts her shoes on, then goes back to bed.

Freddie, get up!

KATHERINE grabs her arm.

FREDDIE   No!! Stand back please.

FREDDIE pulls away.

KATHERINE   Okay, I'm back. About two feet to your left.

FREDDIE   I was trying to do something nice for you. I went to IGA. I wanted to surprise you. Now it's all over Bathurst St.

I was walking home up Bathurst carrying all these bags of stuff.

Little baby corns for the spinach salad. A bundt cake. A voice yelled "Look out!" like really loud. (*THE ENTITY shouts "Look Out" to FREDDIE.*) "LOOK OUT!" I jumped. It startled me. The bags went flying. The tomatoes started rolling across the sidewalk. I just start grabbing them. The voice yells, (*THE ENTITY yells to FREDDIE.*) "YOU'RE ON THE STREET!" So I drop everything, the mushrooms and the *Pet Rock* magazine I bought for us, and then I realize I'm not on the street, I'm on the sidewalk. So I just sort of stand there and say "Asshole!" I try to find the mushroom bag, but I can't find it. So I give up and just keep walking. About a block later I hear him again. And this time, I catch a glimpse of his coat, circling me. I can see him because he's on the outside, running ahead and circling. I turn, put my cane in the air and I tell him "I'll beat the shit out of you if you come anywhere near me again."

Half a block later, there he is again, hiding behind something on the sidewalk. Now, that the boy is nearly dead at this point—I stand there and I contemplate how I will kill him with my cane.

KATHERINE   So what happened?

FREDDIE   *(back in bed)* I ducked into a store and tricked him into thinking I was crossing the road.

KATHERINE   So he was gone after that?

FREDDIE   Yeah, I guess so. Right now I hate everybody and in this condition I think it's best for everybody if I remain still, under a duvet, unstartled.

KATHERINE   Would you like some tea?

FREDDIE   I would like some tea.

KATHERINE   Would you like an Arrowroot cookie?

FREDDIE   I would like an Arrowroot cookie.

scene twenty-eight

The Dark Thief

FREDDIE sits in the dark.

THE ENTITY explores FREDDIE's face with a light.

FREDDIE   It's waiting for me. Lurking in the shadows. It's waiting for me to stop. Stop feeling, stop caring, stop wanting, stop loving. It would have me shrink. I can't escape it. It's inside of me.

FREDDIE catches a glimpse of THE ENTITY.

Suddenly, the lights go off. FREDDIE crawls across the floor in the darkness to find her coat. She stands and puts it on.

scene twenty-nine

Escape from The Dark Thief

The Dyke Bar. Dance music blares.

FREDDIE alone with her cane, alone at centre. She is nauseous, she stumbles, she collapses.

scene thirty

The Light Bearer

FREDDIE at a new THERAPIST's office (played by THE ENTITY).

THERAPIST I'm a little concerned about your reason for coming here. Your message said that your friend wanted you to come. When I hear that I hear "I don't really want to be here"

FREDDIE You have good hearing.

THERAPIST So why are you here?

FREDDIE I don't know. My life. It's not a bad life. I loved my life.

THERAPIST And now you're blind.

FREDDIE Look, I'm not blind. I can see. Differently than you, but I can see.

THERAPIST Yes. Quite differently. I'm a total.

FREDDIE A total what?

THERAPIST Blind. I'm totally blind.

> *Long pause. FREDDIE begins to cry.*

The Kleenex is down to your right.

scene thirty-one

Freddie's Room

It is quite dark. FREDDIE pulls papers and pencil from her knapsack and writes frantically in very large letters, a word per page.

With each word, THE ENTITY, upstage of the scrim, holds a card to the light.

DEAR
GOD
WHAT
ARE
YOU
FUCKING
THINKING.

> *KATHERINE appears dimly behind the scrim.*

KATHERINE Freddie?

FREDDIE *(suddenly)* I need to not see you so much.

Pause. It grows darker.

KATHERINE   Can you see my face?

FREDDIE   No. The light is too dark.

KATHERINE   Do you know that I'm crying?

FREDDIE   No, it's not in your voice. In the dark, I don't even know if you're still there. In fact, maybe you've quietly slipped away. *(pause)*

You see, you didn't say anything just now and I don't even know if you're there. *(pause)*

Is your face all squished up in horror. It is, isn't it. *(pause)*

It would be nice if you would tell me. I can't see, you know!

KATHERINE   Shut up! Just shut up! If you could see me you would know. You'd see the look on my face. You'd see my eyes and you would know. I'm sorry I don't have the words.

KATHERINE leaves.

FREDDIE sits alone. Night is falling. FREDDIE scrambles round the room, picking up the papers, putting on her coat and gathering her things.

THE ENTITY has entered the room and stops her from leaving. FREDDIE and THE ENTITY struggle. THE ENTITY, with great strength, pushes FREDDIE to the ground.

Finally, FREDDIE surrenders. In the darkness we hear a cry of pain.

THE ENTITY places her hand on FREDDIE's head. THE ENTITY exits.

FREDDIE is left lying on the floor.

The lights slowly brighten from here to the end.

scene thirty-two

A Different Hospital

FREDDIE wakens in a white room. There is a big window, which fills the room with light.

NURSE 1 and 2 appear upstage of the scrim.

NURSE 1   Hello, Frederica. How are you feeling this morning?

FREDDIE   Fine.

NURSE 1   You haven't come out of your room for several days.

FREDDIE   Oh.

NURSE 1   Can you spell world backwards?

FREDDIE   D L R…

NURSE 2   Hello, Freddie. How are you feeling this morning?

FREDDIE   Fine, thank you.

NURSE 2   Are you attending the seminar this afternoon? We're making fridge magnets at four.

FREDDIE   No, thank you.

NURSE 2   You haven't eaten in several days. Are you seeing things?

NURSE 1   Freddie, the police are coming to take you to our seminar. Fridge magnets at four.

FREDDIE   I don't need fridge magnets. I don't put little notes on my fridge any more.

NURSE 1 and 2 leave.

FREDDIE stands, looks out of the window. She watches out of the window for quite a while.

scene thirty-three

Elegy

FREDDIE stands front of the window.

FREDDIE   If I close my eyes and practice, practice feeling with my heart, my soul, my desire in the dark. If I practice and touch, practice and love I can stay with the light.

The sun is warm. It's always been warm.

My dear beloved sight.

You allowed me to feel freedom in my body. You protected me. You loved a clear goal and the passage forward. The five ball in the corner pocket, the end of the dirt path to the maple tree, the walk across the bar to the girl. Sight loved her best friend's smile, the space between her grandmother's front teeth, the red ring left on cigarette butts. The morning sun on the crystal water, the laughing reflections in the sky. Sight drank the world in so deeply that no passing can ever erase it. You did not live long, but you did live well. In peace may you find new life.

FREDDIE hears the geese flying overhead and sees them clearly with her ears. THE ENTITY watches the geese from upstage of the scrim.

Look at the geese.

The lights fade to darkness

The end.

Privilege

Corrina Hodgson

Introduction:
Privilege

Corrina Hodgson's *Privilege* (2004) revisits the "coming-out story" of the "disturbed" adolescent school girl by having her protagonist Ginny expose the prejudices which still surface when girls are discovered engaging in same-sex acts. Riffing on the ongoing denial of the existence of female-female sexual desire, Hodgson uses Ginny's situation to interrogate the stereotypical reactions to sexual activities that fall outside heteronormativity. However, she also makes it clear that Ginny's hallucinatory reactions are aimed at breaking down any kind of restrictive labelling that would explain away such joyful sexual experimentation.

First she sets up a deceptively realistic situation in which we watch the very articulate fourteen-year-old Ginny as she undergoes a therapy session with the psychologist Dr. Jameson in his carefully furnished office. The fact that she has to visit him in order to avoid being expelled from her Catholic private school establishes the basic premise that she is being put on trial for her, as yet unnamed, offense. But if everything points to Ginny as the psychopathic-pervert her mother Pam envisages, Ginny herself refuses to take on the labels that are proffered. Her smart-ass answers which get right to the point of owning up to the fact that she was making out with her friend Nat in the school bathroom immediately diffuse the shame she is supposed to feel. What emerges instead is that the real wound she is suffering from is her abandonment by her father who has recently left the family.

At the mercy of her friend, her mother, her school, her doctor and later, her lawyer, Ginny reverts to the world of her imagination. Characters appear and disappear at random depending on Ginny's thoughts. First, we realize that Ginny's mother Pam only materializes in the Doctor's office when Ginny feels her intrusive presence. Her very unreliability as a stage presence reinforces our sense of her chronic neglect and abuse of her daughter. Parallelling her career-driven mother's failure to mother her is the equally painful fact of her abandonment by her adored father. Ginny, for all her bravado, is revealed to us as someone who is lost in a maze that she can't make sense of. Much of the dramatic tension that we feel arises from the slippages that keep occurring as Ginny tries to negotiate her way through the memories and thoughts that crowd into her mind as she answers the Doctor's questions. Ginny's own inability to find a level of reality she can exist in is brought home when she leaves the Doctor's office to pay a visit to the other set location—Nat's bedroom—only to find that she has been banished from this space.

What the play captures is the maelstrom of bizarre imaginings that she falls into as a result of the fact that her experiences have been both vilified and erased from existence. Framing her excursions into an endless series of hallucinatory visions of all the possible permutations and combinations of sexual behaviours that the other characters might or could perform is the moment when Dr. Jameson steps out of the office to take a call during their session. This temporary abandonment leads her into spinning a whole set of scenarios which all portray him as a sexual deviant who preys on adolescent girls. The most coherent through-line that this stereotyping leads to is her flirtation with him and the ensuing accusation she makes against him of sexual assault when he rejects her advances. As she imagines the entire scenario where his reputation is entirely destroyed, she brings into focus the ridiculous discrepancies between the responses to her accusations against him for his alleged advances to her, and the accusations against her for her sexual act with Nat. With typical fourteen-year-old logic, she asks why her lies about him would be believed when the truth of what she and Nat did cannot even be countenanced.

But she is just as relentless in refusing to play the defence card that her pushy dyke lawyer tries to impose upon her when she insists that Ginny self-identify as a lesbian to improve her chances of winning her court case against the Doctor. Ginny's hallucinatory excursions into the policing of sexual behaviours are intercut with her nightmarish reactions to her friend Nat's obsession with prom night. Finally these scenes become completely intertwined after Ginny attacks the Doctor with her vibrator, and rushes Nat at her prom. Then Elaine and the Doctor meet and play an extended scene where Elaine gets to interrogate the Doctor who role-plays Ginny, followed by one in which the Doctor puts Ginny on trial for her sexual deviance. By the time the characters have begun to role-play each other, the frenzy has mounted to the place where everyone has come under attack—except possibly Nat who continues to look for the conventional outcome.

When the parentheses ends as Ginny comes to the realization that everyone is scared about their own sexuality, she returns to her session with Dr. Jameson and learns that she has misinterpreted his actions and that he really is the kind supportive single dad that she wishes she had. It is at this point that Ginny finally gets "real" as she exits to Nat's bedroom. She and Nat now replay the original incident where they make love. Full of youthful joy and innocent experimentation, the scene forces us to recontextualize everything that has happened before.

photo by Jill Boettger

Corrina Hodgson

Bio and Artist's Statement

Corrina Hodgson is a Toronto-based playwright whose works have been produced across Canada (Toronto, Winnipeg, Edmonton, Calgary, Kamloops, Vancouver) and the United States (Seattle, Allentown, Off-off Broadway), as well as on CBC Radio One. She is the past winner of the Jane Chambers International Playwriting Competition, The Solo Collective's Monologue Competition, and Theatre BC's National Playwriting Competition. Corrina teaches a playwriting class called "Subverting the Canon: Writing Plays as though Race, Class, Gender, and Sexual Orientation Mattered." She is a graduate of UBC's MFA in Creative Writing, and has been a part of professional playwriting units at the University of Lethbridge, Buddies in Bad Times Theatre, and Nightwood Theatre.

•

I don't know what got me started thinking about things, but in 2001, I was suddenly obsessed with how young women's sexuality was represented in theatre. From my perception, young women's sexuality was either entirely ignored, or portrayed as something to be taken advantage of. In the plays I read, young women were either asexual, or victimized. A young woman saying, "I'm horny," was unacceptable, but that same young woman saying, "I was raped," became a voice that could not be argued with. I wanted to create a play that broke this dyad, and sat down to work on *Privilege*. It is my hope that the audiences who see it experience a young woman who, while confused about her identity, is not victimized by her sexuality—a young woman who not only knows about vibrators, but has the guts to steal one, and knows that it is the best present you can give a friend. And, ultimately, a young woman who recognizes that while being queer is scary, it's just as scary—and, therefore, just as normal—as anyone else's sexual awakening. Finally, with the decision to move that first scene between Nat and Ginny to the end of the play, it is my hope that audiences recognize how ultimately joyful a young woman's experience of climbing into bed with another woman is, and how tragically society can screw it all up.

Production Information

Privilege was first produced as *Unbecoming* as part of the SummerWorks Theatre Festival (Toronto), in the backspace of Theatre Passe Muraille, in 2004, with the following company:

GINNY	Jordana Commisso
NATALIE	Lindsey Clark
DR. JAMESON	Larry Smith
PAM/ELAINE	Lesley Dowey
Production Dramaturge	Corrina Hodgson
Textual Dramaturge	Amanda McCoy

Characters

Ginny, 14 years old. A very bright, very troubled young woman. Has just been forced into therapy at the beginning of the play.

Dr. Thomas Jameson, Ginny's psychologist. A warm man in his early to mid 40s, Dr. Jameson has seen it all and heard it all. He has endless patience and a nice sense of humour. It should be easy for an audience to see how a young woman could fall for him.

Natalie Collins, 14 years old. Ginny's best friend and classmate. Natalie may be lacking Ginny's large intellect, but she understands society and wants more than anything else to fit into it.

Pam, Ginny's mother. A heavy-drinking, professional woman who obviously has no idea how to begin to parent a child like Ginny. Pam has turned bitterness into an art form. Her husband has just left her and she's convinced her child will be the death of her.

Elaine Cooperman, Ginny's lawyer in Act Two. A hip, urban professional woman with a knack for double speak.

Note: The same actor plays Pam and Elaine.

PRIVILEGE

scene one

The stage is divided into two worlds. On one side is an office. On the other, a bedroom.

The office has all the markings of a successful psychology practice. Degrees framed on the wall, a large van Gogh painting, two plush chairs, and an almost overpowering wood desk. A laptop computer and various files adorn the desk.

DR. JAMESON sits on one of the chairs. GINNY, 14, stands near his desk. She is in a private school uniform—kilt and blouse. Her backpack is slung over one shoulder.

GINNY's mother, PAM, appears behind GINNY.

DR. JAMESON   So, Ginny, what brings you here today?

GINNY   My mother.

PAM   Behave.

GINNY   She drove me.

DR. JAMESON   Does your mother usually drive you places?

GINNY   Well, let's see. I'm one year and seven months away from being allowed to drive legally, and I may be into a lot of different things, but doing time for hot-wiring my own mother's car isn't one of them, so YEAH, she tends to drive me places. You gonna analyze that for some deeper meaning?

PAM   *(to DR. JAMESON)* Do you see how it is?

GINNY plops into a chair.

DR. JAMESON   We have more pertinent things to discuss, don't we, Ginny?

GINNY   My friends call me Ginny. You're not my friend.

PAM   Virginia. Really.

DR. JAMESON   Would you rather I call you Virginia?

GINNY   No. I'd rather you didn't call me anything at all.

DR. JAMESON   I have a daughter your age. Olivia. Her mother and I call her Liddy. To everyone else she's Olivia.

GINNY   Fine, call me Olivia.

DR. JAMESON   Do you smoke? You're welcome to smoke here, if you wish.

PAM   She does not smoke.

GINNY   I'm not old enough to smoke.

PAM   It has nothing to do with your age.

DR. JAMESON   I suspect you're capable of many things beyond your age. You tested very bright. IQ 148. 150 is genius.

GINNY   I missed it by TWO points?

PAM   Might as well have been twenty. If you missed it, you missed it. I need a cup of tea.

> *PAM exits.*

DR. JAMESON   You're obviously an intelligent young woman.

GINNY   Isn't gonna help me much if I'm expelled in Ninth Grade, now is it?

DR. JAMESON   Your mother told me that you weren't—

GINNY   Yeah, yeah. She stepped in. Saved my butt with a big fat cheque, so as I'm only suspended.

DR. JAMESON   But you still wear your uniform?

GINNY   Oh, I still have to go to school. Just not allowed to go to class. How much do you cost?

DR. JAMESON   One hundred dollars per session.

GINNY   That's not bad. My mother thinks I'm worth a hundred bucks an hour, huh?

DR. JAMESON   I'm sure your mother would not put an hourly price on your worth.

GINNY   Oh. So it's you who does that?

DR. JAMESON   The exchange of money between a psychologist and his, or her, client ensures that the relationship is professional rather than personal.

GINNY   What's wrong with personal relationships?

DR. JAMESON   Personal relationships are inappropriate in a therapeutic setting.

> *Pause.*

Why don't you tell me why you were suspended?

GINNY   Like you don't already know? Like my mother didn't tell you?

DR. JAMESON   I would like to hear it from you.

GINNY   What'd she tell you?

DR. JAMESON   (*opening the file*) One day last month, I believe it was a Tuesday, during lunch hour—

GINNY   Without your notes. If you can.

DR. JAMESON   (*closing the file*) You were caught in a fight with a classmate.

> *GINNY walks around the office, poking at objects.*

GINNY   A fight with a classmate, huh? Were those her exact words?

DR. JAMESON   I'd have to consult my notes for her EXACT—

GINNY   You don't have to play nice. I was caught pounding the CRAP outta a classmate. Isn't that what my mother told you?

DR. JAMESON   Not in so many words.

GINNY   But it wasn't just a "fight," was it?

DR. JAMESON   No.

GINNY   I knew it. My mum hasta make everything EXCITING.

DR. JAMESON   So your mother lied to me. Why?

GINNY   (*picking up a photo from DR. JAMESON's desk*) This your wife and kid?

DR. JAMESON   That's Julia and Olivia, yes.

GINNY   You ever lied about Olivia?

DR. JAMESON   Not intentionally.

GINNY   What would she have to do, for you to lie about her? Something shameful. Something that embarrassed you.

DR. JAMESON   Do you think your mother is ashamed of you?

GINNY   I think she's embarrassed by me.

DR. JAMESON   Your fighting embarrasses her?

GINNY   A girl fighting would embarrass my mother, sure. But I already TOLD you that's not what happened. You're not very good at this listening thing, are you?

DR. JAMESON   What did happen?

> *Pause.*

I'm listening.

> *GINNY walks back to the chair and sits in it.*
>
> *PAM appears.*

GINNY   Last month—you're right, it was a Tuesday—I was caught making out with a classmate in the bathroom.

> *PAM exits.*

Way worse than beating someone up, wouldn't you say?

DR. JAMESON   Actually, I'd say it was pretty normal.

GINNY   Oh, would you?

DR. JAMESON   Girls your age are naturally curious about sex, and—

GINNY   I'm tainted, if you ask Sister Mary Henry.

DR. JAMESON   Is she the one who caught you?

GINNY   Oh yeah. Thought she was gonna have a freakin' heart attack on the spot. Acting like she's never seen anything like that before. Or done it. I mean, please, everyone knows Nuns are lezzies.

DR. JAMESON   Are you?

GINNY   Does it matter?

DR. JAMESON   That's your decision.

GINNY   Well, I don't think it does. We were just fooling around. I mean, I was just hanging out with Nat.

DR. JAMESON   Nat?

GINNY   Natalie Collins. The classmate. My co-conspirator. Although she's not getting any grief.

DR. JAMESON   Why don't you tell me about your father?

> *Pause.*

Your parents are divorced, is that right?

> *Pause.*

Your mother told me that your father disappeared about three months ago. And that just before he left, he took you on a camping trip. Is that right? Ginny?

GINNY   I TOLD you, only my friends call me Ginny.

> *Pause.*

DR. JAMESON   I'm getting the feeling that you don't want to talk about your father.

GINNY   You're not so stupid after all.

> *GINNY meanders about the office, then stops at the laptop on his desk.*
>
> *DR. JAMESON gets up and stands beside her.*

This is nice. Can you burn CDs on it?

DR. JAMESON   I wouldn't know.

> *GINNY tries to open the laptop, but DR. JAMESON holds it down.*

So if your father is off limits, what *would* you like to talk about?

> *GINNY sits.*

> *DR. JAMESON stays at his computer. He presses some buttons.*

GINNY   You're not really married, are you?

DR. JAMESON   You don't think so?

GINNY   No. I KNOW you're not married. I know you live in a small brownstone apartment on Rosemount Drive with Olivia. I wonder if you ever *were* married? Maybe you were and maybe one day your wife woke up and decided that she didn't love you or Olivia anymore and just took off.

DR. JAMESON   Is that what happened with your father?

GINNY   Don't you wanna know how I know all that?

DR. JAMESON   I assume you looked it up in the phone book.

GINNY   I was a bit surprised, I hafta admit. I thought you wouldn't be listed, being a shrink and all. But then, you're not a real shrink, are you? Psychologist, not psychiatrist. Is your wife dead?

DR. JAMESON   We're separated. The divorce hasn't gone through yet.

GINNY   But Olivia gets to live with you?

DR. JAMESON   For now. Would you like to be living with your father?

GINNY   What if I did? Its not like he wants to live with me.

DR. JAMESON   How do you know that?

> *Pause.*

Have you asked him?

GINNY   I'd have to find him first, wouldn't I? Besides, I'm not pretty like Olivia.

DR. JAMESON   You're a very pretty girl.

GINNY   You probably have to say that. It's part of what you get paid for.

DR. JAMESON   I don't get paid to lie to my clients.

GINNY   No. But you probably don't get paid to tell them they're ugly either.

> *GINNY steps into NATALIE COLLINS's bedroom. GINNY looks around for her friend, but she is not there. As GINNY turns to leave, NAT enters.*

NAT   What're you doing here?

GINNY   What d'you mean? This is what I do. I come here.

NAT   Yeah, well. You can't anymore.

>*GINNY returns to DR. JAMESON's office. Her mother is collapsed in the chair that GINNY was sitting in.*

GINNY   Nice. Got another "A" today. French. 89. One off A+. I know it's still not an A+, only an A. D'you think you could make it to the Science Fair? Mum?

>*PAM moans lightly.*

Dahling. So lovely to see you. I would love to stay and chat but truly, your life is so terribly boring I don't think I could stand it. Just have another drink and write me another cheque, would you, dahling? Toodle-oo.

>*PAM opens her eyes.*

Oh, sorry.

PAM   Ginny?

GINNY   No. It's the Easter Bunny.

PAM   Well, good to see you're in your usual high spirits. Be a doll and get me some water.

GINNY   Do you want to know what I did today?

PAM   *(pause)* Was it something important?

GINNY   No.

PAM   Because you know how I hate forgetting important things.

>*Pause.*

Was I supposed to drive you somewhere?

GINNY   No.

PAM   It wasn't one of your violin things, was it?

GINNY   No, Mum. That's at the end of the year.

PAM   Ginny, I don't have time for these games. This Peterson case is going to keep me reading all night and—

GINNY   It's the Science Fair, okay? It's a stupid Science Fair.

PAM   Did you place?

GINNY   No.

PAM   Well then why would I want—

GINNY   We haven't been judged yet.

PAM Let me know when you are. I'm sure you'll do well. You always do.

> *GINNY plops into the chair and resumes her session with DR. JAMESON.*

DR. JAMESON You used to spend a lot of time with your father.

GINNY Used to. Past tense.

DR. JAMESON What did you do together?

GINNY Father-daughter stuff.

DR. JAMESON And what do fathers and daughters do?

GINNY If you have to ask, I pity your daughter.

> *Pause.*

I don't know. We used to fly kites. We make our own.

DR. JAMESON Did you make a kite the last weekend you went camping with your father?

GINNY Yeah.

DR. JAMESON What else did you do?

GINNY We went fishing. I caught two bass. Landed them by myself.

DR. JAMESON Did your father say anything? Or maybe do something? Something unusual?

> *Pause.*

Ginny?

> *There is a loud knock on the door.*

Will you excuse me?

GINNY Yeah, sure.

> *DR. JAMESON exits. He can be heard talking offstage in a stern, but muffled voice.*
>
> *PAM appears. She looks around, confused that DR. JAMESON is not there.*

PAM Well, isn't this the height of professionalism. He's left the little psychopath alone.

GINNY I'm not a psychopath.

PAM Just a pervert.

GINNY Thanks, Mum.

PAM   Grab your stuff.

GINNY   I'm in the middle of something here—

PAM   I'm not in the mood for games. I have a terrible headache—

GINNY   Hangover.

PAM   I've been in court all morning.

> *PAM opens DR. JAMESON's laptop and clucks her dismay.*

Good Lord. I should phone the police.

> *GINNY looks over her mother's shoulder. She's shocked and intrigued.*

That's the truth about the man who you think is helping you. Now will you come with me, please?

> *GINNY continues to stare at the laptop. Suddenly she realizes she can't hear Dr. Jameson talking anymore. She panics and runs back to her seat. As she sits DR. JAMESON re-enters.*

DR. JAMESON   Sorry about that.

GINNY   Whatever.

DR. JAMESON   So, where were we?

GINNY   You wanted to know if I was having sex with my father.

> *Pause.*

Only you said it better. Nicer.

DR. JAMESON   Your mother is concerned.

GINNY   My mother is ALWAYS concerned. Doesn't mean anything.

DR. JAMESON   When you got back from camping with your father, did you try to kill yourself?

GINNY   Is that what she told you?

DR. JAMESON   She told me that you attempted suicide by swallowing a bottle of Tylenol.

GINNY   Wow. I'm impressed. She's never said that before. She's always called it my "accident."

DR. JAMESON   Did you try to kill yourself?

GINNY   No. I just wanted her to stop drinking and pay some attention.

DR. JAMESON   Your mother drinks?

GINNY   Like a fish. Unless she has something or someone to distract her. And once my father took off, it was up to me.

DR. JAMESON That was a pretty dangerous way to get your mother to sober up.

> *Pause.*

GINNY You don't really wanna talk about this, do you?

DR. JAMESON And what do I want to talk about?

GINNY Sex?

DR. JAMESON What would you like to talk about with regards to sex?

GINNY Do you think I'm sexually attractive?

DR. JAMESON I—I don't know that that is an appropriate question for me to answer.

GINNY Why not? Why is something sexual automatically something bad?

DR. JAMESON Well… well, it's not.

GINNY So?

> *Once again the lights come up on NAT's bedroom. NAT sits on her bed, pinning a pattern onto soft pink satin material. GINNY enters.*

NAT You can't be here.

GINNY That's just school.

NAT It's not just school, Ginny. It's, like, life. I think you should go home.

GINNY And I think YOU should go back to BEING MY FRIEND, Nat.

NAT Shhhhh.

GINNY I didn't DO anything you didn't WANT.

NAT So what? So this is all MY fault?

GINNY No. But it's not mine, either.

NAT I know.

GINNY So how come *you* didn't get in any trouble at school?

NAT I did.

GINNY You didn't get suspended, did ya?

NAT You probably talked back to them when they were yelling at you.

GINNY What'd you do? Cry?

> *NAT shifts uneasily from foot to foot.*

NAT Did you see? I picked the material for my prom dress.

> *NAT shows GINNY the pink satin.*

GINNY   It's real pretty.

NAT   You're lying I can tell.

GINNY   I saw you eating lunch with Eleanor Lightbody today.

NAT   Well I can't eat lunch with you, can I? Besides, Eleanor's okay.

GINNY   She's a stuck-up princess.

> *Pause.*

Did Robbie ask you?

NAT   Nah. Not yet.

GINNY   That's kinda an important step.

NAT   I KNOW.

> *Pause.*

I hafta go to chapel after lunch every day.

GINNY   And what? Pray for your soul? I hafta see this shrink.

NAT   A shrink?

GINNY   Well, he's like a shrink. I don't know what he is. I hafta talk to him.

NAT   About me?

GINNY   About everything.

NAT   Ginny. Are you going to tell him what we did?

GINNY   Nat, EVERYONE knows what we did. We got CAUGHT.

NAT   Yeah, but you can't keep talking about it, or no one'll ever forget.

GINNY   Don't worry. I'll tell him you were a friend. *(pause)* Cuz you WERE a friend. Once.

NAT   Is he cute?

GINNY   I hadn't thought of that.

NAT   Well is he?

GINNY   Yeah, I guess. He's old.

NAT   Old-old. Or just old-grown-up-old?

GINNY   Old-grown-up-old.

NAT   Cool.

> *Pause.*

GINNY   Nat? What are you doing?

NAT This is what girls DO. They talk about boys. They get married. They have babies. This is what we're SUPPOSED TO DO.

GINNY Really? Well have you decided where you and Robbie are going to do it?

NAT Omigod. Don't talk about THAT.

GINNY I thought it was what we were SUPPOSED TO DO. *(pause)* Besides, it's gonna happen.

NAT NO IT'S NOT.

GINNY I betcha he thinks it's gonna happen.

NAT He hasn't even asked me out yet.

GINNY So? You think that means he doesn't think about it?

NAT Do you think about it?

GINNY What?

NAT What.

GINNY Of course I do. Don't you?

NAT Maybe. Sometimes. Mostly I think of holding hands though. Or kissing.

GINNY Yeah. Me, too.

> There is a loud banging noise of someone drying pots in the kitchen below.

NAT Oh man. You gotta go.

GINNY Nat, we've been friends since kindergarten. Your mum's always liked me.

NAT Things are really messed right now.

GINNY Nat?

NAT Yeah?

GINNY You really wanna get married and have a baby?

NAT Totally. I mean, not right now.

GINNY Well, obviously.

> Pause.

If that's really what you want, then you're gonna hafta put out for Robbie.

NAT Why? Guys like to marry virgins.

GINNY Guys like to marry girls who pretend they're virgins.

NAT My mum was a virgin. She told me.

GINNY What else is she gonna tell you? *(pause)* You gonna tell your kid about you and me?

NAT Well, no... but that's different... that's...

> *NAT sits on her bed and resumes pinning the pattern.*

GINNY I almost forgot. I brought you something.

NAT My mum was a virgin, okay?

GINNY Okay.

NAT She's not like your mum. She doesn't lie.

GINNY OKAY.

> *Pause.*

NAT What'd you bring?

GINNY Close your eyes.

> *NAT closes her eyes. GINNY pulls out a "personal massage" device and places it in NAT's hand.*

NAT What is it?

GINNY Can you guess?

NAT No.

> *GINNY turns the device on. It buzzes and vibrates.*

Omigod! Shh. Shh. Shut it off. Omigod. What the hell is that?

GINNY It's a massage tool.

NAT For my... neck?

> *GINNY turns it on again.*

Omigod. You're too much. How much did this thing cost?

GINNY It was free.

NAT Free?

GINNY Uh-huh.

NAT What, they were giving out vibrators at the Bay today?

GINNY It's not a vibrator. It's a personal massage tool. For your neck.

NAT You stole it.

GINNY Uh-huh.

> *NAT looks at the vibrator in her hand. Turns it on and off a couple of times.*

It's yours.

NAT   Oh, no. Ginny, you hafta take it with you.

GINNY   I got it for you.

NAT   If I get caught with it—I'm in too much trouble already.

> *GINNY takes the vibrator and puts it back in her bag.*

It was really sweet of you, though.

GINNY   Yeah, well. Later, I guess.

> *GINNY returns to her session with DR. JAMESON.*

So? Why is something sexual automatically something bad?

> *Pause.*

You told me earlier that you thought I was pretty. Why is it okay for you to tell me that, but it's not okay to answer whether or not you think I'm sexually attractive?

DR. JAMESON   That's a very good question.

GINNY   So, do you?

DR. JAMESON   I'm still not sure that I'm entirely comfortable with it.

GINNY   Never mind. I already know. I'm a pervert, I'm tainted. Nothing I haven't heard already.

DR. JAMESON   Ginny—

GINNY   Do you touch your daughter?

DR. JAMESON   How do you mean?

GINNY   I mean do you TOUCH her? Do you hug her? Do you kiss her?

DR. JAMESON   Within the boundaries of a normal parent-child—

GINNY   YES. You don't have to pervert everything you know.

DR. JAMESON   No, of course not. I mean…. Yes. Yes I touch my daughter.

GINNY   She's lucky. After I turned eleven, my dad stopped touching me. Completely. Wouldn't even kiss me goodnight.

DR. JAMESON   Girls your age go through a lot of changes. And sometimes that makes people uncomfortable. Especially fathers, and especially with daughters. They no longer are certain of appropriate behaviour. And, unfortunately, that means they don't touch at all. That doesn't mean, however, that there's anything wrong with you.

GINNY   Does my mother know she's paying you a hundred bucks an hour to tell me that the world's screwed up and that there's really not much wrong with me?

DR. JAMESON   To be perfectly honest, I don't think there is much wrong with you.

> *GINNY returns to NATALIE's bedroom. She flips through NAT's CDs. Occasionally, she will pick up a CD that grabs her interest, and pull out the liner notes.*
>
> *NAT sits on her bed, reading a magazine. She's reading it very intently, as though trying to memorize it. She practices smiling a couple of times. Big thousand-watt smiles. NAT stands up and slowly walks by GINNY. She flashes her one of those great big smiles.*

GINNY   Okay, yeah.

NAT   Yeah?

GINNY   Like, a seven.

> *NAT nods, taking this in. She returns to studying the magazine. She stands and hikes her skirt up.*

That's not obvious.

NAT   Hey, it says.

> *She picks up the magazine and reads.*

Become more irresistible! SHOW A LITTLE LEG, wear higher heels, the redder your lipstick the more available and noticeable you will be.

GINNY   Red lipstick is gross. You know, you're going to a lot of trouble for nothing.

NAT   It's not for nothing.

GINNY   Oh, sorry, it's for ROBBIE.

NAT   He's *gotta* ask me.

GINNY   You going to his school's debating thing?

NAT   Uh-huh.

GINNY   And, lemme guess, you gonna wait around after?

NAT   Don't have to. Eleanor's fixed it so that a group of us are going for burgers after. And she says he'll come. For sure.

GINNY   Oh, and anything Eleanor says…

> *NAT goes back to her reading. GINNY goes back to looking at the CDs.*

Why don't you just go up to him and say, *Hey Robbie, are you attracted to me?*

NAT Omigod, you are so messed. You don't just go up to some guy and say *Hey, do you like me?* That's crazy.

GINNY Oh yeah, and walking and smiling, and wearing bright lipstick, and all that stuff is sooo normal.

NAT It is.

> *Pause.*

It completely is, Ginny. It's what everyone does. It's what guys expect. It's called "The Mating Ritual" or something.

GINNY So it's all about lying.

NAT Hey, yeah. But nice lying.

> *GINNY returns to her session with DR. JAMESON.*

GINNY Does that smoking offer still stand?

DR. JAMESON It does.

GINNY Good. Cuz I freakin need a smoke.

> *GINNY goes back to her bag and pulls out a cigarette. PAM appears. She sees GINNY with the pack of cigarettes. GINNY sees her. There is a moment of standoff, then GINNY lights the cigarette and blows smoke toward her mother.*

PAM Very mature.

DR. JAMESON When did you start smoking?

GINNY Coupla years ago.

PAM You look like a hooker.

GINNY I used to steal them from my father. Pall Mall unfiltereds. Talk about head rushes.

DR. JAMESON Did your father know you smoked?

GINNY Omigosh NO. He'd a cuffed me up the head.

DR. JAMESON Did your father hit you?

GINNY It's an expression.

PAM Doesn't mean he didn't hurt you.

> *Pause.*

Why don't you tell him? Get it off your chest.

GINNY   I'm getting really tired of everyone thinking that my father did something terrible to me. It's like you WANT him to have done something.

PAM   It'd be a nice excuse for your behaviour.

DR. JAMESON   Ginny, your father takes you camping for the weekend. When you return, he disappears and you try to kill yourself. Now, three months later, you're sitting in my office after nearly being expelled for having a rather indiscreet affair with a classmate at school. Some people might say you're crying out for help and that it stems from something that happened on that trip.

>*GINNY flashes DR. JAMESON one of the huge grins that NAT was practicing earlier.*

GINNY   You didn't notice.

DR. JAMESON   What?

GINNY   My lipstick. It's called "Purple Passion." It tastes like grape.

>*PAM exits.*

DR. JAMESON   Really.

GINNY   You wanna taste?

DR. JAMESON   How would I taste your lipstick?

GINNY   *(pulling the tube from her backpack)* You could put some on. If you want.

DR. JAMESON   Your lipstick is for you to enjoy.

GINNY   *(getting up)* Suit yourself.

>*GINNY returns to NATALIE's bedroom. NATALIE sits on her bed and finishes her dress.*

Okay, so like, you get Robbie in the burger booth. Ooh. Then what?

NAT   I dunno. I tell him… I tell him that he made a good argument.

GINNY   What are they debating?

NAT   How would I know?

GINNY   You think maybe you should find out?

NAT   I'LL LISTEN. They're gonna be talking about it for, like, two hours, right? *(pause)* Besides, it's not like I hafta be smart with Robbie.

GINNY   Just pretty.

NAT   Well, yeah.

GINNY   At least you're good at that.

NAT   Wanna see my dress?

> *NAT holds up her finished dress.*

GINNY   If Robbie doesn't ask you...

NAT   Yeah?

GINNY   D'you think maybe we could...

> *Pause.*

Never mind. He'll ask you for sure.

NAT   Yeah!

GINNY   And you know what else? I don't think you hafta do all those stupid moves, Nat. I think you just hafta get him to spend time with you. Cuz anyone who spends time with you—

NAT   The moves are important.

GINNY   Okay.

NAT   Cuz otherwise he'll think I'm, like, inexperienced or something.

GINNY   I thought guys liked virgins.

NAT   Yeah, virgins. Not complete newbies. *(pause)* He needs to know that he could definitely feel me up.

GINNY   Get out.

NAT   And that I'll kiss him with tongue.

GINNY   Are you for real? Why not just go all the way?

NAT   You're joking. *(pause)* If I go all the way, then my hymen will break. As soon as THAT happens, I'm not a virgin anymore. I can do whatever I want, as long as my hymen stays in place. The Bible says so.

> *Pause.*

GINNY   Okay, wait a minute. Does that mean we're VIRGINS?

NAT   Of course we're virgins.

GINNY   Even though we... did what we did.

NAT   Please, that so does not count.

GINNY   Why not?

NAT   Cuz it wasn't real.

GINNY   What was it, then?

NAT   I don't know. Practicing.

GINNY   Practicing. *(pause)* For when it really is real. When it really counts. *(pause)* I gotta go. I'll see ya around.

NAT   You don't hafta leave, Ginny. *(pause)* I don't want you to leave.

> *Pause.*

Besides, I need you here. To help me test it.

GINNY   Test what?

NAT   My moves. You hafta tell me how everything works.

GINNY   I've already seen them.

NAT   Only one at a time. We don't know how it works all together yet, do we?

> *NAT fusses with her hair and hikes up her skirt. She walks by GINNY and flashes her a huge smile. GINNY smiles back. NAT walks up to GINNY and stops. She stands with one hip thrust out—adjusting a couple of times to make sure she's got it just right.*

Hey.

GINNY   Hi.

NAT   I like your shirt.

GINNY   It's my uniform.

NAT   I know. But the way you wear it. Looks like more than just a uniform, you know? Not a lot of people can do that.

> *NAT bites her lip obviously and brushes a strand of hair from her face. Pause.*

Now you say something nice to me.

GINNY   Right.

> *Pause.*

Your skin.

> *NAT nods, encouraging GINNY to continue.*

It's soft.

NAT   Really?

GINNY   Yeah. And your teeth. I like how even they are. And that you're pretty, but you're never stuck up about it. Not like Eleanor.

> *Pause.*

You're the prettiest girl in the school. And when you talk to me or hang out with me, you make me feel important.

NAT You are important.

GINNY And I like how I can just hang out with you and how we don't hafta have anything planned but we can still have fun together. I liked it when we'd have fun together.

> *Pause.*

I really should go.

NAT Ginny—

> *GINNY grabs NAT and kisses her. NAT kisses back, but then breaks it off. NAT wipes her mouth as though she's just eaten something sour.*

What'd you hafta go and do that for? WE WERE PRETENDING. You were supposed to be helping me. THIS ISN'T HELPING. Why do you hafta ruin everything? We can't be friends, Ginny. WE CAN'T EVEN BE FRIENDS.

> *NAT collapses on her bed.*

> *GINNY returns to her session with DR. JAMESON.*

DR. JAMESON Ginny, I know I've been encouraging you to think of your sexual desires as a normal part of your growth and development—

GINNY Uh-oh. I hear a "but" coming.

DR. JAMESON Not a "but" exactly. Have you ever heard of transference?

GINNY Nope.

DR. JAMESON In the therapeutic process it is not uncommon for the client to experience feelings toward the therapist that would otherwise be directed—

GINNY *(picking up photo of Julia and Olivia)* Is this your only photo?

DR. JAMESON I have numerous photos.

GINNY On your computer?

DR. JAMESON Well, sure.

> *Pause.*

Ginny, why don't you come sit back down?

GINNY I thought I was free to move wherever I wanted in here.

DR. JAMESON We seem to be getting distracted. Why don't we focus on the issue at hand?

GINNY Which is?

DR. JAMESON You.

GINNY But I'm a normal, healthy, developing girl, doc. What is there to discuss?

DR. JAMESON   I'm not sure that you're a HAPPY normal, healthy, developing girl.

> *Pause.*

Are you happy?

GINNY   Not particularly.

DR. JAMESON   I could help you be happy, Ginny. I'd *like* to help you be happy.

GINNY   I'd like that, too.

DR. JAMESON   What makes you happy?

GINNY   Coming here.

DR. JAMESON   Well, that's a good start.

GINNY   Talking to you.

DR. JAMESON   Is there anything else, aside from our sessions that make you happy?

GINNY   Not wearing any panties. They're so confining. Wouldn't you say?

DR. JAMESON   I, uh, you find undergarments restrictive?

GINNY   Terribly. My favourite thing to do is to go somewhere very serious, and not wear any panties. Like church say. And I watch the priest up at the altar, being all pious and everything, and I know, I just KNOW that he wouldn't be pious for very long if he knew I was naked under my skirt.

DR. JAMESON   You like knowing that the priest has sexual desires.

GINNY   Yeah. Sexual desires for ME.

> *Pause.*

I like knowing I've got something that someone wants.

> *Pause.*

And that someone might get, if he plays his cards right.

> *Pause.*

Do you play cards?

DR. JAMESON   No.

GINNY   That's a shame.

> *GINNY goes back to DR. JAMESON. She stands a few feet in front of him and starts inching her skirt up.*

Cuz I'm ready to play.

> *The skirt gets dangerously close to indecent. DR. JAMESON grabs GINNY's hand to stop her from revealing any more.*

DR. JAMESON   Are you offering to sleep with me?

GINNY   I'm sure it'd make a nice change from your daughter.

DR. JAMESON   I think we're done for the day.

> *She moves around the desk and embraces him.*

GINNY   You telling me you're not into this?

> *Pause.*

You telling me you don't want this?

> *Pause.*

Cuz I'm not hearing you say anything.

DR. JAMESON   *(removing himself from the embrace)* Don't do this.

GINNY   I know what you like.

DR. JAMESON   You've made an error in some assumption—

GINNY   And I'm okay with it.

DR. JAMESON   GO HOME. Ginny, please, go home now.

> *Pause.*

I—I'm sorry. I didn't anticipate… I—I'll call your mother later in the week—

GINNY   Don't call HER.

DR. JAMESON   And I'll give her some referrals. There are some very good doctors who can help—

GINNY   You're going to get rid of me?

DR. JAMESON   I think it would be best if someone else took over.

GINNY   YOU CAN'T DO THIS.

DR. JAMESON   I'm sorry, Ginny.

GINNY   You can't do this. You can't just toss me away.

> *Pause.*

You're gonna be sorry. You're gonna be so so so SORRY.

scene two

DR. JAMESON packs his office into boxes, while NAT gets ready for the prom.

ELAINE COOPERMAN appears. She is a hip, professional woman in her mid-thirties. A lawyer. She sits across from GINNY.

ELAINE   Now, Ms. McLean. After leaving Dr. Jameson's office on the day that the events transpired, can you tell me what happened?

GINNY   Well, I—I was really upset, right? And Marie was there.

ELAINE   And Marie is—?

GINNY   His receptionist. I exited Dr. Jameson's office quickly, because I was very upset. And in the waiting room, I encountered his receptionist, Marie.

ELAINE   And what happened with Marie?

GINNY   Well, I couldn't stop crying, right? So she sat me down and gave me some Kleenex. My blouse was undone from when I—when HE—undid it. I'd forgotten about it. So she did it up and she asked me what had happened.

ELAINE   And did you tell her what Dr. Jameson had done?

GINNY   No.

ELAINE   No?

GINNY   I was too upset. I could only cry. I couldn't even speak or breathe. So Marie called my mother.

ELAINE   And did you tell your mother what had happened?

GINNY   No. Well, not for a coupla days. But even then, I didn't exactly tell her.

ELAINE   Mmm. Not good. Try again.

GINNY   When I was still upset two days later, my mother sat me down and started asking me questions? That's when I knew I had to talk about what happened?

ELAINE   Yes. Much better. *(pause)* So you waited two days—TWO WHOLE DAYS—before you told anyone the events that had transpired in Dr. Jameson's office?

GINNY   Yes, I—I guess I didn't think anything bad had happened.

ELAINE   Dangerous.

GINNY   Maybe I didn't remember what had happened?

ELAINE   No, definitely not. They'll bring up mental instability and ask how you know that what you remembered is what actually happened. *(pause)* Besides, you did remember, didn't you?

GINNY   Yeah.

ELAINE   Okay. So, why would you have thought that nothing bad had happened?

GINNY   Cuz he was my doctor, right? Cuz I trusted him.

ELAINE   Is there anything that he said, that you can think of, that might be important to our case?

GINNY   He told me he thought that I was pretty.

ELAINE   You're kidding?

GINNY   No.

ELAINE   BEAUTIFUL. That's beautiful. *(pause)* Oh, Ginny. You're making your lawyer a very happy woman.

>   *Pause.*

How're you holding up?

GINNY   I'm kinda fried.

ELAINE   Okay. We can review more later. But I want to talk to you about your clothes.

GINNY   My CLOTHES?

ELAINE   Yes, we have to do something about your image.

GINNY   My image.

ELAINE   The press is paying a lot of attention to you these days—

GINNY   I know. I told them not to.

ELAINE   Oh no, no. We want to build on that momentum. Feed into it. In a lot of ways trials take place outside the courtroom. Especially these kinds of trials.

GINNY   But you said I couldn't talk to them.

ELAINE   You can't. Well, not about anything to do with the case. But you can talk around them. No facts. All impressions. But you gotta start wearing pants.

GINNY   Pants?

ELAINE   We wanna play up the dyke angle. Make people aware as early as possible that you're not into boys. That way we shoot down any arguments of you seducing him or asking for it.

GINNY   I'm not a dyke.

>   *Pause.*

ELAINE   That… incident with your friend, Natalie. That was a one-time thing.

GINNY   With Nat? No. It happened a coupla times.

ELAINE   A couple?

GINNY   Okay, maybe like twelve or fourteen.

ELAINE   Then you're a dyke.

GINNY   No, really, I don't think—

ELAINE   Look, Ginny, normal teenagers get to take their time owning and discovering their sexuality. We don't have that luxury, okay? If you're not willing to self-identify, then we might as well drop all charges.

GINNY   Can we do that?

ELAINE   NO. *(pause)* I'm one myself. *(pause)* A dyke.

GINNY   You are?

ELAINE   Yes. But you can't repeat that, alright? I have a certain professional reputation that needs to be maintained. You won't say anything, will you?

GINNY   No, of course not.

ELAINE   Good. Because it's nothing to be ashamed of. You got that?

GINNY   Yeah, I guess.

ELAINE   Alright. So, pants. I wanna see you in pants next time you're here, got it?

scene three

The prom. Cheesy music is playing too loud and lights from a disco ball smatter the stage.

NAT looks around, then spots someone and smiles and waves. GINNY (as Robbie), dressed in a tuxedo, approaches her.

GINNY   I can't find the punch.

NAT   Oh, that's okay. I'm not thirsty anyway.

GINNY   Yeah, but it's prolly spiked.

GINNY goes to search some more, but NAT grabs her arm.

NAT   Robbie—

Pause.

GINNY   Kinda boring, sober. Dontcha think?

Nat smiles and bites her lip—as she was practicing in Scene One.

NAT   Maybe we could *(pause)* dance?

GINNY   Well, uh we could I guess. Music sucks though.

NAT   I don't really care about the music.

GINNY   I got an idea. Maybe you and me could go and hang out in my car.

> *Pause.*

I got a coupla CDs there. Good ones.

NAT   Smashing Concrete?

GINNY   Uh-huh. You like those guys?

NAT   Oh YEAH. They're, like, my favourite.

GINNY   That's very kewl. Cuz most chicks find 'em too heavy.

NAT   I think they're just right.

GINNY   Alrighty then. What're we waiting for? Let's blow this pop stand.

NAT   Robbie, wait.

> *Pause.*

We just got here. And I'd kinda like to dance, first.

GINNY   Whoa, Nat. What're ya doin'?

NAT   What d'you mean?

GINNY   I mean, I thought you were more mature. I thought you were a *very* mature girl. That's what I heard.

NAT   What'd you hear?

GINNY   That you were kinda experimental. Kinda kinky.

NAT   Well, it's wrong.

GINNY   That's too bad.

NAT   I mean—

GINNY   Cuz I was really starting to dig you.

NAT   I dig you, too, Robbie.

GINNY   Then how come you're making me suffer through this kindergarten prom?

NAT   It's MY prom.

GINNY   With its sissy music.

NAT   Why don't you request something? And then you can dance with me. Maybe even a slow dance.

GINNY   What and rub my woody against you? Thanks anyway.

Pause.

I'll be in the car for a little while. If you wanna grow up anytime soon, come join me.

GINNY exits.

scene four

GINNY (as Ginny) is at DR. JAMESON's house.

GINNY   I totally thought you'd be in jail. I mean, don't they put all sex offenders in jail?

DR. JAMESON   Alleged.

GINNY   What?

DR. JAMESON   Alleged sex offender. We haven't gone to court yet.

GINNY   Right. But still, don't they…. OH, did you pay bail?

DR. JAMESON   No, I did not pay bail.

GINNY   Something's gone wrong.

DR. JAMESON   You don't suppose it has anything to do with you LYING?

GINNY   Are you mad?

Pause.

I KNOW I fucked up. I didn't mean to.

DR. JAMESON   You didn't *mean* to? What exactly did you think would happen when you went to the POLICE and accused me of those things?

GINNY   I didn't go to the police, my mother did, OKAY?

DR. JAMESON   You had to talk to them. You had to tell them the same lies. Over and over again.

GINNY   I wouldn't have done it if I'd had any idea how it was gonna all pan out.

DR. JAMESON   You're a bright girl, Ginny. What did you think would happen?

GINNY   You figure it out. I mean, I'm caught having sex, full out SEX, in the bathroom at school, and nobody talks about it. No, more than that. Everyone LIES about it.

So you tell me why people wouldn't have the same reaction. Huh? Why the exact same thing wouldn't happen? I mean, I didn't even say we had sex. Not even sex. Just kissing.

DR. JAMESON   You think the court gives a flying fuck how far we supposedly went?

GINNY   Of course they do. I mean, everyone kisses. You don't get a reputation with kissing.

DR. JAMESON   No? Well you can DESTROY a reputation with kissing.

GINNY   I'm sorry. I didn't KNOW that. Nobody explained it.

DR. JAMESON   But you knew that you were lying. *(pause)* Why am I bothering? You're not even supposed to be here. Ginny, leave. Okay?

GINNY   But I want you to know that I'm sorry.

DR. JAMESON   So you've said.

GINNY   You don't believe me.

DR. JAMESON   Or maybe it just doesn't matter. Maybe I am already about to lose my practice, my job, my life, my DAUGHTER. Never mind spending fifteen years behind bars for something I didn't do. Do you know what they do to child molesters in prison, Ginny?

>   *Pause.*

And maybe I know that some spoiled little lying bitch saying that she's SORRY is not going to solve any of this.

GINNY   I don't think that's very nice.

DR. JAMESON   LEAVE.

scene five

>   *The Prom. NAT is standing, watching everyone dance, trying to decide whether or not to join ROBBIE in his car. ELAINE approaches her.*

ELAINE   Hey.

NAT   Hi.

ELAINE   I like your dress.

NAT   It's for the prom.

ELAINE   Yeah, but the way you wear it. Looks like more than just a prom dress. Not a lot of people can do that.

NAT   Whoa.

scene six

DR. JAMESON, dishevelled and really needing sleep, stands in an office. An office chair, its back to him, is in the corner.

DR. JAMESON   Alright, yes. I am attracted to teenage girls. Sexually. And, yes, my wife and I separated because of it. I TOLD her. I told my wife. Because that's the kind of man I am. And allow me to point out that never once did she express concern for our daughter. No. Olivia lived with me. And that was fine with everyone. Until this, this demon child, walked into my office. She's the one with problems, okay? I mean, not to suggest I don't have problems. I know how society looks on me. Not so different as how I look on myself. But the bottom line is that I OWN my problems. I own them, and I confront them, and I talk about them.

Everybody has something about them that makes them ashamed. That sickens them. EVERYBODY. And if anyone thinks they don't, I pity them. Because they are so deep in denial they aren't really living. But I want to make it very VERY clear that I have never acted upon my attraction to these girls. I accept societal norms and I live my life by them.

The office chair spins around to reveal ELAINE sitting, listening, and taking notes.

ELAINE   Okay, that's great.

DR. JAMESON   Even if I think society is wrong. Even if I think they are making a gross mistake, allowing such beautiful, fragile, young women to learn about sex at the hands of bumbling, overeager, selfish teenage boys.

ELAINE   No. Now that's pushing things.

DR. JAMESON   I wouldn't be like that. I would be gentle. I would take care. Not to inflict any pain, any of my own desires, upon these blossoming, beautiful girls.

ELAINE   Dr. Jameson?

DR. JAMESON begins to touch himself through his clothing.

Oh, really. This is…

ELAINE exits.

scene seven

The prom. NAT leans against the wall, watching everyone else dance and have fun. DR. JAMESON (as Robbie) appears and puts an arm around her.

NAT   I thought you'd gone to your car.

DR. JAMESON   Not much fun sitting in a car by myself.

NAT   I'm sorry. I—

DR. JAMESON   Oh, no. You don't need to apologize, Natalie. In fact, I think you're owed an apology. Was I a complete jerk?

NAT   Not *complete*.

DR. JAMESON   D'you suppose you could find it in your heart to forgive me? To give me a second chance?

NAT   Yeah, I guess. *(pause)* But could you maybe not keep touching my breast like that?

DR. JAMESON   Was I—? Did I—? Oh dear. I wasn't aware.

NAT   No, no. It's okay. Not a big deal.

DR. JAMESON   Quite the contrary, Natalie. I think your body is a huge deal. It's so very lovely and precious. And valuable. D'you see how everyone else is looking at us?

NAT   No.

DR. JAMESON   Sure they are. Kyle Watters, over there in the corner.

NAT   Kyle's weird. He always stares.

DR. JAMESON   And Bobby Kinsey. And Michael Dern. Joey and Jeffrey and Theo. Don't tell me you can't see how they're all staring.

NAT   I guess. I never noticed before.

DR. JAMESON   Do you know why they're staring?

>   *NAT shakes her head "no."*

Because of you. Because they all wish they were me. That's how lucky I am, how lucky you've made me.

>   *Pause.*

NAT   I feel pretty lucky, too.

DR. JAMESON   Well, good. This is going to be a very special night for us, isn't it? Now, how about a dance?

NAT   I thought you didn't want to dance with me.

DR. JAMESON   There is nothing I would like better than to dance with you. What d'you say?

>   *NAT takes DR. JAMESON's arm. He leads her onto the dance floor and they dance.*

NAT   Robbie? Thanks for coming back in here. You seem so different now. So much more grown up.

DR. JAMESON   I *am* grown up, Natalie. I'm in Grade Eleven, remember?

> *NAT and DR. JAMESON continue to dance, as the lights come up on:*

scene eight

> *GINNY and ELAINE are in ELAINE's office. GINNY is wearing the tuxedo pants from her scene with NAT at the prom.*

ELAINE   The pants are definitely an improvement.

GINNY   They are?

ELAINE   They give you a tougher edge. A bit more butch. I look at you in those pants and I am able to believe that you seduced Natalie Collins.

GINNY   But I didn't.

> *Pause.*

I didn't.

ELAINE   Ginny. I've seen pictures of Natalie.

GINNY   Yeah, I know. I showed them to you.

ELAINE   Well, she's definitely the more traditional femme of the two of you. Not to suggest that you're not very attractive in your own way.

GINNY   What difference does that make? So Nat's pretty. Nat's always been pretty.

ELAINE   Pretty equals passive. Passive equals femme. Femme equals NOT the initiator of any sexual interaction.

GINNY   What?

ELAINE   You're young. It's to be expected. One tends to reject the longstanding tenets of one's community before learning to fully appreciate them. Who says all adolescent rebellion takes place in the home, hey?

GINNY   My "community" is my school. The nuns. The church.

> *ELAINE bursts out laughing.*

ELAINE   Oh. Oh, that's priceless.

GINNY   It's TRUE.

ELAINE   Ginny, THEY DON'T WANT YOU.

GINNY   No, they just don't want me having sex.

ELAINE   Is there a difference? Are you not a sexual creature?

> *Pause.*

It's alright. I understand your dilemma. I was a cheerleader myself. Why don't we move on? We have a lot to cover today. (*pause*) I want to talk to you about your make-up.

GINNY   Don't you want to talk about the case?

ELAINE   We are talking about the case. Now, for all intents and purposes, you need to stop wearing make-up.

GINNY   Why?

ELAINE   Because it makes you look too much like a girl.

GINNY   But I AM a girl.

ELAINE   Yes, but you're the boy-girl.

GINNY   I'm pretty sure I'm all girl.

ELAINE   No, Natalie is the all girl. She's girl-girl, you're boy-girl.

GINNY   We're BOTH girls.

ELAINE   Oh, Ginny. Why do you have to make this so difficult. It's not just you, I realize, it's your entire generation. (*pause*) As your lawyer, I am forbidding you from wearing make-up.

GINNY   Can you do that?

ELAINE   I just did.

GINNY   Ho-okay.

ELAINE   Good, it's settled. Now, the exception is for the press.

GINNY   I wear make-up for the press?

ELAINE   Yes, but subtle. Maybe some mascara. A touch of rouge. Some clear lip-gloss. Nothing over the top. Just enough to let them know that you're not confused about your gender.

GINNY   I'm not.

ELAINE   Of course not. And, if you are, just look down the next time you're in the bathtub. Now, then, let's go from the beginning.

scene nine

GINNY stands in front of DR. JAMESON. She is pointing her vibrator at him with great menace.

DR. JAMESON   Someone is going to get hurt if you don't put that thing down.

GINNY   Well I don't think it'll be me.

DR. JAMESON   Ginny, you don't want me dead.

GINNY   Don't bet on it.

DR. JAMESON   If I'm dead, I can't take you back as a client.

GINNY   You're not gonna anyway.

DR. JAMESON   I wouldn't be so sure. Life has a funny way of working out.

GINNY   Meaning what?

DR. JAMESON   Meaning anything's possible.

GINNY   You're just desperate. You don't really mean any of this.

DR. JAMESON   PUT THAT THING DOWN.

> *GINNY lowers the vibrator, but keeps holding it.*

Thank-you.

GINNY   Maybe I could kill you. Do you think?

DR. JAMESON   You seem to be doing a fine job of it, with or without a weapon.

GINNY   Oh poor YOU.

DR. JAMESON   Yes, Ginny, poor ME. I know this is going to come as a terrible shock to you, but this little drama that you have created—

GINNY   I didn't do it.

DR. JAMESON   You're not some victim whose been cornered into something you didn't want to do—

GINNY   They like me better if they think I am.

DR. JAMESON   Can you take the focus off yourself for one second? This isn't about you.

> *GINNY raises the vibrator again, pointing it at DR. JAMESON.*

GINNY   I'm very important right now. When I speak, people listen. They stick microphones in my face. They write down things I say.

DR. JAMESON   You're a good story on a slow news day. Bravo. We should all aim so high in life.

GINNY   Are you making fun of me? Are you making fun of me, you weaselly little PEDOPHILE.

DR. JAMESON   Hebophile.

GINNY   What?

DR. JAMESON   A pedophile is attracted to children. A hebophile is attracted to adolescents.

GINNY   Oh, and that's so much better.

DR. JAMESON   There's a difference.

GINNY   Not much of one. Not enough of one to save your life. If I killed you right now—

DR. JAMESON   You're not going to kill me, Ginny.

GINNY   You know what everyone would think? Everyone would think, GOOD. GOOD I'M GLAD HE'S DEAD. One less CREEP in our society. Our streets, our LIVES are safer with him dead. People like him are DANGEROUS. They should all be rounded up and SHOT. They don't DESERVE to be ALIVE.

DR. JAMESON   I never did anything to you.

GINNY   Don't think that matters.

DR. JAMESON   I never would.

GINNY   You know that for sure?

DR. JAMESON   I do.

GINNY   For 100% sure?

>   *Pause.*

Yeah, that's what I thought.

>   *GINNY brings the vibrator to within inches of DR. JAMESON's face.*

DR. JAMESON   You don't kill a man because of something he MIGHT do. We all have the potential to do dangerous things, Ginny. If you kill me, you're going to have to kill everyone. Everyone on this whole planet.

GINNY   I'll start with you.

>   *GINNY turns the vibrator on, but it won't start. She tries two more times.*

Dammit.

DR. JAMESON   Get out of here.

GINNY   Oh it was so good, too. Meaningful.

DR. JAMESON   GINNY.

GINNY   Yeah, yeah. I'm going.

>   *Ginny exits. Lights come up on:*

scene ten

The prom. NAT stands in the parking lot. GINNY (as Ginny, but still dressed in the tuxedo pants) approaches.

NAT Robbie?

GINNY NO, it's Ginny.

NAT Ginny?

GINNY Yeah, your ex-best friend.

NAT What are you doing here?

GINNY My vibrator's dead.

NAT YOUR vibrator?

GINNY You wouldn't take it, remember? So I figured—

NAT Gross.

GINNY It's not like you used it. How come you're all dressed up like that?

NAT Um, for PROM?

GINNY Omigod, that's right. Hey, how's it going?

      NAT shrugs.

  Nat?

NAT I dunno. It's not like I thought it would be.

GINNY It's not the best night of your life?

NAT No.

GINNY How come you're not inside?

NAT Oh, you know. Just wanted some fresh air.

GINNY Robbie inside?

NAT No. He's in his car.

GINNY His car? What the hell is he doing—? Oh. OH.

NAT Yeah.

GINNY Why didn't you say so? Didn't mean to hold you up or anything.

NAT I'm not sure I wanna go.

GINNY Are you joking? This is what you've been waiting for all year.

NAT Right.

GINNY Did you decide how far you were willing to go?

NAT Yeah.

GINNY Okay, then. Go on.

> *NAT takes a deep breath and walks toward the car. She calls back:*

NAT Ginny? I miss you.

GINNY *(pause)* I'm right here.

scene eleven

> *DR. JAMESON approaches ELAINE.*

DR. JAMESON Hey.

ELAINE Hi.

DR. JAMESON I like your shirt.

ELAINE I don't play with boys.

DR. JAMESON Me neither.

ELAINE That isn't even remotely funny.

DR. JAMESON Oh. Sorry. *(pause)* Can we try it again?

ELAINE I don't think so.

scene twelve

> *ELAINE and DR. JAMESON (as Ginny) are in ELAINE's office.*

ELAINE Oh, Ginny. Ginny Ginny Ginny. So much better. You're not the same little girl who first walked into my office, are you?

DR. JAMESON I'm not?

ELAINE Those pants. That face—not a stitch of make-up. You've even adjusted the length of your hair. Bravo. Bravo, Ginny. You're well on your way to becoming a WOMAN.

> *DR. JAMESON sits down. He starts to cross his legs at the knee.*

Ah-ah-ah.

> *DR. JAMESON uncrosses his leg and hesitantly tries to cross it at the ankle.*

Mmm No.

> *DR. JAMESON plants both feet firmly on the floor. ELAINE grabs his knees and foists his legs apart.*

There we are. Why, hello Ginny. With very little imagination, I can almost see something dangling between your legs.

> DR. JAMESON *snaps his legs shut.*

Now, now. Don't be shy. You aren't PACKING, are you? You naughty girl.

DR. JAMESON   You mean, like, luggage?

ELAINE   Luggage?

DR. JAMESON   You know, for a trip.

ELAINE   You're not planning a trip, are you?

DR. JAMESON   No. I mean, prolly after graduation.

ELAINE   You're not going anywhere, kiddo.

DR. JAMESON   I'm not?

ELAINE   And jeopardize your trial? Most certainly not.

DR. JAMESON   But graduation's not for another four years.

ELAINE   These things have a way of dragging on.

DR. JAMESON   For FOUR years?

ELAINE   What's four years in the grand scheme of things? A mere drop in the pond of life.

DR. JAMESON   Four years is MAJOR. I'll be, like, eighteen in four years.

ELAINE   Such a baby.

DR. JAMESON   At eighteen? I don't think so. I'll be done with school. I'll prolly have a car. My own apartment, and a—a—a...

ELAINE   A girlfriend?

DR. JAMESON   N—no.

ELAINE   A boyfriend?

DR. JAMESON   NO.

ELAINE   A puppy?

DR. JAMESON   Okay, yeah. I could handle that.

ELAINE   The perfect butch choice.

DR. JAMESON   I'm sorry?

ELAINE   Butches have puppies. Femmes have kitties. Oh, it's so exciting, Ginny. You fit the stereotypes like a glove.

DR. JAMESON   I SEDUCED HIM. Omigod. I just said it. WOW. That felt great.

ELAINE   I hope you're not saying what I think you're saying.

DR. JAMESON   Uh-huh.

ELAINE   Okay. Okay, we'll deal with it.

DR. JAMESON   I walked into his office and I complimented him on his tie. And I wore my new lipstick. Yeah, LIPSTICK. And I jacked my skirt waaaaaay up—

ELAINE   ENOUGH.

DR. JAMESON   How's the stereotype doing now?

ELAINE   Why would you do such a thing?

DR. JAMESON   Hmm. Probably transference.

ELAINE   No. Transference means you *fantasize* about your shrink.

DR. JAMESON   Good point. Transference combined with an unresolved Electra complex in an already narcissistic personality.

>   *Pause.*

Just a guess, anyway.

ELAINE   I don't know what kind of sick little game you're playing—

DR. JAMESON   Ask Dr. Jameson, you don't believe me.

ELAINE   He's a PERVERT, Ginny. I'm hardly going to take his word as gospel.

DR. JAMESON   So, I guess you'll just hafta believe me, huh? I'm telling you the truth.

ELAINE   You'd better not be.

DR. JAMESON   Yeah, well. That seems to be everyone's reaction when I'm honest.

ELAINE   Ginny. Ginny Ginny Ginny. We all have moments in our past—indiscretions—that we'd rather not dwell on. Sadly, they almost always involve men. Why, when I was in college, I attended a fraternity party.

DR. JAMESON   You did? Did you do anything?

ELAINE   No. But I attended it. (*pause*) Point is, we don't discuss these incidents.

DR. JAMESON   The incidents with boys?

ELAINE   Yes. They're not for public consumption.

DR. JAMESON   But it's okay to talk about the incidents with girls?

ELAINE   Oh YES. We talk freely about those. With whoever will listen.

DR. JAMESON   See, that didn't work for me. I wasn't allowed to talk about Nat with anyone. Not even with her.

ELAINE   Surely you must have spoken to someone about it. You told me.

DR. JAMESON   No, I—I think you read it in my file.

ELAINE   Oh, that's right. Well, you COULD have told me.

scene thirteen

GINNY and DR. JAMESON are at his home.

GINNY   You were so nice to me. You listened to me. You never got mad. I could talk to you about ANYTHING.

DR. JAMESON   I was doing my job, Ginny.

GINNY   So… what… you treat all your clients like that?

DR. JAMESON   Yes.

GINNY   You know what hurts the most? What hurts the most is that I was liking how you kept telling me that I was normal. I believed that. But you wouldn't know normal if it bit you in the ass, would you? I mean, it's kinda hard to take comfort in the fact that a sexual pervert finds you sexually normal. I think the two kinda cancel each other out, don't you?

DR. JAMESON   Oh, Ginny. I was hoping it wouldn't come to this. But, yes, it's true.

GINNY   What is?

DR. JAMESON   You. You're sexually abnormal. You're a freak. Warped. You frighten even me.

GINNY   You're lying.

DR. JAMESON   Afraid not. Just didn't want to say so earlier. I was hoping to lull you into a false euphoria about yourself, then jump in and tinker with your sexual depravity before you woke up and realized what was going on.

GINNY   There's nothing wrong with me.

DR. JAMESON   Quite the contrary. Being sexually attracted to Natalie—

GINNY   Nat's attractive—

DR. JAMESON   Seducing her.

GINNY   Okay. WOULD EVERYONE STOP SAYING THAT?? SHE showed ME the magazines. She had the them between her mattresses. We looked at them. TOGETHER. We decided to fool around. TOGETHER. I DID NOT SEDUCE NAT.

DR. JAMESON   Yeah, tell that to the judge.

GINNY   What are you talking about?

DR. JAMESON   Save it for the trial, Ginny.

GINNY   You're the one on trial.

DR. JAMESON   Me? Why in God's name would I be on trial?

GINNY   Cuz, cuz of the photos. On your computer.

DR. JAMESON   Research, Ginny. I'm a psychologist. I have to expose myself to all sorts of pornographic material, so that I am not shocked when one of my clients references a particular sexual act or fantasy.

GINNY   Bullshit.

DR. JAMESON   Afraid not. (*pause*) You probably shouldn't say any more. I'm one of the Crown witnesses for the prosecution at your trial.

GINNY   I'm not on trial.

DR. JAMESON   You've got a lawyer, don't you?

GINNY   Yes, but—

DR. JAMESON   Well, only people on trial have lawyers.

GINNY   No—

DR. JAMESON   Are you going to argue with me over this? I'm the adult. I think I know best, don't you?

GINNY   M—maybe? (*pause*) What, what'm I charged with?

DR. JAMESON   Sexual awareness at an unlawfully young age.

GINNY   And you're one of the witnesses against me?

DR. JAMESON   Yes.

GINNY   Kinda sucks.

DR. JAMESON   I was never your psychologist, Ginny.

GINNY   I'm pretty sure you were.

DR. JAMESON   No, I just appeared to be. I was always gathering evidence of your sexual deviance for the court.

GINNY   Oh shit. You've got a ton of ammo, dontcha?

DR. JAMESON   Yes. You made my job very easy, Ginny.

GINNY   Oh maaaaan, my mother's gonna flip. And she was so excited when she thought I'd been assaulted. (*pause*) Is there any way that maybe you could, um, lie?

DR. JAMESON   Absolutely not.

GINNY   Why not? I lied. I said you'd sexually assaulted me. Everyone believed me.

DR. JAMESON   Would they have dared to doubt you? Even if they doubted you privately, there's no way in hell anyone is going to risk their reputation by doubting you publicly.

GINNY   So, so why can't you do the same thing?

DR. JAMESON   Because I am approximately 30 years too old and the wrong gender to get away with it.

GINNY   Fuck.

DR. JAMESON   Yeah.

> *GINNY starts to exit. DR. JAMESON calls her back.*

Ginny, wait—

GINNY   Yeah?

DR. JAMESON   I want you to know that I am risking my professional reputation here. But I happen to think that you are a special young lady whose been given a particularly rough time for no good reason. So—

> *Pause.*

So. How would you like it if I didn't testify against you?

GINNY   Oh, would you do that? Would you?

DR. JAMESON   I think I could be persuaded to.

GINNY   Omigod. How can I ever thank you?

DR. JAMESON   Well, nothing comes for free, right?

GINNY   Sure.

DR. JAMESON   So, all you need to do is sleep with me.

GINNY   What?

DR. JAMESON   Sleep with me and I won't testify against you. Sleep with me and I won't tell a soul about your sexual deviance, your sexual awareness at an unlawfully young age. What d'you say, Ginny?

GINNY   Um.

DR. JAMESON   Come on, baby girl. Come to Daddy. Come to Daddy.

scene fourteen

The prom. NAT (as Robbie) sits smoking a cigarette on the hood of Robbie's car. GINNY (as Nat) goes to put an arm around NAT/Robbie, but NAT/Robbie pulls away.

NAT   Don't.

GINNY   Robbie—

NAT   Leave it alone, Natalie.

GINNY   Robbie, look at me. (*pause*) Do I look upset?

NAT   N—no.

GINNY   No.

NAT   Yer prolly blissed. You prolly can't wait to get home and phone all your girlfriends and tell them about your prom date who couldn't get a hard on.

GINNY   Why would I do that?

> *Pause.*

NAT   Everyone knows prom is for sex.

GINNY   Says who?

NAT   EVERYONE. It's been a blast. I'll catch you later.

> *NAT (as Robbie) starts to leave. GINNY (as Nat) grabs her arm to stop her.*

GINNY   Kiss me.

NAT   Whatever.

GINNY   Omigod. Omigod. You're scared.

NAT   Bullshit.

GINNY   You are. You're SCARED. I was so caught up in me being scared that I never even thought—

NAT   I don't know what you're talking about.

GINNY   I'm talking about knees turning to Jell-o. I'm talking about not being able to catch your breath. I'm talking about what everyone thinks and what everyone says being the most important thing in the world.

NAT   Yeah, well. You're talking too much.

> *Nat exits.*

GINNY   You are, Robbie Manslow. You're scared. You're just as scared as Natalie Collins. And Virginia McLean. And Dr. Thomas Jameson. And every other human being on the face of this planet. You're scared of me. You're scared of sex. You're scared of it happening. You're scared of it never happening.

> *GINNY continues talking, but as GINNY now. All the other characters return to themselves, and repeat their lines from earlier.*

NAT   What'd you hafta go and do that for?

GINNY   Of drowning.

DR. JAMESON   I think we're done for the day.

GINNY   Of getting lost.

NAT   WE WERE PRETENDING.

GINNY   Of people leaving.

DR. JAMESON   Don't do this.

GINNY   Of being left alone.

NAT   You were supposed to be helping me.

GINNY   You're scared of it all.

NAT   THIS ISN'T HELPING.

DR. JAMESON   GO HOME, Ginny.

GINNY   I just never thought.

DR. JAMESON   Please, go home now.

GINNY   I just never.

> *ELAINE/PAM appears, and takes a step toward GINNY.*

It's okay. You don't hafta protect me.

> *ELAINE/PAM disappears. GINNY returns to her session with DR. JAMESON.*

DR. JAMESON   Sorry about that.

GINNY   Whatever.

DR. JAMESON   So, where were we?

GINNY   You wanted to know if I was having sex with my father. Only you said it better. Nicer.

DR. JAMESON   Your mother is concerned—

GINNY   My mother is ALWAYS concerned. *(pause)* It's a bit rude for you to leave the room during a session?

DR. JAMESON   Well, yes.

GINNY   Brave, too.

DR. JAMESON   Brave?

GINNY   I coulda stolen something.

DR. JAMESON   I trust you.

GINNY   Or snooped.

DR. JAMESON   You're welcome to look around.

GINNY   On your computer say.

> *GINNY gets up and approaches the laptop. DR. JAMESON follows her.*

You get nervous whenever I'm near the computer.

> *GINNY tries to open the computer, but DR. JAMESON holds it down.*

Yup. I'd say there's something here you don't want me to see. Maybe it's something you're ashamed of?

DR. JAMESON   I do have a personal life, Ginny.

GINNY   I know. *(pause)* It involves sex with teenage girls, doesn't it?

DR. JAMESON   I beg your pardon?

GINNY   That's why you think I'm normal, right? Cuz you're really, really perverted. Whereas I'm only a bit perverted, so compared to you, I seem normal. Don't worry, I don't think you were lying on purpose.

DR. JAMESON   Ginny—

GINNY   Don't bother. I've already seen them.

DR. JAMESON   Them?

GINNY   The pictures? On your computer? The ones you're scared I'm gonna see? I already saw them. While you were out schmoozing with whoever knocked on the door.

> *DR. JAMESON opens his computer. GINNY is confused by what she sees.*

That's not—where are?—but I just saw them. There was porn—I swear. I swear, I'm not making this up. My mother—I mean, well, why would you hide this? It's just an email.

DR. JAMESON   It's a *personal* email to my daughter, Olivia. Telling her that I can't drive her to ballet tonight, so she should phone her mother for a ride. Unfortunately, this damn machine keeps going offline every time I press "send," so the email won't go through. I didn't want to turn the machine off before I sent the email—

GINNY   I don't feel good.

GINNY walks back to her seat.

DR. JAMESON   Long and short of it being that Olivia never received the email and thought I was going to drive her, so she came by. She knows better than to knock when this door is closed, but given the circumstances—

GINNY   I swear to you, I saw—

DR. JAMESON   Sometimes we see what we want to see. Or what we need to see.

GINNY   Why would I—?

DR. JAMESON   You said something about your mother. Perhaps she could join us for a session?

GINNY   She'd never come near here. She'd be afraid of catching some crazy germ. Besides, she thinks you're a quack.

DR. JAMESON   Really?

GINNY   Yeah. But like I said before, she usually gets it wrong. Like with my dad, right? Like how she thinks he did something to me.

DR. JAMESON   But he didn't?

GINNY   Sure he did. He left. Isn't that enough?

> *GINNY steps into NATALIE's bedroom. NAT sits on the edge of the bed, flipping through a magazine. GINNY picks up the phone and sits down in front of an open phone book.*

NAT   I don't like any of them. *(pause)* And they're all so expensive.

GINNY   *(on the phone)* Hi, Ian? Oh, sorry.

> *GINNY hangs up the phone.*

That's not him, either.

> *She crosses out a number in the phone book and starts dialing another one.*

NAT   Don't worry, you'll find him. *(pause)* Betcha I could make a dress.

GINNY   On average, it's eight "McLean's" per city. About 76 cities per province makes 608 McLean's per province—

NAT   Did you just do that in your head?

GINNY   Duh. No answer. *(GINNY hangs up the phone and makes a note in the book.)* So, six hundred and eight times thirteen provinces and territories is seven thousand, nine hundred and four McLean's in the country. That's do-able, right?

NAT   I dunno, Ginny. That's a lot.

NAT returns to her magazine. GINNY picks up the phone and dials the next number.

GINNY   Hello, may I please speak to Ian? Ian McLean. Okay, thanks.

She hangs up the phone and crosses out another name.

NAT   It's not just about the dress, you know. It's the whole look. Hair, shoes, handbag.

GINNY   School's barely started, Nat. Prom is, like, ten months away.

NAT   You've got your plan. Why can't I have mine?

GINNY   Yeah, but my plan is to find my father. You're planning for prom. Not even prom. JUNIOR prom.

NAT   It's still prom.

GINNY   Whatever.

NAT   You know there's a flaw in your system.

GINNY   My *system*?

NAT   Yeah. Your track-down-your-dad-through-the-phonebook system.

GINNY   Really?

NAT   Your dad's been gone for, what, a month?

GINNY   Six weeks.

NAT   Same diff. He won't be in the phone book. You've gotta live somewhere for, like, at least a year before you're in the phone book.

GINNY   You think I don't know that?

NAT   So why you calling, then?

GINNY   You know your mum's the same as mine, right? She's never going to let you go to prom.

NAT   You're just saying that cuz you know I'm right about your dad.

GINNY   I'm saying it cuz it's true.

Pause. NAT puts the magazine down. GINNY starts flipping through NAT's CDs.

NAT   Look, I'm sure your dad'll be home soon, anyway.

GINNY   Since when do you like Smashing Concrete?

NAT   Oh, I dunno. It looked cool.

GINNY   You got it cuz Robbie Manslow listens to it.

NAT   Whatever.

GINNY   Whatever. You know it. Cuz anything Robbie Manslow does is so cool. Cuz he's so handsome and I want to be his girlfriend cuz my name is Natalie Collins and I'm the only girl in high school who's never been kissed.

NAT   Except for Virginia McLean.

GINNY   Yeah, well. *(pause)* You're the one with the little-Miss-Innocent reputation.

NAT   Yeah, right.

GINNY   Little-Miss-Goody-Two-Shoes.

NAT   Okay, stop. *(pause)* Besides, that was junior school. That doesn't count anymore.

GINNY   What d'you mean, *doesn't count*?

NAT   I mean it's like we're starting all over again. We're not who we used to be.

GINNY   That's not true.

NAT   Yes it is. Everything's changing.

>   *Pause.*

I wanna show you something.

GINNY   What kind of something?

>   *NAT pulls a couple of magazines from between the mattress of her bed. She gives one to GINNY.*

Where'd you get these?

NAT   Tommy moved out for college, and my mum cleaned his room. I found them in the garbage.

GINNY   You stole your brother's porno mags outta the garbage?

NAT   Yeah.

GINNY   Sweet.

>   *GINNY continues to look through the magazine. NAT picks one up and does the same.*

Wow. She's pretty, um…

NAT   Flexible?

GINNY   Yeah. *(pause)* It's gotta hurt.

NAT   Majorly.

GINNY   It always hurts the first time. For everyone.

NAT   Duh. *(pause)* I don't think this is her first time.

GINNY   Just think, Nat, this is gonna be you and Robbie by the end of the year.

>   *NAT punches GINNY in the arm.*

NAT   I'm not a slut.

GINNY   Never said you were. *(pause)* Everyone knows you do it at prom.

NAT   Says who?

GINNY   *Everyone.* It's what prom is for.

NAT   *(turning pages)* Lookit this one.

GINNY   Oh. Actually, that doesn't look *so* bad.

NAT   Ew.

GINNY   Why "ew"? Cuz they're using their mouths?

NAT   Well, yeah.

GINNY   They look like they're enjoying it, don't they?

NAT   I think they're paid to look like that.

GINNY   Nah. They're into it. You can totally tell.

NAT   Hey. How come she doesn't have any hair?

>   *GINNY puts her magazine down and looks over NAT's shoulder at the magazine NAT is holding.*

GINNY   Weird. I don't know.

NAT   I thought everybody got hair. When they grew up.

GINNY   Maybe she's albino.

NAT   D'you think so?

GINNY   I don't know. *(pointing to another picture)* But thank God I don't have as much as that. Ew. That's just not right.

NAT   How much do you have?

GINNY   What? Hair? Enough.

NAT   Show me.

GINNY   You wanna see my pubic hair?

NAT   Uh-huh.

GINNY   Whatever.

NAT   I'll show you mine.

GINNY   Okay sure.

NAT   You first.

GINNY   I don't think so.

NAT   Yeah but you're gonna like double cross me or something.

GINNY   I won't.

NAT   Same time.

GINNY   Deal.

> *They undo their kilts and peek at one another.*

Yours is blonde.

NAT   Cuz my hair is.

GINNY   *(realizing)* Oh.

NAT   When did you get yours?

GINNY   It's been a while now. You?

NAT   Same.

GINNY   Wanna see what it's like?

NAT   What what's like?

> *GINNY picks up a magazine and shows it to NAT.*

Do you?

GINNY   I don't care.

NAT   Me neither.

GINNY   I'll go first.

NAT   Okay.

GINNY   Okay. Get in bed.

NAT   Just a sec.

> *NAT goes to her CD player.*

My mum might come home.

GINNY   When?

NAT   Not for a while. It's just in case. When do you hafta be home?

GINNY   I don't think it matters. My mum's on one of her spa days.

NAT   Oooh. Lah-di-dah.

NAT puts on a CD.

GINNY   Are these them?

NAT   Uh-huh. Smashing Concrete.

GINNY   They're not so bad.

> *GINNY crawls into the bed. NAT removes the magazines and crawls in beside her.*
>
> *Black.*
>
> *The end.*

About the Editor

Rosalind Kerr teaches in the Drama Department of the University of Alberta. She is the co-editor of *Staging Alternative Albertas: Experimental Theatre in Edmonton* (Playwrights Canada Press, 2002) and is also editing the forthcoming: *Queer Theatre* in the series "Critical Perspectives on Canadian Theatre in English" for publication in 2007.